KEEPING THE LOCK IN WEDLOCK

A Critical Analysis of the Doctrine of Dr. James D. Bales on Divorce and Remarriage

THOMAS B. WARREN, PH.D.

NATIONAL CHRISTIAN PRESS, INC.
P.O. Box 1001 **Jonesboro, Ark., 72401**

KEEPING THE LOCK IN WEDLOCK

Printed in the United States of America

Second Printing

ISBN 0-934916-26-8

Printed by McQuiddy Printing Co., Nashville

CONTENTS

FOREWORD

The Fuqua Position—1954

In December, 1954, it was my privilege to write the "Foreword" to the *Warren-Fuqua Debate*. I made clear in that "Foreword" that the fundamental point in the discussion is the sphere (or realm) of application of divine law: Where are God's laws applicable? To whom do God's laws apply? Do God's laws apply to non-Christians? If God's laws on *any* subject apply to *non-Christians*, then His laws regarding *marriage* must have application to *non-Christians* as well as to *Christians*. On the other hand, if God's laws regarding marriage apply only to Christians, then His laws in general apply only to Christians. I concluded that it is clear that the fundamental point in this problem is the sphere (or realm) of application of divine law. not necessarily so

In that "Foreword" we sought to emphasize brother Fuqua's position. He affirmed that non-Christians (people in the world) are "not under Christian law," that they "are under civil law exclusively," that "the world is in no sense under any law from Christ," that "God has placed the world as such under civil law exclusively," that those in the world have no "law from God on any subject," that "Gentiles or other aliens are without law to God," that "after baptism Christ's law takes over," that "no specific sins, like fornication, could be levied against people in the world."

Bales' Position

Now, February 29, 1980—twenty-five years later—I am writing another "Foreword" for another book written by Thomas B. Warren, which book is designed to refute much the same *basic* doctrine—which will be explained below—as that held and preached by brother E.C. Fuqua.

Brother Bales would not like for me to say that he believes and teaches the Fuqua doctrine. In fact, since the *Warren-Fuqua Debate* I have not come across a single person who admits to believing the Fuqua doctrine! Suppose we try to explain the particular difference between the Fuqua position and brother Bales' position.

(1) Brother Fuqua believed and taught that the law of Christ does not apply to non-Christians—that Mt. 19:9 does not apply to non-Christians (those persons in the world). Brother Bales also believes and teaches that the law of Christ does *not* apply to non-Christians—that Mt. 19:9 does not apply to those persons in the world. On this *basic view* there is identity.

(2) Brother Bales believes and teaches that *Mt. 19:9* applies ONLY to the case in which a *Christian* is *married* to a *Christian*—that it has *no application what-*

internal laws of the covenant

soever to the case in which a *Christian* is *married* to a *non-Christian*, or to the case in which a *non-Christian* is married to a *non-Christian*. So far as I know (or can recall) brother Fuqua *would apply* Mt. 19:9 to the *Christian* who is married to the non-Christian. On this point, *there would be a difference* between brother Fuqua and brother Bales.

(3) Both brother Bales and brother Fuqua realized (realizes) that God commands ". . .all men everywhere to repent," and that repentance presupposes the fact of sin. Both men wrestled with the problem: if *non-Christians* are not amenable to the law of Christ, how do they become sinners? Brother Fuqua answered: they become sinners by violating *civil law*—that aliens are under *civil law exclusively*. However, brother Bales stresses: ". . .it has never been my position that the world is under civil law only" (*Not Under Bondage*, page 10). Rather, brother Bales holds that aliens become sinners because of violation of the "law in the heart." Thus, Bales and Fuqua differ in regard to *how the alien becomes a sinner*.

(4) Brother Fuqua sought to build his case upon the alien-under-civil-law-exclusively idea, and brother Bales seeks to build his case upon two foundation factors: the "law in the heart," and I Cor. 7:10-13. Thus, another point of difference.

It is clear, therefore, that *brother Bales' view of the relationship of the gospel to the alien (non-Christian) is identical to that of brother Fuqua. Brother Bales' view of the relationship of Mt. 19:9 to the alien is identical to that of brother Fuqua.*

I, personally, have never dealt with or examined a doctrine which is more devastating to the pure gospel of Christ than is this doctrine espoused by brother Bales.

Brother Bales' Erroneous Concepts

We believe that brother Bales is wrong—

1. In his concept of the *Great Commission*;
2. In his concept of man's *amenability* to the gospel of Christ;
3. In his concept of "the law written in the heart";
4. In his views regarding the teaching of Mt. 19:9;
5. In his views regarding the teaching of I Cor. 7:10-15;
6. In his distinction between "invitation" to come into the covenant, and the *things* to be taught those who are in the covenant;
7. In his concept of the teaching of I Cor. 7:15;
8. In his concept of *obligation* in relation to *qualification*;
9. In his concept of the nature of revelation.

More specifically, we believe that brother Bales is wrong in his teaching—

1. That *not all* accountable persons are amenable to *all* the gospel of Christ;
2. That Mt. 19:9 applies ONLY to the case in which a *Christian* is *married* to a *Christian*;
3. That the *guilty party* (of Mt. 19:9) has a *scriptural* right to remarry;
4. That I Cor. 7:10-11 *does not* apply to *all* "the married," but applies *only* to the case in which a *Christian* is *married* to a *Christian*;
5. That Paul, in I Cor. 7:10-13, teaches that Mt. 19:9 applies *only* to the case in which a *Christian* is *married* to a *Christian*;
6. That people in the world who have put away their companions (regardless of the number of times, and regardless of the causes) may—upon becoming Christians—*continue* in the remarriage without sin (or, with God's approval); or
7. That neither Christ ~~nor Paul~~ ". . .legislated on divorce and remarriage between two people who are outside of Christ's covenant";
8. That the *deserted believer* of I Cor. 7:15 may, with God's approval, remarry;
9. That no person can be *obligated* to do something which he is *not qualified* to do.

Brother Bales Must Prove. . .

In order for brother Bales to establish his case he must prove (but he CANNOT prove) at least the following things:

1. He must prove (but he cannot prove) that men in the world (i.e., non-Christians) are not amenable to the law of Christ; internal laws of the covenant
2. He must prove (but he cannot prove) that the Great Commission (Mt. 28:18-20) says: teach. . .baptize . . .teach some more;
3. He must prove (but he cannot prove) that there is such a thing as "the law written in the heart," by violation of which people in the world become sinners;
4. He must prove (but he cannot prove) that people in the world *do not* become sinners by violating *the law of Christ* (the gospel);
5. He must prove (but he cannot prove) that Mt. 19:9 applies ONLY to the case in which a Christian is married to a Christian; — where is the evidence that refutes his position
6. He must prove (but he cannot prove) that I Cor. 7:10,11 teaches that Mt. 19:9 applies *only* to the case in which a Christian is married to a Christian;
7. He must prove (but he cannot prove) that I Cor. 7:

10,11 applies *only* to the case in which a Christian is married to a Christian (that it does not, and that it CANNOT apply to ALL "the married");

8. He must prove (but he cannot prove) that "the rest" (of I Cor. 7:12) means "mixed marriages," and cannot possibly mean the rest of the questions or the rest of the cases;
9. He must prove (but he cannot prove) that a distinction exists between the "invitation" to obey the gospel and the *command* to obey the gospel;
10. He must prove (but he cannot prove) that I Cor. 7:15 teaches (in spite of what Mt. 19:9 says) that the deserted believer can scripturally remarry, upon the grounds of the desertion alone;
11. He must prove (but he cannot prove) that no man is obligated to do something which he is not qualified to do;
12. He must prove (but he cannot prove) that God involves Himself in contradictory revelation;
13. He must prove (but he cannot prove) that from Pentecost (of Acts 2) to the time that God revealed to Paul the information contained in I Cor. 7:10-13—a period of at least several years—no apostle (or other inspired teacher) ever applied the teachings of Mt. 19:9 to a non-Christian, and that IF an apostle (or other inspired teacher) *ever did* apply the teaching of Mt. 19:9 to a non-Christian that that apostle (or that inspired teacher) was guilty of teaching FALSE DOCTRINE!

Warren belives it did not apply to marriage contracted under Law up until ~AD60

In this amazing book brother Thomas B. Warren deals (in great detail) with these matters, and with so many more.

Can Warren prove that he did apply this teaching?

The Purpose of This Book

Recently, brother James D. Bales has published a book which he entitled *Not Under Bondage*. In this book (to use his own words) he stresses: "I accept the Spirit's harmony of Matthew 19:9 with I Corinthians 7:12-15. Christ's legislation had reference to two people in the covenant who are married, but not with mixed marriages. Paul legislated on a different category of marriages, i.e. the mixed marriages. Neither legislated on marriages in the world" (pages 40,41). "It is my conviction that Christ's legislation on this subject is for marriages between Christians, and not for aliens, or for a mixed marriage" (page 44). "One can summarize my book by saying: *First,* Christ in His personal ministry legislated on marriage, divorce and remarriage for two Christians. (I Cor. 7:10-11). *Second,* Paul legislated on marriage, divorce and remarriage for the Christian married to a non-Christian. (I Cor. 7:12-15). . .It should be observed that neither Paul nor

Christ legislated on marriage, divorce, and remarriage for two unbelievers" (page 10).

There you have it in a nut-shell! No one has to guess or to wonder as to what brother Bales is saying. They can read it in his own book.

Thus, brother Warren's book is intended to be a thorough refutation of *Not Under Bondage* and other material brother Bales has written on divorce and remarriage. It is intended to be a "critical analysis of the doctrine of Dr. James D. Bales on marriage, divorce and remarriage."

I would especially like to call the reader's attention to the fact that brother Warren has proved in this book that brother Bales' doctrine on divorce and remarriage *implies* that *denominationalism* (with all of its urging {by its preachers} (1) that men reject the gospel plan of salvation and accept the doctrine of salvation at the point of faith before and without being baptized and (2) that men reject the church for which Jesus died and accept humanly-originated churches) is NOT SINFUL!

It seems simply *incredible* to me that a man such as brother Bales would espouse a doctrine which implies such!

Brethren everywhere ought to be (and we predict, will be) truly grateful for this wonderful work which brother Warren has produced under extremely difficult circumstances. May God richly bless this tremendous work to His glory, and to the salvation of men. May it contribute mightily to "the home as God would have it be."

—Roy Deaver

PREFACE

This book has two basic purposes: (1) to set out and *demonstrate* the basic Biblical proposition (doctrine) on divorce and remarriage and (2) to set out and *refute* the basic proposition advanced and propagated by brother James D. Bales.

I propose to accomplish these purposes by: (1) setting out Biblical evidence which proves that the proposition (on divorce and remarriage) which I will affirm is true. In doing this, I will show that—since it is contradictory of Bales' view—such proves Bales' doctrine to be false, and (2) by doing four other things, to show that the *conclusion* demanded by the truth presented is that *Bales' doctrine is false*.

This will all be accomplished in six main *parts*, which are divided into twenty chapters and are supplemented by twenty-five appendices. It is hoped that these appendices will help to make the total book a sort of "handbook" on the question of divorce and remarriage.

I want to make as clear as I possibly can—with all of the sincerity I can muster—that I love and appreciate James D. Bales for his life in defense of the faith. It is clear to me that he is wrong—"dead wrong" —on the question of divorce and remarriage. And he is wrong in a way that has very serious implications both for the church and for the world.

But these facts do not detract from my love and concern for him and for all who may accept and follow his teachings. I love him still and—if I know my own heart—I know that I would do any righteous thing to help him wherever and whenever he may need my help.

Yet, as a servant and soldier of Jesus Christ, I dare not let my love for him (and others) lead me to fail to oppose the error he has espoused and taught. I love him as a brother and friend and, yet, I must oppose the false doctrine which he is now teaching on divorce and remarriage.

Even though I have been planning for a number of years to arrange my affairs in such fashion as to enable me to give a large portion of my time to what I regard as the greatest threat to the church and to the spread of the gospel in the world today—I refer to atheism, agnosticism, modernism, etc.—I have felt that I simply *must* take the time to write this book even though we are deeply involved in arranging public debates with atheists and agnostics of world stature in the academic world. This I feel we simply *must* do—or see the church dwindle to a relative handful during the coming half century (or less).

After one has read this book—and has seen for himself the serious, far-reaching false doctrines which are implied by brother Bales' false doctrine on divorce and remarriage—it may be the case (as I hope it will) that he will ask, "Why would *anyone* accept such a doctrine as that advanced by brother Bales?" Of course, neither I nor any other mere human being can know the heart of another person, but it does *seem* that some people accept certain views simply because they *want* to believe them. For example, some people, it seems, accept the doctrine that men are saved from sin by faith only simply because such is a doctrine which they *want* to believe. As one well-known theologian put it, the doctrine of salvation by faith only is one which is "very full of comfort." Believing it enables the one who believes to accept the view that many who, in rebellion to God, have *refused* to obey Christ by being baptized (cf.: Acts 2:38; 22:16; 10:48) to be saved.

In much the same way, it seems that some people abhor the very thought of having to teach and/or preach that *any* marriage is adulterous and must be severed. A doctrine such as that advanced by some today is "very full of comfort" to them—they feel that they can say of *any marriage* that "it is acceptable to God—stay in it; don't break it up." Some seem even to take pride in having told various couples not to break marriages which violate Matt. 19:9.

The doctrine, on divorce and remarriage, which is advanced by brother Bales is just such a doctrine—i.e., "very full of comfort" to those who have married in violation of plain teaching of the gospel (law) of Christ or who have loved ones who have done so. But, eternity will reveal such to have been nothing more than self-deception. Human doctrines do not change God's laws—they only lull the humans involved into being self-satisfied while they are in rebellion against Christ. I say this lovingly—and as kindly as I know how—but I also say it firmly: men must not pervert the gospel to fit the lives of ungodly, worldly men and women (Rom. 12:1-2).

The prophet Samuel stated the case very well when he said, "Behold, to obey is better than sacrifice, and to hearken than the fat of rams " (I Sam. 15:22). Rebellion against the word of God is a terrible thing indeed.

I cannot close this preface without expressing my deepest gratitude to a number of people. I cannot name them all, but I must name: (1) my wife, Faye (whose faithfulness to Christ and loyalty to me and our children defy my adequate description), who did much of the early typing; (2) brother Roy Deaver, whose Biblical scholarship has been such a help to me as we discussed various crucial matters; (3) brother Andrew Connally, whose wise counsel and encouragement meant so much to me; (4) brother W. D. Jeffcoat, who tirelessly xeroxed crucial research materials; (5) brother Malcolm L. Hill, President of Tennessee Bible College, for his encouragement to me during the entire writing of this book, (6) our three children and their spouses who also encouraged me, and (7) the entire staff of Tennessee Bible College —a group which truly loves the truth and the cause of Christ.

I offer a special note of gratitude to those who helped me proof-read the manuscript (Roy Deaver, Andrew Connally, and W. D. Jeffcoat) and to Linda Lipe, who did some of the first and all of the final typing.

As I close this Preface, I want to make it clear that in no statement in this book do I mean for what I have said to reflect adversely in any way upon the *character* or the *motivations* of brother Bales. I oppose the *doctrine* which he teaches as strongly and firmly as I know how—yet, I *love him* as a dear friend and beloved brother in Christ. But, as surely as denominationalism is sinful and as surely as *all* marriages today which violate the law of Christ are sinful, just so is brother Bales' doctrine on divorce and remarriage sinful. If the matter were not so serious, I would not take time from my efforts to fight atheism, agnosticism and modernism to write this book.

It is my earnest and sincere prayer that God will use this book to His glory and the salvation of men and women.

Thomas B. Warren
March 6, 1980

PART I

SOME INTRODUCTORY MATTERS

CHAPTER I

A BRIEF INITIAL LOOK AT WHAT THIS BOOK IS ALL ABOUT: THE DOCTRINE OF JAMES D. BALES ON DIVORCE AND REMARRIAGE.

In Chapter VIII the doctrine of James D. Bales on divorce and remarriage will be set out in precise propositional form. It seems good, however, to give the reader at least a brief, initial insight into just what that doctrine is. It seems good also to set out briefly, some of the historical background of this problem.

1. *Historical background to this problem.* Down through the years, members of the Lord's church have generally understood (1) that the law of Christ (the gospel)[1] is addressed to all men, (2) that Matthew 19:9 is a constituent element of the law of Christ, (3) that Matthew 19:9 makes clear that the only *scriptural* ground for divorce and remarriage for people living today is that of *fornication*, and, therefore, (4) that all who put away their companions on any ground other than fornication and marry another, commit adultery in so doing (and *keep on committing* adultery as long as they ~~stay in the second marr~~iage). *the original marriage is in fact.*

However, within the past few years there have occurred various brief "bursts" of effort to persuade members of the church to accept the view that the Bible teaches that at least *some* people can—with *God's* approval—divorce and remarry on some ground other than fornication.[2]

In this book, interest is particularly directed toward the doctrine of brother James D. Bales (Professor of Christian Doctrine, Harding University, Searcy, Arkansas). This is the case for at least three reasons: (1) it seems clear to this author that others who have attempted (by different arguments) to show that at least some people can (with God's approval) divorce and remarry on some ground other than fornication have all been clearly shown to have failed in their efforts and that such failure has been at least *generally* recognized —however, it seems that perhaps a rather large number of people are pinning their hopes (for grounds other than the fornication stipulated by *Jesus* in Matthew 19:9) on the efforts of *brother Bales*; (2) brother Bales has written an enormous amount of material on the subject and (in typescript form) has sent it to many brethren all over the country, and (3) brother Bales has affirmed positions (explicitly and implicitly) which contradict truly crucial, fundamental Bible teaching

For these and perhaps other reasons, the author feels that his (Bales') material must be reviewed and refuted.

In his written material on this topic, brother Bales has given a great deal of attention to the work of other brethren—especially, it seems, to that of brother Roy Deaver and this author. Both of us are always happy to have others review our work—provided they do not *misrepresent* what has been taught—for the desire of each is to teach only truth.

2. *Some of the basic elements of Bales' doctrine.* It will be shocking, no doubt, to many people to learn that brother Bales actually teaches what he does. In Chapter VIII, it will be *proved* that brother Bales teaches the doctrines listed just below. Here, the point is to simply let the reader know that he *does* teach these doctrines, shocking as it may be to most Christians. Brother Bales teaches (explicitly and/or implicitly) that:

(1) The New Covenant (the law of Christ, the faith, the word, the truth, the gospel, etc.) is addressed *only* to *Christians*, and, therefore—

(2) No *non-Christian* living today is amenable to (under) the law of Christ (the gospel);

(3) Non-Christian *Gentiles* living today are amenable to (under) the "law written on the heart" and are *not* amenable to the *law of Christ* on *any* subject;

(4) Non-Christian *Jews* living today are amenable to (under) the law of Moses and are not amenable to the law of Christ (the New Covenant) on any subject.[3] And, thus—

(5) No *non-Christian* living today (whether Gentile or Jew) *can violate* the law of Christ (the New Covenant, the gospel) (cf. Rom. 3:19; 4:15);

(6) No *non-Christian* living today (whether Gentile or Jew) can *obey* the law of Christ (the New Covenant, the gospel) (cf. Rom. 3:19; 4:15); and, thus—

(7) No *non-Christian* living today can *be saved* (because, not being amenable to the gospel, he cannot obey it (Rom. 3:19), and he cannot be saved without obeying the gospel (Mark 16:15-16; II Thess. 1:7-9; John 8:32).

(8) No *non-Christian* living today *sins* when he enters a mere human denomination. (This is the case, brother Bales teaches, because he is not amenable to the law of Christ and, thus, cannot sin in violating it.)

(9) No *non-Christian* living today sins when, in preaching Baptist doctrine, he urges men to *reject* Jesus' *plan of salvation* (Mark 16:16) and to *accept* the Baptist doctrine that alien sinners are saved at the point of faith before and without being baptized. (This is the case, brother Bales teaches, because he is not amenable to the law of Christ, and, thus, cannot sin by

violating it).

(10) No non-Christian living today sins when, in preaching Baptist doctrine he urges men to reject *the church* purchased by the blood of Christ and to enter the Baptist church. (This is the case, brother Bales teaches, because he is not amenable to the law of Christ, and thus, cannot sin by violating it.)

(11) No non-Christian living today sins when he uses instrumental music in the worship of God. (This is the case, brother Bales teaches, because he is not amenable to the law of Christ and, thus, cannot sin by violating it.)

(12) No non-Christian living today sins when, in preaching Roman Catholic doctrine, he urges men to accept the view that the Roman Pope is actually the Vicar of Christ on earth. (This is the case, brother Bales teaches, because he is not amenable to the law of Christ and, thus, cannot sin by violating it—and—the law he is under, according to brother Bales, does not have any stricture against such.)

(13) No non-Christian living today is amenable to Matthew 19:9, brother Bales teaches, and, thus, does not sin when he marries in violation of its teaching.

(14) No unmarried Christian is amenable to Mt. 19:9 and, thus, does not sin when he marries in violation of its teaching. (For example, given Bales' doctrine, a Christian who had never married could, with God's approval, marry a non-Christian divorcee who had been put away for fornication!)

(15) Only Christians who are married to Christians are amenable to Matthew 19:9 and, thus, only Christians married to Christians can sin in violating its teaching.

(16) No Christian living today who is married to a non-Christian is amenable to Matthew 19:9, and, thus, no Christian married to a non-Christian can sin by violating the teaching of Matthew 19:9.

(17) No non-Christian living today who is married to a Christian is amenable to Matthew 19:9 and, thus, no non-Christian living today who is married to a Christian can sin by violating the teaching of Mt. 19:9.

(18) No non-Christian living today who is not married is amenable to Matthew 19:9 and, thus, no non-Christian living today who is not married can sin by violating the teaching of Matthew 19:9.

(19) Jesus Christ, through His gospel, does *not* have all authority in heaven and on earth (as He claimed in Matthew 28:18).

(20) Jesus Christ does not have authority over all flesh (as is taught in John 17:2).

(21) Jesus Christ is not now "King of kings and Lord of lords" (as is taught in Revelation 19:16).

(22) The law of Christ (the faith, the gospel) is not universal (as is taught in Mark 16:15; Matthew

28:18-20; Luke 24:45-49; Acts 1:6-8; Isaiah 1:1-4).

(23) "The *gospel* of Christ" is one body of teaching but "the *doctrine* of Christ" is another (distinct—not the same) body of doctrine ("Neo-Ketchersidism").

(24) "Neo-Fuquaism": no non-Christian is amenable to the law of Christ on any subject. In order to be amenable to the New Covenant, one must be "in" the New Covenant (i.e., must be a *Christian*).

(25) Thus, since instruction to be baptized is a part of the New Covenant, *Christians*—not *non-Christians* are to *be baptized!*

(26) In a marriage in which fornication occurs, the *guilty* party is just as free to marry again as is the *innocent* party.

3. *What one must do to accept and follow Bales' doctrine.* To say that brother Bales has taught the truth on divorce and remarriage is to obligate oneself to believe, live by, and urge others to accept and live by the doctrines set out in 2 above. What right-thinking person is prepared to do so? Brother Bales has claimed that at least one faculty member in each of our Christian colleges agrees with the doctrine on divorce and remarriage which he (Bales) teaches. (If such be the case, this author calls for them to openly identify themselves.) It seems impossible to conclude—in the light of his great work in learning and teaching truth in the past—that even brother Bales, after he has seen what he has taught *implicitly* by his *explicit* statements, will accept it. Surely, as his honesty and love for God and truth in the past has led him to renounce a false position he had held and tried strenuously to defend, his honesty and love for God and truth will lead him to renounce this unscriptural doctrine before even more souls are deceived into accepting it and, thus, to living in adultery (Colossians 3:5-7; cf. Rev. 21:8).

4. *Why do some people believe this doctrine?* This question might be answered by answering the question, "Why do men accept the doctrine that men are saved at the point of faith before and without being baptized into Christ?" The answer is, as a leading theologian said, "It is very full of comfort." It is what men *want* to hear. They do not *like* the strict plan of salvation set out by our Lord (Matthew 7:13-14; Mark 16:15-16; John 3:3-5, et al.). Holding to "salvation by faith only," preachers can "preach into heaven" many who have rejected *the will* of God (Matthew 7:21). Many do not *like* the truth that there is: (1) one—and only one plan of salvation, (2) one—and only one *faith*, (3) one—and only one church and (4) one—and only one—ground for divorce and remarriage.

Without the slightest challenge of the motive of *anyone*, it might be noted that even *honest* people can be misled when they *want* to believe a certain doctrine—especially when it is taught by a well-trained man in whom they have great confidence (Ezek. 14:4).

It is well known that some people have "run" from one preacher to another until they finally found one who would tell them that it would please God for them to marry even though such a marriage would violate the teaching of the law of Christ. How happy they are then to obey what is obviously a false doctrine and, yet, which they very likely have convinced themselves to be the will of God. All such should note Rev. 21:8.

5. *We must beware lest we become a Jezebel or a Balaam.* To teach people that they can marry with God's approval when the Bible teaches otherwise is to fall into much the same pit as (1) Jezebel—who taught Christ's servants to commit fornication (Revelation 2:20) and (2) Balaam—who taught Israel to commit fornication (Rev. 2:14).

While it is certainly the case that it is sinful to *forbid* what God allows (I Timothy 4:1-5; Galatians 2:3-5), we must not become so apprehensive of doing such that we *allow* what God has *not authorized* or has even *forbidden!*

6. *The results of Bales' doctrine.* If it is indeed the case, as has been set out above, that brother Bales has taught (explicitly and/or implicitly) the doctrines ascribed to him, then the situation is *most serious indeed.* The Bible teaches that those who live and die as fornicators will be lost forever (Revelation 21:8; cf. Gal. 5:19-21).

7. *Does brother Bales really teach the above?* The answer is, yes. Proof that such is the case will be set out in succeeding chapters. But it was felt that the reader from the very outset should have some insight into various elements of brother Bales' doctrine.

Footnotes

[1]Chapter X will discuss this matter in detail—i.e., that the gospel, the faith, the law of Christ, the word, the word of God, etc. all refer to one and the same body of doctrine.

[2]Chapter II involves a more detailed account of some of these efforts.

[3]Bales might deny this point by saying that he holds that the Jews were under the Law of Moses only until the destruction of Jerusalem. But the fact remains that in answering questions which this author sent to him, Bales said (in an answer to T.B.W. question no. 14), "There is enough truth in the Old Testament *today* (emphasis T.B.W.) to condemn the Jew." But no one can be condemned by a law to which he is *not*

amenable (Rom. 3:19; 4:15; I John 3:4). Of course, Hebrews 10:9 makes clear that even Bales' position that the Law of Moses remained in force until the destruction of Jerusalem is also false. Bales has admitted that the *entire* Law of Moses had to be done away before the New Covenant could come into force and before *any* of the Law of Moses was done away.

To conclude that a particular law of Christ is limited to a particular group in no way commits one to the position that aliens are amenable to no law of Christ on any subject.

CHAPTER II

BALES' DOCTRINE EASILY REFUTED

Chapter IV of this book will be devoted to showing (1) how to *demonstrate* a doctrine or proposition (i.e., prove it to be *true*) and (2) how to *refute* a doctrine or proposition (i.e., prove it to be *false*). That material is relevant to this present chapter.

1. *A brief preview of showing Bales' doctrine to be false.* However, as a sort of brief *preview* of what is to come (in much more detail) in the remainder of the book, the author wishes to point out that two of the ways a doctrine (or proposition) can be shown to be false are (1) proving that it *implies* a false doctrine[1] and (2) by proving that the *contradictory* of it is the conclusion of a sound argument.[2] It is possible (and actually quite easy) to use both of these ways[3] in proving brother Bales' doctrine to be false.

2. *An example: Baptist doctrine on the plan of salvation is false.* Baptists teach that the alien sinner (non-Christian) is saved at the point of faith, before and without being baptized. Here is a brief, precisely stated argument which proves Baptist doctrine false: (1) If Baptist doctrine is true, then the alien sinner is saved at the point of faith before and without being baptized; (2) It is *false* that the alien sinner is saved by faith before and without being baptized (the fact that in Mark 16:16 "is baptized" is an aorist participle (in the original Greek) *proves* that being baptized *cannot* occur *after* salvation); therefore, (3) Baptist doctrine is false.[4]

3. *Bales' doctrine is just as easily proved false.* The doctrine of brother Bales on divorce and remarriage is as easily shown to be false as is Baptist doctrine on the plan of salvation: (1) If brother Bales' doctrine on divorce and remarriage is true, then the New Covenant (the law of Christ, the gospel, the faith, the word, the truth) is *not addressed to all men* (whether Christian or non-Christian); (2) It is *false* that the New Covenant is not addressed to all men (Mk. 16:15-16; Mt. 28:18-20); therefore, (3) brother Bales' doctrine on divorce and remarriage is false.

The reader must understand that this argument and a number of others (all *conclusive* in proving his doctrine false) will be set out *in detail* in later chapters. This *brief* look at *one* argument is given here so that the reader may gain some grasp of how easily refuted is the Bales' doctrine.

One might wonder: If it is so easily defeated, why do more? Why, in effect, "kick" an argument after it is already "dead"? More is given because some people have questions which may not, in their minds, be settled by the above argument. This may be the case simply because (1) they do not understand what brother Bales' basic proposition is[5] or (2) even if they *do* know what his basic proposition *says*, they may not *understand* some of the crucial *implications* of that proposition, or (3) even if they do know what his basic proposition is and even if they do understand the crucial implications of it, they may not understand why the argument set out above refutes his basic proposition. For these—and perhaps other—reasons, the entire book, not only this one chapter, will be written.

Footnotes

[1]This is the case because any doctrine which implies a false doctrine is itself false. (See details in Chapter IV and Appendix Q.)

[2]This is the case because the conclusion of any sound argument must be true. See details in Chapter IV and Appendix Q.

[3]And others besides. See succeeding chapters.

[4]Set out in symbolic terms, the argument looks like this:

(1) ${B_1}^D \supset A^{F \cdot \sim B_2}$

(2) $\sim A^{F \cdot \sim B_2}$

(3) $\therefore \sim {B_1}^D$

Where ${B_1}^D$ = Baptist doctrine (is true).

$A^{F \cdot \sim B_2}$ = the alien sinner is saved at the point of faith before and without being baptized.

$\sim {B_1}^D$ = Baptist doctrine (is false).

[5]Bales' position will be set out in precise detail in Chapter VIII. A *listing* of various elements of his doctrine has already been set out in Chapter I.

CHAPTER III

THE PROBLEM IN GENERAL

1. *The basic question set out.* As this author sees the matter, the basic question which men face (as pertains to what *the Bible* teaches about divorce and remarriage) is: "Is it the case that *all* persons (whether Christian or non-Christian) who, in violating the law of Christ (specifically, in divorcing and marrying again on some ground other than fornication in violation of Matthew 19:9) are involved in sinful practices and/or sinful relationships and/or sinful states *are* persons who are instructed by that law to cease those sinful practices, to get out of those sinful states, and to sever those sinful relationships?"

2. *Reaction to this question.* It is true, of course, that "counting noses"—that is, the tallying up of the number of people who either do or do not believe a particular doctrine—is *not* the way to arrive at truth. A man may hold to a view with which the rest of the world disagrees and yet be holding to the truth. The Bible teaches men not to follow a multitude to do evil.

Yet, it is not without some significance that at least during this author's almost thirty-five years of preaching and defending the gospel of Christ, almost every member of the Lord's church understood what some other member meant when he asked—concerning some divorced person (whether Christian or non-Christian) who was soon to be married—"Did he (she) have *scriptural* ground for divorce and remarriage?" Almost every member of the Lord's church during all those years understood that the questioner was asking, "Did he (she) put away his (her) companion on the ground of *fornication* (the sexual unfaithfulness of the one put away)?"

But, to use an expression found in one Baptist manual, "now it is different." In recent years, a number of false doctrines have been advanced with the claim made by the exponents of each particular doctrine that that doctrine showed that the basic question (set out above) should be answered *negatively*. And, even though this author is certain that the question should be answered *affirmatively*, he wants to make clear that he does *not* challenge the *honesty* of those who advance the theories.

Considering the number of false theories presently being advanced and the zeal, in propagating those theories, which characterizes those who teach them, it should be of some value to note a number of the theories which have been advanced by brethren in an effort to establish the view that God allows some ground other than fornication for divorce and remarriage.

3. *Some false theories on divorce and remarriage listed and briefly explained.*

(1) *No ground at all for divorce and remarriage.* One brother, whom this author met in public oral debate on the matter, advanced the theory that there is absolutely *no ground at all* for divorce and remarriage—not even sexual infidelity on the part of one's spouse. (Of course, this theory is at the "opposite end of the totem pole" from the theory being considered in this book.) He based his theory on his contention that Matthew 19:9 was a part of the law of Moses—not a part of the law (gospel) of Christ.

(2) *No non-Christian is amenable to (under) the law of Christ, but is under civil law only.* Brother E. C. Fuqua (whom this author also met in written debate on the subject of divorce and remarriage)[1] advanced the theory that even though Matthew 19:9 is a part of the law of Christ (not a part of the law of Moses) and even though Matthew 19:9 *does* teach (for those who are *amenable to* it) that fornication is the *one* and *only* ground for divorce and remarriage, *non-Christian* persons simply are *not amenable* to Matthew 19:9, because they are not amenable to the law of Christ *at all,* but are amenable to *civil law only.* Brother Fuqua asserted that non-Christians are not amenable to God on *any* subject!

(3) *Sin is not imputed to non-Christians.* During a college lectureship, I heard another brother argue that even though non-Christians *are* amenable to (under) the law (gospel) of Christ—and of Matthew 19:9—nevertheless it is the case that God does not *require* of *non-Christians* that they live up to the high standard set forth in the gospel of Christ. This is made clear, the brother alleged, by the fact that even though it is true that non-Christian men *sin* when they violate the teaching of Matthew 19:9, God *does not impute* that sin to them if it occurs while they are *non-Christians.* This is made clear, he said, by the fact that God does not require people who unscripturally married (while they were non-Christians) to separate. But the brother merely *assumed* this doctrine, he did not prove it.

(4) *The guilty party (in a case of sexual unfaithfulness) is as free to marry again (with God's approval) as is the innocent party.* The effort to prove this theory is based more upon a mere *analogy* than upon the Scriptures. (Note: many who try to use analogies do not really understand them.) It is alleged that—just as when two people are handcuffed together, if *one* of them is freed from the handcuffs, then the *other* one, of necessity, must also be freed—if the *innocent* party is freed (to marry someone else) when his (her) companion has been put away for fornication, then the *guilty* party of necessity must also be freed to remarry, because, if one is free, the other must also be free. This theory implies that if a husband and wife

It is obvious that bro Warren does not understand this position.

grow weary of their marriage and each of them wishes to obtain a divorce in order to marry someone else, then, to do this *with God's approval* they could simply agree that *one* of them would *commit fornication* and—lo!—*both* of them would be *free to marry someone else!* This doctrine implies that two men can "swap wives" (and children) and then merely say, "I'm sorry" and continue to live with the second wife and have *God's approval* while doing so! Does anyone need the degradation of this viewpoint explained to him? (At least some men who advance this view admit that *all* men (both *Christian* and *non-Christian*) are amenable to Matthew 19:9.

(5) *Unscripturally divorced and remarried couples may continue in the second marriage without any further sin.* So far as this author knows, those who advance this view also admit that *all* men (both Christian and non-Christian) are amenable to the law of Christ (including Matthew 19:9). If indeed it is the case that one can divorce in violation of Bible teaching and then marry in violation of Bible teaching and yet *continue in that unscriptural marriage without any further sin,* it is difficult (indeed, impossible) to see *any* value to the Bible.

(6) *The "application" (set out by Paul in I Corinthians 7) countermands the "concept" (set out by Jesus in Matthew 19:9) as regards divorce and remarriage.* One brother, the preacher for a congregation which serves thousands of Christian college students (the congregation of which brother Bales is a member), holds that, although *all* men (whether Christian or non-Christian) are *amenable to* Matthew 19:9 (thus contradicting theory (2) above and theory (7) below), the instruction which is set forth in Matthew 19:9 (what this brother refers to as the *concept*) is "*countermanded*" by Paul in I Corinthians 7. It must be noted that since "countermand" means "to contradict, to revoke," this brother thus alleges that Paul *contradicts* what Jesus plainly taught. Thus, our brother is faced with a dilemma. To be consistent with this theory, he must affirm either (a) that the Bible is the word of God and, thus, (since the Bible contradicts itself) that God is a *liar* or (b) that God does not lie, thus, (since the Bible contradicts itself) the Bible is *not* the word of God. (This theory has been refuted in detail in this author's book of charts.)

(7) *Matthew 19:9 is a "covenant passage" to which only Christians who are married to Christians are amenable. This* theory, taught by brother James D. Bales,[2] entails at least the following points (listed in Chapter I and to be elaborated upon in Chapter XIV): (a) no *non-Christian* is amenable to the law of Christ, (b) thus, since Matthew 19:9 is a part of the law of Christ, no *non-Christian* is amenable to Matthew 19:9; (c) the *only* persons who are amenable to Matthew 19:9

are *Christians* who are *married* to *Christians*, (d) no *Christian* who is *not married* is amenable to Matthew 19:9;[3] (e) no *Christian* who is *married* to a *non-Christian* is amenable to Matthew 19:9; (f) since sectarians (Baptists, Roman Catholics, Pentecostals, et al.) are *not Christians* (and, thus, given this theory, are *not* amenable to the law of Christ), they do *not sin* when, in preaching their sectarian doctrines, they urge men to *reject* the *gospel* plan of salvation and to *accept* such *sectarian* doctrines as the theory that non-Christians are saved (from sin) at the point of faith before and without being baptized in the name of Christ (Acts 2:38; 10:47-48); and (g) *non-Christian Gentiles* living today are amenable to the "law written on the heart" and are not amenable to the law of Christ. (This author will have more to say—when he discusses this view in detail in later chapters—regarding brother Bales' view of the status of *non-Christian Jews* living today as relates to the law of Christ. At any rate, he does clearly teach that *non-Christian Jews* were still amenable to (under) the law of *Moses—not* the law of *Christ*—until the destruction of the Temple of Jerusalem. (In taking this position, he unequivocally contradicts truth which he formerly taught on this important question); and (h) by *implication*, he also teaches (following Leroy Garrett and Carl Ketcherside) that a definite distinction must be made between the *gospel* of Christ and the *doctrine* of Christ. In doing so, he not only teaches that particular error but also involves himself in a self-contradiction while doing so.

Detailed proof of the above matter—with refutation thereof—will be set out in later chapters. The implications of the above elements of this doctrine—advanced by brother Bales—are shocking indeed. But this author's love for him personally and this author's respect for his faithful work accomplished during years past cannot be allowed to deter him (this author) from refuting Bales' false teaching on this most important matter (I Timothy 6:12; Jude 3). Further proof of the need of the refutation of brother Bales' doctrine is seen in the fact he has argued a number of doctrines which contradict the truth which he himself formerly taught (and, it is supposed, still does on every subject except divorce and remarriage). But details of these matters must await the discussion in later chapters.

Footnotes

[1]This debate is available in book form: Thomas B. Warren and E. C. Fuqua, *Divorce and Remarriage: Are non-Christians Amenable to the law of Christ?* National Christian Press, Inc. P.O. Box 1001, Jonesboro, Ak. 72401.

[2] James D. Bales (a professor of Christian Doctrine at Harding University, Searcy, Arkansas) has written (1) a great mass of material in typescript form (which he has widely circulated, attacking what has been taught by this author, brother Roy Deaver and others, and (2) a book on the subject *Not Under Bondage*, hereinafter referred to as *NUB*. See also my remarks in the Preface.

[3] Thus, given this theory, a young unmarried Christian would be free (in God's sight) to marry a non-Christian who had divorced on some ground other than fornication. Of course, this is a false position.

CHAPTER IV

THE IMPORTANCE OF THE GENERAL PROBLEM SEEN IN THE IMPLICATIONS OF *ONE* OF THE FALSE THEORIES LISTED IN CHAPTER I

1. *The theory identified.* The false theory which shall be noted in this chapter is that of brother E. C. Fuqua, who was editor of *The Vindicator* for many years. Brother Fuqua was one of the most able, bold, and valiant fighters for the truth of the New Testament plan of salvation and of the New Testament church who has lived in the twentieth century.

He wrote many articles in *The Vindicator* which exposed the fact that denominationalists (such as Baptists, Pentecostals, Jehovah's Witnesses, Catholics, et al.) violated the law (gospel) of Christ by preaching their *human* (not authorized by the Bible) "churches," and by being involved in their human acts of worship (not authorized by the Bible). He printed many of these articles in tract form, and they were used to teach the truth in many countries around the world. As a very young preacher, I personally learned a great deal from his pungent, forceful and truthful writings.

He also engaged in a number of debates in defense of the truth on such matters as the plan of salvation, the Lord's church as over against denominationalism, instrumental music in worship, the Sabbath or the Lord's day, et al.

A debate of particular significance, in my judgment, was his debate with Dr. L. S. Ballard, one of the most able defenders of Baptist doctrine of his day. In that debate (printed in *The Vindicator* and later in book form), brother Fuqua affirmed that the Bible teaches that *all* people (whether *Christian* or *non-Christian*) who enter the Baptist church *sin* in so doing. In *proving* that proposition, brother Fuqua used, *not civil law*, but the law (gospel) of Christ! This author contends that bro. Fuqua defended the *true* position in that debate. Brother Bales teaches, by implication, that brother Fuqua taught false doctrine in that debate. This author urges the reader to obtain and study carefully the *Fuqua-Ballard Debate* on the Baptist church and remember, while doing so, that brother Bales agrees with the Baptist preacher in that debate.

In his tract on instrumental music, brother Fuqua said that no more flagrant sin is committed in "all of Popery" (i.e., by Catholics) than is committed by Protestants (such as Baptists, Methodists, et al.) when they introduce instrumental music into the worship of God! (Brother Bales, to be consistent with his doctrine on divorce and remarriage, must deny that Protestants and Catholics sin when they use instrumental music in the worship of God.)

Perhaps at this stage the reader is asking, "Well what's wrong with that? Is it not the case that anyone

(Christian or non-Christian) who enters the Baptist church *sins* in so doing? And, is it not the case that Protestants (who are, of course, non-Christians) sin when they introduce instrumental music into the worship of God?" The answer, of course, is, "Yes!" to *both* questions.

Then, the reader might ask, "Why point out what brother Fuqua wrote on those two matters?" Because he did, in principle, just what brother Bales (whose doctrine on divorce and remarriage is under critical review in this book) did with his (Bales') writings on divorce and remarriage: he rejected truth which he formerly taught.

2. *How this worked in brother Fuqua's case.* It must be noted (in this chapter) how this works in brother Fuqua's case, and in following chapters, it will be noted how it works in brother Bales' case.

Let it be noted carefully, that in fighting the errors of denominationalism, brother Fuqua recognized (and used) the truth that *all* men (whether Christian or non-Christian) were amenable to (under) *the law (gospel) of Christ!* Not one time did he ever say such a thing as, "Non-Christians do not sin when they enter the Baptist church because no non-Christian is amenable to the law (gospel) of Christ"! Never did he say such on *any* subject—*except* that of *divorce and remarriage!*

It seems to this author that the question of divorce and remarriage has a sort of strange power to "befuddle" even some wise, able, and otherwise faithful men.

The reader should note carefully how brother Fuqua rejected (by contradicting) the truth (on divorce and remarriage) which he so powerfully used to refute denominationalism. When writing on divorce and remarriage—*not* on *denominationalism*—some of the errors he taught are: (1) "While in the world, people cannot be *with* or *without* 'a Scriptural cause' for anything, seeing they are *not under Christian law*, but under *civil law* exclusively" (*The Vindicator*, Oct., 1951, p.6). (2) "All his law and legislation are exerted in the church, and over its members exclusively; so that the world is in no sense under any law of Christ" (Ibid., p. 5). (3) "God has placed the world as such under *Civil law* exclusively" (Ibid.). (4) "Nor do I find where those in the world are given any law from God on any subject. Gentiles or other aliens are without law to God" (Ibid., May, 1950, p. 12). (5) "Thus if a man marries a woman, then leaves her in destitution for another, he sins against Civil Law—God's only law in the world" (Ibid., Feb., 1952, p. 6). (6) "Baptism is the dividing line between the world and the church (I Cor. 12:13). {This one statement is true, T.B.W.} Up till then, Civil laws control. After baptism, Christ's law takes over" (Ibid., Dec., 1951, p. 2.). (7) "That being true, nothing done in the world was looked upon as a sin, for it *transgressed no law* from Him" (Ibid., Oct., 1951, p. 4). (8) "Therefore, no specific sins, like fornication, could be levied against people in the world" (Ibid.). (9) "They were not 'living in adultery' in the world, because *adultery* is a violation of God's specific law; and people in the world are not under any specific law from God. They are not therefore required to repent of any specific sins" (Ibid., Aug., 1951, p. 3).[1]

From the quotations stated above, it is clear that brother Fuqua affirmed the following propositions as comprising his basic position: (1) The world (i.e., all *non-Christian* adults) is under civil law *exclusively* and will be judged *solely* by that law; (2) The world is *not* under *any* law from God or Christ on *any* subject, and so *no non-Christian* can violate *the law of Christ* on *any* subject; and (3) The salvation of a *non-Christian* does *not* involve his repenting of *any specific* sins, and, thus, (4) no *non-Christian* is under the obligation to sever sinful relationships (as viewed by the law of Christ) which were entered while he is (was) in the world.

Even casual thought by anyone who knows anything about the Bible and logic will easily enable such a person to see the terrible self-contradictions in which brother Fuqua involved himself. If no non-Christian is under law from Christ on *any* subject (as brother Fuqua alleges when writing on divorce and remarriage) and if, as he further alleges, the law of Christ does not "take over" until *after* baptism, then it follows that *the law* (instruction) one obeys to be saved (become a child of God) is *no part* of the *law of Christ*. But in Romans 8:2, Paul makes clear that men are saved by the law of the Holy Spirit (the word of God, Eph. 6:17; that is, the law—gospel—of *Christ*).

Brother Fuqua *taught* the *truth* (that all men now living—whether Christian or non-Christian—are amenable to the law of Christ) when he was debating *Baptists* and other denominationalists, but he *rejected* that same truth (by contradicting it) when he wrote on the subject of divorce and remarriage. (This author does not propose to judge *why* such was the case, but he does know that it happened.)

It was indeed a sad state of affairs when brother Fuqua, upon being faced with the dilemma of choosing to say either (1) that his affirmation in regard to the (Baptist church) with the Baptist, Dr. Ballard, was false or else (2) to say that his affirmation with this author (on divorce and remarriage) was false, refused to face the force of that dilemma but chose to *invent* what he called an "ecclesiastical realm," to which he said all denominationalists belonged. In spite of the fact that for many, many years he had rightly taught that every responsible adult is either in the *world* or the *church*, in debate with this author he pitiably took the position that denominationalists were neither in the world nor the church! (The reader should watch for information in a later chapter as to how brother Bales reacts to this same basic problem.)

This author urges the reader to study carefully *The Warren-Fuqua Debate*[2] in order to get the force of the implications of brother Fuqua's doctrine.

While reminding the reader that *any* doctrine which *implies* a false doctrine is itself false, this author here calls attention to just a few of the implications of brother Fuqua's theory that all non-Christians are amenable to (under) civil law only and are amenable to (under) no law from Christ on any subject: (1) since instruction to be baptized is a part of the gospel (law) of Christ, brother Fuqua's theory implies that no *non-Christian* can be baptized in the name of Christ unto the remission of sins. (But Peter said they could, Acts 2:38.); (2) thus, given brother Fuqua's theory, no non-Christian can be saved (since no one can be saved without being baptized, John 3:3-5); (3) thus, given Fuqua's theory, in spite of Christ's death on the cross and the sending of His law (gospel) into all the world, all of mankind is in a helpless, hopeless situation—*no one* can be saved; (4) given brother Fuqua's theory, the gospel (law) of Christ is *not* to be preached to *every* creature but only to a *part* of mankind (the church) (but *Jesus* said that *the gospel* should be preached to *every* creature, Mark 16:15); (5) brother Fuqua's theory, in contradictory fashion, implies that *Christians* are to *be baptized* (this is the case because, he says, only *Christians* are amenable (under) to Christ's law (the gospel) and yet the *instruction* to *be baptized* is a *part* of *the gospel* (Mark 16:15-16); (6) brother Fuqua's theory denies that Christ has *all authority* in heaven and on earth (but Christ said that He did, Matthew 28:18-20) and brother Fuqua's theory denies that Christ is "King of kings and Lord of lords" (Revelation 19:16); (7) since he teaches that one can continue (with God's approval), after being baptized, in a relationship which violates the law of Christ (provided that relationship was entered before baptism), brother Fuqua's theory implies that one can (with *God's approval*) be in and remain in the Baptist church, after being baptized into Christ. Such implications prove the falsity of brother Fuqua's theory (Acts 13:8-12; II John 9-11). And there are many others of perhaps equal interest. (The reader should carefully study them on pages 155 and 156 of *The Warren-Fuqua Debate*.)

3. *The value of the preceding material in this chapter*. First, as was noted above, a great value in considering brother Fuqua's theory is seen in the fact that (1) *brother Bales'* theory is so *very close* to that

of brother Fuqua (the two theories do differ slightly, and that difference will be noted in following chapters). However, since the Warren-Fuqua debate in 1954, this author cannot recall that he has ever met even one person who would say that he believed, without reservation, the theory advanced by brother Fuqua. On the other hand, the view which this author upheld in that debate is the view generally held by conservative brethren around the world.

Second, a great value in analyzing (even though briefly) brother Fuqua's theory on divorce and remarriage (and seeing some of the unscriptural positions—both explicit and implicit) is that such an analysis will be of so much help in our critically analyzing the doctrine taught by brother James D. Bales on the same subject. This is the case, as noted just above, because the position held by brother Bales is so close to that of brother Fuqua. And this is the case in spite of the fact that brother Bales denies a fundamental proposition affirmed by brother Fuqua; viz., that all non-Christians are under *civil* law *exclusively* and are not under law from *God* on any subject. Brother Fuqua accepts *this* proposition; brother Bales denies it. Brother Fuqua held that all *non-Christians* are under *civil law* only, but brother Bales holds that non-Christians are under what he calls "the law on the heart" (although according to some of his statements, he teaches that non-Christian Jews living today are still amenable to the law of Moses)—not under the law of Christ on any subject.

Nevertheless, it is the studied opinion of this author that brother Bales' position is so close to that of brother Fuqua that his (Bales' position) can be labeled accurately as "neo-Fuquaism" (i.e., a new, slightly different form of the Fuqua doctrine on divorce and remarriage).

As was stated earlier, in espousing this neo-Fuqua doctrine (which, as shall be proved later, may also be accurately termed "neo-Ketchersidism"), brother Bales has rejected (by contradicting them) many crucial fundamental truths which he formerly so ably taught and defended. It is sad, indeed, that such is the case, but nevertheless, it is true.

And, so, having looked briefly at a false theory on divorce and remarriage which (this author claims) is so very close to that of brother Bales, attention is now directed to the three-fold task of (1) presenting the case which shows what the true (i.e., Biblical) position on divorce and remarriage actually is; (2) setting out what the position of brother Bales actually is (often, all that is needed for many people to see that a particular doctrine is false, is to simply *understand* what the doctrine *really is,* what it really says), and (3) giving the proof that brother Bales' doctrine on divorce and remarriage is false.

However, before that three-fold task is undertaken, it seems necessary to give some attention to two questions: (1) How does one *prove* that a particular proposition (doctrine) is *true*? and (2) How does one *prove* that a particular proposition (doctrine) is *false?* Adequate answering of these two questions should be helpful to the reader in correctly evaluating whether what is claimed for the propositions (that of brother Bales and that of Thomas B. Warren). The question is: does *the Bible* teach that either one of them is true? This question will be answered in subsequent chapters.

Footnotes

[1] It should be noted that Bales agrees with Fuqua in a number of crucial, false positions.

[2] Thomas B. Warren and E. C. Fuqua, *The Warren-Fuqua Debate*, (P.O. Box 1001, Jonesboro, Ark.; National Christian Press, 1955).

CHAPTER V

WHAT IS MARRIAGE? WHEN DOES IT OCCUR?

This chapter will by no means say all that *might* be said on this important subject. To hold this book to a reasonable length, the author wishes to come to the heart of the matter which seems crucial to the problem at hand.[1] Thus, in this chapter, two questions will be asked and answered: (1) What are the various ways in which the word "marriage" is used? and (2) When does a *God*-approved marriage occur? In response to the second question, a precise logical argument, showing the truth of the matter will be set forth.

1. *Various ways of using the word "marriage."* The word "marriage" is used in the Bible and in other literature (and speech) in a number of ways. These ways cannot be understood by anyone who does not also understand (a) that there is such a thing as a *scriptural* marriage (that is, one which is *authorized*—approved—by God in the scriptures, the Bible), (b) that there is such a thing as an *unscriptural* marriage (that is, one which is *not* authorized—and, thus, is condemned—by God in the scriptures, the Bible), and (c) that a marriage may be *authorized* by the Bible and yet *not* be an *ideal* marriage (in the sense that it fails to bring the joy, the pleasure, the emotional and spiritual support, etc., which God ideally wishes for every authorized marriage to have.)[2] {It is surely obvious to the thinking person that if the word "marriage" is to be confined to reference to unions of men and women which *God* has brought about (i.e., that God has actually "joined together" the man and woman involved), then there could be no such thing as an *unscriptural* marriage for *all "marriages"* would (given the above stricture) be *scriptural*. Even the Bible itself uses the word "marriage" to refer to unions which God condemns (Matt. 14:4; Mk. 6:17-18).}

(1) *The word "marriage" is used to refer to the relationship (union) which results from God's actually joining together two eligible (by the Bible standard) people (man and woman) as husband and wife (Matthew 19:6).* *God* never "joins together" two people in marriage when either *one* or *both* of them is *not eligible* (by the *Bible* standard) to be married. It would be good to note at this point that according to *Bible* teaching only the following people are eligible to be married (a) Those who have *never* been married at all (I Corinthians 7:28), (b) those who have been married but whose companion has been put away because of *fornication* (marital unfaithfulness) (Matthew 19:9; 5:31-32), and (c) those who have been married but whose companion has *died* (Rom. 7:1-4). All of these persons (described under a, b, and c above) will form (if they marry

another person who is *also eligible* according to Bible teaching) an *authorized* (scriptural) union when they marry. (All other persons *sin* when they marry.)

(2) *The word "marriage" is used to refer to the relationship which results when a civil government (or even a religious institution) recognizes it as a legal relationship (that is, one which has been formed according to the laws of whatever civil government it involved—even though that relationship violates God's (Christ's) law, as set forth in the gospel.*

a. The reader should note carefully that Jesus Himself used "marry" to refer to an act (resulting in a relationship) which violated His law. He said ". . .and shall *marry* another, committeth adultery" (Matthew 19:9). Jesus plainly intimated that the persons involved possibly were about to *marry*, but he also said that in doing so, the parties *commit* (Greek, keep on committing) *adultery!* Thus, Jesus made clear: (a) that the word "marry" *can* be used to refer to what people do even when they *violate* His (Christ's) law and (b) that they keep on committing adultery as long as they maintain that unscriptural marriage. So, it is clear that to refer to a union as a marriage is *not necessarily* to say that the "marriage" is *acceptable to God.*

It should be noted (a) that *any* marriage between a man and woman which involves even *one* partner who is *not* eligible (according to Bible teaching) is *unscriptural* and (b) that *any* union which men may refer to as "marriage" which involves two people of the *same sex* (homosexual relationship) is also *unscriptural* (according to Bible teaching *no one* is *eligible* to marry a person of the *same sex*). *Every* marriage either is *authorized* by the Bible (that is, is *scriptural*) or is *not authorized* (that is, is *not scriptural*). A man will go to hell for being "married" to a *woman* to whom he has *no scriptural right* to be *married,* just as he will if he is "married" to a man (as some homosexuals *claim* to be *"married"* today). The burning question in both cases is: does *the Bible* approve of the union? Adulterers who die not having repented of that adultery will be lost (Revelation 21:8). In the same way, homosexuals living in a homosexual relationship who die *not having repented* of that union will be *lost* (I Corinthians 6:9-11; Romans 1:18-32; Matt. 19:4; I Cor. 7:2)!

b. Another case in point is that of Herod, who the Bible teaches had *married* his brother Philip's *wife*, Herodias. It must be noted that John the Baptist had told Herod, "It is *not lawful* (emphasis, T.B.W.) for thee to have her" (Matthew 14:5). The Greek word translated "have" at least almost always (when used in connection with a man "having" a woman or a woman "having" a man) means "to be married to." (See lexicons and critical commentaries.) John simply told Herod that it was *not lawful* for him (Herod) to be "married" to

Herodias, whom the Bible refers to as "his brother Philip's wife" (Matthew 14:3) even though the Bible also says that Herod had "married" her (Mk. 6:17-18). Thus, even the Bible itself uses the word "marry" to refer to a relationship that is strictly *unlawful* in the sight of God. So, *men* can use the word "marry" to refer to the forming of unions of which God does *not* approve. Some very interesting questions arise here: (a) What *law* was referred to? The law of *God? Civil* law? Obviously, it was the law of *God!* John told Herod that it was *not lawful* (that is, not lawful according to the law of God) for him (Herod) to have Herodias, his brother Philip's *wife!* (b) Can a woman be properly referred to as the "wife" of two men at the same time? In one sense "Yes" but in another sense "No." There can be a *linguistic* referral to a relationship as "marriage" even when *God* has *not joined the two together*. But, if one means to say (by using either "marry" or "marriage") that the people involved in the relationship have been "joined together" by *God* (so that they are actually *married* in a sense *approved by God*) when such is *not* really the case, then the use of "marry" or "marriage" in such cases is *not correct!* Thus, the fact that one can use "marry" or "marriage" in a *linguistic* referral (without meaning to say that *God approves* of it) does not *necessarily* mean that no *sin* is involved. Thus, the Bible says that Herod had "married" his brother's *wife* even though it was "not lawful" for Herod to "have" his brother's wife. So, in one sense, Herodias *was* Herod's *"wife"*, but, in another sense, she was *not* his *wife*.

Someone may object by saying, "But Matthew 14:3-4 does *not* say that Herod was *married* to Herodias; it only says that Herod *had* her." It has already been pointed out that the word "have" when referring to a man "having" a woman should be taken to mean that he is married to her *unless* there is some *compelling* reason not to do so. However, as implied above, the matter can be laid to rest once for all by simply noting that the Bible says, "For Herod himself had sent forth and laid hold upon John, and bound him in prison for Herodias' sake, his brother Philip's wife, for he had married her" (Mark 6:17). Note that: (a) she is referred to as *"Philip's wife,"* (b) Herod had *"married" his "brother's wife"* and (c) in doing so, Herod had done that which it was *"not lawful"* for him to do. (In connection with these points, the reader should also carefully consider I Corinthians 5:1-13. A detailed analysis of that passage will be set out in Appendix B.)

Thus, it is clear that the words "marry" or "marriage" may be used to refer to unions which *men* regard as *acceptable* but which *God* does *not* recognize as *acceptable!* If, for example, the state of Nevada should pass a law that one *man* may "marry" another *man*—and, thus, the inevitable result would be that *newspapers* would refer to two men as being *married* to one another—this would *not* mean that Christ's law (the gospel) teaches that such would be acceptable to God.

It is worth repeating: each and every marriage either *is* authorized by the Bible or it is *not* authorized by the Bible! What *men* do in rejecting and/or in trying to modify the word of God (that is, as to their own beliefs and/or practices) does not change one word of Bible teaching!

It is further worth repeating that the *only* persons who are *truly married* (that is, *married with scriptural authorization for such*—that is, with *God's* approval, and are thus "joined together" by God) are people who were *eligible* (according to *Bible* teaching) to be married and who have married others who were *eligible* (according to *Bible* teaching) to be married. No other persons are *truly married* in the sense of having been "joined together" by God. This alone should "lay to rest" Bales' quibble in regard to the use of the expression "homosexual marriage." (see more in Appendix H.)

It is further worth repeating that the only persons (whether Christian or non-Christian) who are eligible (according to Bible teaching) to be married are: (a) those who have *never* been married (according to scriptural authorization), (b) those who have been married but whose companion has *died*, and (c) those who have been married but who have put away their companion because of *fornication*.[3]

(3) *A third way the word "marriage" is used is to refer to the relationship which results when two people call their relationship a marriage even though (a) God condemns it (because it violates His law), (b) the civil government involved does not recognize it as a legal marriage, and (c) society in general does not recognize it (the relationship) as an acceptable "marriage."* But to use the word "marriage" to refer to such a union does not necessarily mean that the speaker or writer holds that the two people have been "joined together" by God (Matt. 19:6). God "joins together" only an eligible man to an eligible woman.[4] Mark knew this when, under the guidance of the Holy Spirit, he penned the words recorded in Mk. 6:17-18. To be consistent with his contentions,[5] Bales should charge Mark with holding that Herod's was a "real marriage"—that is, that God had actually "joined together" Herod and Herodias (Herod's brother's wife)!

2. *When does a God-approved (scriptural, authorized by Bible teaching) marriage occur?* In answering this question, two points will be made.

(1) *A scriptural (authorized, approved by God) marriage occurs when God "joins together" (as husband*

and wife) a man and a woman, each of whom is eligible (according to Bible teaching) to be married to the other. Although the Bible does not explicitly say, "Thou shalt have a marriage ceremony," it clearly implies that there must be some sort of ceremony, even if such should be nothing more than an agreement that when the two jump over a broomstick at the same time they will be married. It is altogether proper (in spite of brother Bales' efforts to ridicule the necessity of any sort of ceremony) that a preacher (or, say, a justice of the peace) say (to an eligible couple who have clearly agreed to the significance of the ceremony and the concluding pronouncement), some such statement as, "I now pronounce you husband and wife." When that pronouncement is made to (or over) such an eligible man and an eligible woman (in the face of their mutual understanding of the significance of such), the man and the woman will be "joined together" (by God) as husband and wife. (This is the case in spite of brother Bales' contention that a man and woman do not become husband and wife until after they have had sexual intercourse with each other for the first time. Bales takes the ridiculous position that a man must have sexual intercourse with a woman as a prerequisite to her becoming his wife. This position implies that God requires that a man and woman must commit sin in order to get married—i.e., they must commit fornication in order to get married.)

(2) It is true (a) that God did not specify details of a marriage ceremony and (b) that God did not specify who was to "say" the ceremony, but it is also true (c) that some sort of ceremony is demanded (otherwise the couple would never know just when they became husband and wife—for example, if, as Bales contends, a man and woman are not married until after their first sexual intercourse, exactly when does marriage occur: {1} after they are sexually joined but before either one has experienced orgasm? {2} only after both of them have experienced orgasm? {If so, and if certain reports given to gynecologists and psychiatrists are true, then since some women experience orgasm—if ever—only after years of "married" life, a man and woman could live together for years without being married.} {3} only after at least one of them has experienced orgasm? or {4} just when? Let Bales answer!) and (d) that men are to obey civil law (Romans 13:ff), as long as that law does not violate God's law (Acts 4:18; 5:29).

3. *Bales' position demands that men and women commit fornication and/or laciviousness in order to get married.* Brother Bales argues that men and women do not become husband and wife until the completion of their first union in sexual intercourse. This implies a number of absurd (and false) positions. (a)

It implies that when a minister "says" a marriage ceremony, he should not (at the close of the ceremony) say, "I now pronounce you husband and wife." Rather, he should say something like this, "I now declare that John and Jane have openly and publicly declared their intentions to become husband and wife at some time in the near future—that time may be later tonight (after they are in their motel room), or it may be as long as a year or two from now." (b) This ridiculous position advanced by brother Bales, also implies that even though a man and woman are not yet married to one another, that—provided they intend to become husband and wife by their first completed act of sexual intercourse—they may go to a motel room together and do many things with and to each other in order to bring about sexual excitement. Given brother Bales' theory, they may, for example, before they become husband and wife, be involved in the most intimate sexual activities (short of actual sexual intercourse) which are (or may be) involved in sexual foreplay which ordinarily precedes actual sexual intercourse. All of these things —given brother Bales' theory—can be done with God's approval before and without their becoming or being husband and wife!

A careful, honest reading of such passages as Galatians 5:19-21 and Revelation 21:8 make clear that such is simply not the case. For a man to fondle the breasts and genital area of a woman who is not already his wife is for him to be guilty of lasciviousness (the unchaste handling of males and females, Galatians 5:19-21). Bales' theory implies that, before becoming husband and wife, a man and woman may stand in each other's presence absolutely naked and fondle each other —all with God's approval.

Brother Bales' theory requires that men and women must be guilty of both lasciviousness and fornication in order to get married! Thus, his theory is false for it implies false doctrine (I Cor. 6:18).

4. *Let it be noted once and for all that sexual intimacy is a privilege of marriage; sexual intimacy is not what marries men and women.* The Bible plainly teaches a number of things which consitute proof that sexual intimacy is a privilege of marriage and that sexual intimacy is not what marries men and women.

(1) *The Bible teaches that one can be involved in sexual intercourse without being married.* To the woman of Samaria, Jesus said, "Thou saidst well, I have no husband; and he whom thou now has is not thy husband. . ." (John 4:17-18). She was evidently living with a man but was not married to him—at least she had not been joined to him by God.

(2) *The Bible teaches that one can be married without having engaged in sexual intercourse.* Before

Joseph and Mary came together sexually, an angel said to Joseph, ". . .fear not to take unto thee Mary thy wife: for that which is conceived in her is of the Holy Spirit" (Matthew 1:21). At that time Mary was a virgin (Matthew 1:23). Having been given this instruction, Joseph arose and "did as the angel of the Lord commanded him, and took unto him his wife; and knew her not till she had brought forth a son; and he called his name Jesus" (Matthew 1:24-25). The statement that Joseph "knew her not till she had brought forth a son" means that *Joseph did not have sexual intercourse with Mary until after Jesus was born!* Yet, the Bible makes clear that Mary was his wife before Jesus was born—that he "took unto him his wife."

Thus, it is clear that sexual intercourse is a privilege of marriage and is not what marries a man and woman. Two eligible partners marry each other by pledging themselves—each to the other—to become husband and wife and to live as such.

But, given brother Bales' theory, if because of the illness of either one (or both) of the two immediately after the marriage ceremony (or for some other reason—such as a crippling accident) the man and woman mutually agreed (as per I Corinthians 7:1-5) to forego sexual relations for a brief period of time, they would still not be married until after their first sexual relation. Further, given Bales' theory, if the man were killed in an automobile accident before the two had sexual intercourse, the woman would not be his wife and, so, would have no right to his estate.

Brother Bales' theory implies that God requires men and women to commit sin in order to get married. Any doctrine which implies such a doctrine is false! Thus, the doctrine of James D. Bales on marriage is false.

Footnotes

[1]J. D. Bales has discussed at considerable length the fact that the author of this book (T.B.W.) has, in responding to false doctrine on divorce and remarriage, used the term "homosexual marriage." See Appendix H for this author's additional response to Bales' effort in regard to this matter.

[2]For a more detailed discussion of this point see Roy Deaver, "What is Marriage?" in *The Home as God Would Have It and Contemporary Attacts Against It*, edited by Thomas B. Warren and Garland Elkins (National Christian Press, Inc., Jonesboro, Arkansas, 72401).

[3]This will be proved in Chapters XI and XII.

[4]See Appendix H for further discussion of this matter.

[5]Ibid.

PART II

HOW TO DEMONSTRATE A DOCTRINE

AND HOW TO REFUTE A DOCTRINE

CHAPTER VI

THE CRUCIALITY OF THE LAW OF RATIONALITY AND THE LAWS OF THOUGHT IN THE LEARNING OF TRUTH

1. *The law of rationality.*

(1) *The law of rationality explained.* Although it is no doubt the case that all men are, at some time or other, irrational in their basic response to a given problem and/or situation, every man ought to strive earnestly to be rational.

But what is to be rational? To put the matter quite simply, to be rational is to draw only such conclusions as are warranted by the evidence. When one is a rational person, he says, in effect, to himself, "My conclusions must not outrun the evidence which is relevant to the truth of the question at hand!"

On the other hand, to become irrational is (1) to reject the proper roles of evidence, reason, and conclusion and (2) to hold that faith (Christian faith, that is) must involve the espousal of some inadequately supported conclusion by some "leap into the dark" beyond the evidence. Such a viewpoint is definitely contradictory of the Bible (which teaches men to "prove all things. . ." I Thessalonians 5:21; cf: Acts 17:11).

The law of rationality (I Thessalonians 5:21; Acts 17:11) demands that the Bible be studied carefully, systematically, and prayerfully. This means (1) that the evidence (as to what the Bible actually says explicitly) must be gathered (learned) and (2) that the one who has gathered the evidence must then handle that evidence correctly (logically)—i.e., one must reason correctly about the evidence. It is not enough merely to have learned that the Bible explicitly says thus and so. The task of Biblical interpretation is not finished until that evidence has been properly handled.

(2) *The importance of the law of rationality.* The importance of this law (or principle), which is self-evidently true, is made clear by the following truths: (a) Only God's truth (the Bible) can free men from sin (John 8:32), (b) one must learn not only what the Bible says but also what it means (Matthew 22:29), (the present time is one of enormous proclamation of error—both philosophical and theological, both in and out of the Lord's church), and (c) Christians must not

only preach the truth in a positive way, but they must defend that truth against challenges to it (Mark 16:15-16; Jude 3; I Peter 3:15).

If one rejects the law of rationality, then he holds that logical (valid) reasoning is irrelevant to the search for truth, and if he rejects logic, then he rejects evidence as being of any value, and finally, if he rejects evidence, then even conversation about truth and falsity becomes nonsensical.

The importance of the law of rationality is further seen in the words of Jesus (recorded in Matthew 4:1-11). After the devil had quoted from Psalm 91:11, Jesus said, "Again it is written. . ." and quoted from Deuteronomy 6:16, showing that the Deuteronomy passage modified the surface meaning of Psalm 91:11 (Matthew 4:1-11). Thus, it is clear that, in order to understand the Bible, one must know not only what the Bible says explicitly but also what it implies by its explicit statements.

Since the Bible is the product of the Holy Spirit, it contains neither false statements (premises) nor invalid arguments in the presentation of God's case. No one can understand the Bible without recognizing that all the Bible teaches, it teaches either explicitly or implicitly.

To say that something is taught *explicitly* is to say that it is stated in so many words (i.e., the point is made clear without the reader (or listener) having to exercise his powers of ratiocination (reasoning) in order to deduce (infer) some proposition which is not already part of that explicit evidence. To say that some proposition (or the conjunction of a number of propositions) *implies* another proposition is to say that it is impossible for the proposition(s) which serves as evidence to be true without the conclusion also being true.[2]

The reader should also study the material in some standard logic textbook on the three laws of thought (the law of identity, the law of excluded middle, and the law of contradiction).[3] For propositions, the *law of excluded middle* says: every precisely stated proposition is either true or false. For propositions, the *law of contradiction* says: no proposition can be both true and false, in the same respects.

2. *Some special points on logic.*

(1) *The importance of logic.* Even some Christians have been so misled by false philosophy and false theology, that they reject logic as having a crucial role in an adequate method in learning what the Bible teaches. But without the power to reason logically (i.e., in a valid way) one could not know: (1) that God exists, (2) that the Bible is the word of God, (3) that God is infinite in all of His attributes, (4) that

Jesus Christ is the Son of God, (5) that one must be baptized to be saved, etc.

(2) *Some crucial definitions. Logic* is that discipline which attempts to determine whether conclusions are warranted from some given evidence. Thus, logic deals with the *relationship of propositions,* some of which serve as *evidence*, and others which serve as conclusion(s). Validity and soundness apply to arguments. To say that an argument is *valid* is to say that *if* the *premises* (the supporting propositions) are true, then the *conclusion* must also be true. An argument is *sound* if it is the case both that the *argument is valid* and *all* of the *premises are true*. Only sound arguments prove their conclusions. Invalid arguments prove nothing. These are some of the crucial reasons why logic (and its proper use) is so very important. Men who have the truth do not disparage logic. In fact, as one well-known philosopher said, "No man ever turns against reason until reason turns against him."

In this review, it will be pointed out from time to time how very little attention brother Bales gives to the setting out of arguments in precise logical form. In order to determine what he (Bales) is arguing, one usually must read through long sections of his books and, then, in the absence of brother Bales' himself having set out his arguments (if any) in precise logical form, the reader himself must perform that task—i.e., the reader must formulate the argument(s) which brother Bales should have formulated in the presentation of his own case.

This writer does not wish to be unfair, with brother Bales. It certainly is true that he is aware (I judge this from what he has told me personally) that the proper use of logic is important. It is just that he does not give precise formulations of his own "arguments." He writes long discourses with no "three-line arguments" by which his efforts may be quickly tested for validity and soundness. It has been well said that while four hundred pages of crowded fact and loose argument may deceive many people, when that same material is reduced to a three-line syllogism, its validity or invalidity is usually easily seen by at least most people.

It is the judgment of this writer that the absence of such precise argumentation in brother Bales' work on divorce and remarriage is very significant and some who say, "His argument proves his case," could not even set out his argument for Bales has not set it out and neither have his followers. Strictly speaking —in a technical sense—brother Bales has no precisely stated, logical argument on this matter.

(3) *A final word on logic*. To learn truth, one must (1) *gather* the relevant *evidence*, (2) using that evidence, write an *argument* and prove that that

argument is *valid* and (3) *prove* that *all* of the *premises* are *true*. (Points (2) and (3) are involved in the proper handling of the evidence.) When one has correctly done these three things, he has a *sound argument* which *proves* that the *conclusion* of his argument is *true*. Until one does this, even though he may write hundreds of books and millions of words, *he has not proved his case*.[4]

Brother Bales has *not* proved his case—he has not set out a sound argument, the conclusion of which is his basic proposition.[5] He has not truly acted in harmony with the law of rationality (I Thess. 5:21).

Footnotes

[1]Much of the material in this chapter is from the author's book on hermenutics, *When Is An "Example" Binding?* National Christian Press, Inc., P.O. Box 280; Jonesboro, Arkansas 72401.

[2]A more detailed discussion of this matter can be found in standard logic textbooks.

[3]These laws have relevance both to objects and propositions. The basic concern in this book will be with propositions.

[4]See more details of this in the author's book, *When Is An "Example" Binding?* Chapter II.

[5]More on this in Chapters XIV and XV.

CHAPTER VII

HOW TO PROVE A PROPOSITION TO BE TRUE

There is hardly any problem which could compare in importance with that suggested by the title of this chapter. The reader should study carefully not only this chapter but, if he should be interested in more detailed treatment of the same topic, he should study Appendix I on Logic and—perhaps—even a textbook on logic.

1. *Some introductory material.* In chapter XV, it will be shown that brother Bales (1) failed to set out a specific, precise proposition to affirm and prove and (2) failed to set out a sound argument by which to prove his proposition. In failing in these two points, brother Bales failed to prove his case.

2. *"Logophobia"—the fear of logic.* A proposition (doctrine) is shown to be true if (1) that proposition is the conclusion of an argument, (2) the argument is valid, and (3) all of the premises are true. Revelant to this is Kahane's statement that a "proof of an argument is a list of sentences all of which are either premises of the argument or else follow from previous sentences on the list by valid argument forms (rules of inference), where the last sentence on the list is the conclusion of the argument."[1]

So, to prove that a proposition is true, one must (1) *gather* the relevant evidence and (2) correctly *handle* the evidence (i.e., reason about the evidence in a valid way—cf. I Thessalonians 5:21). *There is no other way to prove that the Bible teaches a certain doctrine.* Obviously, this requires that those who wish to learn truth will both recognize the value of and utilize the principles of valid reasoning (logic).

But, it seems that some are afflicted with a very dangerous theological disease: "logophobia." "Logophobia" is the fear of and/or the rejection of the cruciality of the role of *valid reasoning* in arriving at the truth. Dr. A. G. N. Flew, of England stated it well when he said, "To be illogical, therefore, is to be stupid, or to be incoherent, or to be insufficiently concerned about truth, or all three together."[2]

Many people erroneously think that they are being simple and, thus, clear, because they reject logical reasoning. Actually, some even boast of having nothing to do with logic. The appalling ignorance of such a position—especially on the part of one who claims to follow the gospel of Christ (I Thessalonians 5:21)—is simply outrageously inexcusable. Almost always such people try to establish their case (obviously, inconsistently so, even in attempting such an endeavor) by the use of invalid arguments. But *invalid* arguments prove nothing (except, perhaps, the ignorance of those who are victims of "logophobia").

Professor Flew again stated the case well when he said, "Certainly it is true that those who speak thus disrespectfully of logic or tolerantly of contradiction usually do so, either because they do not much care whether what they say is true, or because they have little or no comprehension of what logic is."[3]

He goes on, "What is obnoxious, and what merits all the abuse in the stockpile, is wilful maintaining of preconceptions against the weight of the evidence."[4]

But what if one simply "shrugs off" (rejects as non-essential or irrelevant) logical (valid) reasoning? Then he rejects the very way by which Jesus Himself (and the Holy Spirit, the Apostles, and the prophets) proceeded (Acts 2:22-40; I Thess. 5:21). No honest man could continue to do such after he learned the truth of the matter. Let no child of God be guilty of rejecting the Bible way (of proving things, I Thessalonians 5:21) but accepting the devilish philosophy of existentialism, with its basically anti-logic—and purely subjective—approach.

Thus, may it be emphasized, as a summary of the matter, that (1) "logophobia" is the fear and/or the rejection of the cruciality of the role of valid reasoning (logic) in the learning of truth, and (2) to be *illogical* is to be either: (a) *ignorant*—of the crucial role of logic, or (b) *stupid*—i.e., to be simply unable to grasp the essentiality of valid reasoning in arriving at truth, or (3) *incoherent*—i.e., simply unable to "fit things together," or (4) *unconcerned*—i.e., not really caring whether what one holds is true or false, or (5) *concerned*—i.e., about something else more than one is concerned about truth!

Thus, he who speaks disparagingly of valid reasoning—or if he is not disturbed by the fact that his position involves self-contradiction and/or implies a logical contradiction—then he shows that he (1) has little or no concern as to whether what he holds is true, (2) has little or no understanding of what logic really is, and (3) that he is more "wedded" to a human theory than he is to Christ—that he will continue to hold to a false position even in the face of a sound argument which proves that his position is false. How sad for any Christian to become a victim of the "disease" of the mind called "logophobia."

Remember, no man ever knowingly turns against reason until reason turns against him. This is why one often hears some exponent of error say, "Oh, he uses logic! All logic does is confuse the issue. He should become as I am—i.e., irrational!" But if this author were to ask such a misguided person why he (this author) should also become irrational, the man would be inconsistent (self-contradictory) if he tried to give a reason. Why is this the case? Because giving reasons (evidence) for holding that a position should be accepted as true is a rational activity—not an irrational one. To try to be irrational is to become a victim of nonsense.

Yet, many Christians try to maintain their position on divorce and remarriage while being very strong "logophobiaists" (irrationalists). No doubt, the Lord's church will suffer severly during the next few years because of this stupidity! Any man who is unconcerned as to whether his argument is valid or invalid, sound or unsound is indeed a dangerous man so far as the kingdom of God is concerned. He himself will draw many wrong conclusions and, no doubt, will lead many others to follow him—especially when the issue involved is one frought with such emotional aspects as is that of divorce and remarriage. But God's law is not changed by human feelings and/or desires. That law will meet men at the Judgment, unchanged by human emotions—even emotions about marriage.

3. *How to prove that a proposition is true.* Some on this subject has already been said in the preceding section. Yet, at least a little more needs to be said because: (1) this author has a proposition (doctrine) to be proved and (2) brother Bales has a proposition (doctrine) to be proved. The reader must understand the obligation which falls upon the shoulders of the respective disputants in order to know which (if either) has succeeded in proving his own proposition to be true.

By way of repetition, the task can be summarized by noting (1) that each must recognize and honor the "law of rationality," (2) that each must gather the evidence which is relevant to each respective proposition, and (3) that each must properly handle the evidence gathered; i.e., he must reason about it in a valid way, drawing only such conclusions as are warranted by the evidence. (This means that if either is to prove his proposition, he must show that it is the conclusion of a sound argument.)

It must be noted that in gathering the evidence, one must consider (1) the *lexical* evidence (the meaning of the words involved), (2) the *syntactical* evidence (the evidence of the way the words are put together to form sentences) (3) the *contextual* evidence (i.e., the evidence of both the immediate and remote context), (4) the *historical* evidence (i.e., the evidence of the circumstances which call forth the writing of a certain thing), and (5) the *analogical* evidence (i.e., the whole trend of scripture which would be weighted toward a certain viewpoint).[5]

4. *How should one react to efforts to persuade him to accept certain positions?* When other people seek to persuade one to accept a certain position, how should he react?

First, one must be careful that he does not accept a view just because (a) it is a popular view, or because (b) one wants to believe it, or because (c) it involves emotional factors, or because (d) it "seems" right to him, or because (e) it is taught by people one "likes," or because (f) not to accept it would involve one in a confrontation with exponents of that view.

5. *Some further thoughts about arguments.* It is very important for one to understand a number of crucial matters on arguments. Among these are the following.

(1) Arguments (in logic) are comprised of propositions, some of which serve as premises (evidence) and one of which serves as the conclusion.

(2) An argument is valid when the truth of the premises guarantees the truth of the conclusion.

(3) An argument is sound when the argument itself is valid and the premises are true. (Thus, a sound argument must have a true conclusion.)

(4) An argument can be persuasive (i.e., people, may be persuaded to accept its conclusion) even if it is not sound.

(5) An argument can be sound but not persuasive. (Jesus and His disciples often presented sound arguments which were rejected by their auditors. Cf. Stephen {Acts 7}; Paul {Acts 14:1-7; 17:1-9}.)

(6) One can be pleasing to God only by being persuaded by sound arguments (I Thessalonians 5:21; Acts 17:11; 2:22-47; I John 4:1; Acts 20:28 ff; John 6:26; 20:30-31).

(7) It is possible for a valid argument to have a false conclusion (cf., atheists and the "problem of evil").

(8) It is possible for an invalid argument to have a true conclusion.

6. *Assertions without knowledge.* Surely Abraham Lincoln was correct when he asserted that a man who contends that a given position is true without knowing that such is the case is, in fact, guilty of falsehood and, even if the position is true, then he is still not excused or justified in asserting that to be true which he did not know to be true.[6]

7. *The value of a precise logical argument.* Josiah Stamp correctly said that a fallacy that would be obvious to every one in a three-line syllogism "may deceive the elect in four hundred pages of crowded fact and argument. . ." Stamp went on to say that he thought that it is a "useful exercise for any of us. . . to reduce any book of whose conclusions we are doubtful into a set of formal syllogisms and lay bare the bones of the argument."[7]

8. *Summary as to how to prove a proposition is true.* Basically there are three ways of showing that a proposition (as it relates to Bible teaching) is

true: (1) show that it is *stated explicitly* in the Bible, (2) show that it is *implied*[8] by *explicit* statement(s) in the Bible, and (3) show that it is the *conclusion* of a *sound argument*—i.e., the argument is valid and all of the premises are true.[9]

To put the matter in a simple way, it has been made clear that, to prove that a proposition (which relates to Bible teaching) is true, is to show that it is the conclusion of a sound argument which involves true premises which relate to Bible information.

Who presents a sound argument in regard to divorce and remarriage: James D. Bales? Thomas B. Warren? Neither? The remainder of the book should answer this question.

Footnotes

[1]Howard Kahane, *Logic and Philosophy* (Belmont, Ca., Wadsworth Publishing Co., 1978, 3rd edition).

[2]A. G. N. Flew, *Thinking Straight*.

[3]Ibid., p. 18.

[4]Ibid., pp. 29-30.

[5]Cf.: W. D. Chamberlain, *An Exegetical Grammar of the Greek New Testament*.(New York, The Macmillan Co., 1952), pp. 3-5.

[6]Cf.: Flew, *Thinking Straight*, p. 15.

[7]Quoted by Prof. Max Black (Cornell University) in his book *Critical Thinking*, p. 13.

[8]To say that proposition q is implied by proposition p is logically equivalent to saying that it is impossible for proposition p to be true and proposition q to be false. $\{(p \supset q \equiv \sim(p \cdot \sim q)\}$. See Appendix I, on "Logic" and Chapter XVIII for more details.

[9](2) and (3) are basically the same procedure.

CHAPTER VIII

HOW TO PROVE A PROPOSITION TO BE FALSE

The importance of Chapter VIII certainly compares in importance with that of Chapter VII. It is no doubt the case that one needs to be able to prove that the proposition (doctrine) which he himself affirms is true. At times, it may be equally important to refute the proposition which is affirmed by an opponent in a dispute.

1. *Some introductory material.* In Part V, four chapters will be devoted to refuting the doctrine of Dr. James D. Bales on divorce and remarriage. His *basic proposition* (which this author has been forced to formulate—since brother Bales himself did not do so) will be set out and explained in Part IV, Chapter XIV. His failure to prove that proposition will be shown in Chapter XV.

Then in Part V, brother Bales' basic proposition will be refuted (proved to be false).

In Chapter XVI-A and XVI-B it will be shown that brother Bales' doctrine is false because it denies plain Bible teaching. (Any doctrine which denies plain Bible teaching is—and must be—false.[1])

In Chapter XVII, it will be shown that his doctrine is false because it implies false doctrine, and any doctrine which implies a false doctrine is itself false.

In Chapter XVIII, it will be shown that his doctrine is false because it implies and/or involves logical contradictions, and any doctrine which implies a logical contradiction is itself false.

In Chapter XIX, it will be shown that his doctrine is false because he *admits defeat* in a number of ways.

In connection with the showing (in Chapter XV), of brother Bales' inability to prove his own doctrine, these refutations of that doctrine (in Chapters XVI-A, XVI-B, XVII, XVIII, and XIX) will really complete the case against his false doctrine.

In the face of such damaging evidence against the Bales' doctrine, it will require extreme prejudice to accept and/or continue to hold onto it.

Of course, the reader must judge for himself as to whether the case against brother Bales' doctrine is as strong as the claim herein made.

Since much of the material in this chapter somewhat overlaps with the material set forth in Chapter VII (e.g., the material on contradiction), it will not be necessary to go into as much detail in this present chapter.

2. *Ways of showing that a proposition is false.* The two main purposes of this book are: (1) to prove

Again, where is the critical analysis, the head-to-heAd confrontation with BAles position focusing on text itself.

that "Proposition TBW" (the basic one affirmed by the author of this book) is true and (2) to prove that "Proposition JDB" (the basic one affirmed by brother Bales) is false.

In Chapters X, XI, XII, and XIII "Proposition TBW" will be proved to be *true*, and in Chapters XVI-A, XVI-B, XVII, XVIII, and XIX, "Proposition JDB" will be proved to be *false*.

3. *How will "Proposition JDB" be proved to be false?* "Proposition JDB" will be proved to be false in these ways: (1) by showing that it *contradicts* an *explicit* statement in the Bible,[2] (2) by showing that it implies a *false doctrine*.[3] (Any doctrine which implies a false doctrine is itself false.), (3) by showing that it implies (or involves) a *logical contradiction*,[4] and (4) by showing that it involves *admissions of defeat*.[5]

4. *Conclusion of this chapter.* In this chapter, it has been shown that there are at least four ways of refuting a doctrine. All of these ways will be used (in Chapters XVI-A, XVI-B, XVII, XVIII, and XIX) to prove that "Proposition JDB" is false.

Footnotes

[1]See Appendix I on "Logic" for more details.

[2]$\{Q\cdot(P\equiv\sim Q)\}>\sim P$ (where "Q" stands for a proposition which is taught either explicitly or implicitly in the Bible) The reader who has not studied logic in a formal way can easily understand the argument without studying this more technical material.

[3]$\{(P>Q)\cdot\sim Q\}>\sim P$ (Where "Q" stands for some proposition which is implied by Bales' basic proposition.)

[4]$\{P>(X\cdot\sim X)\}>\sim P$ (Where $(X\cdot\sim X)$ stands for a logical contradiction implied by Bales' proposition.)

[5]Note: a fifth way might be considered (i.e., by showing that it contradicts another proposition which has already been proved to be true), but since this way so nearly parallels another and since the refutation is complete without it, this way will not be considered here.

PART III

THE TRUE BASIC PROPOSITION ON DIVORCE AND REMARRIAGE

SET OUT, EXPLAINED, AND DEMONSTRATED

CHAPTER IX

THE CRUCIAL ISSUES INVOLVED IN THE TRUE BASIC PROPOSITION

The proposition to be set out and defended in this book is held by the author to be true and to be demonstrable as such. Part III will be devoted to that demonstration (proof).

Because the proposition involved is rather long, the author will use numbers and paragraphs in order to make it easier for the reader to follow and understand it. The proposition is long because, as should be clear to any honest person who sees the basic issues in this problem, not only is the question *divorce and remarriage* at stake, but as logically prior to that question, the additional question as to who (among those living today) is *amenable to* (under) the New Covenant (the law of Christ, the gospel of Christ, the faith, etc.) is also at stake. More will be said toward the clarification of this point after the statement of the proposition.

1. *The true basic proposition set out.* The proposition (in regard to the crucial matter of divorce and remarriage) which the author of this book holds to be true is now to be stated. This author holds that the following proposition—which will hereinafter be referred to as "Proposition TBW," in order to easily distinguish it from the basic doctrine of J. D. Bales, which will hereinafter be referred to as "Proposition JDB"—accurately sets forth *the Biblical position* on the matters which are most crucial to this entire problem.

"Proposition TBW" will be comprised of (a) *Sub-Proposition R, an opening general statement* in regard to amenability to the law of Christ, (b) *Sub-Proposition S*, which relates that amenability (to the law of Christ) to the question of denominationalism, and (c) *Sub-Proposition T*, which relates that amenability (to the law of Christ) to the specific question of divorce and remarriage.

Of course, Sub-Proposition T is the element of "Proposition TBW" which is most relevant to the basic problem with which this book deals, but it is very important for the reader to understand that the entirety of "Proposition TBW" is necessary to a proper treatment of the question at hand. (This same importance will, later in the book, be attached to the entirety of "Proposition JDB.")

"Proposition TBW" reads as follows: The Bible teaches that:

(SUB-PROPOSITION R of "Proposition TBW")

(1) All men (whether Christian or non-Christian) living today are amenable to (under) the New Covenant (the law of Christ, the gospel, the faith) and—thus,

(SUB-PROPOSITION S of "Proposition TBW" follows)

(2) That all men (whether Christian or non-Christian) living to day

a. Commit sin when they *establish or enter or support* (by, for example, preaching the doctrines of) any religious institution (such as the Baptist Church and/or the Roman Catholic Church) which is *not authorized* by the New Covenant (the law of Christ); and—

b. Commit sin when they (as, for example, Baptist preachers living today sin—by violating the law of Christ—when, in preaching Baptist doctrine) urge other men:

(a.) To reject the *gospel plan of salvation* and to accept the Baptist doctrine that alien sinners (non-Christians) are saved at the point of faith in Christ before and without being baptized in the name of Christ, and/or—

(b.) To reject *the church* which was purchased by the blood of Christ and to enter the Baptist Church and to remain in it until death, and/or—

(c.) To reject the *worship* authorized by the New Covenant and to worship God by singing with the accompaniment of mechanical instruments of music, and/or—

(d.) To reject the *way of life* authorized and demanded by the law of Christ (cf. I John 1:7; Gal. 5:19-23) and to urge others to accept the view that no sin from murder to adultery to idolatry can endanger the salvation of one who has been born again (II Pet. 2:20-22);

(SUB-PROPOSITION T: The Bible teaches)

(3) *That*—as regards marriage, divorce, and remarriage—all persons (whether Christian or non-Christian) who, in violating the teaching of the law of Christ (specifically, in divorcing and marrying again on some ground other than *fornication*, in violation of Matthew 19:9), are involved in sinful practices and/or sinful states and/or sinful relationships are persons who are instructed by that law to cease those sinful practices, to get out of those sinful states, and to sever those sinful relationships.

2. *The true basic proposition explained.*

Is bro Bales desperately looking for a way around Matt 19 or rather has an honest examination of I Cor 7 forced him to his conclusions?

Admittedly, "Proposition TBW" is more lengthy than is usual for propositions to be proved or disproved. But this proposition is as long as it is because of various positions taken (explicitly and/or implicitly) by brother Bales.

As did brother Fuqua, he (Bales) seeks desperately to find some way of offering to people some ground other than the one—and only one—allowed by Jesus for divorce and remarriage (Matt. 19:9) namely, that of *fornication* on the part of the one put away. (As was stated earlier, Bales' position can accurately be branded "Neo-Fuquaism.")

To find (and establish) that some *other* ground or grounds actually are allowed by God, brother Bales must do something about Matt. 19:9 for it obviously teaches {see Appendix A} that, for all who are amenable to its teaching, fornication is the one and only ground for divorce and remarriage. (Even brother Fuqua admitted that.)

So—no doubt in all honesty—brother Bales has come up with the following positions (as to what the Bible teaches on this matter).

(1) No *non-Christian* is amenable to (under) the New Covenant (the law of Christ).

(2) Thus, no *non-Christian* is amenable to the teaching of Matthew 19:9.

(3) Not even all *Christians* are amenable to the gospel (law) of Christ, but—Bales affirms— only *Christians who are married to Christians* are amenable to Matthew 19:9.

(4) The gospel (law) of Christ contains *no* legislation to any *non-Christian*. (This is the case, he alleges, because one cannot be under the New Covenant until he is "in" the Covenant. But, if his allegation is true, then *Christians* are to be baptized. Since this is false, Bales' doctrine is false.)

Other points in Bales' doctrine will be set forth and criticized in subsequent material. It will suffice, for the purposes involved at this point, to set out those indicated above, and those suggested by the questions below.

The crucial issues for which one should look in a discussion of marriage, divorce and remarriage are pin-pointed by the following questions.

1. Is it the case that men are amenable only to the law which is addressed to them? (Cf.: Rom. 3: 19; 4:15.)

2. If a law is *universal*—that is, if it is addressed to all men—then is it not the case that all men are amenable to (under) that law? (Cf.: Mk. 16: 15-16; Matt. 28:18-20.)

3. If the gospel (law of Christ) is a universal law—that is, if it is addressed to all men—then is it not the case that all men (whether Christian or

non-Christian) are amenable to (under) the law of Christ?

4. If all men are to be taught to observe "all things whatsoever" Jesus commanded (as a part of the New Covenant) during His earthly ministry, then is it not the case that (since Jesus *did* teach *Matthew 19:9* during his earthly ministry) *all* men living today (whether *Christian* or *non-Christian*) *are* amenable to the teaching of Matthew 19:9?

Conclusion

The reader must beware lest anyone (by an appeal to emotions, hardships, etc.) blind him to the fact that the issues cited above (and even others) are crucially involved in the problem of marriage, divorce and remarriage. Brother Bales has tried to make it appear that, for example, denominationalism is not at all involved in the problem. Material which will be set out in following chapters will prove that brother Bales is wrong about that—just as was brother Fuqua. Fuqua could not handle both problems (divorce and remarriage and denominationalism) and neither can Bales. This is the case because their positions on divorce and remarriage are false. This truth will be proved in chapters yet to come.

Warren assumes that everything in NT Message is Addressed to Aliens.

CHAPTER X

THERE IS ONE—AND ONLY ONE—BODY OF DOCTRINE FOR MEN LIVING TODAY: THE GOSPEL OF CHRIST (THE LAW OF CHRIST)

I. Some Introductory Matters

In Chapter XI, a proposition which states the truth on Bible teaching regarding divorce and remarriage will be restated and then explained briefly. In Chapter XII, that proposition ("Proposition TBW" as over against "Proposition JDB" which sets out brother Bales' doctrine) will be demonstrated (shown to be true).

What will be set out in this present chapter is actually a crucial element in the argument which is to be used to prove that "Proposition TBW" is true. However, since the particular matter to be discussed in Chapter XII is so lengthy, in order that the "flow" of the argument (which is to be set forth in Chapter XII) be allowed to be as uninterrupted as possible, it was decided to discuss the proposition (which not only serves as the title of Chapter X, but also is crucially involved with several premises in the argument which proves "Proposition TBW") in detail here in Chapter X. This procedure will enable this author to refer to the material in Chapter X without having to repeat it in Chapter XII.

II. Some Additional Introductory Matters

1. *The proposition to be proved in Chapter X set out and explained.*

(1) *The proposition (premise) which will be proved in this present chapter is:* "There is one—and only one—body of doctrine for men living today: the gospel of Jesus Christ (the law of Christ)."

(2) *What this proposition means.* The proposition stated in (1) above means simply that the gospel of Christ (the law of Christ) is the one—and the only—law which God has for all men living today. (Of course, the law of Christ authorizes civil law, Rom. 13:1-7.) All men (whether Christian or non-Christian) are amenable to (under) that one law, and, thus, all men (whether Christian or non-Christian) who violate—by either thought or action—its teachings sin in so doing.

Since the New Testament uses a number of terms and/or expressions in describing the message of Christ which was preached and/or taught during New Testament times, this proposition also entails the affirmation that all of these expressions (such as "the gospel," "the faith," "the truth," "the law of Christ," "the doctrine of Christ," et al.) refer to one and the same body of doctrine. If this is true—and it is—then Bales' doctrine is false.

Brother Bales' allegation to the effect that gospel and doctrine are to be distinguished is simply not true. More of brother Bales' error on this point will be set out in Parts IV and V.

2. *The task involved in dealing with this proposition.* Since the proposition affirms that the gospel (law of Christ) is the one and only body of doctrine which God has addressed to all men living today, and since a number of different terms are used in the New Testament to refer to what was preached and/or taught by Christ's faithful disciples during New Testament times, if it can be shown, in regard to each of these expressions, (a) that it was *to be preached* to both *non-Christians* and *Christians*, (b) that both non-Christians and Christians could (can) *be saved* by it, and (c) that both non-Christians and Christians will *be lost* if they reject it, then it will have been shown: (a) that all of the terms and/or expressions refer to one and the same body of doctrine, (b) that that one body of doctrine is addressed to all men (whether non-Christian or Christian) and, thus, (c) that all men (whether non-Christian or Christian) are amenable to (under) that one body of doctrine (the gospel, the faith, the word of God, the law of Christ, et al.).

Since brother Bales stakes his case on his allegation that *non-Christians* are *not* amenable to (under) the law of Christ (the doctrine of Christ), it is imperative that it be shown that "the gospel," "the law of Christ," "the doctrine of Christ," "the faith," "the word," "the word of God, et al., all refer to *one and the same body of doctrine*. If this is true—and it is true—then the distinction which brother Bales implies exists between "gospel" and "doctrine" simply does not exist. (Brother Bales' doctrine on this point will be discussed in detail in Part IV and V. In this present chapter, the main look is at the affirmative (TBW) case. Some of the terms will be discussed in detail; others will be discussed enough only to show the point under consideration.

III. The Proposition Stated

The proposition to be proved in this present chapter, Proposition A (which will be a constituent element in the argument which proves "Proposition TBW") is stated as follows: (a) "The law of Christ, the gospel of Christ, the doctrine of Christ, the faith, the truth, the New Covenant, the word (as well as the message designated as "Jesus," "Christ") are all one and the same body of doctrine, and (b) that law (the law of Christ) is God's one and only law for men living today, and, thus, (c) all men living today are amenable to that one law (the law of Christ), and (d) that law (the law of Christ) instructs all men living today as to (1) how they must live in order to please God (i.e., not sin), (2) what they must do to become saved (i.e., to become a Christian) after having fallen into sin, and (3) what they must do in order to stay saved (i.e., to live the faithful Christian life),"[1]

IV. Proposition A Explained

In the material to be presented here, the following terms and/or expressions will be considered: "the gospel," "the doctrine of Christ," "the faith," "the word," "the law of Christ," "the truth," "the New Covenant," "Jesus," "Christ." It will be shown that each one of these terms and/or expressions refer to one and the same body of doctrine. It will be shown that in regard to each one of them, with reference both to the non-Christian and to the Christian, these things are true: (1) each is to be preached to and/or taught to both the non-Christian and the Christian, (2) each is shown to be the means of salvation both to the non-Christian and the Christian, and (3) any person (either non-Christian or Christian) who rejects any one of them will be lost.

Thus, it is clear that the law of Christ (God's one and only law for men living today) instructs all men living today as to (1) how they must live in order to please God (i.e., not sin), (2) what they must do to become saved (after having fallen into sin) and (3) what they must do in order to stay saved (i.e., to live the faithful Christian life).

V. Proposition A Proved

The proposition is shown to be true by the following material.

1. *"The gospel of Christ."*
   (1) *The gospel and non-Christians.*
      (a) *The gospel is to be preached to non-Christians* (Mk. 16:15; Acts 16:10; I Corinthians 4:15).

The gospel is to be preached to *every creature* (person) in *every nation* (cf. parallel account of the great commission in Matthew 28:18-20). The challenge is hereby offered to brother Bales (or to any one else) to name one responsible, adult person now living on earth who is not amenable to (under) the gospel! Jesus addressed it to all men and, thus, all men are amenable to (under) the gospel (Mk. 16:15-16; Romans 3:19; 4:15).

(b) *Non-Christians will be saved by the gospel if they believe and obey it (Mark 16:15-16; Acts 14:21;*

II Thessalonians 2:14; Romans 1:15-17. Jesus made clear that every non-Christian who believes and obeys the gospel will be saved (Mark 16:15-16). Paul made clear that men are called by the gospel (II Thessalonians 2:14). The challenge is hereby offered to brother Bales to name even one non-Christian, responsible adult person now living on earth who would not be saved if he believed and obeyed the gospel! Brother Bales cannot meet this challenge, for Jesus taught that all such would be saved (Mark 16:15). God does not lie (Hebrews 6:18); all who come to Him in faithful obedience will be saved (cf. John 6:37).

(c) *Non-Christians will be lost if they reject the gospel (II Thessalonians 1:7-9; Mark 16:15-16; cf. Acts 3:22).* The challenge is offered to brother Bales to name one responsible non-Christian living today who will not be lost if he does not believe the gospel. He cannot meet the challenge, for the Bible teaches that those non-Christians who reject the gospel will be lost. He is further challenged to name one man now living who will not be lost if he does not obey the gospel.

(2) *The gospel and Christians.*

(a) *The gospel is to be preached to Christians.* Paul said he was ready to preach the gospel to the Christians in Rome (Romans 1:15). Paul also taught that the Christians at Corinth had stood and were standing (perfect tense, indicating a completed action with an abiding result) in the gospel (I Corinthians 15:1). The Christians in Corinth were abiding (standing) day-by-day in the gospel. This could not have been the case if Christians are not amenable to the law (gospel) of Christ—one can neither obey nor disobey a law which is not addressed to him (Cf. Romans 3:19; 4:15).

(b) *Christians can be saved by the gospel.* Further, to the Christians at Corinth, Paul said that they were being saved (present passive indicative—the present tense indicating linear, abiding or continuous action) by the gospel (I Corinthians 15:2). Thus, Christians are amenable to the body of doctrine which is called in the New Testament "the gospel." The challenge is hereby offered to brother Bales to name one Christian now living on earth who is not amenable to the gospel.

(c) *Christians will be lost if they reject—do not obey—the gospel.* All who do not obey the gospel will be lost eternally (II Thessalonians 1:7-9). Paul rebuked some Christians who did not walk "uprightly according to the truth of the gospel" (Galatians 2:14). The expression "the truth of the gospel" means "the truth which is the gospel" (genitive of apposition or identification). The challenge is offered to brother Bales to name one Christian now living on earth who will not be lost if he rejects the gospel!

(3) *Some significant facts about the gospel.*

(a) *It should be noted* that "the gospel" and "the word" are clearly indicated in Hebrews 4:2 to be the same body of doctrine. Also, "the word" and "the gospel" are seen to be the same body of doctrine by a comparison of Mark 16:15 ("the gospel" was to be preached to every creature) and Acts 8:4 (the disciples went everywhere preaching "the word").

(b) *In Acts 14:21-22*, it is made clear that "the gospel" and "the faith" are one and the same body of doctrine.

(c) *In I Timothy 1:10-11*, Paul makes clear that "sound doctrine" and "the gospel of the glory of the blessed God" are one and the same body of doctrine. (Cf. Matthew 28:18-20, which will be discussed in Chapter XVI-B and Appendix T.)

(d) *In Colossians 1:5*, Paul makes clear that "the word," "the truth," and "the gospel" are all one and the same body of doctrine. In this passage, the expression "of the truth" is the genitive of identification—that is, "the word which is the truth." Further, the expression "the gospel" is also genitive of identification, making the entire expression read, ". . .the word, which is the truth" and "the truth, which is the gospel." Thus, since things equal to the same thing are equal to each other, and since "the truth" is equal both to "the word" and to "the gospel," it follows that "the word" and "the gospel" are equal to each other (that is, they are one and the same body of doctrine). Consider also Mark 16:15-16; I Timothy 3:14-15; and II Timothy 2:15.

(e) *In Acts 14:21-22*, it is made clear that "the faith" and "the gospel" are one and the same body of doctrine. Further, since men obey: "the gospel" in being saved (Mark 16:15-16) and since non-Christians were obedient to "the faith" in becoming Christians, it is clear that "the gospel" and "the faith" are one and the same body of doctrine. From the same passage (Acts 6:7), it is also clear that "the word" is one and the same body as "the faith" and, thus, that "the word" and "the gospel" are one and the same body of doctrine (teaching).

2. *"The doctrine of Christ."*

(1) *"The doctrine of Christ" and non-Christians*

(a) *A crucial element in brother Bales' effort to prove his doctrine of divorce and remarriage is his erroneous exegesis of Matthew 28:18-20.*[2] Brother Bales thinks that, according to this passage, Jesus told His apostles, first, to teach all nations, then second, to baptize those whom they have taught, and, third, to teach (regarding their responsibilities now that they are Christians) those whom they have already baptized. Even though it is true that God's people are to teach every person in every nation, to baptize every penitent believer (Mark 16:15-16; Acts 2:38), and to continue to teach those who are baptized (after they are baptized, II Timothy 2:1-2; Galatians 1:6-9), it is not true that Matthew 28:18-20 teaches such. Brother Bales' erroneous exegesis of Matthew 28:18-20 is absolutely necessary to his false contention that non-Christians are not amenable to the law of Christ, to his contention that neither Christ nor Paul legislated on divorce and remarriage as far as non-Christians are concerned. But his exegesis of Matthew 28:18-20 is incorrect in that he fails to take into account the fact that both "baptizing" and "teaching" are present participles in the original Greek and, thus, cannot refer (as brother Bales claims) to action which is subsequent to the action of the main verb.[3] The main verb is "make disciples" (ASV from *mathēteuo*). Thus, neither the "teaching them to observe all things whatsoever I command you" nor the "baptizing them" can occur after the action of the main verb—that is, neither the teaching (here referred to) nor the baptizing can occur after the making of disciples! Yet, brother Bales' entire case depends upon the "teaching" occurring after the people are made disciples (Christians) by being baptized. The truth of the matter is: both "baptizing" and "teaching" are present participles used in a modal sense that is, to explain how something is to be accomplished—e.g., "Go beautify the barn, cleaning and painting it" (neither the cleaning nor the painting come after the beautification, but are the means by which the beautification is brought about). Thus, the "teaching" (from *didasko*, which means the delivery of a didactic discourse {doctrine} which is to be delivered to those not yet baptized) is to include "all things whatsoever I (Jesus, T.B.W.) commanded you." Since Jesus taught Matt. 19:9, the "all things" which Jesus said are to be taught to non-Christians includes Matt. 19:9, which brother Bales claims is addressed only to Christians who are married to Christians and, thus, not to non-Christians at all.[4] Bales' case falls on this single point!

But, since a special section on Matthew 28:18-20 is planned for later in the book,[5] it must suffice here to point out that the Bible teaches that "doctrine" is to be taught to non-Christians! In denying this point, brother Bales joins hands with such false teachers as Leroy Garrett and Carl Ketcherside, both of whom long have attempted to persuade the Lord's people to accept doctrine which is false.[6]

(b) *Doctrine is to be taught to the non-Christian.* According to Acts 5:21-29, an angel of the Lord told the apostles, "Go ye, and stand and speak in the temple to the people {obviously non-Christians, T.B.W.} all the words of this life." About daybreak the apostles entered the temple and taught (from *didasko*). Later, this report was given of the apostles' activity, "Behold the men whom ye put in the prison are in the temple standing and teaching (from *didasko*) the people" (Acts 5:25). Thus, they were delivering the *doctrine of Christ* to *non-Christians*!—a thing which brother Bales alleges cannot be done.[7] (Let it be noted that if Bales cannot prove his point on this matter—and he cannot—then his whole case falls!) Still further, in the same context, the captain with the officers brought the apostles before the council, and the high priest said to them, "We straitly charged you not to teach (from *didaskō*, T.B.W.) in this name: and behold, ye have filled Jerusalem with your teaching {*didachēs* translated "doctrine" in K.J.V., T.B.W.} and intended to bring this man's blood upon us" (Acts 5:28). It is clear that the preaching of the crucifixion is designated in the New Testament as "doctrine."

Bales is wrong. According to Acts 13:6-12, the proconsul was converted by Paul's delivering to him "the doctrine (*didachē*) of the Lord" (13:12). Clearly the "doctrine of Christ" was taught to non-Christians! Also note: Acts 17:19; Romans 6:7-18; Matt. 28:18-20. Brother Bales and Leroy Garrett are wrong in teaching that "doctrine" is to be taught only to Christians and that "gospel" is to be preached only to non-Christians.[8] In former times, brother Bales, in commenting on John 6:44-45, both recognized and taught the truth that the doctrine of Christ can be taught to non-Christians.[9] Now, he rejects the truth which he formerly taught—at least when he is on the divorce and remarriage question. (It is the prayer of this author that he will once again recognize and teach the truth which he taught in times past.)

(b) *Non-Christians can be saved by the "doctrine" of Christ.* This has already been proved by Matthew 28: 18-20; Acts 5:17-29; and John 6:44-45. Other passages are also relevant to this same point. For example, after Jesus had taught what is set out in Matthew 7: 13-14 and 7:24-27, the Bible says that "when Jesus had ended these sayings, the people were astonished at his doctrine {from *didachē*} for he taught {from *didaskō*} them as one having authority. . ." (Matthew 7:28-29). Thus, it is clear that the "doctrine" of Christ is to be taught to non-Christians and that non-Christians can be saved by the "doctrine" of Christ. Thus, Bales' doctrine is wrong.

Also, it should be noted that Jesus' teaching on marriage is referred to as "doctrine" (Matthew 22:33). Compare also: Mark 1:22; 4:2; 11:18 ("doctrine," from *didachē*, is used to refer to the parable of the sower). Thus, Bales' doctrine is wrong.

(c) *Non-Christians will be lost if they reject the "doctrine" of Christ.* In the accounts of the

Great Commission, Mark's record has Jesus teaching that every non-Christian who does not believe the gospel will be damned (Mark 16:15-16). Matthew's record teaches that, to be made a disciple (be saved, become a child of God in this context), one must accept the teaching (doctrine) of Christ. Thus, since both accounts refer to one and the same body of teaching (making "gospel" and "doctrine" the same body of teaching), it is clear that non-Christians who reject the "doctrine" of Christ will be damned. (Compare: Acts 3:22.)

(2) *The "doctrine of Christ" and the Christian.*

(a) *The doctrine of Christ is to be taught to Christians.* Without any detailed discussion here, this point is clearly taught in the following passages: II John 9-11; Titus 2:1; II Timothy 2:2; Colossians 2:22; Acts 2:42; 17:19; Romans 16:17-18; II Timothy 4:2; Titus 1:9 (Cf. *didaskalia* "word" and "doctrine"); I Timothy 1:10; I Timothy 4:6; Titus 2:1 (*didaskalia*).

(b) *Christians can be saved by the "doctrine of Christ."* This truth is made clear in at least the following passages: II Timothy 3:16-17; II Timothy 4:3; I Timothy 4:1; Titus 1:9; Acts 2:42. To be saved, Christians must live faithful (to the doctrine of Christ) unto death (Revelations 2:10; Galatians 6:7-9).

(c) *Christians will be lost if they reject the "doctrine of Christ."* This truth is made clear in the following passages: II John 9-11; Matthew 15:9; Titus 1:9-11 (note: to "gainsay" = to "contradict" sound doctrine).

(3) *Some further points about "the doctrine of Christ."* A fair reading of I Timothy 4:1-6 makes clear that the expressions "the faith" (vv. 1,6 obviously in contrast to "the doctrines of devils", v. 1), "the word of God" (v. 5), and "good doctrine" (v. 6) are all used to refer to the same body of teaching. To make known "the faith" is to make known "the word of God" and "the doctrine of Christ." The "doctrine of Christ" (II John 9-11) is the doctrine which has Christ as its author and supporter (John 7:17; Acts 13:12; II John 9; Thayer *Greek Lexicon*, p. 144; cf. John 18:19-20).

Thus, it is clear that "the doctrine of Christ" (in its full connotation) refers to: (a) all that is necessary to avoid sin in the first place, (b) all that is necessary to become saved after falling into sin, and (c) all that is necessary to staying saved after becoming a Christian. Thus, "the doctrine of Christ" includes His teaching on divorce and remarriage and all men (whether Christian or non-Christians) are amenable to it. (Matt. 28:18-20; Mk. 16:15-16; Acts 17:30-31.) This point is destructive of Bales' doctrine.

In the treatment of the two expressions considered above, more detail was given than will be given to the various expressions yet to be discussed. This lessening of detail is not, by any means, brought about because there is less information in the Bible on them. Rather, it has been decided upon to avoid tediousness. It has been shown what can be done with each of the foregoing and following words. Thus, an outline approach with the following terms which are used to refer to the one body of doctrine will be sufficient. Especially is this case since so many references to the scriptures will be made.

3. *"The Faith."*

(1) *"The faith" and non-Christians.*

(a) *"The faith" is to be taught to non-Christians.* This truth is made clear in at least the following passages: Acts 15:6-9; 13:8; 13:4-12; 14:21-22; 18:5-11; 24:24-25; Galatians 1:23; 3:14; 3:23-27.

(b) *Non-Christians can be saved by "the faith."* This truth is made clear in at least the following passages: Acts 6:7; 13:7-8; Romans 3:25; 3:30-31; 5:2; 10:8; Galatians 3:23-27.

(c) *Non-Christians will be lost if they reject "the faith."* This truth is made clear in at least the following passages: Galatians 3:23-27; Acts 24-25; 6:7; II Thessalonians 1:7-9 ("the gospel" = "the faith" Acts 14:21-22).

(2) *"The faith" and Christians.*

(a) *"The faith" is to be taught to Christians.* This truth is made clear in at least the following passages: I Timothy 6:10; Acts 14:21-22; Galatians 6:10; I Timothy 4:1; Titus 1:13-14. ("the faith" = "the truth").

(b) *Christians can be saved by "the faith."* Philippians 1:27; 3:9; Acts 16:5; ("the faith" = "the word of God," Acts 6:7) Colossians 1:22-23; 2:6-7; Ephesians 3:17; 6:16; II Corinthains 13:5; Romans 11:20; I Corinthains 16:13; II Corinthains 1:24; I Timothy 3:9; 4:1,6; 6:12; II Timothy 4:7; Titus 2:1-2; Acts 16:5.

(c) *Christians will be lost if they reject "the faith."* This truth is made clear in at least the following passages: Jude 3; I Timothy 6:10,12; 4:1; 5:8; 6:10; Acts 14:22; II Timothy 4:6-8; I Corinthians 16:13; I Peter 5:8-9; I Timothy 1:19; II Timothy 3:7-8; I Timothy 6:21 (cf. II Timothy 2:18 re "the truth").

(3) *Some further points about "the faith."* Paul plainly teaches that there is "one faith" (Eph. 4:5). By this means that there is one body of doctrine which Christ has for the whole world. That one faith is exactly the same thing as "the word of God," "the doctrine of Christ," "the gospel," et al. It is the one body of doctrine which is to be preached to all men

(with proper explanation as to application), and it is the one body of doctrine for which we are to earnestly contend. (Cf. Acts 6:7; Jude 3; Galatians 3:23-27). Note Romans 10:8 which reads "the word is nigh thee, . . .that is, the word of faith (that is, the word which is the faith {genitive of apposition or identification}) which we preach."

It is certain, therefore, that "the faith" (in its full connotation) refers to: (a) all that is necessary to avoid sin in the first place, (b) all that is necessary to become saved after falling into sin, and (c) all that is necessary to staying saved after becoming a Christian. Thus, "the faith" includes the teaching of Christ on divorce and remarriage, and all men (whether Christian or non-Christian) are amenable to it. Thus, Bales' doctrine is wrong.

4. *"The word," (the word of God, the word of truth).* "The word of God" and "the faith" are one and the same body of teaching (doctrine): "The word of God increased; and the number of disciples multiplied in Jerusalem exceedlingly; and a great company of the priests were obedient to the faith" (Acts 6:7). Cf. Romans 10:8: the word which is the faith.

(1) *"The word" and non-Christians.*

(a) *"The word" is to be taught to non-Christians.* This truth is made clear in at least the following passages: Acts 2:41; 6:2,4,7; 8:4; 13:4-8,12; 14:25; 24:24; Romans 10:17; Luke 8:11; Ephesians 6:17; Hebrews 4:12; (Cf. Isaiah 2:1-4).

(b) *Non-Christians can be saved by "the word of God." This truth is plainly taught in the following passages:* Acts 2:41; 6:7; 8:4; 16:31 (Cf. Isaiah 2:1-4); 13:4-12. Colossians 1:5-6; James 1:18-21; I Peter 1:22-25; 3:1; II Corinthains 5:19; Ephesians 1:13; Philippians 1:14; I Thessalonians 1:6. (Cf.: "word of truth," John 16:12-13; Romans 10:17).

(c) *Non-Christians will be lost if they reject "the word."* The Bible plainly teaches that non-Christians who do not both believe and obey the word of God will be lost. This truth is made clear in at least the following passages: John 12:48; Acts 13:4-12 (note verses 8-10); 3:17-26 (note verse 22).

(2) *"The word" and Christians.*

(a) *The word is to be taught (and/or preached) to Christians.* This truth is made clear in at least the following passages: II Timothy 4:1-5; I Thessalonians 2:13; Hebrews 2:1-4.

(b) *Christians can be saved by "the word."* That Christians who faithfully live according to the word of God will be saved is made clear by the following passages: I Timothy 4:5; II Timothy 4:1-5; Titus 1:9; I John 2:5.

(c) *Christians will be lost if they reject the word.* That Christians who become unfaithful (that is, they come to reject the word of God) will be lost is plainly taught in the following passages of scripture: II Timothy 4:1-5; Acts 3:22; James 1:21-22.

(3) *Some other truths in regard to "the word of God."*

(a) *"The word" is the same body of doctrine as "the faith"* (Romans 10:8—the genitive of identification). Thus, since there is one—and only one—"faith" (Eph. 4:5), there is one—and only one—word!

(b) *"The word" is the same body of teaching as "sound doctrine"* (II Timothy 4:1-5; Acts 13:5,7,12).

(c) *"The Word" is the same body of doctrine as "the gospel."* Jesus commissioned the apostles to preach "the gospel" (Mark 16:15). Yet, the disciples went everywhere preaching "the word" (Acts 8:4). Thus to preach "the gospel" is to preach "the word" and to preach "the word" is to preach "the gospel." (Cf. Acts 15:7; the word which is the gospel {genitive of identification}).

(d) *The apostles preached "the gospel"* on the day of Pentecost (Acts 2:1-41). On that day, they preached to non-Christian Jews. But that same message was preached to the Gentiles: ". . .and he made no distinction between us {Jews} and them {Gentiles}, cleansing their hearts by faith {Greek: by the faith}" (Acts 15:9). Thus, it is clear that "the word," "the gospel," "the faith," and "the doctrine of Christ" are all *one and the same body of teaching.* This is indeed a most crucial truth not only for the matter at hand (divorce and remarriage) but also for any Bible subject. It refutes Bales' doctrine, which depends upon a distinction between "gospel" and "doctrine."

5. *"The law of Christ."*

(1) *"The law of Christ" and the non-Christian.* This truly is a crucial point. Brother Bales and those who stand with him deny that the non-Christian is amenable to (under) "the law of Christ." Brother Bales holds that the law of Christ is addressed only to Christians. But, in so holding, he makes a far-reaching mistake, for "the gospel," "the word," "the faith," "the doctrine," and "the law of Christ" are all one and the same body of teaching. The significance of this fact is truly special.

(a) *"The law of Christ" is addressed to the non-Christian.* In Old Testament times, the prophet Isaiah prophesied that ". . .out of Zion shall go forth the law, and the word of the Lord from Jerusalem" (Isaiah 2:3). It is clear that "the word of the Lord" and "the law" (that is, of Christ—the law of Christ) are one and same body of teaching. It has already been proved that "the word" of the Lord is to be preached (during the gospel dispensation) both to non-Christians and to Christians. It follows, then, that "the law of the Lord" (i.e., the law of Christ) is to be preached to non-Christians. In fact, in Isaiah 2:2, the prophet says (referring to the time when "out of Zion shall go forth the law"), ". . .and all nations shall flow into it." Thus, "the word" of Christ, "the gospel" of Christ, and "the law" of Christ are all one and the same body of teaching. Brother Bales joins liberals Garrett and Ketcherside in teaching that "the gospel" of Christ is one body of teaching and "the law" of Christ is another body of teaching. It should come as no surprise to the informed that Garrett and other liberals have now commended brother Bales for his having come to this position. It is clear (from James 1:21-25) that "the word" of Christ and "the law" of Christ are one and the same body of teaching. Romans 8:1-2 also makes clear that "the law" of Christ is to be preached (and/or taught) to non-Christians. "The law of the Spirit of life" (mentioned in Romans 8:2) is the law of the Holy Spirit (the Spirit of life—the Spirit who is the source of life), and the law of the Holy Spirit is the word of God (Ephesians 6:17). It has already been proved (in preceding sections) that "the word" is "the gospel." Thus, if "the word" is "the gospel." and if "the word" is "the law" (of Christ) then it follows that "the gospel" of Christ and "the law" of Christ are one and the same body of doctrine.

Thus, since non-Christians are to have "the gospel" preached to them (Mark 16:15), and since "the gospel" of Christ and "the law" of Christ are one and the same doctrine, then it follows that "the law" of Christ is to be taught to all non-Christians! Bales' doctrine is false.

(b) *Non-Christians can be saved by "the law of Christ."* The apostle Paul said, "There is therefore no condemnation to them that are in Christ Jesus. For the law of the Spirit of life in Christ Jesus made me free from the law of sin and death" (Romans 8:1-2). Thus, non-Christians are saved (become Christians) by obeying the law of Christ. Bales' doctrine is false.

(c) *Non-Christians will be lost if they reject the law of Christ.* Since the law of Christ is the means by which non-Christians are saved (cf., the gospel, Romans 1:15-17), it follows that all who reject it (refuse to obey the plan of salvation which it sets forth) will be lost (cf. Romans 1:15-17 and Mark 16:15-16 in regard to "the gospel," since the gospel of Christ and the law of Christ are one and the same body of teaching).

(2) *The law of Christ and the Christian.*

(a) *The law of Christ is to be preached (and/or taught) to Christians.* The apostle Paul made clear that he (a Christian) was under (amenable to) the law of Christ (I Corinthians 9:21; Romans 3:19).

(b) *Christians can be saved by the law of Christ.* This truth is made clear in James 1:22-25.

(c) *Christians will be lost if they reject the law of Christ.* Since (as has been shown) the law of Christ and the gospel of Christ are one and the same body of teaching, and since both are addressed to Christians (as well as to non-Christians), and since anyone who rejects the gospel will be lost (II Thessalonians 1:7-9), it follows that any Christian who rejects the law of Christ will be lost. This truth is also implied in I Corinthians 9:20-21; James 1:22-25.

(3)*Some further points about the law of Christ.*

(a) *The law of Christ is addressed to all men.* (proved above). Thus, all men (whether Christian or non-Christian) are amenable to its precepts (Rom. 3:19).

(b) *Thus, since Matthew 19:9 is a part of the law of Christ, both Christians and non-Christians are amenable to its teaching.*

6. *"The truth."*

(1) *"The truth" and the non-Christian."*

(a) *"The truth" is to be preached (and/or taught) to the non-Christian* I Tomothy 3:14-15; John 8:32 (Cf. Mark 16:15-16); (Cf. John 1:17; 17:17 {it has already been proved that "the word" is to be preached to the non-Christian so, since "the word" and "the truth" are one and same, "the truth" is to be preached to the non-Christian}; 18:37; Acts 26:25; Romans 1:25).

(b) *Non-Christians can be saved by "the truth."* This is made clear by John 8:32; I Timothy 4:3 (note: "the faith" = "the truth," 4:1,2); I Peter 1:22; John 17:17-19; I Timothy 2:4.

(c) *Non-Christians will be lost if they reject "the truth."* The Bible makes this clear in II Thessalonians 2:10; 2:12; I Timothy 6:5.

(2) *"The truth" and Christians.*

(a) *"The truth" is to be preached (and/or taught) to Christians.* The Bible clearly teaches, that such is the case, in at least the following passages: John 8:32; II Timothy 2:8; II Corinthians 13:8; Galatians 2:5.

(b) *Christians can be saved by "the truth."* This fact is made clear in: John 8:32; Galatians 2:4; I Peter 1:21-25; Ephesians 6:14-15 (note: "the truth" = "the gospel" cf. Colossians 1:5); Galatians 2:5; 2:14; II Timothy 2:15.

(c) *Christians will be lost if they reject "the truth."* That Christians will be lost if, after having become children of God, they apostatize into living lives which are not according to "the truth" is clearly taught in the following: II Thessalonians 2:10-12; I Timothy 4:3; 6:5; II Timothy 2:8; 3:7-8; I John 1:6,8; 2:4,21 (cf.: II Peter 2:20-22, "way of righteousness"). II Timothy 3:7-8; Galatians 3:1; James 5:19; II Timothy 4:4.

(3) *Some further points on "the truth."*

(a) "The truth" is exactly the same body of

teaching as "the gospel," "the word," "the doctrine," "the faith," etc.

(b) "The truth" is God's *one and only law for all men now living* (*The truth* authorizes civil law.)

(c) "The truth" is addressed to all men; thus, all men (whether Christian or non-Christian) are amenable to it (the truth).

(d) Matthew 19:9 is a part of the truth thus, all men (whether Christian or non-Christian) are amenable to it.

7. *"The new covenant."*

(1) *"The new covenant" and non-Christians.*

(a) *"The new covenant" is to be preached (and/or taught) to the non-Christian.* This is made clear in the following passages: Jeremiah 31:31-34 (prophecy of the coming of the new covenant); Hebrews 8:8-10; 9:11-17; 10:9; 10:16-20; Romans 11:26-27; (cf.: Matthew 28:18-20—note discussion above and below). The "new covenant" is simply the last will and testament of Jesus Christ. The expression "the new covenant" is simply another way of referring to the body of doctrine (teaching) which is elsewhere referred to as "the gospel," "the truth," "the doctrine of Christ," "the faith," "the law of Christ," etc.

(b) *Non-Christians can be saved by "the new covenant."* This is made clear in at least the following passages: Jeremiah 31:31-34; Hebrews 8:8-10; 9:11-17; Galatians 4:21-31.

(c) *Non-Christians will be lost if they reject "the new covenant."* This is made clear in the following passages: II Corinthians 3:1-6,14; Galatians 3:17; 5:6.

(2) *"The new covenant" and Christians.*

(a) *"The new covenant: is to be preached (and/or taught) to Christians.* This fact is made clear in at least the following passages: Hebrews 8:8-10; 10:9.

(b) *Christians can be saved by "the new covenant."* That Christians can be saved by "the new covenant" is made clear by: Hebrews 8:8-13; 9:11-17; 10:9-22.

(c) *Christians will be lost if they reject the new covenant and turn aside to something else.* This is made clear in: Hebrews 10:26-29; Galatians 5:1-6.

(3) *Some points to emphasize re: "the new covenant."*

(a) "The new covenant" is exactly the same body of doctrine as "the gospel," "the law of Christ," "the word," "the truth," etc.

(b) All men are amenable to the New Covenant (New Testament).

(c) Since Matthew 19:9 is a part of the New Covenant—not the Old (Mosaic) Covenant, all men living today are amenable to Matthew 19:9.

(d) The Old Covenant and the New Covenant could

not be in force at the same time, for the gospel is a universal law (addressed to all men during the gospel dispensation). This truth is made clear in Galatians 3:23-27; 4:21-31; Hebrews 10:9-10.

8. *"Jesus" ("Lord Jesus," "Christ.")* At times, instead of saying that someone preached "the gospel" or "the word," the New Testament says that someone preached "Jesus," or "Christ," etc.

(1) *"Jesus" and the non-Christian.*

(a) *"Jesus" is to be preached to all non-Christians.* This truth is made clear in Acts 8. The evangelist Philip is said to have preached "Jesus" to the eunuch from Ethiopia (Acts 8:35). When Philip preached "Jesus," he instructed the eunuch that he should be baptized (8:26-40). But this is what one does when he preaches "the gospel" (Mark 16:15-16). "the word of the Lord" (Acts 16:31-34); "the faith" "Galatians 1:23; Cf. 3:23-27). Only some sort of infidel would deny that "Jesus," "the gospel" and "the word of the Lord" are to be preached to all men now living. (Cf.: Acts 8:5; 11:19-25).

(b) *Non-Christians can be saved by the body of teaching referred to as "Jesus."* The New Testament makes clear that when "Jesus" is preached to non-Christians, everyone who believes and obeys that message will be saved (receive remission of sins, be born again, become a Christian—a child of God). This is made clear in Acts 8:26-40; 8:5-13; 11:19-25 (note especially verses 20 and 21: ". . .a great number that believed turned unto the Lord" after "the Lord Jesus" had been preached to them).

(c) *Non-Christians will be lost if they reject "Jesus."* The Bible clearly teaches that non-Christians who do not believe and obey (be baptized into Christ, Galatians 3:26-27) the message of "Jesus" will be lost. To reject "Jesus" is to reject "the gospel." To reject "the gospel" is to be damned (Mark 16:15-16). Therefore, to reject "Jesus" is to be damned.

(2) *"Jesus" and Christians.*

(a) *"Jesus" is to be preached to Christians.* To preach "the gospel" is to preach Jesus Christ (already proved. Cf. Philippians 1:15-17). If Christians reject "the gospel" and follow a perverted gospel, they will be anathema (Galatians 1:6-9). Thus, if Christians reject "Jesus," they will be lost.

(b) *Christians can be saved by the message referred to as "Jesus."* To preach "Jesus" (or "Christ" or "the Lord Jesus") is to preach "the word" (Acts 8:4-5). To preach "the Lord Jesus" is to preach "the word" (Acts 11:19-20). A burning question for brother Bales is: When the disciples preached "the word" (as recorded in Acts 11:19), did they preach "the gospel"? If he says "no," he denies plain Bible teaching; if he says "yes," he gives up his case. Brother Bales cannot avoid impaling himself on one of these horns or the other. His doctrine is false.

(c) *If Christians reject "Jesus," then they will be lost.* It has already been shown that preaching "Jesus" is exactly the same thing as preaching "the gospel." Yet, Paul made clear that if a Christian rejects the gospel, he will be lost (Galatians 1:6-9; cf.: II Thessalonians 2:8-12).

(3) *A further point on "Jesus."* It should be noted that to preach "Christ" is exactly the same thing as to preach "the word" (Acts 8:4-5). Since "the word" is to be preached both to non-Christians and to Christians (Acts 8:4-13; II Timothy 4:1-5), it follows that "Jesus" is to be preached both to Christians and to non-Christians.

One might also consider the force of Matthew 7:21-23 (one must obey "the will" of the Father in order to enter the kingdom) and Acts 5:20 (which contains reference to "all the words of this life").

VI. A Summary Of The Foregoing

The basic proposition (Proposition A) set forth and defended in this chapter ("There is one—and only one—body of doctrine for men living today: the gospel of Christ {the law of Christ}") has been proved by the foregoing material. Since this proposition (and the material which proves it to be true) is so important, it seems appropriate to give a very brief summary of that material and point out at least some of the significance of it. Three passages of scripture will be crucial to this summary: Acts 17:30-31; 14:13-17; and Acts 15:6-9. To conserve space, the author will depend on the reader to read carefully, the passages cited, from his own Bible. These passages should help any honest person to understand some crucial matters about Christ's message to man during the gospel dispensation.

1. *Acts 17:30-31.* In this passage Paul does at least three very important things.

(1) *Paul contrasts two times (periods)*: (a) "the times of ignorance" and (b) ". . .now."

(2) *Paul implies some crucial truth*: the meaning of the two periods. (a) By the expression "the times of ignorance," Paul no doubt referred to the times antecedent to the gospel "time" (period, dispensation). (b) By saying "but now," Paul without doubt referred to the "time" (period, dispensation) in which he (Paul himself) was then living: i.e., the gospel dispensation or age.

(3) *Paul thus implied some very significant facts.* (a) Before Pentecost, God had no universal law;[10] i.e., no single body of doctrine (such as the gospel of Christ) which was addressed to all men in the same sense in which the gospel is addressed to all

men. This means that prior to Pentecost, there was no universal (worldwide, to all men) law to which all men were amenable as is the case with the gospel; for example, the law of Moses was addressed to the Jews, II Corinthians 3:1ff (with provision for non-Jews to become proselytes). (b) But, beginning with Pentecost (and after, until Christ comes again, I Corinthians 15: 23-28), Christ has a universal law (the gospel, the word of God, the law of Christ, etc.)—one which is addressed to all men (Mark 16:15-16). Thus, all men (whether Christian or non-Christian) are amenable to (under) that one law (the gospel, the faith, the law of Christ). Matthew 28:18-20 makes clear that non-Christians are amenable to all things that Jesus commanded (that is, to all things which were to be—and now are—a part of the New Covenant, the gospel, the law of Christ). The reader should also carefully study Acts 1:5-8 and Luke 24:44-49.

2. *Acts 14:13-17*. In this passage, Paul again does three very important things.

(1) *Paul refers to two periods of time:* (a) "in times past" and (b) "the present time," just as he did in 17:30-31.

(2) *Paul (by implication) contrasts these two periods*. (a) "In times past" refers to the time anterior to the gospel age. (b) Paul thus implies a present time—the time beginning with Pentecost and continuing until Christ comes again—i.e., the gospel dispensation.

(3) *There are some crucial implications which follow*. (a) In "times past" there was no universal law which applied to all men—not in Patriarchy, not in the law of Moses.[11] (b) But now—during the gospel dispensation—Christ has a universal law, one addressed to all men (Mark 16:15) and to which all men are amenable (Romans 3:19; Cf.: Matthew 28:18-20; Luke 24: 44-49).

3. *Acts 15:6-9*. This passage makes clear the following truth.

(1) *By Peter's mouth, the Gentiles should hear the word of the gospel* (i.e., the word which is the gospel, 15:7).

(2) *God made no distinction between Jew and Gentile*. Rather, God cleansed their hearts by faith (Greek, "the faith") (15:9). When "the faith" came, the old law (the law of Moses) was done away—the Jews were no longer under (amenable to) the law of Moses but became (at Pentecost) amenable to the law of Christ (Galatians 3:23-27). *All men (whether Jew or Gentile) are now amenable to one and the same body of doctrine: the gospel of Christ!* All men (whether Christian or non-Christian) are amenable to one and the same law (the law of Christ—the gospel). Compare the following: Heb. 10:9; Eph. 2:13-16; Gal. 4:21-31; 3:23-27.

4. *Conclusion*. So, it is clear that the one body of doctrine to which all men are amenable contains: (a) all that is necessary to live above sin, (b) all that is necessary to become saved after having sinned, and (c) all that is necessary to stay saved after one becomes a Christian.

Thus, any alleged present "law written on the heart" which is *separate from* and *different from* the gospel *is simply non-existent!* The gospel (law) of Christ is addressed to all men. The same message (the one body of doctrine—the law of Christ, the gospel) was to be preached to all men—to both Jews and Greeks, to both Christians and non-Christians. The reader should carefully study the following passages: Romans 1:15-17; Mark 16:15-16; Matthew 28:18-20; Luke 24:44-49; Acts 15:6-9; Acts 14:1; 13:44-49; 13:4-12; 11:14; 11:16; 11:18; 20:20-21; 24:24-25 (Felix was a Gentile; his wife was a Jewess); 1:5-8 (". . .unto the uttermost part of the earth"); 2:39 (". . .and to all them that are afar off"); Isaiah 2:1-4; Romans 3:24-27.

In the face of this vast array of evidence, it is difficult indeed to understand how brother Bales could read the Bible and conclude that non-Christians are not amenable to the law of Christ.

Let it be remembered by the reader that the next chapter (XI) will build upon the material in this lengthy chapter (X).

Footnotes

[1]See Appendix K for a chart on these matters.

[2]*NUB*, p. 145-147.

[3]See Greek grammars, such as Ray Summers, *Essentials of New Testament Greek*, p. 90.

[4]This author, in preparing to refute the erroneous doctrine taught by Leroy Garrett in regard to his "anti-located-preacher" theory, saw this truth in regard to Matt. 28:18-20 in 1954. He (this author) wrote J. W. Roberts, professor of Greek in Abilene Christian College, about the matter. In response, he said that he agreed with my conclusion that the two present participles in Matt. 28:18-20 are *modal* as to their basic function.

[5]The reader is urged to study carefully material on Matthew 28:18-20 in Chapter XVI-B and in Appendix T.

[6]Brother Bales has received the endorsement of such "liberal" magazines as *Restoration Review* (edited by Leroy Garrett) and *Integrity* (edited by Hoy

Ledbetter). Such endorsement is significant indeed.

[7] He insists that no one is amenable to the New Covenant until he is "in" the Covenant.

[8] So far as this author knows, Bales does not make the distinction between "preach" and "teach" which Garrett does (or, at least did).

[9] Bales, *Was Christ A Christian?*, p. 74.

[10] See Appendix K for relevant material on eternal principles.

[11] Ibid.

CHAPTER XI

THE TRUE BASIC PROPOSITION ("PROPOSITION TBW") EXPLAINED

Before confining the issue (for this book) to that which pertains more strictly (and technically) to the problem of divorce and remarriage, the author wishes to set out and explain the true proposition which covers what really ought to be covered in a serious discussion of this matter. After the proposition is stated, an explanation will be given as to why such a lengthy (extensive) proposition is needed.

1. *"Proposition TBW" set forth.* This proposition (which might well be referred to as "the extensive true proposition") will be comprised of three sub-propositions: "Sub-Proposition R," "Sub-Proposition S," and "Sub-Proposition T." The entire proposition follows. *Sub-Proposition R*: "The Bible teaches that all men (whether Christian or non-Christian) living today are amenable to (under) one and the same body of doctrine (the gospel of Christ, the faith, the New Covenant, the truth, the doctrine of Christ, the word, etc.)," and thus:

Sub-Proposition S: (the Bible teaches) that all men (whether Christian or non-Christian) living today commit sin when they:

(1) *Establish or enter or support* (by proclaiming and/or upholding the doctrines of) any religious institution (such as the Baptist church, the Roman Catholic church, et al.) which is not authorized by the gospel of Christ, (the law of Christ, the New Covenant) and—

(2) *More specifically,* that Baptist preachers living today sin when, in preaching Baptist doctrine, they urge other men:

a. *to reject* the gospel plan of salvation and to accept the Baptist doctrine that alien sinners (non-Christians) are saved at the point of faith before and without being baptized in the name of Christ, and/or—

b. *to reject* the church which was purchased by the blood of Christ and to enter the Baptist church and to remain in it until death, and/or—

c. *to worship* God by singing with the accompaniment of mechanical instruments of music.

d. *to reject* the way of life authorized and demanded by the law of Christ (cf.: I John 1:7; Gal. 5:19-23) and to urge others to accept the view that no sin from murder to adultery to idolatry can endanger the salvation of one who has been born again (II Pet.

2:20-22).

Sub-Proposition T: (the Bible teaches) that—as regards marriage, divorce and remarriage—all men (whether Christian or non-Christian) who, in violating the law of Christ (specifically, in divorcing and marrying again on some ground other than fornication, in violation of Matthew 19:9) are involved in sinful practices and/or sinful states and/or sinful relationships are persons who are instructed by that law (the law of Christ) to cease those sinful practices, to get out of those sinful states and to sever those sinful relationships.

2. *Why such a lengthy proposition on this subject?* Because the question of who can, with God's approval, divorce and marry again is to inextricably be involved with the question of the applicability of Christ's law during the gospel dispensation—what it is, what it involves, who is amenable to it, etc.—the proposition which adequately sets forth the truth on the matter is somewhat more lengthy than some people expect (or even want) it to be. There are those who wish to avoid—at least as a crucial element in the problem—the matter of Christ's law and man's amenability to it. Brother Bales is among that number, and he seems to think that he can prove his case by the use of I Corinthians 7:10-16 (in conjunction with Matt. 19:9) even if he must "give ground" (admit defeat) on the position for which he contends on amenability to Christ's law. But such is simply not the case. The question of amenability to Christ's law is both fundamental and crucial to this entire question. This was clearly shown in *The Warren-Fuqua Debate*, and the matter is no less crucial as brother Bales tries to establish his case. Brother Bales will not be allowed to cast aside the truth that while other matters are important, the question of amenability to the law of Christ is in fact the most crucial element in this entire problem.

Just as brother Fuqua, in the Warren-Fuqua debate, on divorce and remarriage, contradicted his basic position, as regards denominationalism, in his debate with the Baptist debater (L. S. Ballard), just so brother Bales faces the same problem, and he shall not be allowed to escape it, no matter how much he may complain about the question of amenability being recognized as so crucial.

In debating the Baptists, brother Fuqua affirmed that all who enter the Baptist church sin in so doing, and he (Fuqua) used the law of Christ to show that they did so sin! But it is impossible for them to violate the law of Christ unless they are amenable to (under) the law of Christ.[1] In debating the Baptists, brother Fuqua had no trouble in seeing that all men living today (whether Christian or non-Christian) are amenable to the law of Christ! Yet, when he turned to the divorce and remarriage question, he rejected the truth which he had formerly taught and began to argue that all non-Christians are amenable to civil law only and that no non-Christian is amenable to the law of Christ on any subject! When this self-contradiction was pointed out to him, brother Fuqua (in utter contradiction of both the Bible and his own former true teaching) invented a new realm which he called "the ecclesiastical realm" (i.e., made up of people who are amenable to what he called "ecclesiastical law"). It was a pitiable thing for such an ordinarily outstanding Bible teacher to fall into the espousal and teaching of such error.

Yet brother Bales (and any one who stands with him on this matter) now faces the same predicament: he does not know what to do about establishing religious institutions ("churches") which the Bible has not authorized! He does not know what to do about denominational preachers urging people to reject the Lord's plan of salvation (set out in the Bible) and to accept humanly-originated "plans of salvation." He (brother Bales) does not know what to do about denominational preachers urging other men to reject the Lord's church (purchased by the blood of Christ, Acts 20:28) and to accept (by entering) some humanly originated "church" (denomination). The reader may ask, "Why would brother Bales have such a problem with denominationalism?" For the same reason that brother Fuqua did: he asserts that no non-Christian living today is amenable to Christ's law, and, since he further asserts that non-Christians are under the "law written on the heart" and are not under the law of Christ at all, and, since he further recognizes that his alleged "law written on the heart" does not forbid anyone entering the Baptist church, etc., brother Bales (to be consistent) would have to say that it is not sinful either for a non-Christian to reject the Lord's plan of salvation, the Lord's church, and the Lord's way of worship (set out in the law of Christ, the gospel), or for a non-Christian to urge others to make the same rejection! (Paul condemned, in principle, all such, Acts 13:8-12.) Much more on this matter will come in following material. Bales cannot explain denominationalism in such fashion as to be consistent with his position on divorce and remarriage.

It is my sincere prayer that brother Bales (and any who might follow him in this error) will repent and return to the truth which brother Bales himself has taught on every crucial point involved—when he is not dealing with the problem of divorce and remarriage. Would that he could see the same truth when on that subject.

The plan to be followed here is to deal in the

main body of the book with what the author is calling "Sub-Proposition T" (i.e., the one which deals explicitly with divorce and remarriage) disregarding (at least in the proposition itself) the question of the sinfulness of denominationalism. Denominationalism will be dealt with further in Appendix L. This plan must not for one moment be construed to indicate that the author is making even the slightest concession as to the cruciality of the problem of "who is amenable to Christ's law?" (including the problem of denominationalism). But this plan will permit a little smoother "flow" of argument, strictly speaking, as to divorce and remarriage. Then a study of the appendix will give more information on the matter.

3. *The crucial question to be answered.* The question which is at the very heart of this matter is: "Is it the case that all persons (whether Christian or non-Christian) who, in violating the law of Christ (specifically, in divorcing and marrying again on some ground other than fornication in violation of Matthew 19:9), are involved in sinful practices and/or sinful states and/or relationships are persons who are instructed by that law to sever (get out of) those sinful relationships?"

As will be shown, the Bible answer to this question is, "Yes." But it must be remembered that the question of amenability (to the law of Christ, the gospel) is fundamental to the proper answering of this question. No one can afford to allow anyone to mislead him into concluding that the question of amenability (i.e., "who is under the law of Christ: (1) only Christians? or (2) all men, whether Christian or non-Christian? or (3) only non-Christians?) is not fundamental to finding the true answer to this question.

4. *The true basic proposition which is to be proved (demonstrated to be true).* The proposition the proof of which comprises the main (basic) task of this book is the proposition which (under 3 above) has been designated "Sub-Proposition T." To help keep matters clear, that proposition will be repeated here: "The Bible teaches that—as regards marriage, divorce, and remarriage—all men (whether Christian or non-Christian) who, in violating the law of Christ (specifically, in divorcing and marrying again on some ground other than fornication, in violation of Matthew 19:9) are involved in sinful practices and/or sinful states and/or sinful relationships are persons who are instructed by that law (the law of Christ) to cease those sinful practices, to get out of those sinful states and to sever those sinful relationships."

5. *The true basic proposition ("Sub-Proposition T") explained.* Although the proposition is clearly stated (i.e., it is not ambigious at all), it may be of some value to say a few words about its meaning.

The proposition means, in short, that Matthew 19:9 (as a part of the New Covenant, the gospel, the law of Christ) is applicable to all men, that Matthew 19:9 teaches that the one and only ground for divorce and remarriage which is acceptable to God is that of fornication (marital unfaithfulness, in this case), and that, thus, all men (whether Christian or non-Christian) who divorce and marry again on any ground other than the marital unfaithfulness (fornication) of their wives, commit adultery when they do so, and that, thus, all such are instructed to get out of (sever) all such marriages. Otherwise, they will continue to live in rebellion against Jesus Christ, and, if they die in that state, will be lost (Rev. 21:8; Gal. 5:19-21).

Footnotes

[1]Romans 3:19; 4:15; I John 3:4.

CHAPTER XII

"PROPOSITION TBW" DEMONSTRATED

In Chapter VI of Part II above, the cruciality of the "Law of Rationality" (which says, in effect, that all men should draw only such conclusions as are warranted by the evidence) was discussed. In Chapter VII, it was shown how to demonstrate a proposition (the precise statement of a doctrine)—i.e., how to prove that a proposition is true. In Chapter VIII, it was shown how to refute a proposition—i.e., how to prove that it is false. Chapter VII will be especially relevant to this present chapter (XII) and Chapter VIII will be of crucial importance in Part V (Chapters XVI-A, XVI-B, XVII, XVIII, and XIX).

Since in Chapter X it was proved that Christ has one—and only one—body of doctrine (the gospel) for all men living today and since a proposition which deals with unauthorized religious instructions and practices was discussed in Chapter XI (and will be discussed further in various chapters in Parts V and VI and in Appendix L) this present chapter will be mainly concerned with demonstrating that *Sub-Proposition T* (of "Proposition TBW") which deals more specifically with divorce and remarriage, is true.

I. SOME INTRODUCTORY MATTERS

1. *The crucial propositions in this problem.* In order that the reader may more easily grasp the arguments which follow in the remainder of this book, the basic propositions of both Bales and this author will now be listed. The basic proposition of this author is referred to as "Proposition TBW" and is made up of three sub-propositions: "Sub-Proposition R," "Sub-Proposition S," and "Sub-Proposition T." "Proposition TBW" (with its three sub-propositions) has already been set out in Chapter XI. The basic proposition which precisely states the position upheld by brother Bales will be referred to as "Proposition JDB" and will be made up of three sub-propositions: "Sub-Proposition X," "Sub-Proposition Y," and "Sub-Proposition Z." *Sub-Proposition T* is the proposition which deals most directly on divorce and remarriage affirmed by this author. *Sub-Proposition Z* will be the proposition which deals most directly on divorce and remarriage affirmed by brother Bales.[1] Thus, Sub-propositions R, S, and T are constituent elements of "Proposition TBW" (this author's) and sub-propositions X, Y, and Z are constitutent elements of "Proposition JDB" (that of brother Bales). All elements of both "Proposition TBW" and "Proposition JDB" are very important. Although the other propositions are crucial

to the entire problem, for this author the main (though not the only) task is that of proving "Sub-Proposition T" and for brother Bales the main task is that of proving "Sub-Proposition Z."

2. *A reminder of the cruciality of the Law of Rationality.* The "Law of Rationality" says, in effect, that all men should draw only such conclusions as are warranted by the evidence. To demonstrate that "Sub-Proposition T" (the third main element of "Proposition TBW") is true the author must (1) present a valid argument the conclusion of which is Sub-Proposition T" and (2) prove that all of the premises (propositions which serve as evidence) are true. To say an argument is valid is to say that the truth of the premises necessitates the truth of the conclusion.

3. *The truth of "Sub-Proposition R" and the truth of "Sub-Proposition T" are crucially related.* It is important for the reader to note and remember that Sub-Proposition R is crucially related to Sub-Proposition T. Sub-Proposition R deals with the question of amenability while Sub-Proposition T deals more directly with the specific problem of divorce and remarriage.

4. *"Sub-Proposition R" restated.* In order that this crucial proposition be kept before the reader, at the beginning of proof of Sub-Proposition T, Sub-Proposition R is restated here: "The Bible teaches that all men (whether Christian or non-Christian) living today are amenable to (under) one and the same body of doctrine (the gospel of Christ, the law of Christ, the faith, the New Covenant, the truth, the doctrine of Christ, the word, etc.)"

5. *"Sub-Proposition T" restated.* Although the proof that Sub-Proposition T is true will be set out below in II and III), it seems appropriate that it should be stated here (as it was in Chapter XI). "The Bible teaches that—as regards marriage, divorce, and remarriage—all {persons (whether Christian or non-Christian) who, in violating the law of Christ (specifically, in divorcing and marrying again on some ground other than fornication, in violation of Matthew 19:9), are involved in sinful practices and/or sinful states and/or sinful relationships} are {persons who are instructed by that law (the law of Christ) to cease those sinful practices, to get out of those sinful states and to sever those sinful relationships."}

6. *The question which "Sub-Proposition T" answers.* The question which Sub-Proposition T answers is: "Is it the case that all persons (whether Christian or non-Christian) who, in violating the law of Christ (specifically, in divorcing and marrying again on some ground other than fornication, in violation of Matthew 19:9), are involved in sinful practices and/or sinful states and/or sinful relationships are persons who are

instructed by that law to cease those sinful practices, to get out of those sinful states, and to sever those sinful relationships?"

II. THE SIGNIFICANCE OF PROVING THAT "SUB-PROPOSITION T" IS TRUE

In order to prove that the proposition is true, it will be shown that Sub-Proposition T is the conclusion of a sound argument.[2] When this goal has been reached, it will have shown that Sub-Proposition T is true. (The conclusion of every sound argument is true). And, since it cannot be the case (because they contradict each other) that both Sub-Proposition Z of "Proposition JDB" and Sub-Proposition T are true, proving that Sub-Proposition T is true will also constitute proof that Sub-Proposition Z (the Bales proposition) cannot be true (i.e., that Bales' position on divorce and remarriage is false).

Thus, the significance of this matter must not be overlooked. When Sub-Proposition T is shown to be true, it will have also been shown: (1) that for all persons (whether Christian or non-Christian) living today the one and only ground for divorce and remarriage is fornication (as taught in Matthew 19:9), (2) that it is not possible that any other Biblical passage could authorize some other ground for divorce and remarriage, and (3) that, thus, the doctrine of James D. Bales on divorce and remarriage is false (and is at least to be compared with the doctrines of Balaam, Revelation 2:14; and of Jezebel, Revelation 2:20).

IV. PROOF THAT "SUB-PROPOSITION T" IS TRUE: THE ARGUMENT EXPLAINED

1. *The argument to be used in proving "Sub-Proposition T," will be comprised of ten premises and a conclusion.* Premise one is made up of an "If. . . then. . ." (implicative) statement, the antecedent of which is a compound proposition composed of eight propositions. Premises two, three, four, five, six, seven, eight and nine are simple propositions. Premise ten is the conjunction of premises two, three, four, five, six, seven, eight and nine. The eleventh element of the argument is the conclusion, "Sub-Proposition T." (See Appendix I for this argument set out in symbolic terms.)

2. *A valid argument form.* The form of the argument which will be used to prove that Sub-Proposition T is known by logicians as *Modus Ponens* (or "hypothetical syllogism" in traditional logic). This argument takes the form of "If proposition X is true, then proposition Y is true. Proposition X is true. Therefore, proposition Y is true." The proposition

between the "if" and the "then" is known as the antecedent; the proposition which follows the "then" is known as the consequent. In such an argument, if the antecedent is affirmed, then the argument is valid, and the consequent follows. If the two premises of the argument are proved to be true, then the conclusion must also be true.

In some arguments of this form, the antecedent is made up of more than one proposition. (This means that, in such a case, the antecedent is a compound proposition.) When the antecedent is a compound proposition, then, in order for one to know that the antecedent is true, he must know that all of the sub-propositions which comprise the antecedent are true. Knowing that each of the sub-propositions which comprise the antecedent are true, one can (by the logical move known as "conjunction") prove that the antecedent itself (i.e., the compound proposition) is true.

The argument to be used here (to prove "Sub-Proposition T") will be a Modus Ponens argument (the antecedent will be affirmed) with a compound antecedent.

3. *What the above means as to the argument to be used to prove "Sub-Proposition T" (in the argument referred to simply as "T ").* The argument which proves Sub-Proposition T reads, in ordinary English words, Premise one: "If proposition A is true, and if proposition B is true, and if proposition C is true, and if proposition D is true, and if proposition E is true, and if proposition F is true, and if proposition G is true, and if proposition H is true, then proposition T is true. Premise two: Proposition A is true. Premise three: Proposition B is true. Premise four: Proposition C is true. Premise five: Proposition D is true. Premise six: Proposition E is true. Premise seven: Proposition F is true. Premise eight: Proposition G is true. Premise nine: Proposition H is true. Premise ten: The conjunction of Propositions A, B, C, D, E, F, G and H is true. Conclusion: Therefore, Proposition T (Sub-Proposition T) is true.

This simply means that if the first (the compound) proposition is true, and if each of the sub-propositions which together (conjoined) form the antecedent of that compound proposition (all that comes before the "then"), then Sub-Proposition T must be true!

V. PROOF THAT PROPOSITION "T" IS TRUE.

It should be recalled that the argument which proves proposition T ("Sub-Proposition T") to be true was sketched out above. That the argument is valid was also shown.[3]

The conclusion (T) will now be proved by showing that each of the constituent elements of the argument is true.

1. *Premise 1 of the argument (being used to prove that proposition T (of "the TBW proposition" is true) set out.* This is a lengthy premise because it is composed of nine propositions (eight of which function as premises, and, therefore, as evidence) and one of which functions as the conclusion of the argument (the basic thesis of this book: Sub-Proposition T). The propositions which in conjunction, function as the antecedent (the evidence) of this implicative statement are: A, B, C, D, E, F, G, and H. The proposition which functions as the consequent of premise 1 is proposition T (i.e., Sub-Proposition T). Thus, since the argument is Modus Ponens in form, proposition T also functions as the conclusion of the argument.

Premise 1 is stated as follows: "If the Bible teaches Ⓐ that the expressions and/or terms "the gospel of Christ," "the law of Christ," "the doctrine of Christ," "the faith," "the truth," "the New Covenant," "the word" (as well as the message designated as "Jesus," and "Christ") all refer to one and the same body of doctrine, and if Ⓑ that body of doctrine (the "law of Christ," etc.) is God's one and only law for all men living today, and if, thus, Ⓒ all men living today are amenable to (under) that one law (the law of Christ, etc.) and if Ⓓ that one law (the law of Christ, etc.) instructs all men living today as to: (1) how they must live in order to be pleasing to God (i.e., not to sin at all), (2) what they must do to become saved (i.e., to become a Christian) after having fallen into sin, and (3) what they must do in order to stay saved (i.e., to live the faithful Christian life), and if Ⓔ that all men (whether Christian or non-Christian) who are amenable to the law of Christ (the gospel, the faith, etc.) are men who are amenable to the instruction of that law on divorce and remarriage (including that of Matthew 19:9), and if Ⓕ that any person who is amenable to (under) Matthew 19:9 is a person who is eligible to put away his (her) spouse and to marry another if and only if that party is innocent of marital infidelity (fornication) and if the putting away is done (by the innocent party) for the cause of fornication (on the part of the one being put away), and if Ⓖ that all men (whether Christian or non-Christian who put away their wives on any ground other than fornication (on the part of the one being put away as per Matthew 19:9) are men who commit sin in so doing and who, more specifically, begin sinful practices and/or enter sinful states and/or enter sinful relationships in so doing, and if Ⓗ that all men (whether Christian or non-Christian) who, in violating the law of Christ (the gospel) are involved in sinful practices and/or sinful states and/or sinful relationships are men who are instructed by that law to cease those sinful practices, to get out of those sinful states, and to sever those sinful relationships, then Ⓣ. The Bible teaches, as regards divorce and remarriage, that all men (whether Christian or non-Christian) who, in violating the law of Christ (specifically in divorcing and marrying again on some ground other than fornication, in violation of Matthew 19:9), are involved in sinful practices and/or sinful states and/or sinful relationships are persons who are instructed by that law (the law of Christ) to cease those sinful practices to get out of those sinful states, and to sever those sinful relationships."

2. *Each of the premises proved to be true.*

(1) *Premise one is true.* That the first premise of the argument is true is quite obvious. If "the gospel," "the law of Christ," etc. (as set out above) all refer to one and the same body of doctrine; and if that body of doctrine is God's one—and only one—law for all men living today; and if all men living today are amenable to (under) that one law (the law of Christ); and if that one law instructs all men as to how to live in order to be pleasing to God, what to do to become saved, and what to do to stay saved; and if all men who are amenable to that one law are men who are amenable to the instruction of that law on divorce and remarriage (including Matthew 19:9); and if any person who is amenable to Matthew 19:9 is a person who is eligible to put away his (her) spouse and to marry another if and only if the party who does the putting away is innocent of fornication (marital infidelity) and the putting away is done (by the innocent party) for the cause of fornication (on the part of the one being put away); and if all men (whether Christian or non-Christian) who put away their wives on any ground other than fornication (as per Matthew 19:9) are men who commit sin in so doing and who enter sinful practices and/or sinful states and/or sinful relationships in so doing; and if all men (whether Christian or non-Christian) who, in violating the law of Christ (the gospel, etc.) are involved in sinful practices and/or sinful states and/or sinful relationships are men who are instructed by that law to cease those sinful practices, to get out of those sinful states, and to sever those sinful relationships, then it follows—as a necessary conclusion—that the Bible teaches that, as regards divorce and remarriage, all men (whether Christian or non-Christian) who in violating the law of Christ (specifically in divorcing and marrying again on some ground other than fornication, in Matthew 19:9), are involved in sinful practices and/or sinful states and/or sinful relationships are persons who are instructed by that law (the law of Christ) to cease those sinful practices, to get out of those sinful states, and to sever those sinful relationships.

To understand the devastating (to any opposing view) force of this argument, the reader must recall the fact that the form of the argument is Modus Ponens and that if the two premises of such an argument are proved to be true, then the conclusion must be true.[4] If each of the propositions A, B, C, D, E, F, G and H (which are premises 2, 3, 4, 5, 6, 7, 8, and 9 in the argument—which, along with premise 1, comprise the evidence in the argument) can now be shown to be true, then, by the logical "move" known as "conjunction," premise 10 will also be shown to be true. Then, by recognizing that the antecedent in a Modus Ponens form argument has thus been shown to be true, it will follow that proposition T (Sub-Proposition T), the conclusion of the argument, will have been shown to be true. Thus the case will have been completed.

So the task is now that of proving that Premise 1 is true. This will be done by proving, in turn, that propositions A, B, C, D, E, F, G, and H are true. (It must be remembered that propositions A, B, C, and D have already been proved to be true {i.e., in Chapter XI}).

(2) *Proposition A (premise 2) in the argument shown to be true.* Proposition A in the present argument reads as follows: "The Bible teaches that the expression and/or terms 'the gospel,' 'the law of Christ,' 'the doctrine of Christ,' 'the faith' 'the truth,' 'the New Covenant,' 'the word,' et al. all refer to one and the same body of doctrine."

Proposition A was proved in Chapter X so that there is no need to do so in this chapter.

(3) *Proposition B (premise 3) in the argument shown to be true.* Proposition B in the present argument reads as follows: "The Bible teaches that that one body of doctrine (the law of Christ, the gospel, et al.) is God's one and only law for all men living today."

Proposition B was also demonstrated (proved to be true) in Chapter X. Thus, there is no need to prove it again in this present chapter.

An objection to Proposition B might be raised, by some people, on the basis that men are amenable to (under) civil law. Thus, the objection might go: if there is even one law other than the law of Christ to which men are amenable, then Proposition B cannot be true.

But this objection, if any one should raise it, is easily refuted by pointing out that the law of Christ authorizes the right kind of civil law (Romans 13:1-5; I Peter 2:13-15). Thus, civil law which is in harmony with Christ's law is, in effect, an extension of Christ's law, in the sense that it is authorized by Christ's law (Rom. 13:1-7). Of course, no civil law which contradicts the law of Christ is acceptable to God (Acts 4:18; 5:29).

Thus, the point stands (as proved in Chapter XI) that the law of Christ is God's one and only law for all men now living.

(4) *Proposition C (premise 4) in the argument shown to be true.* Proposition C in the present argument reads as follows: "The Bible teaches that all men living today are amenable to (under) that one law (the law of Christ, the gospel)."

This proposition was also proved in Chapter X. Thus, there is no need to prove it again in this chapter. The proposition stands as proved.

The doctrine of James D. Bales to the effect that only Christians are amenable to the law (doctrine) of Christ is simply false and, thus, should be rejected by all men.

(5) *Proposition D (premise 5) in the argument shown to be true.* Proposition D in the present argument reads as follows: "The Bible teaches that that one law (the law of Christ) instructs all men living today as to: (1) how they must live in order to be pleasing to God (i.e., not to sin at all), (2) what they must do to become saved (i.e., to become a Christian) after having fallen into sin, and (3) what they must do in order to stay saved (i.e., to live the faithful Christian life.)"

Proposition D has also been proved in Chapter X. Thus, there is no need to set out that proof here.

(6) *Proposition E (premise 6) in the argument shown to be true.*

a. *Proposition E stated.* Proposition E in the present argument reads as follows: "The Bible teaches that all men (whether Christian or non-Christian) who are amenable to the law of Christ (the gospel, the faith etc.) are men who are amenable to the instructions of that law on divorce and remarriage (including that of Matthew 19:9)."

b. *The argument (which proves Proposition E) set out.* The argument which proves that proposition E is true reads as follows.

(a) If proposition Ⓘ the Bible teaches that all persons (whether Christian or non-Christian) are persons who are amenable to the gospel, including what is necessary (a) to live a life pleasing to God (i.e., not to sin even one time), (b) to become a Christian (after having sinned), and (c) to live the faithful Christian life, and if Ⓙ the law of Christ (the gospel) includes Matthew 19:9, then Ⓔ the Bible teaches that all men (whether Christian or non-Christian) who are amenable to the law of Christ (the gospel, the faith, etc.) are men who are amenable to the instructions of that law on divorce and remarriage (including that of Matthew 19:9).

(b) Proposition I is true. It was proved to

be true by the material in Chapter X. The proof that propositions A, B, C, and D are true implies that proposition I is also true.

(c) Proposition J is true. (Proved in Chapter X).

(d) Therefore, the compound proposition ("Proposition I is true and Proposition J is true") is true.

(e) Therefore, it follows (by Modus Ponens) that Proposition E (the conclusion of the argument) is true.[5]

C. *The details of the argument (which proves Proposition E) enlarged upon a bit.*

(a) If it is the case that both proposition I is true and proposition J is true, then proposition E is true. This proposition is obviously true.

(b) It is the case that proposition I is true (proved by implication by the proof of propositions A, B, C, and D).

(c) It is the case that proposition J is true. This is seen to be true because: (a) Matthew 19:9 is certainly not mere civil law, (b) Matthew 19:9 is not any alleged "law written on the heart" and (c) Matthew 19:9 is not a part of the law of Moses. (Jesus clearly contrasted Matthew 19:9 with the Law of Moses. Cf., Matthew 5:31-32.)

(d) Thus, the compound proposition I and J is also true. This follows by the logical move known as "conjunction" from premises b and c just above.

(e) Thus, Proposition E is true. This is the case because premise d is the antecedent of the modus ponens form argument which is here being used. And, when the antecedent of a modus ponens form argument is affirmed (in an argument in which the implicative premise is true), then the consequent (in this case Proposition E) must also be true.

(7) *Proposition F (premise 7) in the argument shown to be true.*

a. *Proposition F stated.* Proposition F in the present argument reads as follows: "The Bible teaches that any person who is amenable to (under) Matthew 19:9 is a person who is eligible to put away his (her) spouse and to marry another if and only if that party is innocent of marital infidelity (fornication) and if the putting away is done (by the innocent party) for the cause of fornication (on the part of the one being put away)."

b. *The argument which proves Proposition F to be true set out.* The form of the argument which proves Proposition F is also that of Modus Ponens. (See footnote 6 for the entire argument.)

The first premise of the argument which proves Proposition F is as follows:

(a) If Proposition Ⓚ "all 'exceptive' sentences carry the force (meaning) of if and only if and

(b) if Proposition Ⓛ Matthew 19:9 is an 'exceptive' sentence as pertains to divorce and remarriage," then Proposition Ⓕ "The Bible teaches that any person who is amenable to (under) Matthew 19:9 is a person who is eligible to put away his (her) spouse and to marry another if and only if that party is innocent of marital infidelity (fornication) and if the putting away is done (by the innocent party) for the cause of fornication (on the part of the one being put away)."[5]

C. *The argument shown to be valid.*

(a) *The argument is valid*, because it is Modus Ponens in form (the antecedent is affirmed). Thus, if all of the premises (premises 1, 2, 3 and 4) are true, then the conclusion (Proposition F) must also be true. Thus, in order to prove that Proposition F is true, it remains only to prove that premises 1, 2, 3 and 4 are true. These premises actually involve only two different sub-propositions (Proposition K and Proposition L), so the main task is that of proving those two propositions. However, we must look (at least briefly) at premises 1 and 4 as well as premises 2 and 3.

(b) *All of the premises in the argument are true.*

{1} *Premise 1 is true.* If it is the case (and it is) that all exceptive sentences carry the force of if and only if (i.e., the one and the only one way, door, condition, qualification, etc.) and if Matthew 19:9 is an exceptive sentence (and it is), then it follows (since it has already been proved that all persons—whether Christian or non-Christian—are amenable to Matthew 19:9) that any person (whether Christian or non-Christian) is a person who is eligible to put away his (her) spouse and to marry another if and only if the putting away is done (by the innocent party) for the cause of fornication (on the part of the one being put away.)

To read this proposition carefully and honestly is to see that it is true. It really needs no further explanation or illustration. To refute it, one must refute either (or both) Proposition K or Proposition L. That such cannot be done will be shown in the material just below.

{2} *Premise 2 is true.* Premise 2 is simply the affirmation that Proposition K is true. Proposition K affirms that all exceptive sentences carry the force of if and only if. An illustration will help the reader to understand the meaning. Suppose the teacher of a third grade class in an elementary school were to say to that class, "Any student—except one who needs to go to the restroom—who leaves the room will receive a spanking." To make this statement fit into our "logical machine," it must be "translated" as follows: "All students—except those who need to go to the restroom—who leave the room will be spanked, and no student who leaves the room because of need to go to the restroom will be spanked." Thus, it is clear that, to make the original statement fit into our "logical machine," (in "traditional" logic), the original statement (proposition) must be rewritten as two statements. Or, it could be rewritten as follows, "Any student may leave the room without being spanked if and only if he needs to go the restroom." In other words, the force of the exceptive sentence is to say that there is one and only one ground upon which a student may leave the room without being spanked; namely, the need to go to the restroom.

One of the main reasons why brother Bales has espoused an erroneous doctrine on divorce and remarriage is because he has failed to understand the force of an exceptive sentence.[7] The reader is urged to study carefully additional material in Appendix A (on Matthew 19:9).

{3} *Premise 3 is true.* Premise 3 is simply the affirmation that Proposition L is true. Proposition L says, "Matthew 19:9 is an 'exceptive' sentence as pertains to divorce and remarriage." One has only to read Matthew 19:9 (since, among other things, it says, ". . .*except* {emphasis, T.B.W.} for fornication . . .") Thus, premise 3 is true.

{4} *Premise 4 is true.* Premise 4 is nothing more than the affirmation (by the logical move known as "conjunction") that since it is known both that Proposition K is true and that Proposition L is true, then it is also known that the conjunction of Proposition K and Proposition L is true. (See any textbook on logic.)

Thus, it has been shown: (1) that the argument is valid and (2) that all of the premises (in the argument being used to prove Proposition F) are true. Thus, it has also been proved that Proposition F (the conclusion of the argument) is true.

(8) *Proposition G (premise 8) is true.*

a. *Proposition G stated.* Proposition G reads as follows: "All men (whether Christian or non-Christian) who put away their wives on any ground other than fornication (on the part of the one being put away, as per Matthew 19:9) are men who commit sin in so doing and who, more specifically, begin sinful practices and/or enter sinful states and/or enter sinful relationships in so doing."

b. *Proposition G explained.* This proposition affirms that any person who puts away his (her) spouse and marries another on any ground other than fornication sins in so doing. If this proposition is true (and it is), then brother Bales, at least somewhat like Balaam (Rev. 2:14) and Jezebel (Rev. 2:20), when he urges men and/or women to marry in violation of Matthew 19:9, or to stay in marriages which violate

Matthew 19:9, is guilty of leading people (including some Christians) to commit fornication.

Fornication is the one—and the only—ground for divorce and remarriage. This is the case in spite of the enormous amount of material brother Bales has written denying that such is the case. As will be explained in detail in a later chapter, when brother Bales teaches that there is even one other ground (i.e., other than fornication) for divorce and remarriage, he teaches false doctrine; he in effect, thus leads men and women to commit fornication and/or to live in adultery. Those who espouse and live in harmony with that false doctrine will be lost (Rev. 2:14, 22; 21:8; Galatians 5:19-21).

c. *Proposition G proved.* Proposition G is easily proved because all of the propositions which are involved in that proof have themselves already been proved.

(a) *The proof set out in symbolic terms.* Set out in symbolic terms, the argument which proves that Proposition G is true is in a footnote.[8]

(b) *The proof (argument) discussed in ordinary English.*

{1} *Proof of Premise (1).* An honest and careful reading of this premise will enable any reader to understand that it is true. Its truth is obvious. It is obviously the case that if both Proposition E and Proposition F are true, then Proposition G must also be true. There is really no need to discuss in detail what is obviously true.

{2} *Proof of Premise (2).* Premise (2) is simply the affirmation that Proposition E is true. But Proposition E has already been proved to be true (above, in an earlier section of this chapter). Thus, there is no need to prove it again here.

{3} *Proof of Premise (3).* Premise (3) is simply the affirmation that Proposition F is true. But, again, it is the case that the proposition under consideration has already been proved in an earlier section in this chapter. Thus, there is no need that the proof be given again here.

{4} *Proof of Premise (4).* Premise (4) is nothing more than the affirmation that, given both that Proposition E is true and that Proposition F is true, it follows that the compound proposition (Proposition E and Proposition F) is also true (by conjunction).

{5}*Proof that Proposition G is true.* The basic purpose of this sub-section is to prove that Proposition G is true. Since the antecedent of the first premise has been proved, it follows that the consequent (Proposition G) has also been proved. That proof (which is a Modus Ponens argument form) consists in proving that the basic implicative statement is true and that the antecedent of that implicative statement is true. These two things have been accomplished in this section. Thus, since proving that the two premises (when one of them is the affirmation of the antecedent of the implicative statement) are true also proves that the consequent (the conclusion) of the implicative statement is true, then it is clear that Proposition G has been proved.

(9) *Proposition H (Premise 9) is true.*

a. *Proposition H set out.* Proposition H reads as follows: "All men (whether Christian or non-Christian) who, in violating the law of Christ (the gospel), are involved in sinful practices and/or states and/or relationships are men who are instructed by that law to cease those practices, to get out of those sinful states, and to sever those sinful relationships."

b. *Proposition H proved.* This proposition is clearly shown to be true by the following passages: II Corinthians 6:14-18; I Corinthians 5:1-13; and II Thessalonians 3:6-15. All of these passages make clear that it is sinful for one to be involved in sinful practices and/or to be in sinful states and/or to be in sinful relationships. Some other passages which are relevant to this same point are: Ephesians 5:11; Gal. 5:19-21; Matthew 3:8,11; Luke 3:8; Matthew 6:24; I John 2:15-17; Revelation 21:8; 2:14,20; Galatians 6:7-9; Romans 8:13 and Colossians 3:5-8.

Proposition H has been shown to be true.

(10) *Premise 10 (the conjunction of propositions A, B, C, D, E, F, G and H) is true.* That the conjunction of eight true propositions is true has already been explained. Premise 10 is a compound, conjunctive proposition, made up of eight sub-propositions which, in the material set out just above, have already been proved. Thus, it is clear that Premise 10 is true. (See proof below at footnote 8.)

(11) *Proposition T (Premise 11 --- the conclusion, of the argument, which was to be proved) is true.*

a. *Proposition T set out.* Although Proposition T (Sub-Proposition T of "Proposition TBW") has been stated earlier in this chapter, it seems advantageous for it to be restated here: "The Bible teaches that all men (whether Christian or non-Christian) who, in violating the law of Christ (specifically, in divorcing and marrying again on some ground other than fornication, in violation of Matthew 19:9), are involved in sinful practices and/or sinful states and/or sinful relationships are men who are instructed to cease those sinful practices, to get out of those sinful states and to sever those sinful relationships."

b. *Proposition T proved to be true.* As set out earlier in this chapter, a deductive argument is being used to prove that Proposition T is true. (That argument is a Modus Ponens argument which is set out in a footnote.[9])

c. *The argument explained (again) briefly.* The force of this argument has already been explained earlier in this chapter. It was explained that if each one of the propositions which (in conjunction) comprise the antecedent of the first premise could be shown to be true, then the conjunction itself would have been proved to be true. This, in turn, because the argument is in the Modus Ponens form, would prove that the consequent of that implicative proposition must be true. Thus, since the consequent of that implicative statement (Proposition T) is also the conclusion of the argument, then it has been proved that Proposition T (Sub-Proposition T of "Proposition TBW") is true.

d. *The force of this proof.* It must be realized that the foregoing proves: (a) that the basic affirmation of this book (Proposition—i.e., Sub-Proposition T of "Proposition TBW") has been proved and (b) that it is impossible for any other passage in the Bible to authorize divorce and remarriage on any ground other than fornication!

3. *Why the force of this argument is so important.* Although considerable attention will be given in a later chapter to the importance of (b) under (d) just above, it is good to at least make some note of it here. The basic reason for this is the fact that brother Bales claims that Matthew 19:9 does not make clear that no other passage could so modify (or supplement) the teaching of Matthew 19:9 so as to authorize some ground for divorce and remarriage other than fornication. Brother Bales claims that I Corinthians 7:10-16 proves that grounds other than fornication (e.g., desertion) can also be an acceptable (to God) ground for divorce and remarriage. Further refutation of this contention by brother Bales will be set out in detail in later chapters and Appendices.

(12) *The affirmative case (proof of Proposition T)—i.e., "Sub-Proposition T" of "Proposition TBW"—has been established.* In summary of this chapter, it is simply reiterated (1) that Proposition T (Sub-Proposition T) has been proved and (2) that it is simply not possible (and the Bible be true—which, of course, it is!) for any single passage or any combination of passages to prove that God allows divorce and remarriage on some ground other than fornication.

Thus, the case has actually been closed. Yet, lest some complain that not enough attention has been given to the effort which brother Bales has made to establish his doctrine, Bales' doctrine will be specifically refuted, in even more detail, in the chapters which follow.

Footnotes

[1]"Proposition JDB" (the basic proposition which Bales is faced with trying to prove) is made up of three sub-propositions (X,Y, and Z), which will be set out and critically analyzed in Chapters XIV and XV. Chapters XVI-A, XVI-B, XVII, XVIII, and XIX will also be relevant to "the JDB Proposition," in those chapters, "Proposition JDB" will be refuted.

[2]This recognizes that a sound argument is an argument of which both the following are true: (1) the argument is valid and (2) all of the premises are true. The conclusion of a sound argument is always true.

[3]See footnote 9 below for the argument set out in symbolic terms.

[4]See Appendix for the argument set out in symbolic terms.

[5]Symbolically, the argument takes this form:

(1)	(I·J)>E.	
(2)	I	
(3)	J	
(4)	(I·J)	2, 3, conjunction
(5)	∴E	1, 4, M.P.

[6] Put into symbolic terms, the Modus Ponens form of argument looks like this: p>q; p; ∴q. The particular argument under consideration is set out in this way:

(1)	(K·L)>F	(obviously true)
(2)	K	to be proved.
(3)	L	to be proved.
(4)	(K·L)	2, 3, conjunction
(5)	∴F	1, 4, M.P.

[7]*NUB*

[8]The argument set out in symbolic terms is as follows:

(1)	(E·F)>G	obviously true
(2)	E	proved in previous section
(3)	F	proved in previous section
(4)	(E·F)	2,3, conjunction; so, is true
(5)	∴G	1,4, M.P., thus is true.

[9]

(1)	(A·B·C·D·E·F·G·H)> T	already proved above
(2)	A	already proved above
(3)	B	already proved above
(4)	C	already proved above
(5)	D	already proved above
(6)	E	already proved above

(7) F	already proved above
(8) G	already proved above
(9) H	already proved above
(10) A·B·C·D·E·F·G·H	2,3,4,5,6,7,8,9 conj.
(11) ∴ T	1, 10, M.P. (Modus Ponens)

CHAPTER XIII

BALES' FAILURE TO REFUTE PROPOSITION T—"SUB-PROPOSITION T" OF "PROPOSITION TBW"

I. Bales' task as a negative disputant: To show that the argument used in this book (to prove Sub-Proposition T is true) is not a sound one.

To prove that Proposition T (i.e., Sub-Proposition T of "Proposition TBW") is true, in Chapters X, XI, and XII there was set out: (1) "Proposition TBW," the total basic proposition (comprised of three sub-propositions: R, S, and T) which covers the problem under consideration in this book, (2) the sub-proposition (Proposition T) which most directly and specifically deals with divorce and remarriage (although the other two sub-propositions are crucially relevant to the problem), and (3) the sound argument which proves that Proposition T is true.

The truth that an argument is sound if (1) the argument is valid and (2) all of the premises are true has also been shown. Further, it has been shown: (1) that the argument is valid and (2) that all of the premises (Premises 1 through 10, involving Propositions A, B, C, D, E, F, G and H) of that valid argument have (in Chapters XI and XII) been shown to be true. Thus, the argument itself has been shown to be sound. This fact guarantees that the conclusion of that sound argument is true.[1] Thus, since Proposition T is the conclusion of that sound argument, then Proposition T (as the conclusion of a sound argument) must be true. Thus, the argument (the conclusion of which is that fornication is the one—and only—scriptural ground for divorce and remarriage) has been shown to be sound, guaranteeing that the conclusion of that argument is true.

But brother Bales and at least a few others[2] apparently are not convinced of the truth on this matter even when they are faced with a sound argument. Brother Bales advances certain objections to Proposition T and the argument which proves it.[3] The remainder of this chapter will deal with the main objections he levels against Proposition T and the argument which proves it.

II. How brother Bales might go about trying to undermine the argument used to prove proposition T.

1. *A general look at brother Bales' task.* When a logical, precisely stated argument is presented in proof of a particular proposition (as this author has done in Chapters X, XI and XII), anyone who holds that the effort has been unsuccessful (as brother Bales has

done with the effort in regard to Proposition T) must do at least one of the following: (1) he must prove that the argument which was used in the effort to prove the proposition, is not a valid one or (2) he must prove that at least one of the premises of the argument is false.

2. *A crucial question:* has brother Bales done either one or both of those two things (in 1 above)?

(1) *So far as this author is aware, brother Bales has not made the slightest effort to prove that the argument is not valid.*[4] Even if he did make such an effort, he would fail, because the argument is incontrovertibly valid.[5] So, if brother Bales is to overthrow (refute) Proposition ("Sub-Proposition T" of "Proposition TBW") his effort will have to be based on something other than that of proving the argument to be invalid. Since the only possible alternative for him to use is that of proving at least one of the premises (of the valid argument) to be false, his case of refutation (if he can establish such) must rest on his proving that at least one of the premises (of the valid argument used by TBW) is false. But this, as will be shown, he cannot do. Thus, as will be shown, the case for Proposition T will have once for all been established (even in the face of his strongest objections). And, quite crucially, with this having been done, it will have been made clear that brother Bales cannot use either I Corinthians 7:10-16 (as he tries to do) or any other passage to prove his contention that no non-Christian is amenable to (under) Matthew 19:9 and that the only people who are amenable to Matthew 19:9 are Christians who are married to Christians. In subsequent chapters, the doctrine advanced by brother Bales will be shown, in a more detailed way, to be false.

(2) *Brother Bales has not shown and cannot show that any of the premises (which are used as evidence) in the valid argument are false.* He has not done so, because they are all true. They have all been shown to be true (in Chapter XII).

III. Some things brother Bales has done in his effort to undermine the case for Proposition T.

1. *His charge of a faulty hermeneutic.*

(1) An article by brother Bales, in what is obviously his main effort to overthrow the truth and to sustain his own erroneous doctrine, was "Proving It Too Soon."[6]

To anyone who is even slightly acquainted with the doctrine taught by brother Bales on divorce and remarriage and how he goes about trying to justify that doctrine, the intent of this article by brother Bales is obvious: he wishes to lay groundwork for his (Bales') "uninspired interpretation"[7] of the Bible which involves, among other crucial matters, his contention that the writing of Paul in I Corinthians 7:10-16 so modifies or supplements the teachings of Jesus in Matthew 19:9 as to nullify the force of the fact that Jesus stated an "exceptive" sentence, in Matthew 19:9, in regard to divorce and remarriage.

But brother Bales fails utterly in that effort. In what follows, it will be shown: (1) that the reason for brother Bales' failure (to undermine the universal force of Matt. 19:9—i.e., that it applies to all men) is not due to the fact that he urges men to consider the total evidence of the Bible in drawing conclusions as to what it teaches[8] and (2) that the reason for brother Bales' failure to see the truth on this entire subject of divorce and remarriage is that (among other reasons, which shall not be discussed here—e.g., his doctrine that non-Christians are not amenable to the law of Christ and, thus, are not amenable to Matthew 19:9) he does not take into account the difference between a statement which is universal in form but does not contain an exceptive element and a statement which is universal in form and does contain an exceptive element!

(2) *Why brother Bales fails at this point.* Brother Bales does not fail in his effort to sustain his charge of a faulty hermeneutic because he pointed out that, in studying the Bible, one should take into account the total relevant evidence. As a matter of fact, in presenting what little case he had, Bales quotes from brother David Lipe (who has written on this matter in the book *Your Marriage Can Be Great*, edited by this author, TBW). In writing a chapter in that book entitled, "How to Properly Interpret the Bible," brother Lipe (who is scheduled soon to receive the Ph.D. degree), leaned heavily (and acknowledged such) upon material from this author's book *When Is An "Example" Binding?*, which presents much detail in regard to the very point which brother Bales has questioned. (The reader is urged to read *When Is An "Example" Binding?* in order to see (a) how much stress the author (TBW) gives to the matter of gathering the total evidence and of then reasoning correctly about it, and (b) how misleading brother Bales' effort is in regard to this point.) Brother Bales is sadly and tragically mistaken if he thinks that he must instruct this author along that line. The truth of the matter is, the problem raised here by brother Bales is largely one of logic, and this author (TBW) has not gained the impression that brother Bales has studied deeply in that field. I say that kindly—with love—but brother Bales' attack has necessitated the pointing out of this fact.

(3) *Why brother Bales does fail in his point about "proving it too soon."* Brother Bales fails because he thinks that, in pointing out "that some state-

ments which are universal in form. . .are not actually universal in meaning," he overthrows the force (meaning) of the exceptive element of the statement of Jesus which is recorded in Matthew 19:9. Many others besides brother Bales recognize that there is such a thing as the figure of speech which is called "synecdoche" in which the whole is put for the part or the part is put for the whole, the singular is put for the plural or the plural is put for the singular. All of this is not only granted but is insisted upon here as strongly—if indeed not more strongly—as does brother Bales. But a tragic error made by brother Bales (as concerns Matthew 19:9) is that he ignores the force of the fact that Matthew 19:9 is an exceptive sentence! If brother Bales understood this point, it seems extremely unlikely that he would ever have made the tragic errors which have led him to espouse and teach the erroneous doctrine which he now teaches so strenuously so far and wide, but which, because of his health, he cannot defend in public oral debate.[9]

Let it be noted that Matthew 19:9 quotes Jesus as saying, "And I say unto you, whosoever shall put away his wife, except for fornication, and shall marry another, committeth adultery: and he that marrieth her when she is put away committeth adultery." Quite obviously, this statement is universal in form (that is, the "whosoever" *prima facie* indicates that all men (whether Christian or non-Christian) are addressed by the strictures of this passage.) (Bales recognizes the connotation of universality in the word "whosoever" in Acts 2:21 and Rom. 10:13[10].) But, while this statement (Matthew 19:9) is universal in the sense that it is applicable to all men now living, it is also the case that its basic form (logically speaking) is that of an exceptive sentence. Thus, it is a universal sentence, but it is not merely a universal statement which, as brother Bales alleges, some other statement might modify in such fashion as to demand that it be regarded as a particular statement (i.e., one which refers only to some married men—i.e., given Bales' view: only Christians who are married to Christians); this sentence is also an exceptive sentence! And—note this please!—because this is the case, all men know that no other passage (e.g., I Corinthians 7:10-16, as brother Bales alleges) could possibly nullify the force of the fact that Jesus, in Matthew 19:9, teaches without equivocation that the fornication is the one—and the only—ground authorized by God for divorce and remarriage. Some men—such as brethren Bales, Jerry Jones,[11] Jimmy Allen,[12] James S. Woodroof,[13] et al.—claim that other grounds (such as desertion by a non-Christian or practically anything) are also authorized by the law of Christ. However, in making such a claim they contradict Jesus (Matthew 19:9; 5:30-31).

Although Jesus plainly taught (by implication in Matthew 4:1-11) that to be a good student of God's word, one must not only study carefully the "immediate context" of a passage but the "remote context" as well, it is still the case that one can come to knowledge of a particular truth in a single passage so that he can know that it is not even possible for some passage to modify, say, an exclusive matter (such as baptism in the name of Jesus Christ being the one and only door into the kingdom of God, John 3:3-5) so that it is seen to be not correctly regarded as exclusive.

The author unequivocally declares—without the slightest fear that brethren Bales, Allen, Jones or Woodroof will be able to refute the point—that one can know from John 3:5 that one cannot find in any other single Biblical passage or any combination of Biblical passages teaching which authorizes anyone to teach that any one living today can enter the kingdom of God through any door other than that of being "born of water and the Spirit" (i.e., being baptized in water in the name of—by the authority of—Jesus Christ). Being baptized in water in the name of Jesus Christ is the one—and the only—door into the kingdom (that is, into the church, into being saved)!

Here is a burning question for brother Bales and those who stand with him: "Will you dare to so contradict the Bible as to say that it is even possible, given that John 3:5 is a part of the gospel (the law of Christ), that some other passage in that law could teach that there is some door into the kingdom of God other than that of being 'baptized unto the remission of sins' (Cf. John 3:5; Acts 2:38)?" If he will so dare, then will he dare to affirm the position that the *Bible contradicts itself?*[14] And, it must be noted, if it is even possible that the Bible contradicts itself, then either (1) it is possible that the Bible is not the word of God, or (2) it is possible that God is a liar.[15] And, if any of these men is willing to affirm that John 3:3-5 does not prove that it is not even possible that some other passage could prove that there is some door other than baptism into the kingdom of God, this author asks: would he (they) be willing to affirm such in public oral debate?

The argument refutes—beyond any doubt whatsoever—brother Bales' doctrine on divorce and remarriage. Since each one of the two disjuncts implied by brother Bales' proposition (doctrine) cited above is false, it necessarily follows that the proposition which implies that total disjunct is false. This is the case because any proposition which implies a false doctrine is also false.

But, as is the case with bro. Bales on Matthew 19:9 and the question of divorce and remarriage, almost without exception denominational preachers are not satisfied with the exclusivity expressed by Jesus in John 3:5. Sectarians say, for example, that one can enter the kingdom of God (be saved from past sins) at the point of faith in Christ before and without any further acts of obedience (i.e., before and without being baptized in the name of Jesus Christ, John 3:5; Acts 2:38; 22:16; Mark 16:15,16). Thus, they say, in effect, that one must not "universalize" (note how the thrust of their thought is so similar to the thought of brother Bales on Matthew 19:9 on divorce and remarriage) John 3:5 but must wait for other Bible writers to give additional information so that men can understand "the incomplete" in the light of "the complete." As a general rule, the principle (of inductively considering the evidence of "the remote context") referred to here is true and should be recognized and followed. But, it must always be remembered that there is such a thing as an exceptive proposition and that exceptive propositions are conclusive in regard to the matter(s) about which they express exclusivity! To either reject or ignore this truth is to render one's effort to understand the Bible a hopeless and fruitless one. (Note: Mark 16:15-16 also proves that baptism precedes salvation.)

In the light of the above truth, it must be pointed out that there is no more possibility that brother Bales (or Allen or Jones or Woodroof) will find a Biblical passage which authorizes some ground for divorce and remarriage in addition to the one—and only—ground (fornication) set out by Jesus in Matthew 19:9 than there is that a Baptist preacher will find some Biblical passage, which authorizes some door into the kingdom of God, in addition to the one—and only—door ("being born of water and the Spirit") authorized by Jesus in John 3:5. Neither brother Bales nor Baptist preachers can find that which they claim to find on these respective matters. Romans 5:1 does not teach (as Baptist preachers allege) that there is some door into the kingdom other than that of being baptized in the name of Jesus Christ, and I Corinthians 7:10-16 does not (as brother Bales alleges that it does) authorize some "door" other than fornication into divorce and remarriage. (There are some charts on this matter in Appendix A. They should be helpful to the reader.)

(4) *Further explanation of "exceptive" propositions*. A statement such as "All students except freshmen are eligible to attend the game," is one which actually makes two assertions rather than merely one. For example, consider the statement, "All people except employees are eligible to enter the contest." If one thinks that this statement means nothing more than, "All non-employees are eligible," then he is mistaken. To handle properly (from a logical standpoint) the statement, "All students except freshmen are

eligible to attend the game," one must recognize that the proposition actually makes two assertions: (1) "all non-freshmen are eligible to attend the game, and (2) no freshman is eligible to attend the game."[16]

Another way of putting the matter is to utilize the phrase "if and only if." In doing so, one can rewrite "All except freshmen are eligible to attend the game" in this way: "Any student is eligible to attend the game if and only if he is not a freshman."

(5) *A crucial statement on Matthew 19:9 as an "exceptive" sentence.* What Jesus said in Matthew 19:9 can be written in the following form (which is exactly equivalent to the first part of Matthew 19:9): "Given any divorced man, that man is eligible to remarry if and only if he has put away his companion because of (her) fornication."[17]

Matthew 19:9 can also be stated as follows: "If any man has put away his wife on the ground of her fornication, then he is eligible to marry another—but—if he has not put away his wife on the ground of fornication, then he is not eligible to be married to another."[18] Read in simple terms, this means that if any man (whether Christian or non-Christian) divorces his wife on any ground other than her fornication, he will sin if he marries another! Given the plain teaching of Matthew 19:9,[19] it is utterly absurd for any person who is guided by rational (logical principles) to even look for some so-called later revelation such as I Corinthians 7:10-16[20] to give some ground other than fornication for divorce and remarriage. The only way there could be such a revelation, while Matthew 19:9 is in force, is for one of the following to be true: (1) the Bible contradicts itself and, thus, is not the word of God, or (2) the Bible is the word of God and, thus (given the false position that the Bible contradicts itself), God would be a liar. Since both (1) and (2) are false, any contention which implies that (1) and (2) are true, is false.

So, the reader should note carefully that, since brother Bales' position involves such an implication, it is clear that his position is false (This argument is discussed further in Appendix A.)

And so, to utilize something of brother Bales' language, the question must be asked, "Why should anyone hesitate to give up an uninspired interpretation (that of James D. Bales) in order to accept what is obviously in harmony with plain Bible teaching?"[21] Brother Bales has not merely "proved his contention too soon"—he has not proved it at all! It is strange indeed that Bales would refer to the interpretations of others as "uninspired" and yet not apply that same appellative to his own interpretations.

In respect and kindness, in Christian love for a man whom this author (TBW) has long admired, respected and loved, it is suggested that a little more study of logic in general—and of "exceptive" propositions in particular—could well help brother Bales to see the error of the doctrine he has espoused and is now teaching with such vigor.

It is the earnest prayer of this writer that brother Bales not go into the judgment without repenting of his doctrine on divorce and remarriage (Rev. 2:14,20; 21:8). Think of the great number of people who might be misled by it. So many people want to believe this doctrine because it is so "full of comfort" to those who are living in unscriptural marriages! Because people, generally, want to believe a doctrine such as that taught by brother Bales, many will believe it—even in the face of proof that it is false (Cf.: Ezek. 14:4; II Thess. 2:10-12).

2. *Listing of some other matters which brother Bales levels against the argument which proves Proposition T.* There are some other matters which, in addition to the material set forth in the earlier part of this chapter, might be considered to be negative material (i.e., from Bales) in response to the positive case which has been set forth for Proposition T (Sub-Proposition T of "Proposition TBW"). Yet, since that material will be either (1) reviewed and refuted when it is considered as a part of the affirmative case which brother Bales at least tries to present or (2) reviewed in detail in special sections of the Appendix, no more of that material will be reviewed here as negative material to this affirmative case.

The reader may be assured that the remainder of brother Bales' efforts will fare no better than did those set out and refuted above.

Among the passages used by brother Bales which will receive detailed critical analysis will be the following: Matthew 28:18-20 (a passage on which he leans very strongly but woefully misunderstands); I Corinthians 7:10-16 (compared with Matthew 19:9); I Corinthians 6:9-11 (on which he errs concerning the sins listed and the law of Moses, etc.); I Corinthians 9:20-22 (another passage on which he errs concerning the law of Moses, the law of Christ, etc.); and his erroneous position on "the gospel of Christ" and "the law of Christ."

These and other passages will be discussed in showing (1) that brother Bales does not—and cannot—prove his own affirmative case and (2) that his basic doctrine can actually be refuted (i.e., proved to be false)!

Summary Statement Re This Chapter

In the close of this chapter (which ends Part IV, in which the positive case for the truth of Proposition T has been set forth and demonstrated) the reader should carefully note: (1) that an argument (to prove Proposition T) was set forth and shown to be valid (so far as this author knows, brother Bales has never even called the validity of the argument in question.[22]), (2) that every premise of that argument was proved to be true (brother Bales has made a feeble effort to reply to one or two of these premises. The failure of his efforts to prove his own case will be further discussed in Parts IV and V.) and thus (3) that since the argument is valid and all of the premises are true, the argument is sound and, thus, the conclusion (Proposition T—"Sub-Proposition T" of "Proposition TBW") has been proved to be true. Brother Bales has failed to refute it.

Footnotes

[1]No argument can be sound and the conclusion not be true.

[2]Including brethren Jerry Jones and Jimmy Allen, colleagues of brother Bales in the Bible department at Harding University. Jones is the Chairman of the Bible Department of Harding University.

[3]And, it must be assumed that Jones and Allen concur with him in making such objections. If not, let them speak out to what their objections are, since they agree with Bales' basic position.

[4]The same basic argument form was used in a Forum at which brother Bales was present and also in the charts which were used therein.

[5]That the argument is valid has already been proved in preceding material.

[6]*Gospel Advocate*, January 18, 1979.

[7]Brother Bales refers to the conclusions of those who differ with him on this matter as "uninspired interpretations." Of course, we all admit that our conclusions are not inspired, but such an admission does not mean that we admit that our conclusion is false! It is possible that brother Bales did not realize that we would point out that *his conclusions are no more inspired than are those of the rest of us!*

[8]It just so happens that this author (TBW) has written a book which emphasizes that position over some 166 pages. That book is *When Is An "Example" Binding?* by Thomas B. Warren.

[9]Brother Bales has only recently declined three invitations from three congregations to meet this author (TBW) in public oral debate on divorce and remarriage. He has expressed willingness to debate in writing, and, likely, he and brother Roy Deaver will engage in a written debate.

[10]Bales, *Hub Of The Bible,* p. 77.

[11]Statement to Garland Elkins.

[12]*Commentary on I Corinthians.*

[13]*The Divorce Dilemma.*

[14]As, by implication, did James S. Woodroof, the minister of the College church of Christ in Searcy, Arkansas, in the Memphis Forum of 1978.

[15]But both "horns" of this dilemma for brethren Bales, Jerry Jones, Jimmy Allen, and Jim Woodroof are false: (1) II Timothy 3:16,17; II Peter 1:20-21 and (2) Hebrews 6:18; Titus 1:2; I Samuel 15:29. The Bible is the word of God, and God does not lie!

[16]This exceptive proposition (with its two assertions) can be handled with logical symbolism. See Appendix A for details. This information will be very helpful for those who wish to study these technicalities.

[17]To see the statement written in symbolic terms, Appendix A should be consulted.

[18]This is stated in symbolic terms in Appendix A.

[19]See a detailed discussion of Matthew 19:9 in Appendix A.

[20]I Corinthians was written before Matthew was written.

[21]Sub-Proposition T of "Proposition TBW" has already been proved.

[22]The basic argument has been set forth in this author's earlier writings.

PART IV

THE BASIC COMPOUND PROPOSITION OF JAMES D. BALES ("PROPOSITION JDB") SET OUT AND HIS FAILURE TO DEMONSTRATE IT.

CHAPTER XIV

"PROPOSITION JDB" SET OUT AND EXPLAINED

As was the case with the compound proposition which set forth the Biblical position (Proposition T—i.e., "Sub-Proposition T" of "Proposition TBW") on the question of divorce and remarriage,[1] the proposition affirmed by brother Bales[2] must (because it entails a number of crucial matters) be somewhat lengthy. It may seem to one who has not studied carefully the position advanced by brother Bales, that the proposition which is stated below is too lengthy. But an understanding of the matter makes clear that it is necessary to an adequate discussion of the matter.

In this present chapter, the following matters will be considered: (1) the distinction between "Proposition TBW" and "Proposition JDB," (2) brother Bales' failure to set forth (as he should have done) a precise proposition which adequately describes the doctrine he is upholding, (3) "Proposition JDB" will be stated and "Proposition JDB" will be briefly explained.

1. *The distinction between "Proposition TBW" and "Proposition JDB."* In order for the reader to follow easily the "flow" of the overall argument of this book, it will be necessary to"pinpoint" some distinctions as to propositions used both by this author (TBW) and by brother Bales (although Bales has not precisely stated his).

(1) *The two basic propositions identified.* The overall basic proposition affirmed by this author will be referred to as "Proposition TBW," and the overall basic proposition affirmed (by implication) by brother Bales will be referred to as "Proposition JDB."

(2) *The constituent elements of the two basic propositions.*

a. *"Proposition TBW."* The constituent elements of "Proposition TBW" (as has already been noted) are as follows: (a) "Sub-Proposition R," (b) "Sub-Proposition S," and (c) "Sub-Proposition T" (the proposition most directly concerned with divorce and remarriage. "Sub-Proposition T" has already been proved—Chap. XII).

b. *"Proposition JDB."* The constituent elements of "Proposition JDB" are as follows: (a) "Sub-Proposition X," (b) "Sub-Proposition Y," and (c) "Sub-Proposition Z" (the proposition most directly concerned with divorce and remarriage).

2. *Brother Bales' failure to set forth a precise*

proposition which adequately describes the doctrine he upholds. While a careful study of the various and "scattered" writings of brother Bales does make clear the doctrine which he upholds on the question of divorce and remarriage, if he (brother Bales) has anywhere stated that doctrine in a precise proposition (say, for example, one which could adequately serve as an affirmative proposition in a public debate), it has escaped the attention of this writer, although he (TBW) has tried to read what brother Bales has written. It might be noted that some writers may fall to the temptation to seek to avoid the stating of their doctrines in single, logically precise propositions because, if those propositions are false, it is easier for an opponent to expose the falsity of them. Or, it may be the case that he simply does not realize his responsibility to do such. Men who both feel certain that what they are teaching is true and understand their responsibility as an affirmative disputant do not ordinarily fail to state their position in a logically precise proposition.

3. *Statement of "Proposition JDB"—Gleaned from the various writings of brother Bales*. "Proposition JDB" (which sets out the proposition implied by his writings on divorce and remarriage) is comprised of the sub-propositions: "Sub-Proposition X," "Sub-Proposition Y," and "Sub-Proposition Z." (These propositions will hereinafter usually be referred to simply as Proposition X, Proposition Y, and Proposition Z.) These three sub-propositions make clear some crucial issues which are inextricably connected with brother Bales' doctrine on the divorce and remarriage question.

As was the case with brother Fuqua, when brother Bales is trying to defend his false doctrine on divorce and remarriage, he rejects (contradicts) Biblical truth which, in years gone by and on other subjects, he vigorously and valiantly upheld as truth.[3] Also as did Fuqua, given his past performances (in oral discussions and in written correspondence with this writer), brother Bales can be expected to complain about the question of *amenability to the law of Christ and of unauthorized religions* (e.g., Baptist, Roman Catholic, Islam, et al.) being brought into the discussion, but the reader may be assured (1) that these matters are inextricably related to the question of divorce and remarriage (and to brother Bales' doctrine in particular) and (2) that no amount of complaining from brother Bales will deter this author from keeping it in the discussion and showing just how crucial it is to the whole problem. The question of what to say about men entering denominations, such as the Baptist church (that is, as to whether those who do commit sin in so doing) was a "Waterloo" for brother Fuqua, and it is also one for brother Bales. This writer gives his promise to the reader that such will be the case. And, so it will be with the matter of polygamy! Brother Bales' doctrine gets him into trouble on all of these matters.[4] The reader may be assured that brother Bales' "feet will be held to the fire" on these matters.

(1) "Proposition JDB" (which entails the crucial elements of the doctrine which brother Bales upholds) is as follows:

a. {*"Sub-Proposition X" stated:*} The Bible teaches that no non-Christian living today is amenable to (under) the gospel of Christ (the law of Christ, the faith, the New Covenant, the doctrine of Christ, the word of God, etc.) and, thus—

b. {*"Sub-Proposition Y" stated:*} The Bible teaches that no non-Christian living today sins when he:

(a) Establishes and/or enters or supports (by proclaiming and/or upholding the doctrines of) any religious institution (such as the Baptist church) which is not authorized by the law of Christ (the gospel, the faith)," and—

(b) More specifically, that Baptist preachers living today do not sin when, in preaching Baptist doctrine, they urge other men:

{1} to reject the gospel plan of salvation and to accept the Baptist doctrine that alien sinners (non-Christians) are saved at the point of faith before and without being baptized in the name of Jesus Christ, and/or—

{2} they urge other men to reject the church which was purchased by the blood of Christ and to enter the Baptist church and to remain in it until death, and/or—

{3} they urge other men to worship God by singing with the accompaniment of mechanical instruments of music," and—

c. {*"Sub-Proposition Z" stated:*} As regards divorce and remarriage, the Bible teaches that:

(a) the only persons who are amenable to (under) the teaching of Matthew 19:9 are Christians who are married to Christians.

(b) No Christian who is married to a non-Christian is amenable to the teaching of Matthew 19:9.

(c) No Christian who is not married is amenable to the teaching of Matthew 19:9 (or 5:31-32);

(d) No non-Christian is amenable to the teaching of Matthew 19:9;

(e) If a Christian is married to a non-Christian and if the non-Christian departs, then the Christian is free to marry some one else on the ground of that desertion alone.

(f) If a Christian is married to a Christian and one of them is guilty of marital unfaithfulness (commits fornication), then the guilty party (as well as the innocent party) is free to put away his (her) companion and to marry another (with God's approval).

Let the reader be reminded of these truths (1) "Proposition JDB," which adequately sets forth brother Bales' doctrine, is comprised of "Sub-Proposition X," "Sub-Proposition Y," and "Sub-Proposition Z," and (2) although much of the remainder of this book will be directed toward "Sub-Proposition Z" (which most directly deals with divorce and remarriage) the reader must never overlook the cruciality of "Sub-Proposition X" and "Sub-Proposition Y;" these two propositions are quite fundamental to brother Bales' case.

Since brother Bales holds (1) that no non-Christian is amenable to the law of Christ, (2) that all non-Christian gentiles living today are amenable to (under) not the law of Christ, but to what brother Bales calls "the law written on the heart, (3) that all non-Christian Jews living today are amenable to (under) not the law of Christ but to the law of Moses,[5] then it follows that, since Baptists are not Christians—and, therefore, according to brother Bales' theory are not amenable to the law of Christ—and since brother Bales "law written on the heart" has no strictures against entering the Baptist church, then, given brother Bales' theory, non-Christians who enter the Baptist church and who then urge other men to reject Christ's way of salvation and Christ's church and to enter the Baptist church do not sin in so doing! Let Bales and all who claim to accept Bales' doctrine be prepared to defend this anti-Biblical doctrine!

It seems that many have such "itching ears" to hear an "easy" doctrine on divorce and remarriage that they refuse to see the implications of that "easy" doctrine (which, as brother Bales puts it, holds that non-Christians are not amenable to the high standard set out in the gospel).

Brother Bales' denial that the gospel (law) of Christ is addressed to "every creature" (Mark 16:15-16) is a "pandora's box" of doctrinal error, and all who espouse and teach such are going to have to face what comes out of that box!

The fact that God has one—and only one—law addressed to all men now living and that that law is the gospel (law) of Christ, (as was discussed in detail —and proved—in Chapter X above) is not only crucial to brother Bales case—it is fatal to his case! That such is the case will be demonstrated in Chapters XV, XVI, XVII, XVIII, and XIX.

4. *A more detailed look at "Proposition JDB."* Holding as he does, (1) that no non-Christian living today is amenable to the law of Christ (2) that non-Christians living today are amenable not to the law of Christ but to "the law written on the heart,"[6] and (3) that the only people who are amenable to Matthew 19:9 are Christians who are married to Christians, brother Bales has no way of arguing soundly that such false

teachers as Baptist preachers sin when they urge other men to reject the Lord's plan of salvation and to accept their (Baptists') doctrine of salvation at the point of faith before and without being baptized in the name of Jesus Christ. (Paul makes clear, in Acts 13:8-12, that Bales' doctrine here is false.) Thus, he seeks to avoid this problem by branding it as irrelevant to the question of divorce and remarriage.[7] But he will not be allowed to rid himself of this problem for his doctrine has far-reaching implications. *These implications strike at the very foundation of the law of Christ (the gospel).* The significance of this matter was shown in Chapter X, but there will be more discussion of it in the several Chapters of Part V.

This writer urges the reader to recognize the great danger to the cause of Christ which is involved in brother Bales' doctrine. Compare such passages as Revelation 2:14,20; 21:8; Galatians 5:19-25; Acts 13:8-12.

5. *A summary listing of the crucial points of "Proposition JDB" (and of Sub-Proposition Z in particular).* No one can really understand what this present controversy is all about unless he understands that Bales' position involves affirmations (some by explicit teaching and some by implicit teaching) which are definitely false.

Note the following elements which are involved (either explicitly or implicitly) in brother Bales' position.

(1) Non-Christians are not amenable to (under) the law of Christ (the gospel).

(2) Non-Christian Gentiles living today are amenable to (under) what brother Bales calls "the law written on the heart"—not to the law of Christ (the gospel).

(3) Non-Christian Jews who have lived since Pentecost are amenable to the law of Moses—not to the law of Christ (the gospel). (Note: he, at times, seems to take the position that non-Christian Jews were amenable to the law of Moses only until the destruction of Jerusalem. But more of this later.)

(4) Since one can neither obey nor disobey a law to which he is not amenable, then non-Christians can neither obey nor disobey the law of Christ (the gospel).

(5) Thus, since non-Christians cannot disobey the law of Christ (the gospel), they cannot be lost because of disobeying the law of Christ. If they are lost, it is because they have disobeyed some law other than the law of Christ. (Thus, brother Bales invents the position that non-Christians living (Gentiles, at least) today are amenable to (under) "the law written on the heart"—not the law of Christ.

(6) Also, since non-Christians are not amenable

to the gospel (law) of Christ, then cannot obey the law of Christ (the gospel), and since no lost man can be saved without obeying the gospel (Mark 16:15-16; John 3:3-5; Acts 2:38, et al.), then, given brother Bales position, *no one can be saved!* (Bales' effort to set out an analogy, using the Gentiles becoming "proselytes" of Judaism, fails. More on this later.)

(7) Since brother Bales holds that no non-Christian is amenable to (under) the law of Christ, then it follows that he teaches (at least implicitly) that no non-Christian sins when (if) he establishes or enters or upholds a religious institution which is not authorized by the Bible (e.g., the Baptist church, the Roman Catholic church, the Mormon church, et al.) even though such unauthorized religious institutions ("churches") preach false doctrine urging people to reject the true gospel, the true church, true worship and the true Christian life. Let everyone who says, "I believe brother Bales position," be prepared to defend this doctrine which so plainly contradicts the teaching of Paul in Acts 13:8-12! The alternatives for every person are clear: (1) choose Bales' doctrine (as set out in *NUB* and other of his writings) or (2) choose Christ's doctrine (as set out by Paul in Acts 13:8-12). The choice will be an easy one for every honest person who understands the two positions.

(8) Brother Bales teaches that no one is amenable to (under) Matthew 19:9 except Christians who are married to Christians.

(9) Thus, brother Bales also teaches (at least implicitly) that no Christian who is married to a non-Christian is amenable to Matthew 19:9. Thus, he holds that not all Christians are amenable to Matt. 19:9 even though Bales calls Matt. 19:9 a "covenant passage." How can Bales be consistent while claiming that Matt. 19:9 is "a covenant passage" and then deny that any "in the covenant" (as Bales puts it) are not amenable to Matthew 19:9? This is self-contradiction.

(10) Thus, brother Bales teaches (at least implicitly) that no Christian who is unmarried is amenable to Matthew 19:9 (and thus, according to brother Bales, could—with God's approval—marry a non-Christian person who has been put away for fornication). Let every parent ask, "Do I want my child to be taught that doctrine?"

(11) No non-Christian is amenable to Matthew 19:9 and, so, according to brother Bales, any non-Christian may marry many wives and live in a polygamous state—all with God's approval.

(12) Thus, since brother Bales holds that when one is baptized he does not—to be pleasing to God—have to sever marriages which violate Christ's law if those marriages were contracted before the man was baptized. Note: Bales denies this point when polygamy

is involved. But, the reader may be assured, he will not be allowed to "get away with" the self-contradiction thus involved. More on this later in Appendix P.

(13) No non-Christian who is married to a non-Christian is amenable to any legislation from Christ on divorce and remarriage (or any other of Christ's legislation). Thus, according to brother Bales, non-Christians may live (with God's approval): (a) in "polygamous marriages"[8] (one husband and a multiplicity of wives), (b) in "group marriages" (in which there are, say, five men and twenty women and all of the men have marital (sexual) privileges with all of the women), (c) "trial (companionate) marriages" (in which the man and woman agree to marry for, say, no less than three months and no more than six months, during which time they will decide if they wish to continue the marriage. (Cf. brother G. C. Brewer's debate with Judge Ben Lindsey).

(14) Brother Bales holds that in a case of marital infidelity (fornication), the guilty party is just as free (with God's approval) to marry again as is the innocent party. This means that a forty-year old man who wishes to get rid of his wife in order to be free to marry a twenty-five year old woman may commit fornication for the deliberate purpose of freeing himself to put away his wife and "marry" the younger woman! That such an ungodly doctrine could be believed and/or taught by gospel preachers, elders, and/or professors in a christian college seem simply incredible to this writer. May a sleeping brotherhood awaken to the import of this doctrine!

(15) According to brother Bales' doctrine, two elders in the same congregation could "swap wives" (just as did two famous baseball players a few years ago) by the simple "process" of committing fornication—thus freeing all parties concerned to remarry, with God's approval. This author prays that brother Bales and all who claim to believe what he teaches will realize the error of this doctrine which has claimed their allegiance.

There are other similar positions which are implicitly taught by brother Bales, but, since later chapters will be devoted to these unscriptural liasons approved by brother Bales' doctrine, further discussion will be left for those chapters.

Conclusion of this Chapter

Thus, if brother Bales' doctrine is true, then all of the doctrines listed just above are true. But, those doctrines are false. Thus, Bales' doctrine on divorce and remarriage is false. Christ has all authority in heaven and on earth—His message (the gospel, the law of Christ) is to be preached by His authority to every person in the entire world (Matt. 28:18-20; Mk. 16:15-16; Lk. 24:45-49; Acts 1:1-8). Christ has authority over all flesh (John 17:2). God commands all men everywhere to repent (Acts 17:30-31).

This author prays that brother Bales and all who claim to believe what he teaches face up to the implications of his teaching and realize that he is in error on the question of divorce and remarriage. More on this point will be set out in chapters following.

Footnotes

[1]Set out in Chapter XI above (affirmed by this author, Thomas B. Warren).

[2]Hereinafter referred to as "Proposition JDB" (affirmed by James D. Bales).

[3]More details of this will be set out in Chapter XX.

[4]And other matters in addition to these.

[5]Bales takes this position, by implication, in his answer to a question on denominationalism (p. 1) and in his answer to TBW question 14 (p. 16) of another manuscript. This point—on which Bales vascillates (and is wrong in both basic positions he espouses)—will be set out in more detail in subsequent discussions. He sometimes takes the position that non-Christian Jews were amenable to the law of Moses until after the destruction of Jerusalem. But, in many other of his writings, he teaches the truth that the law of Moses, in its entirety, had to be abolished before the law of Christ could come into force. Likely, if the question of divorce and remarriage had not misled him, Bales would never have espoused these erroneous positions on the law of Moses.

[6]As noted in footnote 5 above, brother Bales also argues that non-Christian Jews did not become amenable to the law of Christ on Pentecost. But, in other places he argues that the law of Christ could not come into effect until after the law of Moses was abolished. This will be discussed later.

[7]Just as did Fuqua (*Warren-Fuqua Debate*).

[8]To avoid confusing brother Bales (who attaches enormous importance to quotation marks), those marks have been used with each type of "marriage" listed!

CHAPTER XV

BALES' FAILURE TO DEMONSTRATE HIS OWN BASIC PROPOSITION

In this chapter, the following things will be accomplished: (1) the reader will be reminded of brother Bales' basic proposition ("Proposition JDB"), which was set out in Chapter XIV, (2) the reader will be reminded of what is required in order to demonstrate a proposition (as was set out in Chapter VII), and (3) the reader will be shown that *brother Bales has not demonstrated his basic proposition.*

1. *Brother Bales' basic proposition.* The basic proposition (which adequately states the doctrine which he upholds on divorce and remarriage) of brother Bales was set forth in Chapter XIV. The reader must have that proposition in mind in order to adequately appreciate what follows in this book. (It would be of value to the reader to go back and re-read that proposition.)

2. *A reminder of what is required to demonstrate a doctrine.* This matter was explained in detail in Chapter VII. Explained in a very simply way, the matter amounts to this: when someone asserts that a given proposition is taught by the Bible, he can prove that such is the case either (1) by proving that the Bible teaches it explicitly (i.e., says it in just so many words), or (2) by setting forth sound argument which has the proposition under consideration as its conclusion (i.e., that explicit teaching of the Bible implies the proposition). For an argument to be sound, it must be the case both (1) that the argument itself is valid (that is, that the truth of the premises guarantees the truth of the conclusion)[1] and (2) that all of the premises are true.[2]

It is the contention of this writer (because he knows it to be the case) that brother Bales not only has not demonstrated that his basic proposition ("Proposition JDB") is true—he cannot do so. This writer claims to know that such is the case, because he claims to know that "Proposition JDB" is false—that it can be refuted.

3. *Brother Bales has not demonstrated that his basic proposition is true.* While it is true that brother Bales has written a "mountain" of material about divorce and remarriage within the last one to two years, nowhere has he set forth the sound argument the conclusion of which is his basic proposition ("Proposition JDB"). He has not done so, for the simple reason that it cannot be done. His doctrine can be refuted (proved to be false—see Chapters XV, XVI, XVII, and XVIII), so, of course, it cannot be proved to be true.

The challenge has been given to brother Bales in the past[3] and it is here repeated: set out the sound argument, the conclusion of which is "Sub-Proposition Z". He cannot answer the challenge, because it cannot be done.

The offering of the above challenge is not for one moment to concede the non-importance of either "Sub-Proposition X" or "Sub-Proposition Y." Both of them are quite crucial, and brother Bales can no more demonstrate either one of them than he can demonstrate "Sub-Proposition Z."

Thus far, all this author has seen from brother Bales is a mass of writing but no sound argument proving his case.

Brother Bales gives very little attention to dealing with arguments in a strictly logical way. Some writers do this sort of thing because they know that their case cannot stand the look of logic. As one philosopher said, in effect, "No man ever turns against reason (logic, TBW) until reason turns against him." (But brother Bales knows that the proper use of logic is crucial to properly interpreting the Bible.)

4. *Summary as to the point under discussion in this chapter.* (1) Let it be emphasized as strongly as it can be emphasized that it is always the obligation of the affirmative disputant to set forth the proof (demonstration) of the proposition which he is affirming! It is not the responsibility of the negative disputant to formulate and write the affirmative disputant's case for him. The affirmative disputant (in this case, it is brother Bales so far as "Proposition JDB" is concerned) may write thousands upon thousands of words (as brother Bales has done) without setting out an argument and proving: (1) that that argument is valid and (2) that all of the premises of it are true. (2) The use of the tactic adopted by brother Bales can be very confusing and misleading to the naive and unwary. They may think that the very large number of words proves what the writer claims for it. But may it be said—kindly and lovingly—as one thinker said, in effect: While 400 pages of crowded fact and argument may deceive the very elect, when the entire matter is reduced to a three-line syllogism (or a precise logical —sound—argument), the "bones of the argument are laid bare" and all honest people may see the unsoundness of it. Brother Bales has not set out a sound argument which proves his proposition (i.e., "Sub-Proposition Z"). Thus, he has failed, and he will continue as a failure since no such argument can be given. (3) Let the reader remember that—so far as the specific problem of amenability to the law of Christ—brother Bales has not given the sound argument which proves that only Christians are amenable to the law of Christ (the gospel). He not only has not done it—he cannot do it. Remember! *Brother Bales has not proved this point!* Who then, can accept his position? (4) Also, let the reader remember that—so far as the specific problem of unauthorized

religious "churches" (such as Baptist, Catholic, et al.)—brother Bales has not given the sound argument which proves that they are not amenable to (under) the law of Christ (the gospel). He not only has not done it—he cannot do it (Acts 13:8-12)! It is incredible to this author that a great gospel preacher (such as brother Bales) who in past years has done so much (as did brother E. C. Fuqua) to show the sinfulness of denominationalism (because it violates the law of Christ!) would—in order to have even a semblance of a case for his theory on divorce and remarriage—now deny many basic truths which he formerly recognized and taught (and likely still does on every subject which does not, in his view, touch the question of divorce and remarriage).

Remember! Brother Bales has not proved this point which is so crucial to his entire case! Therefore, he faces this dilemma: he must affirm either (1) that Baptists are amenable to the law (gospel) of Christ or (2) that Baptists are not amenable to the law (gospel) of Christ. Given his doctrine, Bales is in trouble no matter which one he chooses. If he chooses (1) (that Baptists are amenable to the law of Christ), then he admits defeat on divorce and remarriage because he thus admits that non-Christians are amenable to the law (gospel) of Christ! If he chooses (2) (that Baptists are not amenable to the law of Christ), then he admits defeat in that he denies the plain teaching of such passages as Acts 13:8-12 and Mk. 16:15-16.

The problem faced by Bales can also be set up as follows: If, (1), he holds that Baptists are amenable to the law of Christ, then he implies either (a) Baptists are Christians (i.e., to be a Baptist is to be a Christian—this would follow if Bales' contention that only Christians are amenable to the law of Christ) or (b) non-Christians are amenable to the law of Christ and, thus, to Matthew 19:9. In either case, brother Bales' case is destroyed! If Baptists are not amenable to Christ's law—the position which is consistent with brother Bales position on amenability—then brother Bales teaches the false doctrine that men can urge other men to reject the true gospel of Christ (without being guilty of sin, but see Acts 13:8-12 and Paul's condemnation of Elymas. (There will be more on this later.) (5) And, finally, let the reader note carefully that—so far as the specific problem of divorce and remarriage is concerned—brother Bales has not set out the sound argument which proves (a) that the only persons who are amenable to (under) the teaching of Matthew 19:9 are Christians who are married to Christians (Brother Bales' case absolutely depends on this), and brother Bales is hereby challenged to set out the logically precise, sound argument, the conclusion of which is "Proposition JDB" or even "Sub-Proposition Z," (b) that no Christian who is married to a non-Christian is amenable to the teaching of Matthew 19:9 (again, brother Bales' case absolutely depends on this proposition being true), and again he is challenged to present the proof of it by a sound argument. His mere assertions are worthless. It is sound, logical argument which is required, and brother Bales is urged to face up to this responsibility; (c) that no Christian who is not married is amenable to the teaching of Matthew 19:9. This false proposition is implied by brother Bales basic proposition that Matthew 19:9 is addressed only to Christians who are married to Christians. But brother Bales can prove neither of them. Again, his case is based upon mere assertion—not upon sound argument. (If Bales' doctrine on this point were true, an unmarried young christian man could marry a divorced woman who had been put away because of her fornication and be pleasing to God in so doing! Bales' doctrine clearly implies false doctrine and, thus, is itself false.); (d) that no non-Christian is amenable to the teaching of Matthew 19:9. Where is the sound argument which has been presented by brother Bales which proves this position? It has not been written; it cannot be written; the proposition is false; (e) that if a Christian is married to a non-Christian and if the non-Christian departs, then the Christian is free to remarry on the ground of that desertion alone (no fornication need be involved). This he based on I Corinthians 7:15 but he does not set out a sound argument which has this proposition as its conclusion. Therefore, he has not proved it; and (f) that if a Christian is married to a Christian and one of them is guilty of marital infidelity (commits fornication, Matthew 19:9), then the guilty party (as well as the innocent party) is free to put away his (her) spouse and to marry again (with God's approval).

5. *Conclusion as to this chapter.* In this chapter, the reader has been reminded of what one must do in order to prove that a proposition (which is other than self-evidently true) is true: (1) he must present a precise, logical argument—he must present propositions which are so related to one another that some of them function as evidence (premises) and at least one of them functions as the conclusion; (2) he must prove that the argument is valid (i.e., it must be an argument in which the truth of the premises guarantees the truth of the conclusion), and (3) he must show that all of the premises are true.

Brother Bales has not only not done all of these, he has done none of them in the strict sense. In the sense that he has presented statements which he seems to regard as evidence and other statements which he seems to regard as a conclusion, it might be granted that he has presented an "argument"—at least an argument of sorts. But he has not presented a logically precise and clearly sound argument (which he must if he is to prove his case). He has made no effort to say, "Here is my argument; it is valid; all of the premises are true; therefore, the argument is sound, and I have proved my case."

Thus, instead of meeting his obligation as a disputant, he has contented himself, in the main, with mere assertions—many of which, incidentally, are false—which do not prove his doctrine at all.

Thus, this present chapter has been well entitled: "Bales' Failure to Demonstrate His Own Basic Proposition."

Thus far, in Parts I, II, III, and IV, among other things, the following have been accomplished (1) the true basic proposition ("Proposition TBW")—including "Sub-Proposition T" has been demonstrated; (2) it has been shown that brother Bales has not—and cannot—refute "Proposition TBW" (including "Sub-Proposition T"); (3) it has been shown what brother Bales actually affirms and implies by his basic proposition ("Proposition JDB")—including "Sub-Proposition Z"; and (4) it has been shown that brother Bales has not—and cannot demonstrate (prove) his own basic doctrine to be true.

In Part V (Chapters XVI-A, XVI-B, XVII, XVIII, and XIX, brother Bales' basic proposition will be refuted (proved to be false).

Footnotes

[1]See detailed explanation in Chapter VI.

[2]If even one premise is false, then the argument is not sound and, thus, does not prove the conclusion even if the argument is valid.

[3]In a list of questions posed by TBW to JDB.

PART V

BALES' BASIC PROPOSITION REFUTED (PROVED TO BE FALSE)

CHAPTER XVI-A

BALES' DOCTRINE DENIES PLAIN BIBLE TEACHING

In Part II (consisting of Chapters VI, VII and VIII), among other things the following matters were discussed in some detail: (1) the cruciality of the law of rationality in the learning of the truth, (2) how to demonstrate (prove) that a proposition (doctrine) is true, and (3) how to refute a proposition (doctrine)—i.e., show that it is false.

All five of the Chapters (XVI-A, XVI-B, XVII, XVIII, XIX) in this part (Part V) will deal with point (3) above—i.e., each of the five chapters will deal with some phase of proving that brother Bales' basic proposition is false.

This present Chapter (XVI-A) will deal with the fact that brother Bales' proposition (doctrine) is false by proving that his (brother Bales') doctrine denies plain Bible teaching.[1] Given the compound proposition (in the footnote) this means that if Q is a Bible proposition and P a proposition which is affirmed by brother Bales, and if proposition P is logically equivalent to the contradictory of Q (the Bible doctrine) then brother Bales' proposition P is false. More simply put, it means that if a proposition P which is affirmed by brother Bales denies a proposition Q which is plainly taught (in the Bible) to be true, then Bales' proposition P is false!

Thus, it follows that if it can be shown that any proposition which is crucial to brother Bales' case (on divorce and remarriage) *denies plain Bible teaching*, then it has been shown that brother Bales' proposition is false.

The foregoing paragraph describes the basic approach to this present chapter. Brother Bales basic proposition ("the JDB Proposition") will be shown to be false by showing that it denies plain Bible teaching. Since brother Bales proposition ("Sub-Proposition Z") on divorce and remarriage denies so much Bible truth (truth which brother Bales himself formerly taught—and likely does even now on every subject except divorce and remarriage), this will be shown again and again.

The basic purpose of the five chapters of Part V is not merely to undermine brother Bales argument (although that has already been done in Chapter XV). The purpose here is not to merely show that brother Bales has not proved his own proposition ("the JDB Proposition")—that was done in Chapter XV and more will be done on the matter in later chapters—but the purpose of these five chapters is to show that—without doubt—"the JDB Proposition" is false!

The reader will recall that in Chapter VIII (of Part II) it was shown how a proposition can be refuted: (1) by showing that it *denies plain Bible teaching,* (2) by showing that it *implies a false doctrine,* (3) by showing that it *involves logical contradiction.* Relevant also to these three matters is that of *admitting defeat* either (1) by the way the advocate of the proposition answers questions so as to tacitly admit defeat or (2) by the way he tries to argue his case (i.e., so that he involves himself in tacit admissions of defeat).

Although even just one of these four ways would be sufficient to refute brother Bales' proposition, in Chapters XVI-A, XVI-B, XVII, XVIII and XIX all four of these ways will be utilized in proving that "the JDB Proposition" is false! It gives this author no pleasure at all to do this, but it must be done for the sake of the purity of the church (cf. Revelation 2:24, 20; 21:8; Galatians 5:19-21).

Although there are many plain passages of scriptures which brother Bales denies (contradicts—"countermands" as James S. Woodroof put it), because it seems foolish to be guilty of "overkill" on the matter, only the following passages (the plain teaching of which brother Bales denies) will be dealt with in this chapter: John 17:2; Revelation 19:16; Mark 16:15-16; John 3:3-5; Matthew 19:9; I Corinthians 5:1-13; I Corinthians 6:9-11; 9:20-22.

In Chapter XVI-B (a continuation of the same effort here in Chapter XVI-A), the entire chapter will be devoted to a discussion of Matthew 28:18-20 (a passage which is crucial to Bales' case, but which he woefully misinterprets.

1. *Brother Bales' doctrine denies the plain teaching of John 17:2.* According to John 17:1-2, Jesus said, "Father, the hour is come; glorify thy Son, that the Son may glorify thee; even as thou gavest him authority over all flesh that to all whom thou hast given him, he should give eternal life."

Of the statement which refers to authority, J. W. McGarvey well said, "The gift of authority was bestowed after his resurrection (Matthew XXVIII.18). All humanity was given into his hands that he might give life to that part of it which yielded itself to him in true discipleship."[2] This author agrees with the basic position set out here in regard to the authority referred to in John 17:2 being the same authority as claimed by Jesus in Matthew 28:18-20. In the succeeding Chapter (XVI-B), Matthew 28:18-20 (including the matter of Christ having all authority) will be discussed.[3]

John 17:2 and Matthew 28:18-20 mean that Jesus Christ has all authority over every man now living on earth. And, since He exercises His authority through

His law (the gospel, the faith, the New Covenant; Cf.: John 12:48; Mk. 16:15-16; Rom..8:1-2), and since whatever a law says, it says to them who are under that law (Romans 3:19), it follows that every man now living (whether in or out of the church), is amenable (under) that law.

Since brother Bales denies that Christ has authority over all flesh (he holds that non-Christians are not amenable to the law of Christ), he denies that all men are amenable to Christ's authority. Thus, since one of brother Bales' crucial propositions denies plain Bible teaching, brother Bales' doctrine is false.[4]

2. *Brother Bales' doctrine denies the plain teaching of Matthew 28:18-20.* Since the material in Matthew 28:18-20 which is crucially relevant to the divorce-remarriage question will be thoroughly discussed in Chapter XVI-B and in Appendix T (and shown to be denied by brother Bales' doctrine), it will not be discussed in detail here. Suffice it to say that brother Bales simply does not understand the passage because he fails to see the point to the usage of the *modal participles* in Matthew 28:18-20. Brother Bales' case cannot be established unless he can prove that "teaching (*didaskontes*) them. . ." refers exclusively to time subsequent to non-Christian's being baptized into Christ. And that he cannot do. The reader should carefully and prayerfully study the explanation of Matthew 28:18-20 as set out in Chapter XVI-B in order to see that, once again, brother Bales' doctrine denies plain Bible teaching.[5] His doctrine denies that prior to being baptized non-Christians are to be taught to observe all things (including Matthew 19:9) which Christ commanded (which, of course, are a part of the New Covenant).

3. *Brother Bales' doctrine denies the crucial teaching of Revelation 19:16—therefore his doctrine is false.* In reference to Jesus Christ, the Bible says, "And out of his mouth proceedeth a sharp sword, that with it he should smite the nations: and he shall rule them with a rod of iron: and he treadeth the winepress of the fierceness of the wrath of God, the Almighty. And he hath on his garment and on his thigh a name written KING OF KINGS, AND LORD OF LORDS." (Revelation 19: 15-16). Christ has authority over all men.

4. *Brother Bales' doctrine is false because it denies the plain teaching of Matthew 19:9.* In Chapter XII above, a detailed analysis of Matthew 19:9 (so far as the fact that it makes clear that fornication is the one—and only—ground for divorce and remarriage is concerned) was given. An even more detailed discussion of Matthew 19:9 will be set out in Appendix A.

For the purpose of this present chapter (that of showing that brother Bales' doctrine denies plain

Bible teaching) little more than what has already been said in Chapter XII needs to be said. In that chapter, it was made clear that Matthew 28:18-20 undeniably teaches that all things which Jesus had commanded (relevant to the New Covenant, of course) were to be taught to those who were not yet baptized. Since Matthew 19:9 is a part of such instruction, then Matthew 19:9 is to be taught to those who have not yet been baptized. Brother Bales, in utterly denying the force of the modal (present) participles (as pertains to "baptizing" and especially to "teaching") makes clear that his doctrine is false because every doctrine which denies plain Bible teaching is a false doctrine.

No more really needs to be said, but more will be said because there is so much more.

5. *Brother Bales' doctrine is false because it denies the plain Bible teaching that all men are amenable to the teaching of Matthew 19:9*. In addition to the fact that such is made clear by Matthew 28:18-20 (as has already been discussed in Chapter XII and in point 4 just above), there is also the truth that the passage is seen to be universal by Jesus' use of "whosoever..."[6] This amounts to saying: "All men who put away their wives on any ground other than fornication (marital infidelity) are men who commit adultery (actually, keep on committing adultery) if/when they marry another woman."

Brother Bales' doctrine is false because he denies this plain Bible teaching.[7]

6. *Brother Bales' doctrine is false because it denies the plain Bible teaching that I Corinthians 7:10 refers to all married people—not only to Christians who are married to Christians (as brother Bales alleges)*. Paul, guided by the Holy Spirit, says in very simple language, "But unto the *married* (emphasis, TBW) I give charge, yea not I, but the Lord, that the wife depart not from her husband. . ." Brother Bales' whole case depends upon this passage referring only to Christians who are married to Christians. (This is a vital key in his effort to try to prove that Matthew 19:9 is what brother Bales' calls "a covenant passage." If "the married" in I Corinthians 7:10 refers to any married other than Christians married to Christians, then brother Bales' entire case collapses completely! And what does Paul say? Does he say, ". . .and to Christians who are married to Christians"? No! Absolutely not! He says, ". . .to the married." What married? Any married? Paul refers to all people who are *married in harmony with God's will* (he certainly would not tell those who were living in adultery—Cf. Colossians 3:5—not to depart from their companions!) This covers all of the following cases: (a) Christians who are married to Christians, (b) Christians who are married to non-Christians, (c) Non-Christians who are married to non-

Christians.

The reader may ask, "Can brother Bales set forth an argument which warrants the deduction—even though the passage doesn't say it explicitly—that the passage refers only to Christians who are married to Christians?" The plain answer is, "No—he cannot." He has been challenged to do so and the slight effort he made was pitiable indeed.[8]

7. *Brother Bales' doctrine is false because it denies the plain Bible teaching that God—and His Law—is involved in all lawful marriage covenants (Matthew 19:3-6).* The reader should carefully consider the entire passage Matthew 19:3-12. Special attention is called to 19:6: "So that they are no more two, but one flesh What therefore God has joined together, let not man put asunder." A pertinent passage is found in the Old Testament: "Yet ye say, Wherefore? Because the Lord hath been witness between thee and the wife of thy youth, against whom thou hast dealt treacherously: yet is she thy companion, and the wife of thy covenant. . . Therefore take heed to your spirit, and let none deal treacherously against the wife of his youth. For the Lord, the God of Israel, saith that he hateth putting away. . ." (Malachi 2:14-16).

Brother Bales' holds that the guilty party (in a case of fornication) is as free to marry again as is the innocent party because, he alleges, if either one of a married couple is free to marry another, then the other spouse is also free. But, Bales overlooks the fact God is a party to the covenant involved and thus the guilty party is still bound by Christ's law and is not free to marry again (Cf. Matt. 19:9; 5:31-32).

8. *Brother Bales' doctrine is false because it denies plain Bible teaching that the law of Christ (the gospel) is the one and only law (authorizing civil law also, of course) which God has for all men.* Since the argument set forth in detail in Chapter X proves that the law of Christ (the gospel) is the one and only law which God has for all men, then brother Bales' doctrine that non-Christians are not amenable to (under) the law of Christ but are under what brother Bales' calls "the law written on the heart," then it is obvious that brother Bales' doctrine denies plain Bible teaching and, thus, it is clear that Bales' doctrine is false.

9. *Brother Bales' doctrine is false because it denies plain Bible teaching in regard to the fact that the gospel (the law of Christ) is addressed to all men—not merely to Christians.* Brother Bales, at times, tries to deny this point, but he cannot succeed in such an effort. If he denies that the gospel is addressed to all men, then he obviously contradicts what Jesus said, "Go ye into all the world and preach the gospel to every creature. . ." (Mark 16:15-16). This denial would prove his (brother Bales') doctrine to be false.

If he admits that the gospel is a universal message (i.e., addressed to all men—whether Christian or non-Christian), then he admits defeat by thus admitting that Matthew 19:9, being a part of the gospel, is addressed to all men. He admits defeat in only a slightly different way if he admits that the gospel is addressed to all men but then holds that even though Matthew 19:9 is a part of the law (doctrine) of Christ, it is not a part of the gospel of Christ. In taking such a position he would distinguish as do Garrett and Ketcherside, between "gospel" and "doctrine" (or law) and, thus casts his lot with those liberals.[9]

So, there is no escape for brother Bales here—the gospel of Christ is a universal message, and, thus, his (Bales') doctrine denies plain Bible teaching in regard to that matter (Mark 16:15; Matthew 28:18-20; Luke 24:45-49; Acts 1:1-8; 13:8-12; 17:30-31).

10. *Brother Bales' doctrine is false because it actually denies that Matthew 19:9 is an "exceptive" sentence.* Although this point is actually involved in a point discussed above, it will be advantageous for the reader to recall the argument, set forth in Chapter XII, in which the force of the "exceptive" sentence (i.e., it means "if and only if. . ." or "the one and the only. . .") and that Matthew 19:9 is an "exceptive" sentence, making clear that, for all men, the one and only ground on which a man may put away his wife and marry another is that of fornication.

Since brother Bales' doctrine denies the force of the fact that Matthew 19:9 is an "exceptive" sentence (and thus, he denies plain Bible teaching), then his doctrine is false.

11. *Brother Bales' doctrine is false because it denies that the law of Moses was abolished from the day of Pentecost on.* In his effort to avoid the force of I Corinthians 6:9-11 (which refers to sins committed by non-Christians), Bales denies the truth (taught in Heb. 10:9) that the law of Moses (the Old Covenant) had to be abolished before the law of Christ (the New Covenant) could come into force. While dealing with subjects other than divorce and remarriage, Bales has had no trouble in seeing this truth.[10] But being unable to fit this truth into his present theory on divorce and remarriage, he now claims, in some places, that non-Christian Jews were still under the law of Moses until the destruction of Jerusalem in A.D. 70,[11] but in other places, he holds that non-Christian Jews living today are still under the law of Moses.[12] He does this by implying—by his contention that Jews today violate the law of Moses. But, since one can neither obey nor disobey a law to which he is not amenable (Rom. 3:19), Bales' contention implies that non-Christian Jews living today are amenable to the law of Moses! Yet, in times past, in a number of his books,[13] he teaches the truth

that Christ could not become priest and king until the law of Moses was done away and that Christ became king and priest on Pentecost.

Thus, Bales' doctrine is false because it denies plain Bible teaching. By implication, he denies that the law of Moses (the Old Covenant) had to be abolished in its entirety before the law of Christ (the New Covenant) could come into force.

12. *Bales' doctrine is false because it denies that all men everywhere are commanded to repent.* Bales argues that if one is not qualified (as per the Scriptures) to do a certain thing, then he cannot be under obligation to do whatever it is. No doubt, he takes this position because he tries to avoid the truth that all men are amenable to the law (gospel) of Christ and, thus, are amenable to Matthew 19:9 (which is a part of the gospel of Christ) by countering with the point that non-Christians are not amenable to the instruction of the law of Christ that the Lord's Supper be eaten.[14]

But the Bible plainly teaches that men can be obligated to do what they are not yet qualified to do. Paul said that "the times of this ignorance God winked at (overlooked, A.S.V.); but now commandeth all men everywhere to repent" (Acts 17:30).

The following argument proves that men can be obligated to do what they are not qualified to do.

1. If Ⓐ all men are under obligation to repent, and if Ⓑ one cannot be under obligation to obey any law to which he is not amenable, and if Ⓒ some men are non-believers, and if Ⓓ one is not qualified to repent until he believes, then Ⓔ men can be obligated to do what they are not qualified to do. (This premise is obviously true, for if the four propositions which comprise the antecedent (A, B, C, D) are all true, then the conclusion (E) must also be true.

2. Proposition A (all men—whether non-believer or believer—are under obligation to repent) is true (Acts 17:30-31).

3. Proposition B (one cannot be under obligation to obey any law to which he is not amenable) is true (Rom. 3:19).

4. Proposition C (some men are non-believers) is true (Acts 17:32).

5. Proposition D (one is not qualified to repent until he first believes) is true (Acts 2:38).

6. The compound proposition (comprised of Proposition A, Proposition B, Proposition C, and Proposition D) is true. (This is the case because a conjunctive proposition comprised only of true propositions is itself true.)

7. Therefore, Proposition E (men can be obligated to do what they are not qualified to do) is true. (The truthfulness of Proposition E is implied—by Modus Ponens argument form—by the truthfulness of the ante-

cedent {premise 6 above}.)

Thus, since the New Testament plainly teaches that men can be obligated to do what they are not yet qualified to do, and since brother Bales denies this, he is guilty of denying plain Bible teaching.[15] His doctrine is false.

Conclusion

In this chapter, it has been proved that brother Bales' doctrine is false because it denies plain Bible teaching.

Footnotes

[1]Put in symbolic terms, the logic of this matter looks like this:

$$\{Q\cdot(P\equiv\sim Q)\}>\sim P$$

Where "Q" = a proposition which is taught in the Bible; "P" = the proposition to be shown to be false; "·" = "and"; "≡" means "is logically equivalent to"; and "∿" means "it is false that." The symbolism above, put into ordinary English words, can be read: "If Proposition Q is true and if Proposition P is logically equivalent to the contradictory of Proposition Q, then Proposition P is false."

[2]J. W. McGarvey and P. Y. Pendleton, *The Four-Fold Gospel* (Cincinnati, The Standard Publishing Co.), p. 679.

[3]This matter is discussed thoroughly in XVI-B.

[4]This point is "ungetoverable"—no matter how prejudiced one may be: $\{Q\cdot(P\equiv\sim Q)\}>\sim P$ Neither brother Bales nor anyone else can refute this truth (where brother Bales' doctrine = P.)(See footnote 1 above.)

[5]$\{Q\cdot(P\equiv\sim Q)\}>\sim P$ (this means "therefore brother Bales' doctrine is false.")

[6]Bales admits that "whosoever" has a universal connotation when he writes on the plan of salvation; J. D. Bales, *The Hub of the Bible*.

[7]$\{Q\cdot(P\equiv\sim Q)\}>\sim P$ means: "If the Bible teaches proposition Q and if proposition P (the doctrine under consideration) is logically equivalent to the contradictory of Q, then proposition P is false."

[8]I Corinthians 7:10-16 will be discussed in detail in Appendix C. Also see Appendix D on I Corinthians 7:15.

[9]This author plans a book in which this sort of move will be exposed for the Bible-denying doctrine which it is.

[10]See: *HUB*, passim.; *KPAE*, passim.

[11]See Bales' argument on I Corinthians 9:20-22.

[12]See manuscript on "Denominationalism" and manuscript in answer to question by TBW already documented above.

[13]Note: *The Kingdom Prophesied and Established; The Hub of the Bible*, et al.

[14]See Appendix G for a detailed discussion of the problem being obligated to do what one is not yet qualified to do.

[15]The reader is urged once more to read Appendix G in regard to this matter.

CHAPTER XVI-B

BALES' DOCTRINE IS FALSE BECAUSE IT DENIES PLAIN BIBLE TEACHING—MATTHEW 28:18-20

Since it is obvious (1) that the Bible is the word of God (II Timothy 3:16-17; II Peter 1:20-21) and (2) that God does not lie (Hebrews 6:18; Titus 1:2; I Samuel 15:29), then it is also obvious that any proposition which denies (or contradicts) plain Bible teaching is itself false. This point has already been discussed in detail in Chapters VII and XVI-A.

This present chapter is actually a continuation of XVI-A. but, since (as was stated earlier) Matthew 28:18-20, a passage which is so crucial (as he uses it) to brother Bales' case, but which he improperly explains, it was decided to devote an entire (though brief) chapter to this one passage. This is being done in order to call attention to (1) the cruciality of it for brother Bales' case and (2) the error which is involved in his effort to explain the passage.

1. *Matthew 28:18-20 set out.* In the American Standard Version of the English Bible, Matthew 28:18-20 reads as follows: "And Jesus came to them and spake unto them, saying, All authority hath been given unto me in heaven and on earth. Go ye therefore, and make disciples of all the nations, baptizing them into the name of the Father and of the Son and of the Holy Spirit; teaching them to observe all things whatsoever I commanded you: and lo, I am with you always, even unto the end of the world."

2. *Crucial words in the passage.* No effort will be made here to explain in detail all of the words which are used in this passage. Neither will an effort be made to explain all that might be said about even the most crucial words. However, effort will be made to get at the heart of the matter in regard to the most crucial words in the passage—i.e., what role they play in making clear just what Jesus has said here.

(1) *Poreuthentes* (1 Aorist, passive, participle, nominative masculine, plural of *poreuomai,* meaning "go ye"—or "having gone."

(2) *Mathēteusate* 2nd person, plural, 1 aorist, active, imperative of *mathēteuo,* meaning "make disciples" (in this case, meaning "make disciples" or "make Christians" (children of God) out of individuals of "all the nations"—including both Jews and Gentiles in all the nations (ta ethnē). This means that Jesus, in the giving of the Great Commission, put His disciples under the obligation of trying to convert (make Christians out of) all men in all nations—i.e., both Jews and Gentiles—by making known the gospel. When one compares this statement with the record of Jesus' statement in Mark 16:15-16, it is easily seen that one and the same

message (the gospel, the law of Christ, the faith) is to be preached to "every creature in all the world." Thus, on the very face of the Great Commission, it is clear that one and the same message is to be preached to all men. Even this much proves that brother Bales is wrong. But such error (by brother Bales in not recognizing the universality of the law (doctrine) of Christ) is only the "tip of the iceberg" so far as the mass of false doctrine taught by Bales in connection with the subject of divorce and remarriage.

(3) *Baptidzontes* (present active participle nominative masculine plural of *baptidzo*, meaning "I baptize, I immerse, I plunge, I dip.") In this case (being the present participle), it means, "baptizing." Being baptized is the act of obedience, on the part of the penitent believer in Jesus Christ, which culminates in being saved by the blood of Christ (being added to the church for which Jesus died—Acts 2:38; Mark 16:15-16; Acts 2:47; 22:16; Romans 6:3-5; Galatians 3:26-27; Ephesians 1:7).

(4) *Didaskontes*. (present active participle, nominative plural, masculine of *didasko*, meaning, "teach, deliver a didactic discourse"). Since this is a present participle, the meaning here is: "teaching."

3. *The meaning of this passage*. In this passage, the main verb is "make disciples" (*mathēteuo*, an imperative used transitively—that is, with an object). The two participles ("baptizing" and "teaching") are both present participles used in a modal function—that is, they set forth "the manner in which the given action was performed" (S. G. Green, *Handbook to the Grammar of the Greek Testament*, p. 332). Green gives the following passages which are instances of this modal use of the present participle: (a) Matthew 5:2 ". . . he taught them, saying. . .;" (b) Matthew 19:22: ". . . he went away sorrowful," (c) Matthew 11:25, ". . .he said, having addressed himself to reply, 'he answered and said," (Ibid) Professor A. T. Robertson, long recognized as a truly outstanding New Testament Greek scholar, in his large grammar, says, "See *baptidzontes* and *didaskontes* in Matthew 28:19f. as modal participles."[1]

Green also lists Matthew 28:18-20 as an instance of present participles used as modal participles.

An "everyday" illustration which should help the reader to understand this modal use of the present participle is the following. Suppose a farmer gave his son this instruction, "Beautify the barn, cleaning and painting it." "Beautify" is the main verb in the sentence (an imperative). The participles ("cleaning" and "painting") are modal in their basic function—i.e., they are used to explain how the beautfication comes to fruition. This simply means that the farmer was telling his son to beautify the barn by the means of cleaning and painting it. The farmer was not telling his son to beautify the barn by the single action of cleaning it and, then, after having cleansed (and thus beautified it) to paint it as an action which was subsequent to the action of beautification.

In the same way, in Matthew 28:18-20, the main verb is "make disciples." The two present participles ("baptizing" and "teaching") are modal participles—i.e., they explain what men are to do in order to "make disciples" (Christians) out of non-Christians; viz., by baptizing and teaching them to observe all things whatsoever Christ had commanded them.

Thus, it is clear that, prerequisite to one's becoming a Christian, he must be taught to observe *all things which Christ had commanded* (this being confined, of course, to those teachings which are a part of the *law of Christ—not* of the *law of Moses*). Thus, since Matthew 19:9 is a part of the law of Christ, those on the verge of being baptized are to be taught to recognize and live in obedience to the instructions of Matthew 5:31-32 and 19:9. Obviously this does not mean that the one who is teaching the candidate for baptism must teach him the specific details of every individual or particular instruction in the gospel (as brother Bales falsely represented this writer as doing). But it does mean that Christ expects those who preach the gospel to the lost to so teach that, when the lost confess their faith in Christ (just prior to being baptized, Acts 8:26-40; Romans 19:9-10), they are to have been taught that they are, in that confession, publicly committing themselves to being faithful to Christ—i.e., to all of the law (gospel) of Christ for the rest of their lives.

Brother Bales holds that Matthew 28:18-20 teaches that men are to go teach non-Christians, baptize those they have taught and, then, having baptized them, to teach them to observe all things which Jesus had commanded. It is true that the Bible teaches (1) that the lost are to be taught the gospel (Mark 16:15), (2) that penitent believers are to be baptized (Mark 16:16; Acts 2:38; 3:19), and (3) that after becoming Christians the people are to be continually taught the gospel—but—it is not true that these exact details are taught in Matthew 28:18-20.

The correct exegesis of Matthew 28:18-20 has been given in the second paragraph above. The passage makes clear—by the use of the modal participle—that all non-Christians are to be taught to observe all that Jesus had commanded. The view (advanced by brother Bales) that non-Christians are not to be so taught is simply contradictory of what Jesus plainly taught.[2]

Why cannot brother Bales see the plain teaching of Matthew 28:18-20? In the judgment of this author, it may be that he cannot see it because he is blinded by his presupposition that Christ would not require non-Christians to live up to the standard of marriage, divorce and remarriage which He requires of Christians.

Bales—at least by implication—like Garrett and Ketcherside (who do it explicitly) distinguishes between "the gospel of Christ" and "the doctrine of Christ." The espousal of this error (which, perhaps, among other errors) led Garrett and Ketcherside into the "liberal" error usually referred to as "unity in diversity." Thus, it is not surprising that brother Bales has been highly commended (for his position on divorce and remarriage) by such "liberal" magazines as *Restoration Review* and *Integrity*. (So far as this present writer is concerned, he will become alarmed when such magazines commend him as a teacher.) This author says to brother Bales that he is welcome to such commendations. This author is thankful not to have them. But this author is thankful to have the commendations of men who are truly faithful to the Lord.

ACTS 3:8

Acts 3:8 should help the reader to understand the force of the modal participles as used in Matthew 28:18-20. In Acts 3:8, in regard to the lame man who had been healed, the Bible says that, leaping up, he "stood, and walked and entered (2 aorist, active, indicative of *eiserchomai*) with them into the temple, walking (present active participle) and leaping (present middle participle) and praising (present active participle) God. The three participles function here in a modal sense—that is, they explain how he entered the temple or what he did in entering the temple. In the same way, part of what was done in the making of disciples (making Christians out of them) was teaching them to observe *all things whatsoever Jesus had commanded them* (Matthew 28:18-20). This includes Matthew 19:9.

ACTS 13:45

In this passage, the reader is told that almost the whole city came together to hear the word of God preached. When the Jews saw the multitudes, they were filled with envy, and they spoke against (contradicted) what Paul was saying, covering him with abuse (blaspheming) (present active participle). Here again the present participle functions in a modal fashion. The blaspheming (or "covering him with abuse") is a modal participle which explains how the Jews "spake against these things which were spoken by Paul"—that is, it explains how it was done (just as was the case with Matthew 28:18-20).

I TIMOTHY 1:13

In referring to the fact that the Lord had counted him (Paul) faithful, putting him (Paul) into the ministry, Paul describes himself as having been (in the past) a blasphemer, and a persecutor, and a violent man. "But," Paul goes on, "I obtained mercy, because I did (1 aorist active indicative) it ignorantly (present active participle) in unbelief." Thus, Paul says, in effect, "I did it (did the deeds of a blasphemer, a persecutor and a violent man), functioning in ignorance." This is how he acted as a violent man, etc.—that is, being ignorant of the truth about Jesus while he was persecuting the church.

ACTS 14:21

This passage proves that disciples are made by the preaching of the gospel (cf.: Mark 16:15-16 and Matthew 28:18-20).

Conclusion

These three passages (Acts 3:8; 13:45; and I Timothy 1:13) substantiate the point made above in regard to Matthew 28:18-20. Many years ago (in 1953) when this author was doing some writing against the errors advanced by Leroy Garrett in regard to "preach" and "teach," he (this author) came to the conclusion in regard to Matthew 28:18-20 which has been advanced in this chapter. I sent an explanation of my conclusion to brother J. W. Roberts of Abilene Christian College, asking him to criticize the conclusion that both "baptizing" and "teaching" were modal participles. He replied by saying that he agreed with the conclusion and expressed appreciation for having the point called to his attention.

Matthew 28:18-20 proves that brother Bales is wrong in his theory that Matthew 19:9 is addressed only to Christians who are married to Christians. If Bales' doctrine is true, then Jesus taught falsehood in Matthew 28:18-20. But, Jesus did not teach falsehood in Matthew 28:18-20. Therefore, Bales' doctrine on Matthew 19:9 is false. Bales denies that the gospel (the law of Christ) is the universal message of Jesus Christ. He denies that that one message (the gospel, the law of Christ) is addressed to all men and affirms that no non-Christian is amenable to the law of Christ. Rather, he falsely holds that non-Christians are amenable to "the law on the heart."[3] More will be said on this in later chapters.

Footnotes

[1]A. T. Robertson, *A Grammar of the Greek New Testament In the Light of Historical Research,* (Nashville, Broadman Press, 1934), p. 1128.

[2]In a later chapter it will be made clear that brother Bales is in self-contradiction on this passage. Thus, all men should reject Bales' doctrine. (cf.: Revelation 2:14,20; 21:8).

[3]In some statements (previously noted) Bales implies that non-Christian Jews living today are amenable to the law of Moses. He is hopelessly "mixed up" on this whole matter of amenability.

CHAPTER XVII

BALES' DOCTRINE IS FALSE BECAUSE IT IMPLIES FALSE DOCTRINE

I. *The importance of this point.*

In Chapters XVI-A and XVI-B, it was shown that any doctrine which denies plain Bible teaching is false. It was also shown that brother Bales' doctrine on divorce and remarriage involves him in numerous outright denials of plain Bible teaching.

It should also be recalled that Chapter VI contains a detailed analysis of how to prove that a doctrine is false.

In addition to the way shown in Chapter XVI-A and Chapter XVI-B, another way to prove that a doctrine is false is to show (prove) that it *implies a false doctrine*. Every doctrine which implies a false doctrine is itself false.[1] This simply means that if one knows that proposition p implies proposition q and that proposition q is false, then one can also know that proposition p is false.[2]

Thus, the importance of this matter is made clear: if it can be shown that even one proposition which is crucial (necessary) to the proving of Bales' doctrine on divorce and remarriage is false, then his entire case will have been destroyed.

1. *Bales' doctrine is false because it implies the false doctrine that a non-Christian can be saved without being baptized in the name of Christ.*[3]

The point to be discussed here will be involved in Chapter XVIII also.[4] In this present chapter, it will be the purpose to prove that Bales' doctrine is false because it implies a false doctrine.

As a sort of preface, it will be good to note that the argument, in essence, amounts to this: (1) If Bales' position on Matthew 19:9 and I Corinthians 7:10-15 implies a false doctrine, then Bales' doctrine on divorce and remarriage is false, (2) Bales' position on Matthew 19:9 and I Corinthians 7:10-15 does imply a false doctrine, (3) therefore, Bales' doctrine on divorce and remarriage is false.

It should also be noted that Bales cannot give the premise which warrants the deduction he draws in regard to Matthew 19:9 and I Corinthians 7:10-15.[5]

Relevant to this matter is a statement made by Bales in his latest book.[6] Bales says, "However, I believe that Christ's legislation is for two believers —I learned this from Paul (I Corinthians 7:10-11),[7] and that Paul's legislation is for mixed marriages. (7:12-15) Since neither one of them legislated for the world, I am not thereby given authority to pass such legislation."

By "believer" is meant "Christian." By "mixed marriage," Bales means a marriage of a Christian to a non-Christian (unbeliever). By "the world" is meant "those who are not in the church."

It would be impossible to overestimate the importance of the argument which the reader is about to study. Bales bases his entire case on divorce and remarriage on his erroneous interpretation of Matthew 19: 9 and I Corinthians 7:10-15. Some of the implications of the positions he advances are grossly anti-Biblical. Let the reader carefully note the precise logical argument which is now to be presented. The argument is sound (that is, the argument is valid and all of the premises are true). After the argument is presented, it will be shown that (a) the argument is valid and (b) all of the premises are true. When these two things have been accomplished, then the conclusion (that Bales' position on I Corinthians 7:10-15 implies a false doctrine) is true. Thus, two things then will have been accomplished: (a) that Bales' position on I Corinthians 7:10-15 is false (and, thus, cannot be used to establish his case—all of his quibbling on I Corinthians 7 will have been refuted) and (b) that his general doctrine on divorce and remarriage is false doctrine (every doctrine which implies a false doctrine is itself a false doctrine).

Following is an argument which proves that Bales' statement (quoted above from *NUB*, p. 9) is false. Bales' statement (position) is shown to be false because it implies a false doctrine. In one sense there will be two arguments here but, in another sense, there will be only one argument since the second argument will be an extended proof of the second premise in the first argument. Here are the arguments:

1. If any statement implies that one can get into (enter) the kingdom (church) in any way other than by being baptized into it, then that statement is false (John 3:3-5).

2. Bales' statement re divorce and remarriage (*NUB*, p. 9) implies that one can get into (enter) the church by simply marrying a Christian.

3. Therefore, Bales' statement re divorce and remarriage (*NUB*, p. 9) is false.

A more detailed argument in regard to the same matter follows.

1. If (as Bales contends) Ⓐ it is false that Christ legislated for the world and if (as Bales contends) Ⓑ it is false that Paul legislated for the world, and if Ⓒ Paul did legislate for mixed marriages then it follows (as per Bales) that Ⓓ no non-Christian who is a partner in a mixed marriage is in the world.

2. Ⓐ Bales contends (*NUB*, p. 9): it is false

that Christ legislated for the world.

3. Ⓑ Bales contends (*NUB*, p. 9): it is false that Paul legislated for the world.

4. Ⓒ Paul did legislate for mixed marriages (I Corinthians 7:12-15).

5. It is true that Bales affirms Proposition Ⓐ, and it is true that Bales affirms Proposition Ⓑ, and it is true that Proposition Ⓒ is true.

6. Therefore (given Bales' position in *NUB*, p. 9), no non-Christian who is a partner in a mixed marriage is in the world. (This follows by Modus Ponens, from Premise 1 and Premise 5.)

Proposition D is actually false, but, given Bales' statement in *NUB*, p. 9, it follows as an implication of Bales' statement. Thus, Bales' statement is false.

Since Bales' statement (*NUB*, p. 9) implies Proposition D, another interesting argument presents itself:

1. If Ⓓ no non-Christian who is involved in a mixed marriage is in the world (an implication—which is false—of Bales' statement in *NUB*, p. 9), and if Ⓔ all men are either in the world or the church, then it would follow (given Bales' statement, *NUB*, p. 9) that Ⓕ no non-Christian who is a partner in a mixed marriage is outside the church.

This conclusion (Proposition F) is false, but it is implied by Bales' statement (*NUB*, p. 9). Thus, since it implies a false doctrine, Bales' statement itself is false. Bales holds false positions on both Matthew 19:9 and I Corinthians 7:10-15.[5]

II. *Some propositions which are crucial to Bales' case (doctrine) imply false doctrine.*

1. *Bales' doctrine is false because it implies the false doctrine that no one can be saved.* The Bible plainly teaches that lost men can be saved (Mk. 16:15-16; John 8:32; Luke 24:45-49; Hebrews 7:25). Since this is the case, if it can be shown that Bales doctrine implies that not even one person can be saved, then his doctrine will have been proved to be false.

The following argument proves that Bales' doctrine implies that no one can be saved.[8]

1. If Ⓐ[9] sin is the transgression of God's law, and if Ⓑ where there is no law, there is no transgression, and if Ⓒ everything in a law applies only to those who are under (amenable) that law, then Ⓓ one can neither obey nor violate a law which he is not under (amenable to).

2. Proposition A is true. (I John 3:4).
3. Proposition B is true (Rom. 4:15).
4. Proposition C is true. (Rom. 3:19).
5. The compound proposition A and B and C is true (2,3,4 by conjunction).

6. Therefore, Proposition D is true. (1,5, Modus Ponens).

This argument is valid[10] and all of the premises are true. Therefore, the conclusion must be true!

Then, having proved that Proposition D is true, Proposition D can be used to continue the same argument.

7. If Ⓓ one can neither obey nor violate a law which he is not under (amenable to) and if Ⓔ no non-Christian is under (amenable to) the gospel (law) of Christ and if Ⓕ no one living today can be saved without obeying the gospel (law) of Christ (i.e., the words of Christ), and if Ⓖ every non-Christian sins not by violating the gospel (the law of Christ) but by violating "the law written on the heart" (as Bales puts it), then Ⓗ no one living today can be saved.

8. Proposition D is true. (Already proved above: 1, 6, M.P. also Romans 4:15 is relevant)

9. Proposition E is true—that is, Bales claims it is true. (This proposition, although it is actually false {Mark 16:15; Romans 3:19}, is affirmed by Bales and is a crucial proposition in his total case. It is put here, as a part of this argument to show that one of Bales' crucial propositions implies a false proposition and, thus, is false itself. The reader must be careful to follow the argument.)

10. Proposition F is true (John 3:3-5; Mark 16: 15-16; James 1:23-25; John 8:32; Romans 8:1-2; II Thess. 1:7-9).

11. Proposition G is true—that is, Bales claims it is true (This proposition {like E above} is also false {Mark 16:15-16; Romans 3:19; 4:15; I John 3:4}, but it is actually affirmed by Bales and is a crucial proposition in his total case. So, it is put here—not as a true proposition—but as a part of this argument, to show that one of Bales' crucial propositions is false because it implies a false proposition. The reader must keep this distinction clearly in mind.)

12. Therefore, the conclusion Proposition H is true—that is, implied by Bales' statements (Given the fact that two false premises {E and G} which are affirmed by Bales {not by TBW}, then this conclusion proposition H follows. But, of course proposition H, which affirms that no one living today can be saved—i.e., it is not even possible that any one living today can be saved—is false! That it is false is easily seen from many passages. Some of these are: Romans 1:15-17; Mark 16:15-16; Hebrews 7:25; Matthew 11:28-30; Titus 2:11.) But Bales' doctrine implies this false doctrine.

Thus, since it is clear that Bales' doctrine implies a false doctrine, Bales' doctrine itself is false. No honest, careful student should need any further argumentation in order to reject Bales' doctrine which, in its basic thrust, is like that of Jezebel in that it "seduces" the Lord's servants to "commit fornication" (Revelation 2:20). (Cf. Balak, Rev. 2:14).

In regard to the argument set out just above, it is interesting to counterfactually consider Bales' holding the position that non-Christians are amenable to (under) neither the gospel (law) of Christ nor "the law written on the heart" (as Bales put it) nor the law of Moses. In which case, (1) no one living today could sin—since they would be amenable to no law, (2) no one living today could be saved, and (3) no one living today could be lost. But, given the way Bales actually has it, all men will be lost and no one can be saved! It would be difficult—if indeed not impossible—to find a doctrine more strictly anti-Biblical.

Put into symbolic terms, the arguments look like this:

1.	$B^D \supset \sim S$	proved above. (If Bales' doctrine is true, then no one living today can be saved.)
2.	S	Mark 16:15-16. (But men living today can be saved.)
3.	$\therefore \sim B^D$	1, 2, M.T. (Therefore, Bales' doctrine is false.)

Where (a) B^D = the doctrine of Bales on divorce and remarriage (b) $\sim S$ = it is false that it is even possible that any one living today can be saved from sin, and (c) S = it is possible for some people living today to be saved from sin.

This argument is valid (in the form of Modus Tollens) and all of the premises are true. Therefore, the argument is sound and guarantees the truth of the conclusion (namely, that Bales' doctrine on divorce and remarriage is false).

May any person who leans toward accepting such a doctrine be duly warned by these truths.

2. *Bales' doctrine is false because it implies that Christians can live in polygamous marriages and be pleasing to God in so doing.*

As will be explained in some detail later, Bales woefully crosses himself in the matter of polygamy. In regard to polygamy, Bales (a) contradicts himself, (b) implies false doctrine, and (c) admits defeat (by implication).

Points (a) and (c) will be discussed in later sections, and (b) will be discussed here in this present chapter.[11]

Bales argues[12] (a) that no non-Christian is amenable to the gospel (law) of Christ (b) that no non-Christian is amenable to (under) the high standard of Matthew 19:9,[13] and (c) that no one has a right "to put asunder marriages which took place in the world," even though they do not meet the high standard of

Matthew 19:9 (or even any of the rest of the instructions on divorce and remarriage in the law of Christ). Although Bales—following his usual habit—did not set out his argument in precise logical form, this author will now do it for him so that perhaps, the reader will more easily follow it and not be as likely to be mislead.

If, as Bales asserts, no one has the right to put asunder marriages which took place in the world (that is, on the part of non-Christians), then, if a man married ten women while he was yet in the world (i.e., while he was still a non-Christian), then, given Bales' doctrine, no one would have the right to put asunder those polygamous marriages! Why not, according to Bales? Simply because Bales asserts (in utter contradiction to plain Bible teaching) that no one has the right to put asunder marriages which took place in the world even when those marriages do not meet the high standard of the gospel (law) of Christ.

Thus, Bales' doctrine clearly implies that it is possible for Christians to live (with God's approval) in polygamous marriages. This means that, given Bales' doctrine that no one has the right to put asunder any marriage which took place in the world.[14]

Yet, Bales himself immediately contradicts himself by teaching that "polygamy is not to exist in the church, for each is to have his own mate, not mates (I Corinthians 7:2)."[15]

Thus, in this first Bales' position discussed above, he (Bales) argues that Christians can live (with God's approval) in polygamous marriages.

But, in the second position, discussed above, he condemns polygamy by saying that "polygamy is not to exist in the church. . ."[16]

Then, in what is surely a most surprising move for the followers of Bales, he completely admits defeat by saying, in connection with his contradictory contention that *polygamy is not to exist in the church*, that polygamists who are baptized are to give up their multiplicity of wives on the ground that after one comes "into Christ he is to live by His (Christ's) law for His people."[17] In doing so, Bales utterly rejects the basic foundation upon which his whole case rests; viz., that no one has the right to put asunder any marriage in which only non-Christians are involved. To avoid having to admit to his fellow Christians that his (Bales') doctrine implies the acceptability (to God) of polygamy, he resorts to the claim that the polygamous marriages are to be given up for the one—and only—reason that such marriages violate the law of Christ—a position which utterly contradicts his basic contention on divorce and remarriage.

But Bales seems utterly oblivious to the fact that he has now not only accepted—"lock, stock and barrel"—the very position for which some (Deaver, Warren, Connally, Elkins, Taylor, et al.) have been fighting so diligently, but has also utterly rejected the position for which he himself has fought so hard. Bales is correct in rejecting polygamy for Christians, but his reason for doing so is a direct contradiction of his basic position on divorce and remarriage!

Such is the value of the discussion of Biblical truth and doctrinal error.[18]

His position thus entails, on the one hand, (unbelievably, in the light of the mass of writing on this subject he has done) that baptism somehow renders polygamy to be unacceptable to God—but, on the other hand (by implication from other positions which have been explained above), his position entails that baptism has nothing whatever to do with the acceptability (to God) of polygamy. Thus, he both affirms and denies the same position. It must be remembered that Bales' basic contention is that no matter what the law of Christ says, marriages which are contracted by non-Christians are not affected by Christ's law.

But since in regard to polygamy, he said (on the one hand) that baptism renders it unacceptable to God, then (to be logically consistent), Bales must admit that some (e.g., Deaver, Warren, et al.) are right when they teach that marriages contracted by non-Christians which violate the law of Christ must be severed in order to be pleasing to God.

Thus, in regard to polygamous marriages which are contracted before baptism, Bales faces what, for him, is an absolutely devastating dilemma: either (a) Bales must admit and accept a position which he himself—in another statement—admits is condemned by the gospel (law) of Christ: viz, that Christians can live (with God's approval) in polygamous marriages or (b) Bales will have to admit that he is wrong and that others (Deaver, Warren, et al.) are right on the divorce—remarriage question.

Which "horn" of the dilemma will Bales and his fellows choose? They will be "impaled" (theologically destroyed) no matter which "horn" they choose.

3. *Bales' doctrine is false because it implies that denominationalism is not sinful.* In years gone by, brother Bales, along with all other conservative (faithful) members of the Lord's church strongly and unequivocally condemned denominationalism (religious institutions—such as the Baptist church, the Roman Catholic church—which are not authorized by the Bible) as being sinful. He knew and taught—as did all other faithful gospel preachers—that it is sinful for a man (whether he is a Christian or a non-Christian) to establish, enter, and support (by proclaiming its false doctrines) any denomination.[19]

In times past, brother Bales knew as well as any of us that the gospel (law) of Christ condemns (as sin) the actions of those who seek to lead others to *reject the gospel plan of salvation* (John 3:3-5; Mark 16:15-16; Acts 22:16; Romans 6:3-5; Galatians 3:26-27 et al.) and to *accept the false doctrines* which have been invented by men.

The reader should note carefully that in Cyprus, Elymas the sorcer resisted the efforts of Saul and Barnabas to persuade the proconsul (deputy) to accept and obey the faith (Acts 13:8).

So, the situation here is one in which a non-Christian (whom Bales claims is not even amenable to the law of Christ) fighting strenuously to persuade a man not to accept and obey the gospel plan of salvation. Thus, according to Bales, since Elymas was not a Christian (was not "in the covenant" as Bales likes to put the matter), he (Elymas) could not be guilty of sin by violating the law of Christ, because, Bales argues, no non-Christian is amenable to (under) the law of Christ.

But did Saul (Paul) agree with Bales' doctrine? Absolutely not! Note Saul's reaction to the efforts of Elymas to lead the proconsul to reject the gospel plan of salvation. Being filled with (aorist passive participle of pimpleemi) the Holy Spirit (meaning that the Holy Spirit was guiding Saul in what he was saying), Saul said, "You are a child of the devil and an enemy of everything that is right! You are full of all kinds of deceit and trickery. Will you never stop perverting the right ways of the Lord?" (Acts 13:10).

If Saul was right in what he said, then Bales is wrong in what he now affirms. If Bales is right (in his position on denominationalism), then Saul was wrong in condemning Elymas of sin. Who is right? Of course, Saul is right, and Bales is wrong!

Because this point is so important—because it is so devastating to Bales' whole approach to the problem of divorce and remarriage—it will surely be of considerable worth to the reader to belabor the point a bit more.

In contrast to Bales' practice, let us set up the matter in strict logical form so that all may easily follow—and easily see that Bales is in error.

1. If Ⓐ Bales' doctrine (that no non-Christian is amenable to the law of Christ) is true, then Ⓑ no non-Christian can be guilty of sin for seeking to lead other men to reject the plan of salvation given to men by Christ (Mark 16:15-16; Matthew 28:18-20; Acts 22:16; James 2:24-26; et al.).

2. Proposition B is false (Paul condemned Elymas for trying to persuade a man to reject the faith (Acts 13:8-12.)

3. Therefore, Proposition A is false (1, 2, Modus Tollens.)
This means that if proposition A implies proposition B, and proposition B is false, then proposition A is also false. This is easily proved by the proper logical procedure.[20] Thus since proposition A (Bales' doctrine) implies proposition B (another of Bales' doctrines), and since Acts 13:8-10 proves that proposition B is false, then Bales' proposition A must also be false. But proposition A (that no non-Christian is amenable to the law of Christ) is the foundation rock of Bales' whole theory on divorce and remarriage.

Thus, Bales' theory has been proved—absolutely beyond any shadow of doubt—to be false! Let all who accept his theory be prepared to accept the error which Bales has accepted.

What a tragedy that a man who has for so many years fought for truth with such dedication, should so lose his theological bearing—perhaps because of some emotional impact; e.g., feeling sorry for people who have gotten themselves into unscriptural marital tangles—as to come to the point of teaching a doctrine which implies that, for non-Christians, denominationalism is not sinful!

When one considers the terrible "muddle" into which brother Fuqua fell because his position on divorce and remarriage simply made it impossible for him to teach that for the non-Christian, denominationalism is sinful, it is amazing that Bales would not profit by Fuqua's mistake but has fallen into much the same pit.

Thus, may James D. Bales, Jerry Jones, Jimmy Allen and others who accept his doctrine on divorce and remarriage be warned that that doctrine implies that such men as Billy Graham, Rex Humbard, James Robison, Jerry Falwell, Richard De Haan, and other non-Christian preachers do not sin when they urge men to reject (1) the gospel plan of salvation (which involves the truth that, for the penitent believer, baptism is unto the remission of sins) and (2) the church which Jesus purchased with his own blood (Acts 20:28) and to accept (1) their human plan of salvation (that one is saved at the point of faith before and without being baptized in water) and (2) their human "churches." May God help every member of the church to see the falsity of Bales' position.

4. *Bales' doctrine implies that no woman can become a man's wife without first committing fornication with him.* This matter was discussed in detail in Chapter V. The reader is urged to re-read that chapter if he should not as yet understand the point made here. It should be obvious to a mere tyro in logical thought if, as brother Bales contends, a man and woman cannot

be married to each other until after they have completed their first act of sexual intercourse, then no one can get married without committing fornication.

Thus, if brother Bales doctrine is true, fornication is not sinful (it could not be if God had made it necessary to getting married and also approved marriage). But, fornication is sinful (I Corinthians 6: 9-11, et al.). Therefore, Bales' doctrine is false, because it implies a false doctrine. This argument is set out symbolically below.[21]

Bales' doctrine says, in effect: if God demands that a man must have sexual relations with a woman in order to make her his wife, then what of it? —if God commanded it, that's good enough for me! This false doctrine makes God's law purely arbitrary—or at least possibly so. But, this is an ungodly doctrine, ordinarily taught only by modernists.

The Bible makes clear that sexual intercourse is a privilege of marriage—it is not what marries people. (See more in Appendix H.)

5. *Bales' doctrine is false because it implies that "group marriage" may be approved by God.* Group marriage is practiced in some societies—especially it seems, where the total population is small. In group marriage, a number of men and women all consider themselves to be married—the men to have sexual privilege with all of the women and the women with all of the men. Since brother Bales holds that there is no legislation in the law of Christ to the non-Christian and since there is nothing in what Bales calls "the law written on the heart" which forbids such an arrangement then since (according to Bales' doctrine) the arrangement violates no law, it is not sinful for non-Christians. Further, since Bales' doctrine entails the element that if one married (out of harmony with Matthew 19:9) before he is baptized he may (with God's approval) remain in that marriage after he is baptized into Christ. This means that, according to Bales' doctrine, not only non-Christians but Christians also may live in "group marriages" with God's approval.

This doctrine is so obviously false, so obviously degraded, so obviously anti-Biblical and/or anti-Christian, that little more will be said of it here.

The "upshot" of the matter is: brother Bales' doctrine implies a false doctrine and so, brother Bales' doctrine itself is also false.

What more would anyone need to reject Bales' doctrine outright?

6. *Bales' doctrine is false because it implies that "wife-swapping" may be approved by God.* In his lecture in the 1961 Abilene Christian College Lectureship, brother Bales clearly implied that, in a case of infidelity in a marriage, the guilty party is just as free to marry again (with God's approval) as is the

innocent party. The usual argument for such a conclusion is that since it is impossible for one of the two (husband and wife) to be free without the other one also being free. An illustration involving police handcuffs is usually used in an effort to persuade people to accept this ungodly doctrine. Exponents of Bales' doctrine argue along this line: if man A and woman B are handcuffed together, then no one can free man A from the handcuffs without also freeing woman B from them.

First of all, let it be noted than an illustration does not prove anything; it can only help someone to understand the point being made. So even if the illustration were a true analogy (which it is not—it is a false analogy), it still would not prove the case.

Second, let the utter degradation of this position sink into the minds of the reader. Brother Bales' doctrine implies that if (1) man A is married to woman B and (2) man A no longer cares for woman B, and (3) man A is strongly attracted to woman C, then (4) man A may deliberately commit fornication with woman D for the express purpose of giving himself grounds for divorce and remarriage (on the ground of fornication, as per Matthew 19:9) subsequent to that fornication, with the result that (5) man A will be free to both marry and live with sexually (with God's approval) woman C for the rest of his life on earth.

To perhaps even deepen the impression of the degradation of this doctrine, the reader should note the fact Bales' doctrine would allow two elders in the same congregation to "swap wives" with God's approval. Given Bales' doctrine, if elder A had a very strong sexual desire for the wife of elder B (and wanted to divorce his own wife and marry her) and if elder B had a strong sexual desire for the wife of elder A (and wanted to divorce his own wife and marry the wife of elder A) then the two men could free themselves to "swap wives" (with God's approval) merely by deliberately committing fornication with some woman—any woman—and, then, since according to Bales' doctrine the guilty party is as free to remarry (in a case of fornication) as the innocent, each of the two elders could divorce his own wife and marry the wife of the other. And, the reader should note: all of this would/could be done with God's approval. After the "wife-swapping" had occurred, the two men could live the rest of their lives with their new mates. Bales' doctrine implies that such an arrangement is in harmony with Bible teaching! Allegedly, all they would have to do is to go before the congregation and "confess sin," saying they were "sorry" for what they had done. Believe it who can!

Brother Hugo McCord, in showing the degraded nature of this doctrine, gave this account of a series of events which occurred with members of a congregation. "An elder in a congregation where this writer conducted a gospel meeting quit his wife to 'shack up' with a deacon's wife. In time the elder's wife divorced him, as did the deacon, divorce his wife. Now the elder's wife and the deacon conceivably could fall in love and marry. The apostate elder and the sinful deacon's wife, now living in adultery, could scripturally(?) marry and eliminate their adultery. If they wanted to indicate repentance, they could be restored in the same congregation. According to the nefarious doctrine here under review, a spouse-swapping acceptable to God would have taken place in the congregation.

"If ever there was a 'horrible thing' emanating from some gospel preachers that strengthen evil doers, it is this guilty—may—remarry doctrine (Jeremiah 23: 14)."[22]

Above are a number of proofs that Bales' doctrine implies false doctrine. Thus Bales' doctrine itself has in this chapter again been proved to be false.

There is a great deal more of such material, but this book must have a reasonable limit. So, for this book, the above described doctrines which imply false doctrine are being allowed to be sufficient for the purpose of this book.

The doctrine of James D. Bales on divorce and remarriage is false because it implies false doctrine.

Footnotes

[1]$\{(p \supset q) \cdot \sim q\} \supset \sim p$ Where p is the doctrine under consideration and q is the doctrine implied by p.

[2]See more on this point in Appendix I (on Logic).

[3]Yet, Bales admits baptism is necessary to salvation, *Was Christ A Christian?*, p. 56.

[4]Where it will be involved in proving that Bales' doctrine is false because it implies a logical contradiction. Much of the same material will be used in Chapter XVIII.

[5]See this point discussed more thoroughly in Appendix A, Appendix C, and Appendix D.

[6]*NUB*, p. 9.

[7]He did not learn it from either Paul or from anyone else—the position is false.

[8]Apparently, brother Bales has mailed copies of his material to various people all over the nation. Since he did not designate to whom he sent that material (including personal letters to this author), this author can only hope that those who received his "mail-outs" obtain and study a copy of this present book.

[9]The capital letters in the circles are used to identify particular propositions.

[10]Which means that if all of the premises are true, then the conclusion must be true.

[11]But let it be carefully noted that Bales' case is destroyed by any one (and by all three) of these (a, b, c).

[12]*NUB*, p. 187.

[13]Ibid.

[14]Ibid., p. 187.

[15]Ibid.

[16]Ibid.

[17]Ibid.

[18]Ibid., pp. 187, 188.

[19]See many books and articles by Bales.

[20]See section on "Modus Tollens" in Appendix I on "Logic."

[21]

1. $B^p > \sim F^s$	B^p	= if Bales' proposition is true.
2. F^s	$\sim F$	= then, it is false that fornication is sinful.
3. $\therefore \sim B^p$	F^s	= fornication is sinful.
	$\sim B^p$	= Bales' proposition is false.
	$>$	= if. . .then. . .
	$\sim$	= it is false that

[22]Hugo McCord, "The Guilty Party Is Not Free To Remarry," in G. Elkins and T. Warren, editors, *The Home as God Would Have It and Contemporary Attacks Against It* (Jonesboro, National Christian Press, 1979) p. 242.

CHAPTER XVIII

BALES' DOCTRINE IS FALSE BECAUSE IT INVOLVES LOGICAL CONTRADICTION

I. *The Law of Contradiction—An Introduction.*

1. *The three laws of thought.* Logicians recognize as self-evidently true what are usually referred to as "laws of thought": (1) the law of identity, (2) the law of excluded middle, and (3) the law of contradiction.[1] These laws are actually fundamental to all valid reasoning. Each of them applies both to things and to propositions.[2] These three laws (or principles) are not the only ones used in reasoning, but, as logicians recognize, they "certainly are basic in the sense that all reasoning presupposes them."[3]

It is beyond the scope of the purpose of this book to discuss all three of these laws in detail (although, the fact that each is crucial to correct reasoning is strongly affirmed). Here the main concern—because of its role in proving Bales' doctrine to be false—will be the law of contradiction.

2. *The importance of the Law of Contradiction.* May it be emphasized here that no one can be faithful to God who denounces, rejects, overlooks, or ridicules the restrictions of logic. No one can be faithful to God who remains indifferent to logical demonstrations that his position(s) involve logical contradictions. No one can be faithful to God who maintains—with the knowledge that his position involves such—that the Bible contradicts itself.

To hold that one can maintain a position which involves logical contradiction is to imply either (a) that the Bible is not the word of God—since God does not lie or (b) that the Bible is the word of God and that, thus, since the Bible contradicts itself, God is a liar.

Insofar as this particular chapter is concerned, the basic thesis will be this: the doctrine of James D. Bales on divorce and remarriage is involved in logical contradiction and, therefore is false. This is the case because every doctrine which involves (or implies) logical contradiction is false, and Bales' doctrine does involve logical contradiction (as will be proved in the material which follows in this chapter).

3. *The importance of the Law of Contradiction.* Prof. Antony G. N. Flew set forth some truths in regard to the law of contradiction when he said that (a) to tolerate contradiction is to be indifferent to truth,[4] (b) to tolerate self-contradiction is to make clear either that one cares nothing for truth or that he cares more about something else,[5] (c) to tolerate contradiction is to say, in effect, that anything goes—

nothing is false or wrong,[6] and (d) to tolerate contradiction must be repulsive to anyone who wishes to know what is true and to reject what is false.[7] The stupidity involved in accepting a position which involves (or implies) a logical contradiction is further seen in the fact that any self-contradictory proposition implies any and every other proposition.[8] Thus, if it is proved that Bales' doctrine involves a logical contradiction, it will have also been proved that Bales' doctrine implies: (a) that if the Bible is the word of God, then God is a liar, (b) if God is not a liar, then the Bible is not the word of God. But the consequents (what follows "then") of both (a) and (b) are false. Thus, if it is proved that Bales' doctrine involves and/or implies a logical contradiction, then it will have also been proved that Bales' doctrine itself is false. (If one understands these things, then only ignorance, dishonesty, or stupidity could cause one to accept and/or continue in Bales' doctrine.)

4. *An additional effort to explain the Law of Contradiction.* As noted above, the "law of contradiction" relates both to things and to propositions. (a) For things, the law of contradiction means that "nothing can both have and not have a given characteristic in precisely the same respect."[9] This means—quite simply—that nothing can be both A and the contradictory of A. A man cannot be both in the house and out of the house at one and the same time. (b) For propositions (which is of the greater concern here) the law means that no proposition can be both true and false in the same respects.[10]

II. *Bales' doctrine is false because it involves Logical Contradiction.* Since it has been shown that no statement or proposition can be both true and false in the same respects, it is now time for it to be shown that Bales' doctrine implies logical contradiction.

1. *Bales' doctrine is involved in logical contradiction in regard to his claim of cessation of divorcing and remarrying after one is baptized into Christ.*

(1) In Bales' effort to answer question no. 58[11] *by Thomas B. Warren, Bales said,* "Third, when one comes into Christ one is to cease divorcing and remarrying." (Bales' answer to Warren's question no. 58, p. 43).

(2) Wherein does the contradiction occur? Bales' doctrine entails the following propositions. (a) No non-Christian is amenable to (under) the law of Christ. (b) Non-Christians are not required to live up to the high standard of Matthew 19:9. (c) Thus, non-Christians can divorce and remarry as often as they like and for any "reason" they decide upon. Fornication is not required; burning the toast would be

sufficient. This is the case because, Bales claims, the law of Christ simply does not legislate for non-Christians.[12] (d) By the statement which was quoted above from Bales ("Third, when one comes into Christ one is to cease divorcing and remarrying") Bales evidently seeks to leave the impression that after one becomes a Christian then he must live under a very strict law of divorce and remarriage. In fact, he claimed that one is to cease divorcing and remarrying. The contradiction in Bales' doctrine lies within these positions.

(3) The contradiction explained. It has already been noted (and will be explained in greater detail subsequently in this book) that brother Bales holds (a) that Matthew 19:9 is addressed—not to all Christians (as some loose-reading brethren have understood him to say)—but only to Christians who are married to Christians. Thus, according to Bales, Matthew 19:9 does not apply to (a) Christians who are not married (thus, such Christians, according to Bales, have no responsibility to this passage), (b) Christians who are married to non-Christians.[13] Bales holds that Christians who are married to non-Christians[14] are not governed by Matthew 19:9 and may divorce for any ground—fornication is not required, as per Matt. 19:9. So, given Bales' doctrine, a Christian who is married to a Baptist can put away (divorce) his Baptist wife (even though she is a morally pure woman who is faithful to him with great devotion) simply in order to marry a younger woman—provided he, with the express purpose of being freed from his marriage, commits fornication so that his wife will divorce him.

To clarify this point, let it be supposed that John (a Christian) is married to Mary (a non-Christian) and, in striving to bring about a situation in which he (John) will be freed (from Mary) in order to marry Dorothy (with whom he has "fallen in love") says to Mary, "If I commit fornication with Dorothy, will you divorce me?" Then, when Mary says, "Yes, I will divorce you if you commit fornication," John (because he believes—as does Bales—that in a case of fornication the guilty party is as free to remarry as is the innocent party) commits fornication with Dorothy. Mary then puts John away, John then marries Dorothy. It should be carefully noted that even though Bales admits that John's initial fornication with Dorothy was sin, he (Bales) holds that the subsequent marriage of John and Dorothy was not sin. Thus, according to Bales, becoming a Christian does not mean that one ceases divorcing and remarrying.

And Bales dares to call this a "high standard" of divorce and remarriage. And, he has the incredible audacity to assign that ungodly doctrine as having come from Christ and the Holy Spirit (through Paul in

I Corinthians 7:10-15). (Bales further claims that if a Christian is married to a non-Christian, if the non-Christian departs, then the Christian is free to marry again simply and solely on the ground of the desertion —even if the departed unbeliever is never guilty of fornication. More will be said of this later.)

(4) The contradiction further explained. Perhaps it will be helpful to the reader to understand some further points about brother Bales' position in regard to Matthew 19:9, I Corinthians 7:10-11; 7:12-13; and 7:14-15.

(a) In regard to Matthew 19:9, Bales calls this a "covenant passage" (Which is strictly a misnomer even for his doctrine since he does not think that it applies to everyone in the covenant)—which he curiously holds to be addressed only to (or to have application only to) Christians who are married to Christians. This is a false position,[15] of course, but there is also something else about Bales' view of Matthew 19:9 which is not only false, but curious: he claims that if one Christian is married to another Christian—and, thus, the two are amenable to (under) Matthew 19:9—and one of the two is guilty of fornication, then the "guilty party" (the one guilty of fornication) is just as free to marry again (with God's approval) as is the "innocent party" (the one who has been faithful to his (her) marriage vows).[16] As was explained in an earlier chapter—the details of which will not be repeated here—if a man wanted to divorce his wife and marry another, he could deliberately decide to commit fornication and thus free himself to marry again with God's approval.[17] So, given Bales' doctrine on Matt. 19:9, it is contradictory to say (as Bales does say in answer to Warren's question no. 58) that "when one comes into Christ one is to cease divorcing and remarrying." Thus, Bales' doctrine involves a logical contradiction. He affirms both (a) it is true that when one comes into Christ one is to cease divorcing and remarrying and (b) it is false that when one comes into Christ one is to cease divorcing and remarrying (this is the case because, given Bales' doctrine, any Christian married to a Christian can easily free himself to divorce and marry someone else by deliberately committing fornication so he can {with God's approval} divorce and remarry.) This is a logical contradiction. Bales' doctrine is false.

(5) The contradiction explained still further. According to Bales' doctrine, Matthew 19:9 and I Corinthians 7:10-11 say, in essence, the same thing: (a) both refer to the same statement made by Jesus and (b) both refer only to Christians married to Christians. Thus, I Corinthians 7:10-11 must give the same privilege to any Christian married to a Christian which Matthew 19:9 gives; namely, the right to divorce and

marry again after one has committed fornication in order to free oneself for that very purpose. Thus, given brother Bales' doctrine, I Corinthians 7:10-11 cannot be the passage which teaches that "when one comes into Christ one is to cease divorcing and remarrying." The same logical contradiction is involved here as in Matthew 19:9.

Given Bales' position on divorce and remarriage, not even I Cor. 7:12-13 can cause the one who is baptized to "cease divorcing and remarrying." This is the case because, even though Paul said that if a Christian is married to a non-Christian and the non-Christian is content to dwell with the Christian, then the Christian is not to leave his (her) non-Christian spouse, it remains the case that Bales' doctrine allows the Christian to commit fornication and put away his (her) non-Christian spouse and to marry another. Further, given Bales' view, the fornication would be sin and (perhaps) the divorcing would be sin, but the marrying of another would not be sin. If Bales claims that, given his doctrine, the marrying would be sin, let him explain how (or why) it would be sin! Then, let him answer this question: Would the congregation of which he is a member be under obligation to disfellowship him if he did not repent of and get out of that second marriage? If so, let him explain why.

(6) The contradiction seen in one further point. As previously noted, Bales holds that I Corinthians 7:15 teaches that if a non-Christian deserts his (her) Christian wife (husband) that the deserted Christian is free—solely upon the ground of the desertion—to marry again. (See more on this in Appendix D.) The passage says nothing about any requirement that the Christian be loving, kind, etc. in order to qualify to remarry. Given Bales' position the Christian (baptized believer) could be as "mean as a snake" and deliberately drive the non-Christian away and still be free to remarry—simply on the grounds of desertion.

Bales holds that I Cor. 7:15 makes clear that a Christian who is married to a non-Christian is rendered free to marry someone else on the ground of the desertion of the non-Christian alone—nothing else is required; no presumption of fornication by the departed unbeliever. Just the desertion—that's enough, per Bales! So, even if it is a sin for a Christian to deliberately be mean enough to cause his (her) non-Christian spouse to depart, his (her) marrying again after the desertion (by the non-Christian) will not be sin! Note: this is the "high standard" to which Bales' refers.

Thus, given Bales' view of I Corinthians 7:15 it constitutes a logical contradiction of Bales' answer to question no. 58 by T.B.W. Thus, Bales' doctrine is false.

This alone proves Bales' doctrine is false, but it hardly touches "the hem of the garment" of his false teaching. If there should be a need and if the author's affairs can be arranged in the future to allow the completion of such an activity, he may write a book which is devoted entirely to Bales' self-contradictions regarding divorce and remarriage. There will certainly be plenty of material for such a project.

2. *Bales' doctrine is false because it involves self-contradiction in regard to polygamy and the matter of the law of Christ being retroactive on unbelievers (non-Christians) who have married and/or divorced and remarried out of harmony with the teaching of the law (gospel) of Christ.*

The answers of Bales to two of TBW's (Thomas B. Warren's) questions are relevant here: (a) his answer to question no. 58 (a part of which was considered in the preceding section of this chapter) and (b) his answer to question no. 63.

In order to adequately set the stage for the reader to "see" brother Bales' self-contradiction, it will be necessary to set out both the questions and Bales' answers. (All 76 of the questions which TBW asked Bales were precisely written so that he (Bales) could answer by circling either "T" (to indicate the statement was true) or "F" (to indicate that the statement false).[18] Thus, both questions no. 58 and 63 were "true or false" questions.[19]

As indicated above, on question no. 58, Bales declined to indicate whether he thought the question was true or false (which he should have done because the statement was precisely stated, and—according to the law of excluded middle—every precisely stated proposition is either true or false). However, Bales did write out an answer. Here it is: "First, Matthew 19:9 (I Corinthians 7:10-11) is legislated for two believers and *is not retroactive on unbelievers* (emphasis, T.B.W.) who have been divorced and remarried on some ground other than Matthew 19:9. The unbelievers are not under Matthew 19:9 and therefore have not in the world violated Matthew 19:9. Second, the entire manuscript on *Not Under Bondage* is designed to prove this,. . . Third, when one comes into Christ one is to cease divorcing and remarrying."

TBW question (for Bales) no. 63 reads as follows: "If a man had one hundred wives at the time he was baptized he could (with Christ's approval) continue to live with all one hundred of those 'wives' (having sexual relations with all of them) after he was baptized."

Bales circled "F," thus indicating that he holds that the statement is false. He seeks to clarify his answer by appending a comment. "Comment He could not do this even if he was an Abraham or a David. Polygamy was allowed under the law of Moses, and therefore allowed in Jesus' day. It did not mean that a polygamist could keep a multiplicity of wives when he became a Christian. Once one is in Christ one from there on abides by the commands of Matthew 28:18-20."

Putting together Bales' answers to the two questions manifests a flagrant self-contradiction.

(a) In his answer to TBW question no. 58, Bales takes the position that non-Christians are not under (amenable to) the law of Christ (he specifically designates and equates Matthew 19:9 and I Corinthians 7:10-11) and that the law of Christ (he specifically designates Matthew 19:9 and I Corinthians 7:10-11, but the principle would have to apply or Bales would have no point) is not retroactive in regard to the relationships which one enters while he is yet a non-Christian. Bales takes this false position because he wishes to conclude that if a non-Christian divorces and remarries on some ground other than fornication (in violation of Christ's teaching in Matthew 19:9) then—merely because he entered that relationship before he was baptized—he may remain in it after he is baptized. How does Bales try to justify this flagrant disregard for the authority of Christ (Matt. 28:18-20) and the violation of Christ's plain teaching (Matt. 19:9)? Bales teaches that such is the case because the person entered the unscriptural relationship while he was still a non-Christian (i.e., before he was baptized).[20]

But—surprise! Surprise!—on question no. 63, he affirms that if one violates I Corinthians 7:2 (i.e., by having many mates—instead of just one as the law of Christ teaches).[21] And—surprise of surprises! Bales claims (a) that the law of Christ (I Corinthians 7:2) is retroactive in regard to unscriptural relationships which are entered before one is baptized and (b) that the man must give up having a multiplicity of wives which he married before he was baptized! He clearly implies that the polygamist cannot keep his multiplicity of wives after he becomes a Christian.

By these two answers, Bales involves himself in logical contradiction: (a) Ⓐ (the non-Christian is amenable to the instruction of the law of Christ in marriage) and (b) ~Ⓐ (the non-Christian is not amenable to the instruction of the law of Christ on marriage). Thus, Bales affirms: (a) amenable and (b) not amenable.[22] Put a little more fully, Bales' affirmation means (a) it is true that the law of Christ is retroactive in regard to relationships which are entered before baptism and (b) it is false that the law of Christ is retroactive in regard to relationships which are entered before baptism.

It would be well for every reader to remember the following wise statement by Dr. Flew, "For whenever and wherever I tolerate self-contradiction, then and there I make it evident, either that I do not care at all about truth, or that at any rate I do care about something else more."[23] What is Bales' reason for affirming a logical contradiction?

Now that it has been demonstrated that Bales' doctrine involves self-contradiction, will he (and whatever followers he has) admit it or not admit it? If he admits it (as honesty would demand), will he then (a) tolerate it (i.e., continue to hold to it) or (b) will he admit he is wrong and reject it? If he decides to tolerate it (i.e., continue to hold on to it, to affirm it), will he thus make it evident that he does not care at all about truth or simply that he cares about something else more? If he decides that his doctrine is false, then, being honest, he will surely admit it.

Flew makes another statement worthy of careful consideration when he says, "Generally, therefore, when someone with pretensions to be a thinker either denounces the restrictions of logic, or remains unmoved by charges of self-contradiction, we know what to think."[24] What will Bales leave us to think when we see his reaction to the proof that his doctrine—i.e., what James D. Bales teaches—implies logical contradiction?

3. *Bales' doctrine is false because it implies that it is true that the gospel (law) of Christ is addressed to all men and that it is false that the gospel (law) of Christ is addressed to all men.*[25]

4. *Bales' doctrine is false because it implies (a) that it is true that the New Covenant (the law of Christ) could not come into effect until after the Old Covenant (the law of Moses) was abolished and (b) that it is false that the New Covenant (the law of Christ) could not come into effect until after the Old Covenant (the law of Moses) was abolished.*[26]

5. *Bales' doctrine is false because it implies (a) that it is true the church was established before the law of Moses was abolished and (b) that it is false that the church was established before the law of Moses was abolished.*

6. *Bales' doctrine is false because it implies (a) that it is true that the Scriptures alone constitute the God-given rule of faith and practice for mankind and*[27] *(b) that it is false that the Scriptures alone constitute the God-given rule of faith and practice for mankind.*

7. *Bales' doctrine is false because it implies (a) that denominationalism is not sinful and (b) that denominationalism is sinful.*

This is such an important point that space in addition to that in Chapter XVII will be devoted to it. Except for members of the Lord's church who have become modernists, every Christian known to me who knows anything at all about the Bible knows (a) that all that men do in religion must be authorized by the Bible (see Matt. 28:18-20; Colossians 3:17; Leviticus 10:1-2; I Chronicles 15:1-15; II John 9-11; et al.), (b) that every man (whether Christian or non-Christian) who establishes a "church" (religious institution) which is not authorized by the Bible sins in so doing, (c) that every man (whether Christian or non-Christian) who enters a religious institution ("church") which is not authorized by the Bible sins in so doing (see above passages of Scripture), (d) that every man (whether Christian or non-Christian) who rejects the gospel plan of salvation sins in so doing, (e) that every man (whether Christian or non-Christian) who urges men to obey some plan of salvation other than that one of Jesus Christ sins in so doing (see discussion in Chapter XVII on Acts 13:8-10, etc.).

When Bales is writing or speaking on any subject other than divorce and remarriage, he never makes the mistakes (so far as this writer knows) (a) of affirming that non-Christians can reject the Lord's true plan of salvation and accept a plan of salvation of human invention, (b) of rejecting the Lord's true church and entering one of human origins, and (c) of rejecting the Lord's plan for New Testament worship and introduces instrumental music into worship. (Cf.: Chapter XVII).

But, when he discusses the problem of divorce and remarriage he claims that non-Christians cannot violate the law (gospel) of Christ simply because non-Christians are not amenable to the law of Christ. (This is false, of course, because the gospel (law) of Christ is addressed to all men, Mk. 16:15-16—it is God's one and only law {authorizing civil law also, of course} to all men in the world.)

Facing the dilemma which he faced on the matter of unauthorized "churches," plans of salvation, acts of worship, etc., Bales refused to answer TBW question no. 58. (See footnote.[28])

Bales knows that if he is to have any chance at all of establishing his basic doctrine on divorce and remarriage, he must be able to establish (prove) the proposition: "It is false that all men (whether Christian or non-Christian), in order to be pleasing to God, are required to get out of marriages which violate the law of Christ." But if he holds that that proposition is true, he must (to be logically consistent with his own position) also accept the proposition: "It is false that all men (whether Christian or non-Christian) to be pleasing to God, are required to get out of any denomination (any "church" not authorized by the Bible) whether they entered that "church before or after being baptized in the name of Christ." So Bales wisely (not wise in the true sense, but "wise" if he wants to hold onto his doctrine on divorce and remarriage) refused to answer question no. 58.

Bales has thus fallen into the same "sink hole" into which Fuqua fell. Fuqua devastated the Baptist debater Ballard and proved his (Fuqua's) proposition that all men who enter the Baptist church sin in so doing! But, in proving his case, Fuqua used neither "civil law only" (as Fuqua argued when on divorce and remarriage) nor "the law on the heart" (as Bales does on divorce and remarriage). He used the law of Christ!

Bales cannot admit that non-Christian men sin when they preach anti-gospel plans of salvation and urge men to turn away from the faith without also admitting (at least by implication) that men sin when they marry in violation of the law of Christ.[29]

Let brother Bales and every would-be follower of Bales recognize this burning truth: as surely as you deny that men sin when they violate what the law of Christ teaches on divorce and remarriage (Matthew 19:9), you must (if you are not to foolishly affirm a logical contradiction) also deny that men sin when they urge other men to reject the faith and to accept a plan of salvation of human origin.

Let Bales and all of those who agree with him admit that they cannot consistently contend that non-Christians sin when they urge men (a) to stay out of the true church and (b) to join the Roman Catholic Church.

The "best" Bales can do with this matter is say[30] that they (those non-Christians who reject the Lord's church and join the Baptist church) are "no worse off than they were" before they entered the Baptist church. Of course, they are still lost, because they have not yet been baptized into Christ (Romans 6:3-5; II Timothy 2:10; Galatians 3:26-27)! But that is not the point, and Bales surely must know that it is not the point! The question was not, "Are they still lost?" The question was, *"Do they sin when they reject the faith and enter the Baptist church?"* Do they sin when they urge men to reject the faith and obey human doctrine? Bales cannot answer those questions without either (a) accepting denominationalism or (b) giving up his position on divorce and remarriage.

8. *Bales' doctrine is false because it implies (a) it is true that non-Christian Jews living today are amenable to the Law of Moses and (b) that it is false that non-Christian Jews living today are amenable to the Law of Moses.*

In his effort to avoid the force of I Corinthians 6:9-11 (which clearly shows that non-Christians violated Christ's law), Bales on the one hand, says (a) "There is enough truth in the Old Testament *today* (emphasis, T.B.W.) to condemn the Jew," and on the other hand (b) he claims that the New Covenant could not come into force until the Old Covenant (the law of Moses) was abolished[31] and (c) on still another hand, he claims that the law of Moses remained in force until the destruction of Jerusalem. He further holds that none of the law of Moses could have been abolished until all of it was abolished.

It would be difficult to imagine doctrine with greater chaos. The truth of the matter is (as Bales formerly well argued before he accepted his present theory on divorce and remarriage[32]) the writer of Hebrews says, "He taketh away the first, that he may establish the second" (Hebrews 10:9). The gospel (law) of Christ could not have been in force until after the law of Moses was abolished. Further, since Christ was of the tribe of Judah (not the priestly tribe, according to the law of Moses), He could not have been a priest while the law of Moses was still in force!

Much, much more could be said on this and related topics, but the above is surely sufficient to convince anyone who is convinceable that since Bales' doctrine implies logical contradictions, his doctrine is false.

Let all who might be tempted to fall into the clutches of "logophobia" (discussed earlier) and to say, "Oh, well, so the doctrine is self-contradictory—so what?" remember: *every doctrine which implies a logical contradiction is false itself.*

So, it has been proved (a) that Bales' doctrine implies logical contradiction and (b) since such is the case, it has been proved that Bales' doctrine is false.

9. *Bales' doctrine is false because it implies both (a) it is true that the non-Christian can obey the gospel (law) of Christ and (b) it is false that the non-Christian can obey the gospel (law) of Christ.*

In recognition of the plain teaching of Romans 3:19 and 4:15, Bales recognizes that one can neither obey nor disobey a law which is not addressed to him (and, thus, to which he is not amenable). Yet, while making such an admission of this truth, he contradicts that truth by claiming (a) that non-Christians are not amenable to the gospel (law) of Christ (because, as Bales puts it, they are not "in the covenant") and (b) that non-Christians can be baptized in the name of Christ.

But, if non-Christians are not amenable to the gospel(law) of Christ, then they can neither obey nor disobey that law (Rom. 3:19; 4:15). So, if they are not amenable (as Bales alleges), then they cannot obey it by being baptized (instructions to be baptized are a part of the gospel, Mk. 16:15-16; Acts 2:38). But Bales contradicts this by affirming that they can obey the gospel by being baptized in the name of Christ. (As an effort to sustain this, he offers an unsound rationale based on the theory that non-Christians are merely "invited" to come into the covenant, as Gentiles were "invited" to become Jews. But let Bales remember that no Gentile had an obligation to become a Jew, whereas all men living in the gospel age are under obligation to repent (a part of the gospel, Acts 17:30-32) and to be baptized (Acts 2:38). So, again, Bales contradicts himself.

Bales formerly taught that repentance always demands reformation of life (involving the cessation of sinful practices, the severance of sinful relationships, and the getting out of sinful states). However, he now teaches that it is not always the case that repentance demands reformation of life. (But see Luke 24:46-47; Acts 2:38; 3:19; 17:30-31) Jimmy Allen well said that "repentance is a gospel commandment" and that when one genuinely repents he "will bring forth the fruits of repentance."[34]

10. *Bales' doctrine is false because it implies a logical contradiction in that Bales affirms* (a) that subsequent to the day of Pentecost, non-Christian Jews sinned by violating the law of Moses[35] and (b) that, since the New Covenant came into force on the day of Pentecost, the law of Moses had already been abolished.

11. *Bales' doctrine is false because it implies* (a) that it is true that one cannot be saved unless he is baptized and (b) that it is false that one cannot be saved unless he is baptized.

In many places in many of the books he has written, brother Bales correctly teaches that no non-Christian can be saved without being baptized in the name of Christ. He has formerly taught this truth and, this author feels certain, that he still does teach it. Yet, in his desperate efforts to set out some kind of case for his theory on divorce and remarriage, he contradicts that truth. In regard to what Christ, during His earthly ministry, taught on divorce and remarriage, Bales said that "Christ's legislation is for two believers (Christians, T.B.W.)—I learned this from Paul in I Corinthians 7:10-11, and that Paul's legislation is for mixed marriages (A Christian married to a non-Christian, T.B.W.). (7:12-15.) Since neither of them legislated for the world, I am not thereby given authority to pass such legislation."[36]

The reader should carefully note the position thus taken by Bales: (1) that Christ's legislation (Matt. 19:9, et al.) on divorce and remarriage is only for Christians who are married to Christians (2) that Paul's legislation (I Cor. 7:12-15) on divorce and remarriage is only for "mixed marriages" (a Christian married to a non-Christian), and (3) that neither Paul nor Christ legislated for the world (non-Christians).

The reader should now note these positions set up in a precise logical argument.[37] (1) If Christ in Matt. 19:9 legislated only for Christians married to Christians and (2) if Paul in I Cor. 7:12-15 legislated only for mixed marriages (Christians married to non-Christians), and (3) if neither Christ nor Paul legislated for the world (non-Christians married to non-Christians), then (4) {conclusions} (a) if a non-Christian is married to a Christian, then the non-Christian is not in the world (remember, Bales said that neither Christ nor Paul legislated for the world —so, since, I Corinthians 7:12-13, in a "mixed marriage" {not merely for the Christian in a mixed marriage} is legislation for the non-Christian as well as for the Christian, the non-Christian could not be in the world), (b) since everyone is either in the world or in the church (i.e., either a non-Christian or a Christian), then if the non-Christian is not in the world, he must be in the church, (c) since no one can be in the church without being saved (John 3:3-5; Acts 20:28; Ephesians 2:13-16), then the "non-Christian" is saved merely by marrying a Christian, and (d) if one is saved by marrying a Christian before and without being baptized into Christ, then, it follows that one can be saved without being baptized.

Thus, Bales has affirmed both (a) explicitly that baptism is essential to salvation and (b) implicitly that baptism is not essential to being saved. Since brother Bales' doctrine implies a logical contradiction, Bales' doctrine is false.

This sound argument—the argument is valid and all of the premises are true—proves that Bales' interpretation of I Corinthains 7:10-15 (in connection with Matthew 19:9) is false.

This refutes Bales' case. The above argument proves that brother Bales' argument on I Corinthians 7:10-15 is unsound! Why? Because it clearly implies a logical contradiction and contradicts plain Bible teaching in other passages.

In case brother Bales is tempted to follow the trail which brother E. C. Fuqua[38] chose in an effort to avoid the force of a similiar argument against his (Fuqua's) position (viz., that of inventing a new realm "the ecclesiastical realm") and placing denominationalism between the world and the church (but not in either), it will surely be the case that his position will be rejected by all in the church except liberals and those who intend to hold to a loose (non-Biblical) position on divorce and remarriage no matter what proof of its falsity is given.

12. *Bales' doctrine is false because it implies* both (1) that it is true that Christians are to be baptized and (2) that it is false that Christians are to be baptized.

In his desperate efforts to argue in such fashion as to justify his erroneous doctrine that non-Christians are not amenable to (under) the gospel (law) of Christ —i.e., the New Covenant—on divorce and remarriage, Bales accepted the reprehensible doctrine that no non-Christian is amenable to the gospel (law) of Christ.[39]

Having taken that position, he then faces the task of "propping it up" and staying consistent with it in regard to every point to which it is relevant. This being the case, he involves himself in another logical contradiction in regard to whether a Christian is or is not to be baptized.

First, it should be noted that in some statements, Bales makes it clear that the non-Christian (not the Christian) is to be baptized.[40]

Second, he says, "Just so, baptism is a part of the New Covenant."[41] *Note that point carefully! Bales clearly admits that baptism is a part of the New Covenant!*

Third, since Bales affirms very strenuously that only those "in the covenant"[42] are under (amenable to) the New Covenant and that only Christians can obey the New Covenant. (Note: since Jimmy Allen says that repentance is a gospel commandment, if he (Allen) agrees with Bales, he would be saying that only Christians can repent.)

The above are the three basic propositions in this argument. They will now be used to set forth a precise logical argument which shows that Bales again contradicts himself. Here is the argument.[43]

1. If Ⓚ only those who are "in the New Covenant" can obey the instructions of the New Covenant, and if Ⓛ all of those who are "in the Covenant" are Christians (i.e., members of the Lord's true church), and if Ⓜ baptism is a part of the New Covenant, then Ⓝ Christians are to be baptized in the name of Christ.

2. Ⓚ only those who are "in the New Covenant" can obey the instructions of the New Covenant. (Bales claims this is true—but it is false! It is put here to prove that *Bales' doctrine is self-contradictory*.)

3. Ⓛ All of those who are "in the New Covenant" are Christians (i.e., members of the Lord's true church.)

4. Ⓜ Baptism is a part of the New Covenant.

5. K·L·M (2,3,4 Conjunction)

6. Ⓝ Christians are to be baptized in the name of Christ (A false implication of Bales' doctrine).

Thus, given Bales' doctrine, to this point the argument proves that Christians should be baptized. (It must be made clear that, of course, this doctrine is false, but, if Bales' doctrine is true, then this conclusion also would be true.)

But there is more; the argument continues:

7. Ⓟ Non-Christians are to be baptized in

order to be saved (enter the kingdom, become Christians).[44] This proposition is true, and Bales (in the same book, *WCAC?*) admits it![45]

8. If P Non-Christians are to be baptized in order to be saved, then ∿N it is false that Christians are to be baptized to be saved. (Obviously true.)

9. ∴ ∿N It is false that Christians are to be baptized to be saved.

10. ∴N·∿N[46] (6,10, Conjunction.)

So from the statements made by Bales (cited above), it is clear:

(1) Bales' doctrine on divorce and remarriage is false because it implies a logical contradiction.

(2) Bales teaches Baptist doctrine by implying (as shown above) that Christians are to be baptized.[47]

There is no way that Bales can escape his affirmation of a logical contradiction (or his implication that Baptist doctrine on baptism is true) except by giving up his doctrine on divorce and remarriage.[48] This is said in love and kindness, but, in love for Jesus Christ and the souls of men, it must be said.

In the appropriate footnote, the reader may see this argument set out in symbolic terms so that its validity may be seen at a glance by those who are trained in logic.[49]

Bales further compounds his problem when, in trying to explain about men who live during the time of the New Covenant, he says: (a) "The birth of water and Spirit (baptism in the name of Christ, T.B.W.) was not required in the patriarchal or the Mosaic dispensations. It is required for those under the New Covenant." [50] and (b) "We are commanded to be baptized, but they were not."[51] The reader should note very carefully these two statements from Bales!

Again it must be noted Bales has thrown himself in doctrinal chaos. Note the following points (according to Bales):

(1) No one can obey New Covenant instructions except those who are under the New Covenant.[52]

(2) *Non-Christians are not under the New Covenant* (Bales' position).

(3) So, *Non-Christians cannot obey the instructions (commandments, etc.) of the New Covenant* (Bales' position).

(4) Yet, Bales says, "We are commanded to be baptized. . ."[53]

There arises the burning question as to just whom the "we," in the last quotation above, refers. Given Bales' views that those who are not under the covenant cannot obey the covenant and that non-Christians are not under (amenable to) the New Covenant, it would follow that Bales' "we" must refer to Christians! Again, he espouses Baptist doctrine: that Christians—not non-Christians--are to be baptized! Again, he involves himself in Neo-Fuquaism.

On the other hand, if Bales wishes to avoid espousing and teaching Baptist doctrine, his only alternative is to admit that by his statement "We are commanded to be baptized. . ." he meant that non-Christian adults who have lived since the day of Pentecost (the day the New Covenant came into effect) have been commanded (not merely "invited" as Bales is prone to say) to be baptized in the name of (by the authority) Jesus Christ. And, if this latter is the course he chooses, then he thereby gives up a position (which is absolutely essential to his doctrine on divorce and remarriage): namely, that non-Christians are not under (amenable to) the law (gospel) of Christ. This admission—especially in the light of the truth taught in Matt. 28:18-20 (that is, even before they are baptized, men are to be taught to obey all things that Jesus had commanded the Apostles)—is simply devastating to Bales' view.

Thus, Bales faces a dilemma which simply destroys his doctrine: either (a) accept the Baptist doctrine that Christians—not non-Christians—are to be baptized, or (b) admit that non-Christians are under (amenable to) the law (gospel) of Christ and, thus, give up his doctrine on divorce and remarriage. Which horn of that dilemma will brother Bales choose to impale himself upon? This author lovingly prays that it will be (b) and that the two of us can be united on this question of divorce and remarriage (as we have been on practically everything down through the years).

13. *Bales' doctrine is false because it implies (a) that it is true that the Old Covenant (the law of Moses) was not in force after the day of Pentecost and (b) that it is false that the law of Moses was not in force after the day of Pentecost, (thus it implies another logical contradiction).* This point has been proved in preceding material. Bales' doctrine is false.

Conclusion

There is a very great amount of material which can be used to prove a false doctrine to be false (e.g. atheism—the doctrine that at least one man knows that God does not exist). For example, the following one argument proves that atheism is false: (a) If atheism is true, then subjectivity in ethics is true, (b) If subjectivity in ethics is true, then it is both true that adultery is real (objective) wrong and it is false that adultery is real (objective) wrong. (c) Since all logical contradictions are false, then it is false that it is both true that adultery is real (objective) wrong and false that adultery is real (objective) wrong. (d) If it is false that it is both true that adultery is real (objective) wrong and false that adultery is real (objective) wrong, then subjectivity in ethics is false. (e) If subjectivity in ethics is false, then atheism is false.[54]

Let it be impressed upon the reader that Bales' doctrine has just as easily been proved to be false. Why? Because, like atheism, it implies a logical contradiction. This settles the matter for all honest people:

(1) If Bales' doctrine implies logical contradiction then Bales' doctrine is false.

(2) Bales' doctrine implies logical contradiction.

(3) Therefore, Bales' doctrine is false.

To refute this argument, one would have to show either (or both) (1) that the argument is invalid or (2) that at least one premise is false. Since this cannot be done, the case stands: Bales' doctrine is false.

Footnotes

[1]See any standard textbook in logic for detailed discussion of these three laws.

[2]A "proposition" is a statement which asserts that something either is or is not the case.

[3]Lionel Ruby, *Logic: An Introduction* (Chicago, J. B. Lippincott Co., 1960), p. 262.

[4]A. G. N. Flew, *Thinking Straight,* (Buffalo, Prometheus Books, 1977), p. 15.

[5]Ibid.

[6]Ibid., p. 17.

[7]Ibid.

[8]Thomas B. Warren, *Charts You Can Use In Preaching, Teaching, and Studying on Divorce and Re-Marriage* (Jonesboro, AK., National Christian Press, Inc., 1979), p. 108.

[9]Ruby, *op. cit.,* p. 267.

[10]While one can understand the law without knowing the symbolism, the symbolism is given for those who wish to have it. In symbolic terms, the law of contradiction looks like this (where "p" and "q" stand for propositions: $\{p>(q\cdot\sim q)\}>\sim p$. Read in ordinary English it says: "If proposition p implies the con-

junction that proposition q is true and that proposition q is false, then proposition p itself is false.

[11]From the tract *Some Crucial Questions on Divorce and Remarriage* by Thomas B. Warren (National Christian Press). All the questions were precisely formulated so as to be answered as either true or false (see law of excluded middle). Of the 76 questions asked Bales, he answered (that is, by either "true" or "false") on 46, although he did say some things about some he did not answer.

[12]See *NUB*, p. 9 and a number of Bales' answers to questions by Thomas B. Warren (e.g., no. 61, p. 43).

[13]More details on Bales' position on I Corinthians 7:10-15 will be given later in this book.

[14]It must be carefully noted that Bales admits that every adult is either a Christian or a non-Christian. He further admits that Baptist, Catholics, et al. are not Christians.

[15]It will be dealt with in greater detail in a subsequent chapter.

[16]This has been discussed in some detail in an eariler chapter. One man claimed in a public forum that Bales convinced him that the "guilty party is free" theory is true. See also: Bales' lecture at Abilene Christian College, 1961.

[17]Of course, he would have to say that he was "sorry" about the act of fornication that freed him to remarry. (How that fits into the gospel message is a real mystery!)

[18]Of the 76 questions, TBW answered each and every one with a simple true or false. Of the 76 questions, Bales circled neither "T" or "F" on 30 of the questions (although he did make some comment on some of those which he did not circle.)

It might be of interest to the reader to know that these same 76 questions (some of which Bales answered) were sent almost two years ago to brethren Jerry Jones, Jimmy Allen, Jim Woodroof, and Raymond Kelcy. To date, none of them has answered even one of the questions. This author realizes, of course, that some men are very busy, and they have the right to choose what they will do.

[19]T.B.W. question (for Bales) no. 58 reads as follows: "T. F. One is not required to sever (come out of) any of the relationships which (1) violate the

law of Christ and (2) are entered before one is baptized into Christ." The reader should note that Bales declined to circle either "T" (for "true") or "F" (for "false"). This is extremely important. He knew, no doubt that if he circled either "T" or "F" he would be in big trouble on at least (a) divorce and remarriage and (b) denominationalism and other false religions which are not authorized by the gospel (law) of Christ. (More on this below.)

[20]The reader should note carefully that Bales' entire manuscript of *Not Under Bondage* was designed to prove this—viz., that the law of Christ is not retroactive in regard to relationships which were entered before baptism. More on this later!

[21]Of this matter, Bales say, "Fifth, polygamy is not to exist in the church, for each is to have his own mate, not mates (I Cor. 7:2). Once we come into Christ we live by His law for His people." (*NUB*, p. 187).

[22]Set out in symbolic terms, the matter looks like this:

(1) $B^{D}>(A\cdot\sim A)$, (2) $\sim(A\cdot\sim A)$, (3) $\therefore\sim B^{D}$

In ordinary English, this reads as follows: (1) If Bales' doctrine is true, then it is both true and false that the non-Christian is amenable to the law of Christ. (2) It is false that it is both true and false that the non-Christian is amenable to the law of Christ. (3) Therefore, Bales' doctrine is false.

[23]A. G. N. Flew, *Thinking Straight*, p. 15.

[24]Ibid., p. 17.

[25]

(1) $B^{D}>(G^{AAM}\cdot\sim G^{AAM})$ (2) $\sim(G^{AAM}\cdot\sim G^{AAM})$ (3) $\therefore\sim B^{D}$

Where the symbols have the following meanings:

B^{D} = Bales' doctrine is true.

$>$ = "If. . .then. . ." ; $\sim$ = "It is false that"

G^{AAM} = The gospel is addressed to all men.

$\sim G^{AAM}$ = The gospel is not addressed to all men.

$\sim B^{D}$ = Bales' doctrine is false.

So, the argument proves that Bales' doctrine is false.

[26]

(1) $B^{D}>(C\cdot\sim C)$ (2) $\sim(C\cdot\sim C)$ (3) $\therefore\sim B^{D}$

(i.e., Bales' doctrine is false.)

[27]J. D. Bales, *The Nature of the Word* (Searcy, AK., James D. Bales, n.d.) p. 3; and J. D. Bales *Not Under Bondage* (Searcy, AK., James D. Bales, 1979), passim. Bales' answers to TBW question no. 58.

[28]Question no. 58 has already been discussed. It reads: "T.F. One is not required to sever (come out of) any of the relationships which (1) violate the law of Christ and (2) are entered before one is baptized into Christ." It will be recalled that, while Bales commented on the question, he refused to circle either "T" or "F" for "true" or "false."

[29]Paul taught that such did sin, Acts 13:8-10.

[30]As he did in answering T.B.W.'s questions.

[31]Bales, *The Kingdom Prophesied and Established*. passim.

[32]See, for example, his book, *The Kingdom Prophesied and Established*. Throughout this book, over and over, he argues the truth: the New Covenant could not come into force until the Old Covenant was abolished.

[33]By his argument on Matthew 19:9; I Corinthians 7:10-11; 12-13; 14-15.

[34]Jimmy Allen, *What Is Hell Like?*, pp. 155, 167. But Allen has now repudiated the position on repentance re divorce which he upheld in this sermon.

[35]Pages 14, 15 and 16 of Bales' answer to TBW question no. 14.

[36]*NUB*, p. 9.

[37]At one time, at least, brother Bales was among the strongest defenders of the view that logical reasoning is essential to learning the truth of Bible teaching. But, as someone well said, "No one ever turns against reason until reason turns against him."

[38]Of the theory that non-Christians are not under the law of Christ but under civil law only, brother Guy Woods said that in his more than forty years of preaching, in all of his experience in dealing with foolish and fallacious arguments, he had never examined one more positively and palpably wrong, more sophistical and untruthful, more mendacious and harmful, in its consequences than this. (G. Elkins and T. Warren, editors, *The Home As God Would Have It*, Jonesboro, AK. National Christian Press, 1979, p. 190). Originally,

from Guy N. Woods, *Questions and Answers*. G. C. Brewer said, "The assumption that the language of Christ and of Paul on marriage and divorce was addressed only to disciples or Christians is erroneous. . .but to assume that Christ and Paul did not lay down principles of universal application is both gratuitous and reprehensible." (*Gospel Advocate*, October 1, 1931).

[39] *NUB*, passim; and various manuscripts set to T.B.W., passim.

[40] See a rather full discussion of this point in Bales' book *Was Christ A Christian?* (hereinafter referred to as *WCAC?*), p. 56.

[41] Ibid., p. 57.

[42] As Bales puts it. *NUB*, passim, and various manuscripts, passim.

[43] The encircled capital letters identify propositions—some premises and some sub-propositions of the conclusion.

[44] John 3:3-5; Mk. 16:15-16; Acts 22:16.

[45] *WCAC?*, p. 56.

[46] Note: this conclusion clearly affirms a logical contradiction.

[47] Other than some liberals among us, this author knows of no gospel preacher other than brother Bales who teaches this doctrine, either explicitly or implicitly.

[48] He is in much the same position here as was brother E. C. Fuqua in regard to denominationalism and its errors.

[49] (See main text for meaning of the capital letters)

(1)	$(K \cdot L \cdot M) > N$	
(2)	K is true.	(Bales' position)
(3)	L is true.	
(4)	M is true.	
(5)	$(K \cdot L \cdot M)$	2,3,4, conjunction.
(6)	$\therefore N$	1,5, Modus Ponens.
(7)	P is true.	(John 3:3-5).
(8)	$P > \sim N$	obviously true
(9)	$\sim N$	7,8, Modus Ponens
(10)	$\therefore (N \cdot \sim N)$	6,9, conjunction.

Note: this conclusion, which follows from Bales' statements, affirms a logical contradiction! Therefore,

Bales' doctrine is false.

Thus, it can be stated (where B^D = Bales' doctrine is true) as follows:

(11)	$B^D > (N \cdot \sim N)$	shown above, 1-10.
(12)	$\sim(N \cdot \sim N)$	All logical contradictions are false.
(13)	$\therefore \sim B^D$	11,12, Modus Tollens—i.e., Bales' doctrine is false because it implies a false doctrine.

Note: in order for the reader to understand the argument in the main text, it is not necessary for him to follow this symbolic presentation. This is placed here for those trained in symbolic logic.

[50] *WCAC?*, p. 57.

[51] Ibid.

[52] Bales' material, published and unpublished on divorce and remarriage, passim.

[53] *WCAC?*, p. 57.

[54] Put into symbolic terms, the argument looks like this:

(a)	$A > S$	obvious
(b)	$S > (A \cdot \sim A)$	obvious
(c)	$\sim(A \cdot \sim A)$	obvious
(d)	$\sim S$	b,e, M.T.
(e)	$\sim A$	a,d, M.T.

See *The Warren-Matson Debate* on the existence of God.

CHAPTER XIX

BALES' DOCTRINE IS FALSE BECAUSE HE ADMITS DEFEAT

Since Chapter XX (cf. Part VI, "Some Concluding Matters") will be devoted to a listing (with brief—at most—explanation of any of the points involved) of the blunders, inconsistencies, admissions of defeat, etc. of Bales, it will be necessary to discuss, in this chapter, only a few of his admissions of defeat. By an "admission of defeat" here is meant that by what he has said, either explicitly or implicitly, Bales has actually admitted (tacitly, at least) that *his doctrine is false.*

1. *Bales' doctrine is false because he admits defeat when he admits that the non-Christian is amenable to the law (gospel) of Christ.* Since Bales' position depends upon (a) his denying that the non-Christian is amenable to (under) the law (gospel) of Christ and (b) proving that denial to be in harmony with Bible teaching, for him to admit (either explicitly or implicitly) that non-Christians are amenable to the law of Christ constitutes (for him) an admission of defeat. And, an admission of defeat is tantamount to proof that his doctrine is false.

This first argument will deal with "God's way of pardon for the alien sinners" (as Bales puts it[1]). Bales says, "Second, the refusal to repents seals their (alien sinners, T.B.W.) doom for they are refusing God's way of pardon for the alien sinner."[2] Further, Bales says, "obviously, one today (Bales obviously refers to non-Christians now living, T.B.W.) must obey Christ's law of pardon to the alien sinner to be pardoned, but this does not mean that the alien is under Christ's law of pardon for the Christian or the other commands of Matthew 28:18-20."[3]

That Bales does not understand the force of the modal participles in Matthew 28:18-20 (which make clear that the "all things" which had been commanded the apostles were to be taught to those who had not yet been baptized) has already been thoroughly discussed in an earlier chapter.

Next, it should be noted that Bales obviously understands that "the law of pardon to the alien sinner" is just as much a part of the law (gospel) of Christ as is "Christ's law of pardon for the Christian." Recognizing this truth, a precise logical argument will now be set out which proves that Bales admits defeat on the matter of Christ's way of pardon for the alien sinner.

(1) Either Christ's way of pardon is a part of the gospel (law) of Christ or Christ's way of pardon is not a part of the gospel (law) of Christ.

(2) If it is false that Christ's way of pardon

is a part of the gospel (law) of Christ, then it is also false that Christ has all authority in heaven and on earth.

(3) If it is true that Christ's way of pardon is a part of the gospel (law) of Christ, then if it is false that the non-Christian (alien sinner) can obey the gospel (law) of Christ then it is false that the non-Christian is amenable to (under) the gospel (law) of Christ.

(4) But Christ does have all authority in heaven and on earth (Matthew 28:18-20; John 17:2). (This is a denial of the consequent of premise 2 above).

(5) Therefore, Christ's way of pardon is a part of the gospel (law) of Christ. (This is the case because premise 4 is a denial of the consequent of premise 2.) This denial (because of Modus Tollens forms of argument) means that the antecedent of Premise 2 is false, thus changing the false to true in that antecedent.

(6) If it is false that the non-Christian (alien sinner) can obey the law of Christ, then it is also false that the non-Christian is amenable to the law of Christ. (This is the case because one can neither obey nor disobey a law to which he is not amenable, Romans 3:19; 4:15; I John 3:4).

(7) (It is a crucial element in Bales' doctrine that:) it is false that the non-Christian can obey the law of Christ.[4] (This is the case, Bales alleges, because no one can obey the terms of the covenant until he is "in" the covenant {i.e., who has already become a Christian}.)

(8) Therefore, it is false that the non-Christian is amenable to the law of Christ. (This follows as a conclusion from premise 6 and premise 7, Modus Ponens argument.)

(9) If it is false that the non-Christian is amenable to the gospel (law) of Christ, then it is false that the non-Christian can be saved by the gospel (law) of Christ. (One can be saved only by a law to which he is amenable, Romans 3:19.)

(10) Therefore, given Bales' doctrine, it is false that a non-Christian can be saved by the gospel (law) of Christ. (This follows from premise 9 and premise 8 by Modus Ponens argument.)[5]

Thus, by answering T.B.W. questions no. 51 and 52 as he did, Bales admitted (by implication) that his doctrine on divorce and remarriage is false.

2. *Bales' doctrine is false because he admits defeat when he admits (1) that none of the law of Moses was to pass until all of it passed*[6] *and (2) that all of it passed when some of it passed.*[7]

Since Bales' doctrine depends upon men who have not been baptized into Christ being guilty of sin in having violated some law other than the law (gospel) of Christ, he maintains[8] that even after the day of Pentecost, neither non-Christian Jews nor non-Christian Gentiles were amenable to the law (gospel) of Christ. In some places, he holds that this situation lasted only until the destruction of Jerusalem (approximately 40 years after the day of Pentecost—the day the New Covenant—the law of Christ—came into force and the Lord's church was established.) In at least one statement, he clearly implies that non-Christian Jews living today are amenable to (under) the law of Moses—not the gospel (law) of Christ.

But Bales admits defeat on this entire matter when he admits that the Old Covenant (the law of Moses) had to be abolished—all of it, it must be remembered—before the New Covenant (the law of Christ) could come into force. Bales admits this truth (which actually defeats him) and even correctly cites such passages as Hebrews 10:9 and 2:14-17 to prove that such was the case.

3. *Bales' doctrine is false because he admits defeat when he admits that Saul of Tarsus (a non-Christian Jew at the time) sinned when he persecuted the church and sought to persuade men to reject the gospel.*[9]

To sin is to violate divine law (I John 3:4). No one can violate a law to which he is not amenable (Romans 3:19). Where there is no law, there can be no sin (Romans 4:15).

Bales' doctrine on divorce and remarriage depends upon his proving that no non-Christian (i.e., no one who is not "in the covenant," as Bales puts it) is under (amenable to) the instructions of the New Covenant. Yet, in referring to a time before Saul became a Christian, Bales said of Saul that he was "wicked in persecuting the church. . ."[10] But, since Saul was a non-Christian Jew who was persecuting the church (opposing the law of Christ), in order to sustain his case, Bales would have to prove that Saul; as a Jew, violated the law of Moses—not the gospel (law) of Christ—in "making havoc of the faith" (Galatians 1:23). Yet, Saul as a Jew who knew the law well, lived "in all good conscience" while persecuting the church. (It must be remembered that Bales has also argued that the New Covenant could not have come into force until the complete—the entire—law of Moses had been abolished!) But if the New Covenant was not in force until after the destruction of Jerusalem,[11] Saul could not have obeyed the gospel and been saved (as the Bible teaches he was in Acts 9, 22, 26, et al.) because, given Bales' doctrine—since, according to Bales, the Old Covenant would still have been in effect—the New Covenant (the gospel, the law of Christ) could not even have been in force.

Such is the "muddle" into which false doctrine

throws one!

Bales must admit defeat because—to be honest and consistent—he must admit that the case of Saul shows: (a) that a non-Christian can violate the law of Christ, (b) that non-Christians are amenable to the law of Christ, (c) (thus, he admits) that all men (whether Christian or non-Christian) are amenable to the law (gospel) of Christ, (d) that all non-Christians are amenable to Matthew 19:9 (this is the case because, as was proved in Chapter XIII, Matthew 28:18-20 makes clear that "all things" Jesus taught (which would include Matthew 19:9) were to be taught to those who had not yet been baptized, and (e) that the law of Moses went out of effect before the gospel (law) of Christ came into effect on Pentecost (and, thus, Bales has no way of knowing that the sins referred to in I Corinthians 6:9-11 were not violations of the law of Christ—rather than the law of Moses {for non-Christian Jews} and "the law on the heart" for non-Christian Gentiles {as Bales argues}).

4. *Bales' doctrine is false because it admits defeat in regard to beginning and cessation of effectiveness (being in force) of the main covenants.* In his book on the kingdom, Bales said, "The reason the patriarchal system ended with the establishment of the New Covenant {the law (gospel) of Christ, T.B.W.}, and did not end with the establishment of the old law, was that the law was not for all mankind, but the gospel dispensation was for all mankind."

This statement from Bales is true. It is the truth which he formerly taught but now (by implication in his doctrine on divorce and remarriage) emphatically denies! It is the very point for which this author has been pleading for more than thirty years—and which Bales has only fairly recently come to deny.

The reader should note carefully some of the fatal (for Bales' doctrine) admissions which Bales makes in this statement.

(1) The patriarchal system did not end with the establishment of the old law (the law of Moses).

(2) Thus, the patriarchal system continued on (for Gentiles) even after the law of Moses was established (came into effect).

(3) The law of Moses was for the Jews.

(4) The patriarchal system did end with the establishment of the New Covenant (the law of Christ).

(5) The reason why the patriarchal system did end with the establishment of the New Covenant but did not end with the establishment of the Old Covenant was that the Old Covenant was not for all mankind, but the gospel dispensation was for all mankind—not just for Christians (as Bales now alleges when he writes on the divorce-remarriage question).

This is truly an admission of defeat by Bales.

Conclusion

Again, it has been shown that Bales' doctrine is false—this time by showing that, in trying to make a case for the doctrine he advances, he is forced, by implication at least, to admit defeat (i.e., he is forced to admit that some things he has affirmed are false and some things he has denied are true).

It is tragic that a man with such a great mind now denies so much of crucial doctrine which he formerly taught.

Special Note

The next chapter (XX) will include an incomplete listing (there are too many to list them all) of the *inconsistencies, blunders, self-contradictions, admissions of defeat,* etc. which have been committed by brother Bales in his effort to sustain his case on divorce and remarriage.

Some of the admissions of defeat which could have been discussed in detail in this present chapter, will be merely listed (and, perhaps, briefly explained) in that chapter (Chapter XX).

Footnotes

[1]Bales' answer to T.B.W. question no. 52, (p. 42 of manuscript).

[2]Ibid.

[3]Bales' answer to T.B.W. question no. 51 (p. 39 of manuscript).

[4]See *NUB*, passim; and various unpublished manuscripts, passim.

[5]For those who are trained in logic, the argument is set out here in symbolic terms.

1. The meaning of the symbols used:
   - (1) W = Christ's way of pardon is a part of the gospel (law) of Christ.
   - (2) C = Christ has all authority in heaven and on earth.
   - (3) A^{O} = the alien sinner (non-Christian) can obey the gospel (law) of Christ.
   - (4) A^{A} = the alien sinner (non-Christian) is amenable to the gospel (law) of Christ.
   - (5) A^{S} = the alien sinner (non-Christian) can be saved by the gospel (law) of Christ.

2. The argument set out:

(1)	$W \vee \sim W$	obvious, law of excluded middle.
(2)	$\sim W > \sim C$	Matthew 28:18-20
(3)	$W > (A^{O} > A^{A})$	
(4)	C	Matthew 28:18-20
(5)	W	2,4, M.T. $(\sim\sim W \equiv W)$
(6)	$\sim A^{O} > \sim A^{A}$	Romans 3:19; 4:15.
(7)	$\sim A^{O}$	Mark 16:15-16 (Bales admits this point, question no. 51, 52)
(8)	$\sim A^{A}$	6,7, M.P.
(9)	$\sim A^{A} > \sim A^{S}$	Romans 3:19
(10)	$\therefore \sim A^{S}$	9,8, M.P. (Since this conclusion, which follows from Bales' position, contradicts Mk. 16:15-16, Bales thus admits defeat.)

[6]J. D. Bales, *Christ: The Fulfillment Of The Law And The Prophets,* (Shreveport, Lambert Book House, 1973), p. 23.

[7]Ibid., p. 24.

[8]In some statements—although in other statements he contradicts such.

[9]J. D. Bales, *Saul: From Persecutor To Persecuted* (Shreveport, Lambert Book House, 1975), pp. 4-6.

[10]Ibid., p. 5.

[11]As Bales sometimes implies.

PART VI

SOME CONCLUDING MATTERS

CHAPTER XX

A PARTIAL LISTING OF BALES' INCONSISTENCIES, BLUNDERS, ADMISSIONS OF DEFEAT, IMPLICATIONS OF FALSE DOCTRINE, DENIAL OF PLAIN BIBLE TEACHING, ETC.

The case for the truth and the case against Bales' error has already been set forth in this book. Thus, it might well be concluded that nothing more needs to be said. However, having been the debater, the moderator, and simply a helper (chart artist, advisor, etc.) in many public discussions, the author is convinced of the value (for the auditor of an oral debate, the reader of a published debate, or the reader of a book such as this one) of a gathering of the points which have been made. This seems especially to be so in the case of the blunders, admissions of defeat, etc. made by the man in error.[1]

So, without the slightest intent to be unkind to brother Bales—but only with the hope of helping the reader (and him) to see the truth on this matter—this chapter will consist of a partial listing of the inconsistencies, self-contradictions, blunders, admissions of defeat, etc. which have been made by Bales in his effort to sustain his case.

I feel certain that in making these errors, he did not intend to err from the word of God—his lifetime of faithful teaching and preaching of the true gospel would certainly indicate otherwise—but, nevertheless, he has made them, and it is the responsibility of this writer to make that clear.

It should be noted that no effort will be made to classify the various errors made (i.e., into, e.g., blunders, admissions of defeat, etc.). The errors will simply be listed, without any effort toward either order (of importance, etc.) or classification.

1.*Even though Bales has, in the past, admitted that non-Christians sin when they establish unauthorized "churches" and urge men to enter those churches rather than the true church of Christ, his doctrine on divorce and remarriage makes it necessary for him—in an effort to be consistent with his doctrine that non-Christians cannot violate the law of Christ—to be unable to say that men living today sin when they establish such "churches" as the Baptist Church, the Methodist Church, the Pentecostal Church, et al.* Bales must take one of two positions: either (a) it is not a sin for men living today to invent and establish churches or (b) his doctrine on divorce and remarriage is false.

2. *Along the same line, brother Bales says, by implication—if he is to be consistent—that it is not a sin for a non-Christian to enter ("join") a "church" such as the Roman Catholic Church.* The law of Moses does not forbid such, and Bales' "law on the heart" does not forbid it—so, if the non-Christian is not under Christ's law (as Bales contends he is not), then the non-Christian does not sin when he enters such a "church."

3. *Still along the same line, Bales says, by implication, that if a non-Christian urges men to reject the gospel plan of salvation and to accept the Baptist plan of salvation at the point of faith before and without being baptized into Christ, he does not sin in so doing.* But the Bible teaches that non-Christians do sin when they do such (see the case of Elymas, Acts 13:8-12, and the case of Saul of Tarsus who referred to himself as a sinner because, even in good conscience, he tried to lead men to reject the gospel). In both cases, they violated the law of Christ! This proves that non-Christians are under (amenable to) the law of Christ.

4. *Bales claims that some Jews at Corinth violated the law of Moses after the day of Pentecost—yet, he, in other statements, admitted the truth, taught in such passages as Hebrews 10:9; Colossians 2:14-17; Matthew 5:17-18; Galatians 3:23-25; that the entire law of Moses had to be abolished before the law of Christ could come into effect.* Therefore, the law of Moses was not in effect after Pentecost.

Bales said, in referring to the law of Moses ("the schoolmaster," Galatians 3:22-27) that it "is obvious, therefore, that as long as they were under the schoolmaster, the faith had not yet come. And they were under the law, the schoolmaster, as long as Christ lived (Colossians 2:14-17; Ephesians 2:12-16)." Here brother Bales obviously and plainly declares that as long as the law of Moses (the Old Covenant) was in effect, the law of Christ (the gospel—the New Covenant) could not have been in effect. He further taught that when any of the law of Moses was abolished, all of it was abolished.[2]

Thus, Bales admits that the following argument is obviously sound.

1. If, Ⓐ as long as the Jews were under the law of Moses, the faith (the New Covenant) had not yet come, and if Ⓑ the faith came on the day of Pentecost, then Ⓒ no Jew was under the law of Moses after the day of Pentecost.

2. Ⓐ As long as the Jews were under the law of Moses, the faith (the New Covenant) had not yet come (Galatians 3:23-25).

3. Ⓑ The faith came on the day of Pentecost (Acts 2:1-47; Cf. Gal. 3:23-27).

4. Ⓐ is true and Ⓑ is true. (Premise 2 and 3 by conjunction.)

5. Therefore, Ⓒ No Jew was under the law of Moses after the day of Pentecost.

Thus, Bales is wrong in his contention that non-Christian Jews continued under the law of Moses after the day of Pentecost. Thus, his doctrine on divorce and remarriage is false since his position on I Corinthians 6:9-11 depends on his error on this matter.

5. *Bales claims that there "is enough truth in the Old Testament today {emphasis, T.B.W.} to condemn the Jew."* (Answer to T.B.W. question no. 14). It must be noted that Bales said "today"! But Bales also admits that no one can violate a law which is not addressed to him (and Romans 3:19 makes this clear). Thus, if the Old Covenant (the law of Moses) had to be taken away (abolished) before the New Covenant (the gospel of Christ) could come into effect, then if the gospel came into effect on the day of Pentecost, then no Jew (Christian or non-Christian) can violate the law of Moses today. And, if no Jew living today can violate the law of Moses, then it is clear that brother Bales is wrong in saying that there "is enough truth in the Old Testament today to condemn the Jew."

Bales could have avoided this trouble if he had only remembered a truth which he formerly affirmed: viz., if a principle or precept is found in both the Old Covenant and New Covenant, it is bound on men living today, not because it was in the Old Covenant but because it is now in the New Covenant.

No principle by which God has ever acted has been repealed, for God does not change in His nature and, thus, does not change the principles by which He operates. (This is not to say that God is under some law, for He is not.[3]) So whatever principles were in operation during the Patriarchal Age were also in operation during the Mosaic Age and are now in operation in the Gospel Age. Of course, some specific details of the various laws were (are) different. But, every man living today is under (amenable to) the law of Christ—no one living today is under Mosaic law or Patriarchy.

6. *Bales cannot have it both ways.* On the one hand, he claims that non-Christian men today become sinners just as Paul discussed in Romans 1:18-3:20: (a) the Jews violated the law of Moses and (b) the Gentiles violated "the law on the heart" (as Bales puts it). Bales said, "I cannot go wrong in following Paul's arguments, which he then used to prove that Jews and Gentiles had sinned. . ." So, he claims the same situation prevails today for non-Christians as prevailed for Jews and Gentiles before Pentecost.

Yet, when faced with the clear fact that the law of Moses had to be abolished before the New Covenant could come into effect, he "crawfishes" and says, "If the Jew is not condemned by his failure to live up to the truth which is in the Old Testament, he is condemned by his failure to live up to the truth which is written on his heart because he is a moral being made in God's image." (These points by Bales were made in answer to T.B.W. question no. 14.)

But, I repeat, he cannot have it both ways. Paul condemned the Jew because he had violated the law of Moses (Romans 1:18-3:20). If that law was not even in effect on Pentecost, how can Bales (a) condemn any Jew because of it from then on or (b) condemn any Jew living today because of it.[4]

7. *Bales' doctrine implies that one may deliberately commit fornication in order to give himself a ground which is acceptable to God for divorce and remarriage.* This is a reprehensible doctrine and should be utterly rejected by all men.

8. *This doctrine, in turn, implies that two elders may "swap wives" and, then, having "repented" (and confessed wrong for the fornication) may continue to live with the second wives and continue to serve as elders.* This is another reprehensible doctrine.

9. *Since "the law on the heart" (as Bales calls it) does not condemn polygamy, it follows, given Bales' doctrine, that if a man enters into marriage with, say, ten women before he is baptized, he may continue to live with all of them after is is baptized.* In contradiction to the plain implication of his doctrine (that men who marry in violation of the law of Christ before they are baptized may continue to live with—as husband and wife—those wives after they are baptized), in another place[5] he denies that a man may keep a multiplicity of wives after he is baptized even if he did marry them before he was baptized. Bales no doubt realizes that few—if any Christians (other than some of the liberals among us)—would accept the doctrine of polygamy (that is "too much" even for these brethren), so he simply contradicts a basic, crucial proposition of his entire case, that non-Christians are not amenable to (under) the covenant (because, he says, they are not yet "in" that covenant) and are not required to live up to the high standard set out in the gospel for divorce and remarriage. And he claims further, men who marry while in the world do not have to sever those marriages after baptism even if the marriages do violate the law of Christ. Contradiction again!

But many are set for the defense of the gospel: they are not going to allow brother Bales to have it both ways. If he makes the law of Christ "retroactive" to break up polygamous marriages which were entered before baptism, that same law will be "retroactive" (as some put it) to break up monogamous marriages which violate Matthew 19:9.

So brother Bales faces this dilemma: either (a) accept polygamous marriages in the church or (b) give up his false doctrine on divorce and remarriage.

10. *Bales implied*[6] *that one is not required to sever (come out of) any of the relationships which (1) violate the law of Christ and (2) are entered before he is baptized into Christ.* This doctrine implies that if a man entered the Roman Catholic Church, accepting its view of "the Pope," before he was baptized, then he would not have to get out of the Roman Catholic Church after he was baptized into Christ. According to the plain implications of Bales' doctrine, he could remain in it until death and be saved. Bales, in effect, says that he (Bales) will simply leave judgment to the Lord—that he will not presume to judge such matters (shades of sectarians!) But surely brother Bales has not forgotten that the Lord will judge by His word (John 12:48; cf. Acts 17:30-31), and the Bible makes it clear that such people will be lost. Whatever is not authorized by the word is sinful, and membership in the Roman Catholic Church, the Baptist Church, et al. is certainly not authorized by the Bible. (Cf. II John 9-11).

Bales tries to avoid the force of the above by saying, in regard to a non-Christian entering the Baptist church, that, since he was already lost, he is no worse off after he enters the Baptist Church than he was before he entered. This constitutes what logicians brand a "diverting of the issue"—which takes the following form: A is true (or false) because I can prove B (where the truth of B is not even relevant to the truth of A). The question which was asked of Bales was not: "If a non-Christian enters the Baptist Church, will he still be lost—will he be any worse off than he was before he entered?" That was not the question. The question was, "Will a non-Christian sin in the act of entering the Baptist Church? Will he sin in the act of urging men to reject the gospel plan of salvation and to accept the Baptist plan of salvation?"

Bales again faces a dilemma: either (a) he must accept the position that it is not sin for a non-Christian to enter the Baptist Church and to then oppose the one gospel and the Lord's one true church—in which case, by implication, he must also accept the position that one who is a member of the Baptist Church when he is baptized into Christ may remain in the Baptist church for the rest of his life and still be saved eternally, in which case, he denies Bible teaching (I Corinthians 4:6), or (b) he must admit that a non-Christian sins when he enters the Baptist Church and then opposes the true gospel by teaching Baptist doctrine—in which case, he admits, by implication, that his doctrine on divorce and remarriage is false.

11. *Bales' doctrine implies that "group marriages" (which is sometimes practiced in societies with very small populations) can continue to be practiced by those who are baptized into Christ.* Imagine a group of non-Christians (five men and five women) in which the group considers that all of the men are married to all of the women and, of course, all of the women to all of the men. According to the implications of Bales' doctrine, such an arrangement would not be sinful for non-Christians (It is a kind of polygamy.). Thus, if this group should hear the true gospel and be baptized, they could, according to the implications of Bales' basic doctrine on amenability continue to live in this "marriage arrangement" even after being baptized and have the blessings and approval of God while doing so.

Yet, in other statements, even brother Bales recognizes that such would be wrong by citing I Corinthians 7:2 to make the point that after one enters Christ, he must have no more than one mate.

Again, Bales faces a dilemma: (a) accept "group marriage" or (b) give up his present doctrine on divorce and remarriage.

12. *In response to the request by this author (T.B.W.) to Bales to supply the premises of the argument which proves his conclusion that Matthew 19:9 is a "covenant passage" (that is, it applies not to all people but only to Christians who are married to Christians), Bales responded as follows:*[7]

"(1) Premise: If it is true that Christ's legislation in Matthew 19:9 was legislation for two believers, and not for other marriages, it contradicts this passage to refer it to all marriages."

"(2) It is the case that Matthew 19:9 is legislation for two Christians and not for other marriages. (I Corinthians 7:10-11; 12-15)."

"(3) Therefore, Matthew 19:9 is a 'covenant passage' (that is, it applies not to all people but only to Christians who are married to Christians)."

So far as this author is aware, this constitutes the only time that Bales (either in *Not Under Bondage* or in all of the manuscripts—"tons" of them—which he has circulated) that he has even tried to set out a precisely stated, valid argument (and which is also sound). Sadly, for him, even this one effort fails. It is an invalid argument. It seems that he tried to write an argument in the form of modus ponens, which is: (1) if P is true, then Q is true; (2) P is true; ∴ (3) Q is true. But Bales' argument is in this form: (1) If A is true, then B is true, (2) A is true, therefore, (3) C is true. The reader can easily see that he has "C" where he should have "B" in the conclusion. "B" (in his argument) is the consequent (that which follows the "then," in the first premise) and it simply is not the same thing as "C", in his conclusion. "B" in the first premise could, given Bales' wording, refer either to the "mixed marriages" (Christians and non-Christians) or to "world marriages" (to coin a term), i.e., a non-Christian married to a non-Christian. But neither of these is what Bales needs and neither is what he has in his conclusion. Besides this, Premise 2 in his argument is false.

Until Bales can come up with the sound argument (that is, one in which the argument itself is valid and the premises are true) then he has established absolutely nothing with his "wanderings" on Matthew 19:9 and I Corinthians 7:10-15. One can write 400 pages of crowded fact and argument and yet not prove the proposition which is under question.

In such matters only sound arguments prove anything, and Bales has not supplied such. Perhaps a course in elementary logic for Bales could end this controversy for us all. And we do not intend to allow him to merely assume his case; he is going to have to face up to his responsibility to supply a sound argument, the conclusion of which is his basic proposition.

And so we plead once more for brother Bales to set out a sound argument using I Corinthians 7:10-15 which necessitates the conclusion that Matthew 19:9 has application only to Christians married to Christians. He has claimed for these two passages that they provide an argument which is both decisive and sufficient to establish such, but he has not yet done it, and the challenge is extended to him to "put his hand to plow" to do it!

There are many other such inconsistencies, blunders, admissions of defeat, etc. of which Bales has been guilty, but it seems useless to go on and on piling up evidence that his doctrine is false when such has already been accomplished again and again and again.

Brother Bales' doctrine on divorce and remarriage is false. For one to accept his false doctrine, he must also be willing to accept many other false doctrines—some of which have been set forth in this book. When one accepts a doctrine, he must be willing to accept whatever is implied by that doctrine. Will Bales and those who agree with him do this?

Footnotes

[1]For example, see Thomas B. Warren and Wallace I. Matson, *The Warren-Matson Debate on the Existence of God,* (Jonesboro, AK., National Christian Press, 1979).

[2]Bales, *Kingdom,* p.144; Cf.*Christ: The Fulfill-*

ment of the Law and the Prophets, pp. 23-24.

[3]See discussion of this matter in *The Warren-Matson Debate* and *The Warren-Flew Debate*.

[4]This author urges the reader to study carefully Bales', *The Kingdom Prophesied and Established* in order to see how well, in the past, he taught the truth in regard to the fact that the New Covenant could not come into effect until all of the Old Covenant was abolished.

[5]Bales' answer to T.B.W. question no. 63.

[6]Bales' answer to T.B.W. question no. 58.

[7]Bales' answer to T.B.W. question no. 14, p. 17.

THE APPENDIX

INTRODUCTION TO THE APPENDIX

As has been made clear again and again throughout this book, brother Bales stakes his case, in the main, on two passages of Scripture: (1) Matthew 19:9 and (2) I Corinthians 7:10-15. He also leans rather heavily on his interpretation of Matthew 28:18-20 and Romans 2:14-15.

Since this author holds that enough has already been said in the main text of the book about Matthew 28:18-20 (in which it was proved that "all things" that Jesus had commanded His Apostles were to be taught to those who were not yet baptized), emphasis in this Appendix will be on Matthew 19:9 and I Corinthians 7. This is not to say that the falsity of brother Bales' positions on Matthew 19:9 and I Corinthians 7 has not already been established—such has been done—but, it is felt that some additional explanation of each of these passages (along with another passage which is highly relevant to these two—I Corinthians 5:1-13)—placed in an Appendix for ready reference—would be of special value to the careful student.

Also, a large number of other "special" problems which are crucially involved with divorce and remarriage are considered in some detail in various appendices. This will enable the reader to find what he wishes to find much more quickly than would be the case without it. This means that the book can also function as a handbook on the question of divorce and remarriage.

APPENDIX A

MATTHEW 19:9

In a number of chapters in this book, Matthew 19:9 has been discussed in considerable detail. To this author, it seems clear that enough has already been said to make clear that Bales' doctrine that Matthew 19:9 applies only to Christians who are married to Christians is false!

Much of the material in Appendix A was prepared in chart form for the annual Spring Forum of Harding College of 1977, during which this author (T.B.W.) was to discuss the divorce and remarriage question with brother James D. Bales. However, this author suffered a series of serious illnesses during 1976 and early 1977 and was unable to appear on that Forum. With changes, additions, and deletions to fit the differing doctrine—i.e., differing from that of brother Bales' doctrine for which the charts were originally prepared—more charts were prepared for the Harding Forum of 1978, during which this author discussed the divorce and remarriage question with brother James S. Woodroof. Most of the material in this appendix is taken from those charts, most of which were prepared in early 1977 for the Forum of that year.[1]

Much of the material has been left—for convenience sake—in chart form. Some additional numbering has been done in order to help the reader to follow the line of thought.[2]

The basic argument of the Bible (including Matt. 19:9) on divorce and remarriage for all men living in the Christian (gospel) dispensation has been discussed in detail in Chapters IX, X, XI, XII, and XIII. Matt. 19:9 was discussed in connection with the refutation of Bales' basic proposition in Chapters XIV, XV, XVI, XVII, XVIII and XIX. The reader is urged to recall that material as he reads this present Appendix. Thus, it should be remembered that the chapters listed above constitute a commentary on the charts which follow.

1. *Matthew 19:9 is an "exceptive" sentence* (based on Chart no. 70ff in *Charts*). Given what has already been proved in the chapters listed above (namely, that Matthew 19:9 is a "universal passage"—i.e., it is addressed to all men (whether Christian or non-Christian), then the following argument is crucial:

(1) If Ⓙ all "exceptive" sentences carry the force of if and only if, and if Ⓚ Matt. 19:9 is an "exceptive sentence" as pertains to divorce and remarriage, then Ⓒ any man (whether Christian or non-Christian) is a person who is eligible (according to Bible teaching) to put away his wife and to marry another if and only if the putting away is done (by the innocent party) for the cause of fornication (on the

part of the one being put away). Here is an example of an exceptive statement: "The W's and they only are Z's." This can be written as follows: "A thing is a Z if and only if it is a W."

Just so, the statement, "Those who put away their spouses for fornication and only they are eligible to marry again," can be written as follows: "A person is eligible to marry again (while his spouse is still living) if and only if that person has put away his spouse for fornication."

Usually exceptive sentences are re-written as a pair of statements. For example, "All except A's are B's" is re-written as, "All non-A's are B's and no A's are B's."
{This premise is obviously true.}

(2) Ⓙ All "exceptive" sentences carry the force of if and only if. {This is obviously true from logic and the very meaning of the word "except."}

(3) Ⓚ Matthew 19:9 is an "exceptive" sentence as pertains to divorce and remarriage. {Obviously true, by merely reading the passage.}

(4) It is the case that the conjunction of Proposition Ⓙ and Proposition Ⓚ is true. {This is true because the conjunction of any two (or more) true propositions is also true.}

(5) Therefore, Proposition Ⓒ is true: any man (whether Christian or non-Christian) is a person who is eligible (according to Bible teaching) to put away his wife and to marry another if and only if the putting away is done (by the innocent party) for the cause of fornication (on the part of the one being put away). {That this conclusion is true follows from the fact that the antecedent in premise is affirmed and that, therefore, the consequent (the conclusion C) must also be true. Modus Ponens form of argument.[3]}

The above argument—with the preceding material proving that Matthew 19:9 is addressed to all men—constitutes proof of the Bible position and refutation of Bales' position. But, there is more. Note next Chart no. 70, which sets out, in a graphic way, the essential teaching of Matthew 19:9.

Below are some charts which may be helpful to the reader in understanding Matthew 19:9.

2. AS AN "EXCEPTIVE" SENTENCE, WHAT MATT. 19:9 TEACHES: (70)

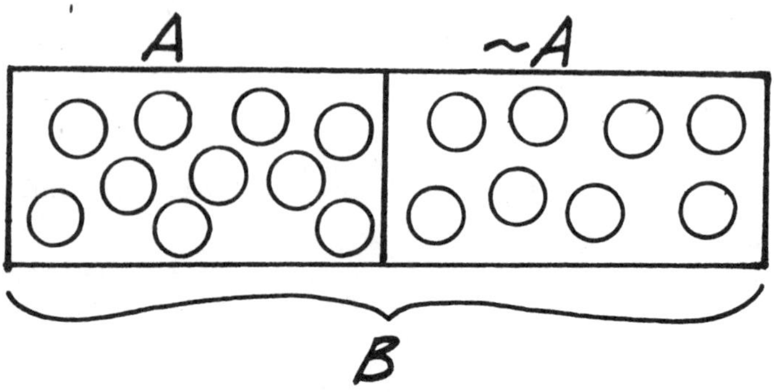

B = ALL PERSONS WHO HAVE MARRIED SOMEONE ELSE WHILE HAVING A LIVING COMPANION (OR FORMER COMPANION). NOTE—SOME IN THIS TOTALITY ARE ADULTERERS AND SOME ARE **NOT**!

A = PERSONS WHO HAVE MARRIED AGAIN BUT WHO DID NOT PUT AWAY THEIR COMPANION BECAUSE OF THAT COMPANION'S FORNICATION — & WHO THUS COMMIT ADULTERY.

~A = PERSONS WHO HAVE MARRIED AGAIN BUT WHO DID PUT AWAY THEIR COMPANION BECAUSE OF THAT COMPANION'S FORNICATION — & WHO THUS DO NOT COMMIT ADULTERY.

3. JOHN 3:5 = AN "EXCEPTIVE" SENTENCE (71)

AN "EXCEPTIVE" SENTENCE: "ALL PERSONS EXCEPT A'S ARE B'S —AND— NO A'S ARE B'S."

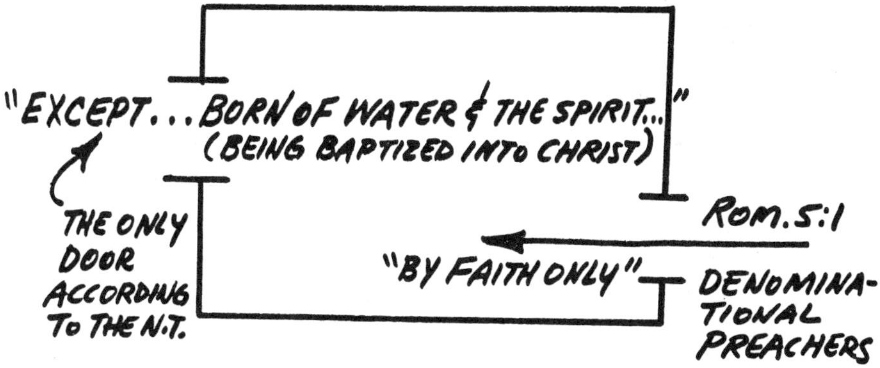

"ALL PERSONS EXCEPT [THOSE WHO ARE "BORN OF WATER AND THE SPIRIT"] ARE [PERSONS WHO CANNOT ENTER THE KINGDOM] - AND - NO [PERSONS WHO ARE "BORN OF WATER AND THE SPIRIT"] ARE [PERSONS WHO CANNOT ENTER THE KINGDOM]."

[CONT'D - NEXT CHART]

4. "EXCEPTIVE" SENTENCES: JOHN 3:5 AND MATT. 19:9 (72)

AN EXCEPTIVE SENTENCE HAS THE BASIC FORCE OF "IF AND ONLY IF".

(1) THUS — JOHN 3:5 SAYS, IN EFFECT: "ONE CAN ENTER THE KINGDOM IF AND ONLY IF HE IS BORN OF WATER AND THE SPIRIT (I.E., IS BAPTIZED IN THE NAME OF CHRIST)."

(2) -AND- MATT. 19:9 SAYS, IN EFFECT, "ONE CAN PUT AWAY HIS (HER) SPOUSE AND MARRY AGAIN WITHOUT COMMITTING ADULTERY IF AND ONLY IF THE PUTTING AWAY WAS DONE BY THE INNOCENT PARTY BECAUSE OF THE FORNICATION OF THE ONE PUT AWAY."

* ANY ONE WHO HOLDS THERE IS SOME OTHER "DOOR" (THAN THE ONE — IN EACH CASE — NAMED BY JESUS) HOLDS THAT JESUS DID NOT TELL THE TRUTH!
* BUT, IN SO DOING, IT IS HE (NOT JESUS) WHO DOES NOT TELL THE TRUTH!!

5. JOHN 3:5 & MATT. 19:9 (CONT'D) (73)

– IF AND ONLY IF –

JOHN 3:5

1. **IF** (S) JOHN 3:5 TEACHES THAT A MAN CAN ENTER THE KINGDOM IF AND ONLY IF HE IS BORN OF WATER AND THE SPIRIT (IS BAPTIZED IN THE NAME OF CHRIST), **THEN** (T) (SINCE THE BIBLE DOES NOT CONTRADICT ITSELF) IT IS FALSE THAT JOHN 3:16 (OR ANY OTHER PASSAGE IN THE BIBLE) TEACHES THAT A MAN CAN ENTER THE KINGDOM BEFORE &/OR WITHOUT BEING BAPTIZED IN THE NAME OF CHRIST.
2. S. "EXCEPT A MAN..."
3. ∴T. 1, 2, M.P.

NOTE: (1) THE ARG. IS VALID.
(2) THE PREMISES ARE TRUE.
(3) –SO– THE CONCLUSION MUST BE TRUE.

[CONT'D – NEXT CHART]

6. JOHN 3:5, MT. 19:9 — CONT'D.

MATT. 19:9 (74)

1. **IF** (U) MATT. 19:9 TEACHES THAT A MAN MAY—WITHOUT SINNING—PUT AWAY HIS WIFE AND MARRY ANOTHER (WHILE THE PUT-AWAY SPOUSE IS STILL LIVING) IF AND ONLY IF THAT PUT-AWAY SPOUSE HAD BEEN GUILTY OF FORNICATION, **THEN** (V) (SINCE THE BIBLE DOES NOT CONTRADICT ITSELF) IT IS FALSE THAT I COR. 7 (OR ANY OTHER PASSAGE IN THE BIBLE) TEACHES THAT A MAN MAY—WITHOUT SINNING—PUT AWAY HIS WIFE AND MARRY ANOTHER (WHILE THAT PUT-AWAY SPOUSE IS STILL LIVING) ON SOME GROUND OTHER THAN THE FORNICATION OF THE PUT-AWAY SPOUSE.
2. U — "...EXCEPT FOR FORNICATION..."
3. ∴ V — 1, 2, M.P.

NOTE: (1) THE ARG. = VALID (2) PREMISES = TRUE (3) ∴ CONCLUSION MUST BE TRUE.

[CONT'D — NEXT CHART]

7. PARALLEL ERRORS ON JOHN 3:5 AND MATT. 19:9 (75)

I. HOW MANY DOORS INTO THE KINGDOM?

JESUS: "ONE AND ONLY ONE: BAPTISM"
FALSE TEACHERS: "OTHERS BESIDES THAT ONE DOOR."

II. HOW MANY DOORS INTO SECOND MARRIAGE (WHILE SPOUSE LIVING)?

JESUS: "ONE & ONLY ONE: FORNICATION."
FALSE TEACHERS: "OTHERS BESIDES THAT ONE DOOR."

8. MATT. 19:9 IS AN "EXCEPTIVE" SENTENCE

(76)

ALL [PERSONS WHO ARE NOT FREE TO MARRY (WHILE THEIR PUT-AWAY SPOUSE IS STILL LIVING)] ARE [PERSONS WHO HAVE PUT AWAY THEIR SPOUSES ON SOME GROUND OTHER THAN FORNICATION] – AND – NO [PERSON WHO HAS PUT AWAY HIS (HER) SPOUSE ON SOME GROUND OTHER THAN FORNICATION] IS [A PERSON WHO IS FREE TO MARRY ANOTHER.]

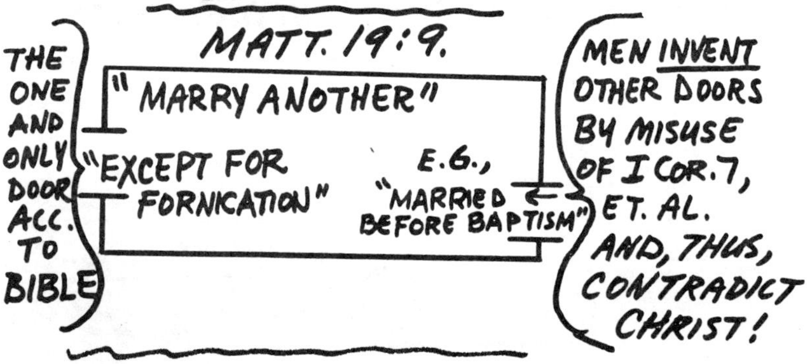

COMPARE CHART 70

9. MATT. 19:9 - AN "EXCEPTIVE" SENTENCE (77)

"ALL [PERSONS, EXCEPT THOSE WHO HAVE PUT AWAY THEIR SPOUSES ON THE GROUND OF FORNICATION ON THE PART OF THE ONE PUT AWAY] ARE [PERSONS WHO COMMIT ADULTERY IF THEY MARRY ANOTHER WHILE THEIR PUT-AWAY SPOUSES ARE STILL LIVING] — AND — NO [PERSON WHO HAS PUT AWAY HIS (HER) SPOUSE ON THE GROUND OF FORNICATION ON THE PART OF THE ONE PUT AWAY] IS [A PERSON WHO COMMITS ADULTERY IF HE (SHE) MARRIES ANOTHER WHILE HIS (HER) PUT-AWAY SPOUSE IS STILL LIVING.]

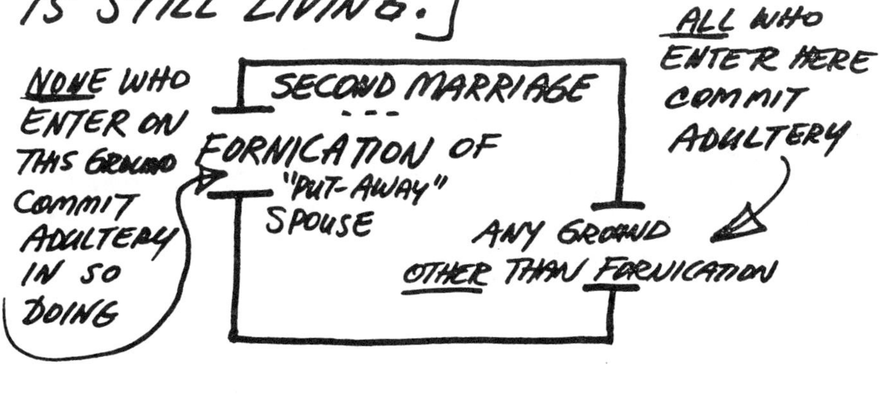

10. A CRUCIAL COMPARISON OF JOHN 3:5 AND MATT. 19:9: (78)

1. IF THERE IS ANOTHER WAY OF ENTERING THE KINGDOM IN ADDITION TO THAT OF BEING BAPTIZED, THEN JOHN 3:5 IS <u>NOT</u> <u>TRUE</u>!

2. IN THE SAME WAY, IF THERE IS ANOTHER GROUND FOR PUTTING AWAY ONE'S SPOUSE AND MARRYING ANOTHER IN ADDITION TO THAT OF THE FORNICATION OF THE PUT-AWAY SPOUSE, THEN MATT 19:9 IS <u>NOT</u> <u>TRUE</u>!

★ BUT— <u>BOTH</u> JOHN 3:5 AND MATT. 19:9 <u>ARE</u> <u>TRUE</u>!!

* BALES ADMITS THIS TRUTH ON JOHN 3:5, BUT HE REJECTS IT ON MATT. 19:9.

11. MATT. 19:9 & LOGIC (80)

1. JESUS' ORIGINAL STATEMENT PUT INTO STRICT LOGICAL LANGUAGE:

"ALL [MEN WHO PUT AWAY THEIR WIVES, ON SOME GROUND OTHER THAN FORNICATION (OF THEIR WIVES), AND MARRY OTHERS] ARE [MEN WHO COMMIT ADULTERY IN SO DOING.]" ☒ TRUE ☐ FALSE

2. THE CONTRAPOSITIVE OF JESUS' STATEMENT:

"ALL [MEN WHO DO NOT COMMIT ADULTERY WHEN THEY PUT AWAY THEIR WIVES AND MARRY OTHERS] ARE [MEN WHO DO NOT PUT AWAY THEIR WIVES ON SOME GROUND OTHER THAN FORNICATION (OF THEIR WIVES) AND MARRY OTHERS.]

☒ TRUE ☐ FALSE

☒ = T.B.W. ANSWER

QUESTION: WHAT ARE BRO. WOODROOF'S ANSWERS??

12. MATT. 19:9: "IF & ONLY IF..." (81)

(1) IF MATT. 19:9 TEACHES THAT THE ONE AND ONLY GROUND (ACCEPTABLE TO GOD) FOR DIVORCE AND REMARRIAGE IS THAT OF ONE'S HAVING PUT AWAY HIS (HER) SPOUSE BECAUSE OF THAT SPOUSE'S FORNICATION, THEN ANY INTERPRETATION OF ANY PASSAGE (E.G., I COR. 7) WHICH CONTRADICTS THAT TEACHING IS A FALSE INTERPRETATION.

(2) MATT. 19:9 DOES TEACH THAT THE ONE AND ONLY GROUND (ACCEPTABLE TO GOD) FOR DIVORCE AND REMARRIAGE IS THAT OF ONE'S HAVING PUT AWAY HIS (HER) SPOUSE BECAUSE OF THAT SPOUSE'S FORNICATION.

(3) ∴ ANY INTERPRETATION OF ANY PASSAGE (E.G., I COR. 7) WHICH CONTRADICTS THAT TEACHING IS A FALSE INTERPRETATION.

NOTE: (1) THE ARG. IS VALID.
(2) THE PREMISES ARE TRUE.
(3) THE CONCLUSION MUST BE TRUE.

13. MATT. 19:9 & VALID REASONING (82)

(1) ALL [MEN WHO PUT AWAY THEIR WIVES ON SOME GROUND OTHER THAN FORNICATION (OF THEIR WIVES), AND MARRY OTHERS] ARE [MEN WHO COMMIT ADULTERY IN SO DOING.]

(2) [JOHN JONES] IS [A MAN WHO (BEFORE HE WAS BAPTIZED) PUT AWAY HIS WIFE, ON SOME GROUND OTHER THAN HIS WIFE'S FORNICATION, AND MARRIED ANOTHER WOMAN.]

(3) ∴ [JOHN JONES] IS [A MAN WHO COMMITTED ADULTERY IN SO DOING.]

14. MATT. 19:9 IN GREEK:

(263)

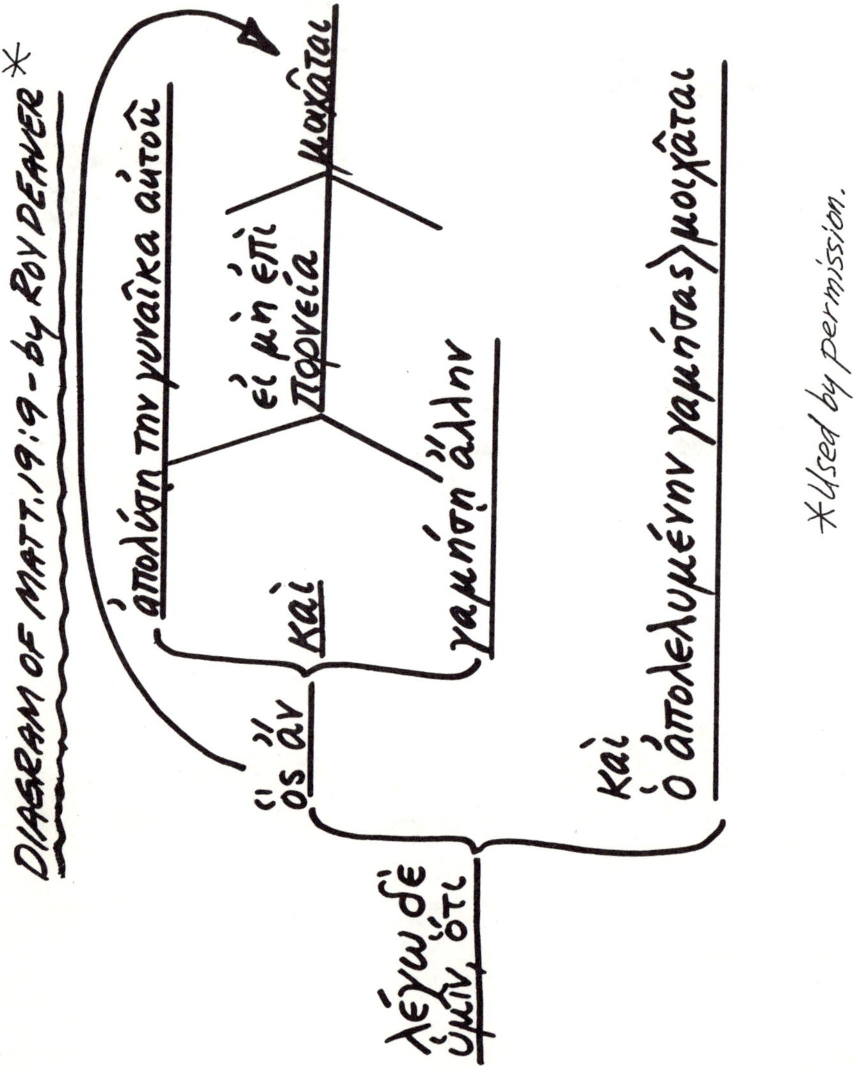

MATT. 19:9 (264)

★ **STATED:** "AND I SAY UNTO YOU, WHOSOEVER SHALL PUT AWAY HIS WIFE, EXCEPT FOR FORNICATION, AND SHALL MARRY ANOTHER, COMMITTETH ADULTERY: AND HE THAT MARRIETH HER WHEN SHE IS PUT AWAY COMMITTETH ADULTERY."

★ **ORIGINAL LANGUAGE CONSIDERED:**

(1.) λέγω δὲ ὑμῖν - "but I say to you. δὲ INDICATES CONTRAST (CF. MT. 5:32). CHRIST'S TEACHING IS HERE SET FORTH IN CONTRAST TO THE MOSAIC TOLERATION. THE ὑμῖν IS A DATIVE CONSTRUCTION, EQUIVALENT TO THE ENGLISH INDIRECT OBJECT.

(2.) ὅτι GENERALLY INTRODUCES A CLAUSE; HERE IT INTRODUCES TWO CLAUSES. THESE CLAUSES ARE DIRECT OBJECTS OF THE VERB "SAY." THE LORD SAYS, I SAY TO YOU (1) WHOSOEVER SHALL PUT AWAY HIS WIFE AND SHALL MARRY ANOTHER - EXCEPT FOR FORNICATION - COMMITS ADULTERY; AND (2) THE MAN WHO MARRIES A WOMAN WHO HAS BEEN PUT AWAY, COMMITS ADULTERY.

(3.) ὃς ἂν - ὃς IS A RELATIVE PRONOUN WHICH WHEN USED WITH ἂν OR ἐὰν AND A VERB IN THE SUBJUNCTIVE MOOD MEANS "WHOEVER" OR "WHOSOEVER".

[MATT. 19:9] [CONT'D]

(4.) ἀπολύσῃ — 3 PER. SING., AOR. ACT. SUBJUNCTIVE OF ἀπολύω, I RELEASE, I DIVORCE, I LIBERATE. (265)

(5.) τὴν γυναῖκα αὐτοῦ - "his wife."

(6.) εἰ μὴ ἐπὶ πορνείᾳ - "EXCEPT FOR FORNICATION."

(7.) καὶ γαμήσῃ ἄλλην - "AND SHALL MARRY ANOTHER.", γαμήσῃ MUST BE CONSIDERED WITH ἀπολύσῃ. THESE TWO WORDS ARE IDENTICALLY RELATED TO THE ὃς ἂν - "WHOSOEVER SHALL PUT AWAY,... AND SHALL MARRY ANOTHER." THE εἰ μὴ PHRASE - "EXCEPT FOR FORNICATION" RELATES IDENTICALLY TO ἀπολύσῃ AND γαμήσῃ - "WHOSOEVER SHALL PUT AWAY HIS WIFE AND SHALL MARRY ANOTHER... EXCEPT FOR FORNICATION...." (γαμήσῃ = I AOR. ACT. SUBJ.)

(8.) μοιχᾶται - "COMMITTETH ADULTERY." IS THE PRESENT TENSE, MEANING: "KEEPS ON COMMITTING ADULTERY." [SEE MORE DETAILED DISCUSSION ON CHARTS].

(9.) καὶ ὁ ἀπολελυμένην γαμήσας μοιχᾶται - "AND HE THAT MARRIETH HER WHEN SHE IS PUT AWAY COMMITTETH ADULTERY."

[CONT'D.]

[MATT. 19:9 - CONT'D.]

ἀπολελυμένην - acc. sing. fem. (266) perf. pass. part. of ἀπολύω, MEANING HERE "THE-HAVING-BEEN-PUT-AWAY (WOMAN). γαμήσας — NOM. MASC. SING. AOR. ACT. PART. OF γαμέω, AND GOES WITH THE DEFINITE ARTICLE WHICH IS MASCULINE. HERE, THE MEANING IS: "THE-HAVING-MARRIED-THE ... (MAN). THE TWO PARTICIPLES HAVE THE FORCE OF: "THE-HAVING-MARRIED-A-HAVING-BEEN-PUT-AWAY (WOMAN)"; THAT IS, "THE MAN WHO HAS MARRIED A WOMAN WHO HAS BEEN PUT AWAY."

(10) μοιχᾶται - [SAME WORD AS USED PREVIOUSLY] - "COMMITTETH ADULTERY." 3 PER. SING. PRES. IND. OF μοιχάω. THE PRESENT TENSE INDICATES: "KEEPS ON COMMITTING ADULTERY." THIS MEANS THAT THE MAN WHO MARRIES A WOMAN WHO HAS BEEN PUT AWAY KEEPS ON COMMITTING ADULTERY.

(11) —SO— MT. 19:9 TEACHES THAT WHOSOEVER SHALL PUT AWAY HIS WIFE,

[MT. 19:9— CONT'D]

AND SHALL MARRY ANOTHER (WOMAN)— EXCEPT ON THE GROUND OF HER FORNICATION— KEEPS ON COMMITTING ADULTERY; AND THE MAN WHO HAS MARRIED A WOMAN WHO HAS BEEN PUT AWAY KEEPS ON COMMITTING ADULTERY. (267)

(12) THE PASSAGE TEACHES:

(1) EVERY MAN (WHETHER IN OR OUT OF THE CHURCH) WHO PUTS AWAY HIS WIFE AND MARRIES ANOTHER WOMAN — EXCEPT ON THE GROUND OF HIS WIFE'S FORNICATION— KEEPS ON COMMITTING ADULTERY.

(2) EVERY MAN (WHETHER IN OR OUT OF THE CHURCH) WHO MARRIES A WOMAN WHO HAS BEEN PUT AWAY (ANY WOMAN WHO HAS BEEN PUT AWAY) KEEPS ON COMMITTING ADULTERY.

(3) EVERY MAN (WHETHER IN OR OUT OF THE CHURCH) WHO PUTS AWAY HIS WIFE BECAUSE OF HER FORNICATION AND MARRIES ANOTHER WOMAN DOES NOT COMMIT ADULTERY.

[MT. 19:9—CONT'D.]

* THE FORCE OF "COMMITTETH ADULTERY" (PRESENT TENSE) IN MATT. 19:9 [CF: 273, 274, 275] (268)

1. μοιχᾶται — "COMMITTETH ADULTERY" IS THE 3 PERS. SING. PRES. IND. OF μοιχάω. THE PRESENT TENSE IS SIGNIFICANT HERE: IT INDICATES CONTINUOUS ACTION. [SEE ALSO CHARTS 128, 129, 130]

2. NOTE: IN N.T. GREEK, THE ACTION DENOTED BY A VERB MAY BE DEFINED BOTH AS REGARDS IT TIME, AND AS REGARDS ITS STATE OR PROGRESS (NUNN, A SHORT SYNTAX OF NEW TESTAMENT GREEK, p. 65).
   (1) ITS TIME MAY BE DEFINED AS PAST, PRESENT, OR FUTURE.
   (2) ITS STATE OR PROGRESS MAY BE REGARDED AS CONTINUOUS
      a. CONTINUOUS OR INCOMPLETED.
      b. PERFECT OR COMPLETE.
      c. SIMPLE OR INDEFINITE (WITHOUT ANY REF. TO CONTINUITY OR COMPLETION).

[MT. 19:9 – CONT'D.]

3. NOTE FURTHER: THE USE OF (269) THE PRESENT INDICATIVE GENERALLY DENOTES ACTION IN PROGRESS OR CUSTOMARY OR REPEATED ACTION.

4. NOTE STILL FURTHER: THE PRESENT TENSE IS OCCASIONALLY USED IN AN AORISTIC SENSE TO DENOTE A SIMPLE EVENT IN PRESENT TIME (CF. MK. 2:5).

5. BUT NOTE STILL FURTHER: IF ANY INDICATIVE IS TO BE PROPERLY REGARDED AS AORISTIC (I.E., AS PUNCTILIAR ACTION RATHER THAN AS LINEAR OR DURATIVE), IT MUST BE BECAUSE THE CONTEXT INVOLVES SOME COMPELLING REASON WHY SUCH IS THE CASE.

6. NOTE STILL FURTHER: THERE IS NO REASON WHATEVER TO REGARD μοιχᾶται IN MT. 19:9 AS AN AORISTIC PRESENT (INDICATING PUNCTILIAR ACTION). RATHER, IT INDICATES CONTINUOUS ACTION; I. E., "KEEPS ON COMMITTING ADULTERY."

7. THUS, THOSE WHO MARRY IN VIOLATION OF MATT. 19:9 "KEEP ON COMMITTING ADULTERY" — AND, IF THEY DO NOT REPENT, WILL BE LOST. — REV. 21:8.

[MT. 19:9—CONT'D.]

8. NOTE STILL FURTHER: (270)

EVEN IF, EX HYPOTHESI, WE WERE TO ADMIT (WHICH, OF COURSE WE DO NOT) THAT μοιχᾶται IS AN AORISTIC PRESENT, THIS STILL WOULD NOT ESTABLISH THE CASE OF THOSE WHO CLAIM THAT ONE CAN PUT AWAY HIS WIFE ON SOME GROUND OTHER THAN FORNICATION AND MARRY ANOTHER.

SEE THIS POINT DEVELOPED ON CHARTS 128, 129, 130—CF.: 273, 274, 275. (SEE book of CHARTS)

(9.) NOTE STILL FURTHER: GREEK SCHOLARS AGREE TO THE POINTS ARGUED ABOVE: CF.: A.T. ROBERTSON, CHAMBERLAIN, SUMMERS, DANA & MANTEY, ROBERTSON & DAVIS, BURTON, NUNN, ET. AL.

[MT. 19:9 – CONT'D]

MT. 19:9 & CONTINUOUS ACTION (271)

MT. 19:9 & TENSE POSSIBILITIES:

BEFORE LORD.

I. HE COULD HAVE USED:

(1.) THE AORIST TENSE (μοιχάσῃ) TO STRESS POINT ACTION: HE HAD USED TWO AORISTS: (1) ἀπολύσῃ (2) γαμήσῃ.

—OBVIOUSLY— IF JESUS HAD WANTED TO STRESS POINT (PUNCTILIAR) ACTION, HE WOULD HAVE USED ANOTHER AORIST TENSE VERB.

(2.) THE FUTURE TENSE (μοιχάσει) TO INDICATE NO SPECIAL REFERENCE TO THE KIND OF ACTION.

(3.) THE PERFECT TENSE (μεμοίχηκεν) TO STRESS COMPLETED ACTION IN PAST TIME WITH SPECIAL EMPHASIS UPON THE CONSEQUENCES.

(4.) THE PRESENT TENSE (μοιχᾶται). ESPECIALLY IN LIGHT OF THE TWO AORIST TENSE VERBS THIS FACT MUST BE SIGNIFICANT.

II. HE DID USE THE PRESENT TENSE (μοιχᾶται).

(1.) HE COULD HAVE USED ONE OF THE OTHERS.

(2) BUT HE DIDN'T! HE USED THE PRESENT!

[MATT. 19:9]

"KEEPS ON COMMITTING ADULTERY." (272)

1. IF (A) ONE CAN "LIVE" IN FORNICATION – AND – IF (B) THE PRESENT TENSE (THE BASIC OR PRIMARY USAGE OF WHICH IS TO INDICATE DURATION OR REPEATED ACTION) IS USED IN REFERENCE TO THE ADULTERY WHICH IS COMMITTED WHICH ONE MARRIES IN VIOLATION OF JESUS' INSTRUCTION RECORDED IN MATT. 19:9 – THEN – (C) ALL PERSONS WHO PUT AWAY THEIR SPOUSES ON ANY GROUND OTHER THAN THE FORNICATION OF THE ONE PUT AWAY ARE PERSONS WHO KEEP ON COMMITTING ADULTERY WHEN THEY MARRY & IMPENITENTLY REMAIN IN THAT SECOND MARRIAGE.
2. A · B. COL. 3:5-7; MATT. 19:9.
3. ∴ C. 1, 2, M.P.

(PUNCTILIAR & LINER ACTION)

ILLUSTRATION OF TENSE CHANGE (273)

★ JOHN 5:8-9: "AND JESUS SAITH UNTO HIM, ARISE, TAKE UP THY BED, AND WALK. AND STRAIGHTWAY THE MAN WAS MADE WHOLE, AND TOOK UP HIS BED AND WALKED."

★ JOHN 5:8-9 (IN GREEK): λέγει αὐτῷ ὁ Ἰησοῦς, Ἔγειραι, ἆρον τὸν κράββατόν σου, καὶ περιπάτει. καὶ εὐθέως ἐγένετο ὑγιὴς ὁ ἄνθρωπος, καὶ ἦρε τὸν κράββατον αὐτοῦ καὶ περιεπάτει.

★ NOTE:

1. ἔγειραι* – AOR. MID., IMPER. 2ND. PER. SING. OF ἐγείρω.
2. ἆρον – AOR. ACT. IMPER. 2ND. PER. SING. OF αἴρω.
3. περιπάτει – PRES. ACT. IMPER., 2ND. PER. SING. OF περιπατέω.

---

* ἔγειρε – 2ND. PER. SING., PRES. ACT. IMPER. IN SOME TEXTS (E.G. NESTLE).

[CONT'D]

(274)

4. <u>ἐγένετο</u> — 2 AOR. MID. IND., 3 PER. SING. OF <u>γίνομαι</u>.

5. <u>περιεπάτει</u> — IMPERF. ACT. IND., 3 PER. SING. OF <u>περιπατέω</u>.

★ <u>NOTE</u>: TO ILLUSTRATE THE FACT THAT OFTEN "A SHARP DISTINCTION IS DRAWN BETWEEN THE AORIST AND OTHER TENSES IN THE SAME CONTEXT," PROF. A.T. ROBERTSON (RECOGNIZED IN ACADEMIC CIRCLES AS ONE OF THE GREATEST GREEK SCHOLARS) USED JOHN 5:8-9. ROBERTSON SAID, "WE SEE A LIKE DISTINCTION [I.E., BETWEEN <u>POINT</u> ACTION AND <u>CONTINUOUS</u> ACTION, T.B.W.] IN JOHN 5:8-9. JESUS SAID TO LAME MAN: 'ARISE, TAKE UP THY BED, AND WALK.' HE WAS TO TAKE UP HIS BED AT ONCE AS A SINGLE ACT (AORIST IMPERATIVE) AND TO GO ON WALKING (PRESENT IMPERATIVE, LINEAR ACTION). IN THE RESULT JOHN KEEPS THE SAME TENSES: 'HE TOOK UP HIS BED (AT ONCE, AORIST INDICATIVE) AND WENT ON WALK-

ING' (IMPERFECT INDICATIVE)." (275)
(A.T. ROBERTSON, THE MINISTER AND HIS GREEK NEW TESTAMENT, p. 94.)

★ NOTE: THIS PASSAGE (CF. MK. 2:9) AFFORDS AN IMPORTANT PARALLEL TO THE TENSE CHANGE IN MATT. 19:9.

★ CF. CHARTS: 268, 269, 270, 271, 274, 276.

★ IT IS CLEAR THAT THE TWO AORISTS DO NOT GOVERN THE PRESENT (SO AS TO NECESSITATE AN AORISTIC PRESENT—I.E., PUNCTILIAR RATHER THAN ITS PRIMARY AND USUAL SENSE OF LINEAR ACTION.

★ JUST SO, THE AORISTS IN MATT. 19:9 DO NOT GOVERN μοιχᾶται ("COMMITTETH ADULTERY")—IT CLEARLY MEANS "KEEPS ON COMMITTING ADULTERY."

MK. 2:9 — PUNCTILIAR & LINEAR ACTION

(276)

★ MK. 2:9: "WHICH IS EASIER, TO SAY TO THE SICK OF THE PALSY, 'THY SINS ARE FORGIVEN; OR TO SAY, ARISE, AND TAKE UP THY BED, AND WALK?

★ GREEK OF MK. 2:9: "...Ἔγειραι καὶ ἆρον σου τὸν κράβββατον, καὶ περιπάτει;"...

★ CRUCIAL WORDS:

1. Ἔγειραι — AOR. MID. IMPER. 2ND PER. SING. OF ἐγείρω. (This is point action, A single act.)
2. ἆρον — AOR. ACT. IMPER. 2ND PER. SING. OF αἴρω. (THIS IS POINT ACTION, A SINGLE ACT.)
3. περιπάτει — PRES. ACT. IMPER. 2ND. PER. SING. OF περιπατέω. (THIS IS LINEAR OR CONTINUOUS ACTION, I.E., "GO ON WALKING".)

★ IT IS CLEAR THAT THE TWO AORISTS DO NOT GOVERN THE PRESENT (SO AS TO NECESSITATE AN AORISTIC [PUNCT.] PRESENT RATHER ITS PRIMARY USAGE OF REFERRING TO LINEAR ACTION.

Conclusion

The material in this Appendix—along with material previously referred to in earlier chapters—proves (1) that fornication is the one and only ground for divorce and remarriage—for any man (whether Christian or non-Christian)—which is acceptable to God and (2) all men who teach otherwise teach false doctrine.

Footnotes

[1]These charts (approximately 300 of them) have been published under the title, *Charts You Can Use In Preaching, Teaching and Studying On Divorce And Remarriage*. (National Christian Press, P.O. Box 1001, Jonesboro, AK., 72401).

[2]It is hoped that the reader will obtain and study a set of the charts.

[3]Modus Ponens argument form:

(a) p>q (b) p (c) ∴q

APPENDIX B

I CORINTHIANS 5:1-13 SHOWS THAT BALES' POSITION ON I CORINTHIANS 7:10-15 IS FALSE

I Corinthians 5:1-13 proves that the position of James D. Bales on I Corinthians 7:10-15 is false. It is significant that this crucial passage (I Cor. 5:1-13) comes in the first Corinthian letter before I Corinthians 7:10-15. Any person reading I Corinthians 7:10-15, should have already read I Corinthians 5:1-13, and a careful, accurate exegesis of I Corinthians 5 will have already shown the reader of I Corinthians 7:10-15 that the doctrine based on I Corinthians 7:10-15 advanced by Bales is false.

In Appendix B, a number of things will be done in regard to the relationship which obtains between I Corinthians 5:1-13 and I Corinthians 7:10-15. These things will be divided into two main headings, with various matters subsumed under each heading.

First, some of the elements of the position set forth by brother Bales in regard to I Corinthians 7 will be set forth.[1] By this the author means that, in order for Bales to know that his position is true, there are certain things which he must know (not merely guess at), but which he cannot know to be true. This point alone is sufficient to show that his "argument" on I Corinthians 7 fails. Yet, as per the fourth point below, his entire case depends upon his exegesis of I Corinthians 7:10-15. Thus, his entire case fails on this point alone.

Second, some things which are clearly taught in I Corinthians 5 which are crucial to the case will be set out and discussed.

Third, some things which no one can know in regard to I Corinthians 5:1-13 will be discussed.

Fourth, it will be shown that I Corinthians 5 destroys the effort of some to use I Corinthians 7 to prove that God will accept some ground other than fornication for divorce and remarriage.

Fifth, information will be set forth which should be helpful to every reader in understanding the force of I Corinthians 5 against the doctrine of Bales on divorce and remarriage.

I. *Various elements of the position held by brother Bales on I Corinthians 7:10-15.*

1. *He holds that I Corinthians 7:10-11 applies only to Christians who are married to Christians.* He claims to have learned this from I Cor. 7:10-15 and that having learned this enabled him to also learn that Matthew 19:9 applies only to Christians who are married to Christians. As pointed out in preceding material,[2] Bales tries to establish this position by claiming (a) that the law (gospel) of Christ simply

does not apply to any non-Christian; the New Covenant, Bales claims, can be obeyed only by those who are "in" the covenant (i.e., only those who are already Christians can obey the New Covenant) and (b) that I Corinthians 7:10-13 makes clear that non-Christians are not under (amenable to) Matthew 19:9. This contention is patently absurd.

Chapter X proved that point (a) above is false, and the arguments set out in Chapters XVII and XVIII show that Bales' position on Matthew 19:9 and I Corinthians 7:10-15 involves both the implication of a false doctrine and the implication of a logical contradiction. Both of these (or either one separately) proves Bales' position on Matthew 19:9 and I Corinthians 7:10-15 to be false and, thus, that his "argument" does not prove his conclusion.

Also, as was discussed in a preceding chapter,[3] Bales, in failing to understand the force of an "exceptive sentence,"[4] thinks that even though Jesus, in Matthew 19:9, said ". . .except for fornication. . ." thinks that Paul, in I Corinthians 7, can give an additional—i.e., one other than fornication—ground for divorce and remarriage. This position implies that the Bible contradicts itself by contending "except" does not really mean "except." Bales seems not to make this mistake on any subject except that of divorce and remarriage. For example, in explaining John 3:3-5, he said, "Jesus said one must be born of water and the Spirit in order to enter the kingdom. He drew the line and said unless one had experienced the new birth he was not in the kingdom. We did not draw the line and we cannot erase it."[5] Thus, it is clear that Bales clearly understood the force of the fact that John 3:5 is an exceptive sentence.[6] Bales knows as well as anyone that he would not accept the "argument" of a Baptist preacher on John 3:5 which parallels his (Bales') argument on Matt. 19:9. If the Baptist preacher said, "I know that John 3:5 says, 'Except a man be born of water and of the Spirit, he cannot enter into the kingdom of God,' and I admit that, just looking at John 3:5 alone, it would appear that the one and the only door into the kingdom is that of being baptized, but you must remember that (in harmony with John 16:12-15—that more things would be revealed to them) Paul, in Romans 5:1 made clear that there is another door—and who knows how many other doors may be revealed in other passages—into the kingdom, namely, that of faith (before and without being baptized in water, cf.: Acts 10:43; 13:39; 16:31; John 5:24; 3:16; et al.)." Of course, Bales no doubt could and would say quite a few things in response to this effort by a Baptist, but one thing he would surely do is explain the power of the exceptive statement which is John 3:5. It means that there is one—and only one—door into the kingdom and no other passage can show otherwise—or else the Bible contradicts itself (which, of course, it does not!). If Bales would only use the same reasoning on Matthew 19:9 which he does on John 3:5, he would know that from Matthew 19:9 alone—before ever even reading I Corinthians 7:10-15—that, given the force of the exceptive sentence in Matthew 19:9, neither I Corinthians 7 nor any other passage could give any ground for divorce and remarriage other than that of fornication!

2. *He holds that Matthew 19:9 and I Corinthians 7:10-11 are, in effect, identical passages (i.e., they refer to the same statement by the Lord).* This has already been discussed in detail and needs nothing further here. It is simply false; Bales has no evidence for drawing such a conclusion.

3. *He holds that Matthew 19:9 (as does I Corinthians 7:10-11) applies only to Christians who are married to Christians and that I Corinthians 7:12-13 applies only to Christians who are married to non-Christians.* He argues from these positions to the conclusion that Matthew 19:9 and I Corinthians 7:10-11 apply only to Christians married to Christians. This has already been shown, in Chapters XVII and XVIII, to be false, so it needs no further discussion here, but more will be given later.[7]

4. *He holds that the law (gospel) of Christ does not legislate for non-Christians—that one must be "in" the New Covenant before he is under (amenable to) it.* Again, this error has already been set out and refuted in preceding material in Chapters XVII and XVIII and needs no further discussion here. His "Neo-Fuquaism" shows through at this point.

5. *He holds that no one who has entered a marriage before being baptized is required (by the Lord) to sever (get out of) that marriage after being baptized.* And this is the case no matter how flagrantly that marriage may violate the teaching of Matthew 19:9. Yet, he claims that men in polygamous marriages must get out of those marriages after being baptized into Christ!

6. *He holds that genuine repentance does not demand the severance of an existing (that is, before and/or at the time of those involved being baptized) relationship even if that relationship violates plain teaching of the New Testament.* He faces a real dilemma here: either (a) he must admit that following baptism those who were Baptists may continue as members of the Baptist Church or (b) he must give up his position on divorce and remarriage. The prediction of this author is—based on some of Bales' statements—that he will try to invent a "new realm" and hold that denominationalism comes in between the world and the church but is in neither. If he does this, he will be only the

second gospel preacher I have known of who has taken this position—the other being brother E. C. Fuqua. This author prays that he will simply give up his erroneous doctrine on divorce and remarriage. He will then be out of the dilemma which now faces him.

7. *He implies (by rhetorical questions) that in a case of fornication in a marriage between two Christians, one of them may deliberately commit fornication for the express purpose of having a ground for divorce and remarriage and, then, be just as free to marry again as the innocent party would be.*[8]

Again, this has already been refuted in previous chapters.

II. *How I Corinthians 5:1-13 refutes the position of Bales on I Corinthians 7:10-15.*

1. *Some things which are taught in I Corinthians 5:1-13.*

(1) I Corinthians 5:1-13 makes clear that it is possible for a Christian to have entered a marriage before he (she) was baptized and yet be required by God to get out (sever himself from) that marriage.

(2) I Corinthians 5:1-13 makes clear that if a Christian is involved in such a marriage, either (a) he must repent of and get out of that marriage or (b) the congregation of which he is a member must withdraw fellowship from him (I Cor. 5:5-7;13).

(3) I Corinthians 5:1-13 makes clear that in such a case, the local congregation (of which the person(s) involved are members) will be regarded by the Lord as being unfaithful, if in the face of the impenitence and lack of reformation of life (severing the marriage) by the offending party, it (the congregation) fails to carry out the action of disfellowship.

Note carefully: this passage makes clear that to be involved (as a partner) in an unscriptural marriage (one which violates the teaching of the law of Christ—Matthew 19:9 in particular) is to be involved in adultery and die impenitent of it is to be lost in Hell (Revelation 21:8; 2:14; 2:20; Galatians 5:19-21; I Corinthians 6:9-11.) All who treat unscriptural marriages as a trivial matter endanger both their own souls and the souls of those who listen to them. (Cf. Balaam, Revelation 2:14, and Jezebel, Rev. 2:20).

2. *In regard to I Corinthians 5:1-13, there are some things which no man can know.*

(1) *No man can know that the passage teaches that the man in question was not legally married to the woman in question.* The passage says, ". . .one of you hath his father's wife." Ordinarily, when the New Testament says of a man that he "has" (Greek, *echein*) a woman, it means that he is married to her. Some scholars have even claimed that it always means married but John 4:18 seems to refute this position.[9]

It is this author's view that the evidence set

out in I Cor. 5:1-13 warrants the conclusion that the man and woman were legally married. An article by brother G. C. Brewer in the *Gospel Advocate*,[10] makes this matter clear. In that article, brother Brewer said, "That this man had married the woman and had not merely been guilty of a single sinful act with her is shown by the expression *'hath his father's wife.'* He had her or was living with her. That the father, husband of the woman, was still living is shown by reference to him 'who suffered the wrong.' (II Corinthians 7:12). In fact, it would not have been *fornication* had the woman been a widow and the man unmarried. It would have been no sin in that case for him to *have* her—that is, to marry her. But the commentaries tell us that the Gentiles—the pagans—considered such a marriage dishonorable even when the father was dead. An inspired apostle, however, would not evaluate a deed according to the pagan sentiment and tradition. When a deed was sinful according to God's law, it was no uncommon thing for Paul to point out the egregiousness of it by showing that even the heathen reprobate it. He did that in this case, but he first condemned it as fornication. *The fact that some of these Christians sought to justify the man in this sin would indicate that he was married to the woman and was not merely cohabiting with her. It is unthinkable that even these Corinthian Christians would seek to excuse such a connection without some pretense of marriage* (emphasis, T.B.W.)."

Brother Brewer goes on, in the same article, to present what he regards as proof that the Corinthian Christians were trying to justify this sin. Among the reasons Brewer cites are: (a) the fact that the Corinthians were not mourning over this sin (I Cor. 5:2), (b) the fact that it is clear that the erring brother had misled some of the brethren and had persuaded them to accept him and his situation, (c) it seems, Brewer says, that the false teacher and those who had been persuaded by him were "broad" and "liberal"—they decided things by their own reason and not by revelation (perhaps by a "law in the heart?") and (d) that some might even have argued (as does Bales in holding that both parties in a case of marital infidelity are free to marry again) that "the act of fornication on the part of the woman undid her marriage to the father, and that the marriage having now been dissolved, she was free to marry her lover!"[11]

The fact the brethren at Corinth were "puffed up" (were arrogant, full of pride) about the matter of the erring brother and the fact that they were not "mourning" over his sin is proof that they were (on some basis) attempting to justify the erring brother and the situation in which he was involved. As brother Brewer points out, this shows that the man was legally married to his father's wife and not merely cohabiting with her. As brother Brewer further said, "It is unthinkable that even these Corinthian Christians would seek to excuse such a connection without some pretense of marriage." It is obvious that the Corinthian Christians—like brother Bales is now doing, no doubt in all good conscience—were trying to justify a marriage which violated Matt. 19:9. But Paul, guided by the Holy Spirit, would have none of that.

Likely, brother Bales will deny that we can know that the two were legally married (he must in order to have even a "ghost" of being able to prove his doctrine). But even if, counterfactually, he should be successful in establishing such a denial, that success will do him no good in proving his position. This is the case because even the possibility that they were legally married (in connection with other matters discussed above) proves that Bales' position is false.

The reader should note carefully (a) that Paul demands that the man and woman cease their cohabitation, and (b) that Paul demands of the church at Corinth that it withdraw fellowship from the man if he does not repent and get out of this sinful situation. The Christians at Corinth should have been shocked at their brother's conduct, but, at first at least, they were not.

Since the evidence is that the two were actually married to each other, (while even the possibility that such was the case is sufficient), on what ground(s) did Paul demand the separation? (This is an extremely important question, because—given Bales' view—if the two were actually married, Paul would have had no ground(s) upon which to demand either (a) that the two separate or (b) that the church disfellowship them if they did not separate!)

In order for Bales to argue that Paul was right in demanding their separation (and disfellowship if they did not), he (Bales) would have to know that the two were not married! And, this he cannot know! In order to emphasize the cruciality of this point in seeing that Bales' case simply cannot be established, the following question is raised. Which of the following passages was the basis on which the separation and/or disfellowship demanded in I Corinthians 5: (a) Matthew 19:9___? (b) I Cor. 7:10-11___? (c) I Cor. 7:12-13___? (d) I Cor. 7:14-16___? (e) I Cor. 7:39___? (f) Rom. 7:1-3___? (g) Mark 10:2-12___? (h) Luke 16:18___? (i) Some other___?

Obviously, given Bales' doctrine, if the two were married then Bales can use none of the above passages as that basis. (Remember, he holds that according to Matthew 19:9—which applies to marriage between two Christians only, as per his view—the guilty party as well as the innocent party is free (with God's approval) to remarry!)

Only when Bales (a) accepts the truth that Matthew 19:9 is addressed to all persons living today and (b) renounces his false views of Matt. 19:9 and I Cor. 7:10-16 can he, too, see the basis upon which this separation was demanded if the couple was married.

Since Bales cannot know that the two were not married, then he cannot know that his view of Matt. 19:9 and I Cor. 7:10-16 is true. If he cannot know that his view of Matthew 19:9 and I Corinthians 7:10-16 is true, then he cannot know that his doctrine on divorce and remarriage is true.

All readers are reminded of the fact that the Corinthian brethren would have already read I Corinthians 5 and I Corinthians 6:9-11 (which see) before they came to the information set out in I Corinthians 7. Therefore, surely even Bales must admit that in his efforts to properly interpret I Corinthians 7, he should take into account the case described in I Corinthians 5. Bales tried to prove his case "too soon" (as he accuses others of doing).

A burning question arises: if Bales were to write a proposition setting forth (as per his view) exactly what would have to be the constituent elements of the total situation of a man and woman who are legally married to each other, to be required by the Scriptures to separate or be lost? Does Bales say, as some have, that all legal marriages may be continued in without further sin?

(2) *No man can know whether the woman involved was a Christian at the time Paul wrote I Corinthians 5.* The passage does not explicitly say whether she was or was not a Christian. Jimmy Allen holds that she may not have been a Christian, for he says, "The woman was probably not a member of the church since no judgment was passed on her (5:12)."[12] If someone were to try to prove that the woman was not a Christian by calling attention to the fact that no punishment for her was noted in the passage, the obvious reply is: (a) the passage does not say she was not punished—information on the matter is simply not given and (b) it must be recalled that (according to Numbers 12) even though both Aaron and Miriam spake against Moses, punishment for Miriam is described but not for Aaron. So, she may or may not have been a Christian.[13]

Since the Bible clearly teaches that the man in this sinful situation was a Christian, if they were legally married (and the evidence shows that they were), then if the woman involved was not a Christian, then—given Bales' position—neither Matt. 19:9 nor I Corinthians 7:10-11 would apply to them, but I Cor. 7:12-13 would. But, if the woman was not a Christian (an "unbeliever") and the two were legally married and the woman was content to dwell with the man, then—given Bales' position—the Christian (the man) should not depart from the non-Christian (the woman). In which case, Paul would have been wrong to demand that they separate. On the other hand, if the woman was a Christian, then—given Bales' position—both Matt. 19:9 and I Cor. 7:10-11 would apply (since it would be a case of a Christian married to a Christian). But, since (a) there is no indication that either of the two was being unfaithful to the other and (b) Bales holds that in a case of fornication, the guilty party is as free to marry again as is the innocent party, even if both the man's father and the father's wife were Christians and if she committed fornication (which she did), then—given Bales' doctrine—if the two would only say "I'm sorry," then they could remain together. But Paul demanded that they separate!

Thus, there is no way Bales can make his unscriptural doctrine fit with that of the Holy Spirit in I Corinthians 5:1-13. This proves that Bales is wrong on I Corinthians 7:10-15 and Matthew 19:9 in particular and his doctrine on divorce and remarriage in general. Bales' doctrine is false.

(3) *No man can know that God accepted a "non-ideal" situation which violated his will.* Again, Jimmy Allen makes an important admission when he says, "They (the Corinthian brethren, T.B.W.) were so broad-minded (they came from a moral background which was the lowest in the then known world), they were not shocked by the sin."[14] (It seems that even today there are some members of the church who are no more shocked by violations of Christ's law on divorce and remarriage (Matt. 19:9) than were the Corinthians!)

But, let it be noted: *men can know that God (1) did not accept this immoral situation, and (2) demanded that the congregation do something about it!* How many congregations of today will do anything about violations of Matthew 19:9?

(4) *No man can know that if they were married that they were married before they were baptized.* But since this passage demands severance of the relationship, Bales must know that if they were married, they were married after they were baptized. But this he cannot know, so *he cannot know that his position on Matthew 19:9 and I Corinthians 7:10-15 is true.*

To sum up the matter, it should be noted: (1) that this author has proved Bales' position to be false, and (2) that Bales cannot prove that his position is true.

(5) *No man can know that, if the woman was also a Christian, whether they were married before or after they were baptized.* The passage simply does not give this information. Yet, Bales' doctrine demands knowledge of such.

To sum up the matter, it should be noted: (1) that to sustain his position on I Corinthians 7:10-15 (that it gives grounds other than fornication for divorce and remarriage) Bales would have to know all of the above points-that is, he would have to know what was the case in regard to each point.[15] Thus, Bales' case falls on this point alone.

An important question is: just what would a Christian have to do today to cause some churches to disfellowship them because of divorce and remarriage?

3. *Since the church at Corinth was instructed to disfellowship this man if he did not repent of his relationship with this woman, if he was married to her (and, as has been shown, he was) which passage would brother Bales hold is the passage which would be the basis of that disfellowship.*

This author says that, if they were married, Matthew 19:9 is sufficient to cover every case of fornication (illicit sexual activity).

Given the true position, the matter is easily settled. But, given Bales' position, it can be only doctrinal chaos. Obviously, Matthew 19:9 would be sufficient but, given Bales' position, what passage is there which would be sufficient to settle the situation described in I Corinthians 5:1-13?

4. *Brief explanation of Chart no. 212.*

The main purpose of this chart is to set out, in a graphic way, the fact that Bales, in order to sustain his position on I Corinthians 7:10-15, (a) must know the details of the situation partially described in I Corinthians 5:1-13 and (b) must be able to give proof of his contentions. But, this he cannot do!

(1) *Explanation of the chart.* In the chart, the "M" stands for the man in the illicit relationship, and "W" stands for the woman. "∿B" stands for "unbeliever" (non-Christian) and "B" stands for "believer" (Christian). On the left side of the chart, we show both the man and woman as non-Christians, but in such a case, we do not know whether they were married at that time or not (we know that it is possible that they were married before either one of them was baptized or after one of them was baptized or after both of them were baptized—if, indeed, the woman was ever baptized).

Note carefully the following: (1) if they were married before either one of them became a Christian, then Bales is obviously wrong on his Matthew 19:9—I Corinthians 7:10-15 doctrine because he claims that Matt. 19:9 does not apply to non-Christians. (2) If they were married before either one of them was baptized and then the man was baptized, then Bales is wrong on his Matthew 19:9—I Corinthians 7:10-15 doctrine (because he has no passage in his theology which would demand a separation in such a case.) (3) If the man was baptized—but not the woman—before they were

I COR. 5— WHAT MUST THEY KNOW ABOUT IT? (212)

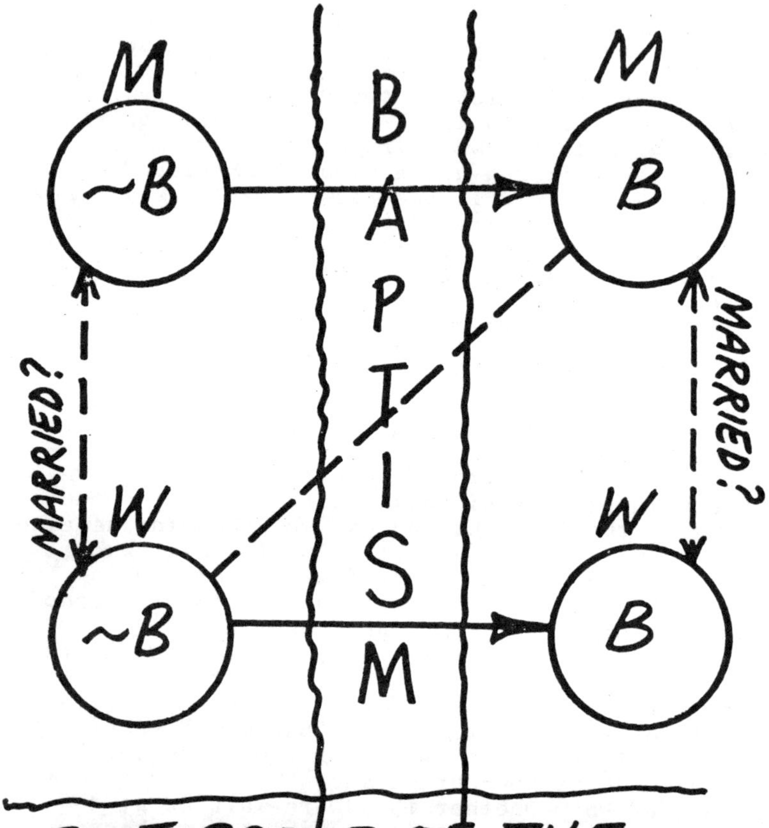

GIVE PROOF OF THE WAY IT WAS!

THEY MUST (TO SUSTAIN THEIR THEORY) BUT THEY CANNOT!!

married, then Bales' position on Matthew 19:9-I Corinthians 7:10-15 is wrong, because he has no passage in his doctrine which would demand the separation which Paul demands in I Corinthians 5:1-13. (4) If they were both baptized before they were married but after their being baptized, they married, then Bales would have no passage to demand a separation, because he holds that the guilty party is as free to remarry as is the innocent party (Matthew 19:9 would then apply, according to Bales, but his "guilty party is free" theory would ruin him here.)

It seems that brethren "jump" all the way from Matthew 19:9 to I Corinthians 7:10-15 and pay no attention to the very crucial statements which comprise I Corinthians 5:1-13. This constitutes rather unfortunate overlooking.

All should remember: according to I Corinthians 5:1-13 God demanded that a church disfellowship at least one of its members who was involved in illicit sexual relations. Matthew 19:9 explains why. I Corinthians 7:10-15 does not. Let that truth be implanted in the hearts of all. Thus, I Corinthians 5:1-13 constitutes a fatal blow to Bales' effort to establish his case for the doctrine that Matthew 19:9 applies only to Christians who are married to Christians. Brother Bales should recognize this and give up his efforts to justify marriages which are sinful in the sight of God.

Bales tries to avoid the problem set out above by claiming that Paul condemned the son's having his father's wife because it was a case of incest. But it is not incest for a man to marry his brother's widow.[16] Evidently, there is a great difference in marrying the widow of one's blood relative and marrying one's blood relative.

Further, the passage which Bales uses in an effort to pass this case off simply as incest (in order to have some explanation for Paul's condemnation of the situation) simply will not do.[17] This passage evidently refers to cases in which it is simply a matter of fornication. Otherwise, there would be a contradiction between Deuteronomy 25:5-10 and Leviticus 18:16; 20:21.

Next, to avoid self-contradiction Bales must know that neither the father nor his wife had been guilty of fornication (marital infidelity) while they were living together. Otherwise, given Bales' doctrine that when, in a marriage between two Christians, either one of them is guilty of fornication and is put away, the marriage bond is broken and both parties (the guilty as well as the innocent) are free to marry! But Bales has no way of knowing this; the Bible simply does not say explicitly whether such was or was not the case.

But, if the Bible teaches either (a) that the

erring brother (who "had" his father's wife) was legally married to the woman or (b) that it is even possible that he was legally married to her, then Bales—given his doctrine on divorce and remarriage—cannot give a sensible explanation as to why Paul condemned the son and demanded that he be disfellowshipped by the church in Corinth.

Of course, if one recognizes the truth that the gospel of Christ is addressed to all men (Mark 16:15; Acts 17:30-31, et al.), including the fact that Matthew 19:9 is addressed to all—not to Christians only (as Bales contends)—then I Corinthians 5:1-13 is easily understood and explained.

Footnotes

[1]This has already been done in Chapter XVII and XVIII, but it seemed good to repeat these elements here for ready reference.

[2]The false positions and logical contradictions involved in such a position have already been exposed in Chapters XVI, XVII and XVIII. That material need not be repeated here.

[3]Chapter XIII.

[4]See this also discussed in Appendix A.

[5]*WCAC?*, p. 56.

[6]See Charts 69-83 (on the force of an "exceptive" sentence) in Appendix A.

[7]However, some additional discussion will be found in Appendix C, on I Corinthians 7:10-15.

[8]See A.C.U. lecture, 1961.

[9]Jimmy Allen, a holder of Bales' doctrine on divorce and remarriage, said, "It is impossible to tell if the brother and woman were legally married or simply living together." *Survey of I Corinthians*, p. 64. Thus, he holds that, for all he knows, the two were married to each other. The importance of this possibility is crucial.

[10]G. C. Brewer, "The Corinthian Case," *Gospel Adovcate*, December 4, 1961, p. 1158.

[11]Ibid, p. 1159.

[12]*Survey of I Corinthians*, p. 64.

[13]Note: it cannot be known if the erring brother's father (whose wife he had) was a Christian. If he were not, then (as per Bales' view) Matthew 19:9 would not even apply to the erring brother's father and his wife.

[14]*Survey of I Corinthians,* p. 65.

[15]Cf.: *Warren-Flew Debate* in which it was proved that atheists cannot know what they must know in order to be truly atheists.

[16]See Deut. 25:5-10; Matt. 22:23-33; Mk. 12:18-27; Lk. 20:27-40.

[17]Lev. 18:7; cf.: 18:16; 20:21; Lk. 20:27-40.

APPENDIX C

I CORINTHIANS 7:10-15

1. *Some Introductory Matters*

(1) *What has been done in preceding material.* Since so much has already been said by way of explaining this passage, and since what has been said destroys the case which Bales seeks to build on it, some consideration was given to not having an appendix on this passage.

First, in Chapters XIV, XV, XVI-A, XVI-B, XVII, and XVIII it was clearly shown that Bales' effort to harmonize Matthew 19:9 and I Corinthians 7:10-15 results in doctrinal chaos.

Second, In Appendix B, it was shown in quite some detail, that, given I Corinthians 5:1-13, Bales' doctrine on divorce and remarriage simply cannot be established. It was shown that the view upheld in this book (that Matthew 19:9 applies to all persons—not only to Christians married to Christians—as Bales affirms) is the only one which clearly fits with the facts in the chapter—i.e., there is nothing in the chapter (I Cor. 5) which is not in harmony with "Proposition TBW," regardless of whether the couple was married or not married.

(2) *What will be done in this Appendix?* The following will be done in the remainder of Appendix C: (a) Bales' view of I Corinthians 7:10-15 will be set forth briefly[1] and (b) the true view of I Corinthians 7:10-15 will be set forth.

2. *Bales' view of I Corinthians 7:1-15.*

(1) The bare facts of Bales' view of the various sections of I Corinthians 7:

(a) Matthew 19:9 and I Corinthians 7:10-11 apply to exactly one and the same "category" of marriage (i.e., both passages apply only to Christians who are married to Christians).

(b) The details of the legislation to that category (referred to in (a) above) are:

{1} The wife is not to depart—but if she should depart, she must remain unmarried.

{2} The husband is not to depart. Bales' alleges that only Christ—not Paul—gave the details of this legislation. (Bales is wrong here; Paul made clear {in referring to himself} that "I give charge. . . . .") Thus, both Paul and Christ gave this legislation.

(c) Bales affirms that I Corinthians 7:12-13 applies to a different category of marriage; viz., that of a Christian married to a non-Christian. He goes on:

{1} Paul said it—but Christ did not. (Bales alleges that Christ did not legislate on the marriage of a Christian to a non-Christian—but he is wrong because Matthew 19:9 covers such marriages.)

{2} If a non-Christian wife is content to dwell with her Christian husband, then the Christian man should not depart.

{3} If non-Christian man is content to dwell with his Christian wife, then the Christian woman should not depart.

(d) On I Corinthians 7:15 Bales alleges that if a non-Christian spouse should depart, then the deserted Christian spouse is free to marry someone else upon the ground of the desertion alone—i.e., even if the departed non-Christian has not been (and is not at any future time) guilty of fornication.

(2) *How Bales "argues" for this view.* In a preceding chapter, it was pointed out that in responding to a challenge put to him (by this author) to write out the premises of a sound argument (a valid argument with all premises true), the conclusion of which is: "Therefore, Matthew 19:9, is a 'covenant passage'—i.e., it applies only to Christians who are married to Christians and to no one else (not even to other Christians)," Bales responded by setting out an invalid (and, therefore, unsound—proving nothing) argument.[2]

It will be recalled that in Chapters X, XI, and XII, this author presented a sound argument which proves "Proposition TBW" (including the point that Matthew 19:9 is addressed to all men, both in and out of the church) is true.

(3) *Another argument against Bales' doctrine.* In addition to the arguments which have already been given in refutation of Bales' doctrine, here is another:

(a) If Ⓐ Matthew 19:9 and I Corinthians 7:10-11 refer to one and the same thing, and Ⓑ if I Corinthians 7:10-11 refers to "the married" (and, therefore, to all married people), then (given Bales' contention at Ⓐ and the truth which is set out at Ⓑ, Ⓒ Matthew 19:9 refers to (is addressed to) all people (both Christian and non-Christian).

(b) A (Bales affirms this proposition.)

(c) B (This proposition is obviously true, Paul says "to the married"—7:10-11.)

(d) A·B (b), (c), Conjunction. (If each proposition separately is true, then the conjunction of the two is true.)

(e) ∴C (a), (d), M.P. (Modus Ponens form argument which is valid. The truthfulness of the compound Proposition A and B demands that proposition C is also true.)

So the basic doctrine of Bales re Matthew 19:9 and I Corinthians 7:10-11 referring to exactly the same thing, along with the truth that "the married" refers to all married people, demands the conclusion that Matthew 19:9 refers to (in addressed to) all people (both Christian and non-Christian).

3. *The truth on I Corinthians 7:10-15 and Matthew 19:9.*[3]

(1) *The general law on all marriage (Matt. 19:6).* Jesus said, "So that they are no more two, but one flesh. What therefore God hath joined together let not man put asunder." (Matthew 19:6). From this general context (19:4-6), it should be noted that Jesus sets forth an argument. That argument, set out in precise logical (modus ponens) form is:

(a) If Ⓐ in the beginning God made a male and a female, and if Ⓑ the relation to one's father and/or mother can be dissolved only by death, and if Ⓒ the relation between husband and wife is even more intimate (close) than that of parent and child, then Ⓓ the obligations of marriage are as binding—and even more so—than those of parent and child.[4]

(b) Proposition A is true (Matthew 19:4).

(c) Proposition B is true (implied by Matthew 19:5).

(d) Proposition C is true (Matthew 19:5).

(e) A and B and C are all true (conjunction from (b), (c) and (d)).

(f) Therefore, Proposition D is true (by modus ponens, from premises (a) and (e).)

The second argument can be set out as follows:

(a) If Ⓓ the obligations of marriage are as binding—and even more so—than those of parent and child, and if Ⓔ husband and wife are one flesh, and if Ⓕ the one flesh relation is to be severed only by the hand of death (which "dissolves the body itself"[5]), then Ⓖ what God has joined together (any marriage of two people who are eligible in God's sight to be married to each other) no man is to put asunder.

Proposition G, then, is the conclusion which is necessitated by the two arguments which are involved in Jesus' statements in Matthew 19:4-6. Thus, God's *general law of marriage* is stated in Matthew 19:6—not in Matthew 19:9, as many have erroneously concluded.[6]

Thus, *God's general law of marriage* is: "what God has joined together let not man put asunder." McGarvey added, "Of course, God who joined together may put them asunder by prescribing the conditions of lawful divorce, but man has nothing to do in the case except to obey God's law."[7]

(2) *Matthew 19:9 is an application of God's general law to a specific situation.* In stating the general law (which applies to all marriages—whether of Christians or of non-Christians), Jesus did not give the details as to what was to be (or could be) done in case one of the parties was guilty of fornication (marital unfaithfulness). Matthew 19:9 is just as universal as is Matthew 19:6, and it makes clear that,

according to the law of Christ, there is one—and only one—ground for divorce and remarriage: viz., that of fornication.

(3) *In I Corinthians 7, Paul does the following:*[8]

(a) He makes reference to God's general law on marriage; he says, "But unto the married I give charge, yea not I, but the Lord. . ." (Cf. I Cor. 7:10-11 and Matt. 19:6 both state God's general law of marriage.) (Note: Paul and the Lord both make this charge. Where did the Lord make it? The record of it is in Matthew 19:6).

(b) Paul makes application of the general law (Matt. 19:6; I Cor. 7:10-11) to three situations about which the Corinthians had asked and to which the Lord had made no specific reference.[9]

The author, in basic agreement with the material stated therein, urges the reader to study carefully the material on I Corinthians 7 in *Marriage, Divorce and Remarriage,* by Roy Deaver.

Conclusion

In regard to I Corinthians 7:10-15, it has been shown (in this appendix, in preceding chapters, in Appendix A, and in Apprendix B):

(1) That Bales' doctrine on Matthew 19:9 and I Corinthians 7:10-15 involves doctrinal chaos.

(2) That I Corinthians 5:1-13 shows that Bales' doctrine on I Corinthians 7 is simply untenable.

(3) What the general law of marriage is (Matt. 19:6; I Cor. 7:10-11).

(4) What is involved in the application of the general law (I Cor. 7:12-15).

Special Argument on "the Rest" in I Corinthians 7:12[10]

The following argument shows that Bales' argument on I Corinthians 7 and Matthew 19 is false.

1. If Ⓐ Bales' doctrine on divorce and remarriage is true, then Ⓑ the expression "the rest" in I Corinthians 7:2 must have a meaning which excludes some marriages from the denotation of the expression "the married" in I Corinthians 7:10 and Ⓒ only Christians who are married to Christians are amenable to I Corinthians 7:10-11 (and Matthew 19:9).

1. $A > (B \cdot C)$

2. It is false that Ⓑ the expression "the rest" in I Corinthians 7:12 must have a meaning which excludes some marriages from the denotation of the expression "the married" in I Corinthians 7:10.

Proposition B is false not only because there is another plausible explanation of the meaning of the term "the rest" but because the total context (which includes both the immediate and remote contexts) but also because the simple truth of the matter is that I Cor. 7:10-11 (in referring to "the married" is addressed to all married people: Christians married to Christians, Christians married to non-Christians, and non-Christians married to non-Christians.) All married people are instructed not to depart from their companions. I Cor. 7:10-11 sets out (as does Matthew 19:6) God's general marriage law and I Cor. 7:12-15 (as does Matt. 19:9) sets out application to some specific cases which are sub-sumed under that general law (which is universal—that is, it is addressed to all men).

3. Since Proposition B is false and every conjunctive proposition which has even one false conjunct is false, it follows that the conjunction Proposition B and Proposition C is also false. $\sim B > \sim (B \cdot C)$

4. Therefore, since every implicative statement (such as Premise 1 in this argument) which has a false consequent (that which follows the "then"—in this case Proposition B and Proposition C) is itself false, then it follows that Proposition A is false. $\{A > (B \cdot C) \cdot \sim (B \cdot C) > \sim A\}$

The entire argument, set out in symbolic terms looks like this:

1.	$A > (B \cdot C)$	Obvious
2.	$\sim B$	I Cor. 7:10-11: "the married" refers to all married people.
3.	$\sim (B \cdot C)$	Rule of conjunction.
4.	$\therefore \sim A$	1,3, Modus Tollens

Since, in the argument above, A (Proposition A) stands for "Bales doctrine on divorce and remarriage is true" and since "$\sim A$" means "it is false that Proposition A is true," it is clear that the conclusion of the above argument is: "Therefore, the doctrine of Bales on divorce and remarriage is false."

When one recognizes that "the rest" (of 7:12) refers to "the rest of the questions which had been asked by the Corinthian brethren", the passage is easily understood. This view of the meaning of "the rest" fits with the fact that Paul discussed in I Cor. 7:10-11 the general law of marriage (in the law of Christ, cf.: Matt. 19:6) and in I Cor. 7:12-15 three applications of that general law to specific situations (note Matt. 19:6 for the situation involving marital unfaithfulness {fornication}). This meaning of "the rest"—in contrast to the position affirmed by Bales—(a) involves no doctrinal chaos on Matt. 19:9 and I Cor. 7:10-15 and (b) is explained in harmony with all other positions affirmed on the entire subject. To establish his case, Bales must know that his explanation is the true one, but this he cannot do.

Some Charts on this Matter

Bales' exegesis of I Corinthians 7:10-15 is set out in a graphic way by the following chart:

I Cor. 7:10-11	I Cor. 7:12-15	No Scripture*
(C) married (C) Bales holds that I Cor. 7:10-11 is a "covenant passage"—i.e., it teaches only in regard to a Christian married to a Christian. Bales holds that Matt. 19:9 is also a "covenant passage."	(C) married (~C) Bales holds that the expression "the rest" proves that "mixed marriages" are not to be subsumed under "the married" of I Cor. 7:10-11. He holds that such marriages are not amenable to the strictures of Matt. 19:9	(C) married (~C) (~C) married (~C) Bales holds that no New Testament scripture is addressed to the non-Christian.
*Bales holds that the law of Christ does not legislate for the non-Christian (*NUB*, p. 9, passim).		

The truth (as per New Testament teaching) is set out in the following chart (see page 226):

God's general law of marriage—stated in Matthew 19:6 and I Corinthians 7:10-11. This general law is addressed to all men (Mk. 16:15-16; Matt. 28:18-20; Acts 17:30-31; Matt. 19:9 {"Whosoever. . ."}, et al.). Therefore, all men are amenable to this general law.

It Covers ALL Marriages

(C) married (C)	(C) married (~C)	(~C) married (~C)
Christian married to Christian	Christian married to Non-Christian	Non-Christian married to Non-Christian

Applications of this General Law to Specific Situations I Cor. 7:12-15

H (C) married W (~C)	W (C) married H (~C)	(C) married (~C)
Christian husband married to non-Christian. If non-Christian is content to dwell with him then Christian is not to leave her.	Christian wife married to non-Christian. If non-Christian is content to dwell with her, then Christian is not to leave him.	If non-Christian is threatening to depart (the Christian will not give up faith), then the Christian to let him (her) depart. The Christian has never been in such bondage as to demand such in order to preserve his (her) marriage.

Application of this General Law to Cases In which Marital Unfaithfulness has occurred Matt. 19:9

(C) married (C)	(C) married (~C)	(~C) married (~C)

In any case in which an innocent party puts away his (her) companion for fornication, the innocent party is free to marry another—but, the guilty party is not.

As noted in preceding material, in order to establish his case brother Bales must know what he cannot know. For example, (1) he cannot know that I Cor. 7:10-11 does not refer to all married people—rather than, as Bales contends, only to Christians married to Christians, (2) he cannot know that I Cor. 7:10-11 is simply a repetition of Matt. 19:9—i.e., that Paul is saying, in I Cor. 7:10-11, what Jesus said in Matt. 19:9, (3) he cannot know that Matthew 19:6 and I Corinthians 7:10-11 are not statements of God's general marriage law, (4) he cannot know that I Cor. 7:12-15 does not refer to some specific applications of God's general marriage law, (5) he cannot know that Matt. 19:9 is not a specific application of that general marriage law, (6) he cannot know that I Cor. 7:10-15 sets out a modification of Matt. 19:9—in the sense of providing for any person, grounds for divorce and remarriage other than that of fornication, (7) he cannot know that Matt. 19:9 does not set out legislation which applies to every "real" marriage, (8) he cannot know that the "bondage" of I Cor. 7:15 refers to the marriage bond (see more on this in Appendix D), and (9) he cannot know that I Cor. 7:15 gives any one the right to divorce and remarry on the ground of desertion alone.

But it is possible for brother Bales to know—if only he will properly gather the Biblical evidence and reason about that evidence correctly—(1) that the gospel is addressed to all men (Mk. 16:15-16), (2) that all men are, therefore, amenable to the gospel (Rom. 3:19), (3) that Matt. 19:9 is a part of the gospel (obvious from Matt. 19:9; 28:18-20; Mk. 16:15-16), (4) that Matt. 19:9 teaches that there is one—and only one—scriptural ground for divorce and remarriage; namely, fornication; (5) that all who divorce and remarry on any ground other than fornication, commit adultery in so doing (Matt. 19:9); (6) that every person who marries someone who has been put away commits adultery in so doing (Matt. 5:32; 19:9); and (7) that, in the light of the force of the exceptive sentence which Matt. 19:9 is, no other passage in the Bible could—without self-contradiction—authorize divorce and remarriage on any ground other than fornication.

Conclusion From The Foregoing Material

The above material proves (1) that Bales cannot establish his position on I Corinthians 7:10-15 and (2) that, as a matter of fact, Bales' position on I Corinthians 7:10-15 in particular is false, and (3) that Bales' doctrine on divorce and remarriage in general—since it depends on his establishing his view of I Corinthians 7:10-15—is false.

Christ's standard for the Christian life in general is high; for example: (1) one must love Christ more than the dearest of human beings (Lk. 14:26-33), (2) one must love Christ enough to go to prison for Him (Acts 21:13), and (3) one must love Christ enough to die for Him (Rev. 2:10). And, Christ's standard for marriage, in particular, is high (Matt. 19:9; 5:31-32). May those who have deceived themselves into thinking that Christ has a low standard for divorce and remarriage beware lest they lose their souls over this matter (Matt. 19:3-12).

Footnotes

[1]The reader is reminded that Bales' doctrine on I Cor. 7:10-15 has already been refuted in preceding chapters and in Appendix B.

[2]See preceding chapters. There is no need to repeat that argument here.

[3]The author hereby expresses great appreciation to brother Roy Deaver for the discussions which we had on this passage. I am indebted to him for the point that "the general law of marriage" is stated in Matt. 19:6 (not Matthew 19:9) and I Cor. 7:10-11.

[4]Cf. J. W. McGarvey, *A Commentary on Matthew and Mark* (Delight, AK., Gospel Light Publishing Co., 1897), p. 164.

[5]Ibid.

[6]Again, the author acknowledges a debt at this point to Roy Deaver.

[7]*A Commentary on Matthew and Mark*,

[8]Again, I am indebted to Roy Deaver for help in this point—but, of course, he is not responsible for any weakness which may be in the author's effort here.

[9]It is a tragic error to conclude that the "application" contradicts the "concept."

[10]Cf. Roy Deaver, *Marriage, Divorce, and Remarriage*.

APPENDIX D

MORE ON I CORINTHIANS 7:15

It is likely that enough has already been said about Matt. 19:9 and I Cor. 7:10-15 that the need for the writing of the material which will appear in this appendix has already been met. However, for some people—especially for brother Bales—this is such a crucial passage to their view of divorce and remarriage, the author has decided to go ahead and put this one into what is already planned to be a rather lengthy list of appendices.

This appendix will entail the answering of three main questions: (1) What does the passage say? (2) What basic question is raised by the passage? and (3) What is the correct answer to the question raised? Since so much else has been and will be said about I Cor. 7, the answers will be as brief as possible.

1. *What does the passage say?* It says, "Yet if the unbelieving departeth, let him depart: the brother or sister is not under bondage in such cases."

2. *What basic question is raised by the passage?* The basic question which is raised by some disputants in the present controversy in regard to this passage is: If a Christian is married to a non-Christian, and the *non-Christian deserts the Christian*, is the Christian then free to marry someone else on the ground of the desertion alone—i.e., even if the non-Christian is not guilty of fornication either before or after the desertion occurs?

3. *What is the correct answer to the question thus raised?* Bales answers "Yes" to the above question. This author (T.B.W.) holds that the Bible answer is "No."

It will be assumed, in the writing of this present appendix, that the reader will have already carefully read and considered Appendix A (on Matt. 19:9), Appendix B (on I Cor. 5:1-13), and appendix C (on I Cor. 7:10-15). Effort will be made here to avoid needless repetition of material in those three appendices (as well as in various chapters in the main part of the book).

In I Cor. 7:10-11, Paul has set out God's general law on marriage (cf. Matt. 19:6). In 7:12-15, Paul deals with details of cases which had not been previously dealt with.[1]

In I Cor. 7:12-13, Paul has instructed the Christian not to leave the non-Christian companion. But, in 7:14-16, the question arises: "What if the non-Christian is threatening to depart (i.e., to leave the Christian)?" It is crucial to the understanding of I Cor. 7:15 that one understand the question which, by implication, is here raised. It will be of value to look at the passage in the original language (Greek): "ei de ho apistos chōridzetai, chōridzesthō. Ou dedoulōtai ho adelphos ē he adelphē en tois toioutois; en de eirēnē keklēken humas ho Theos."

Now, some crucial words and their significance will be considered.

(a) *choridzetai*. This word is translated "departeth" (A.S.V.). It is the third person singular, present middle indicative of chōridzō.

Given the truth as already set out in regard to such passages as Matt. 28:18-20, 19:4-12; I Cor. 5:1-13; I Cor. 7:10-14, it is clear that "departeth" in this passage is a conative present (a species of the progressive present, Burton, p. 8). The conative present means either that an action is attempted but not accomplished (the action is in progress) or it may mean that an action is being threatened on a contingent basis. In I Cor. 7:15, the expression under consideration clearly means "if the non-Christian companion is threatening to leave the Christian companion unless the Christian forsakes Christ (and begins to live a worldly life with the non-Christian). . ."

Likely, some of the Corinthian Christians were married to non-Christians who were making this very threat (i.e., "you must forsake Christ or I will leave you!"). And, if such were the case (as it no doubt was), then the Christian companion might raise the question: "Is the marriage relationship of such nature as to demand that—perhaps for the sake of children—I must forsake Christ before I would allow my following Him to cause my non-Christian companion to leave?"

This author (T.B.W.) has had, during some thirty-five years of preaching the gospel, a sizeable number of Christians to pose that very question to him. The question was usually raised in such a form as this, "Brother Warren, my name is Mary Jones and my husband is not a Christian. He likes to go to night clubs on Saturday night, to drink whiskey, to dance with other women, and to have me to dance with other men. So far, I have refused to do such things with him, but, now, he is threatening to leave me if I do not join him in such. I have told him that—while I do not approve of what he is doing—I will continue to live with him, but that I want to continue to live the Christian life. But, as you know, we have two children—who love their Daddy—and my husband is now threatening to leave me and the children if I do not begin to go 'honky-tonking' with him. I do not know what to do. I do not want my marriage to break up. I do not want our children to grow up without their father. And, sometimes, I feel that marriage is so important that I must do anything to hold mine together. What shall I do in the face of my husband's threats to leave me if I do not forsake Christ."

In answer to such questions, I have always given the answer which Paul gave to the Corinthians: "Let him depart." So, let the word "depart" now be considered.

(b) *chōridzesthō.* This word is the third person singular, present middle imperative of chōridzō. Given the explanation and illustration just above, it is clear that Paul is saying, in effect, "If your non-Christian companion threatens to leave you (depart from you) if you do not forsake Christ, then let him leave (depart, leave the marriage)." Paul is not demanding that the Christian become agressive and drive away the non-Christian companion. This imperative is what is called "a permissive imperative." In effect, this means, "Let him do so if he insists—i.e., if the non-Christian demands that you forsake Christ and threatens to leave you if you do not, then let him go, but let it be the case that he (the non-Christian)—not you (the Christian)—is the agressor in the case."

Involved in the study of the next word to be considered is Paul's explanation for his answer.

(c) *ou dedoulōtai.* "Is not under bondage. . ." Dedoulōtai is the third person singular, perfect passive indicative of douloō. The basic meaning of this word relates to slavery, to be in the bondage of slavery. The use of the perfect tense indicates a completed action with an abiding result. So, by saying that the Christian "is not under bondage in such cases," Paul is simply saying to Christians, "If your non-Christian spouse threatens to leave you (unless you forsake Christ), you must understand that, as a Christian, you are to be faithful to Christ no matter what the cost—even if it means that your marriage is broken up (or that you go to prison, Acts 21:13; or that you lose your life, Rev. 2:10). You are not now and you never have been under such slavery (bondage) to your marriage as to compel you to forsake Christ in order to maintain (continue) it. You are a slave to Christ (Rom. 6:18-22), but you are not a slave to your non-Christian companion so that you must forsake Christ in order to hold him (Lk. 14:26-33; Acts 21:13; Rev. 2:10).

So, in the light of Paul's words here, when Christians have asked this author (T.B.W.) about what to do in the face of threats of a non-Christian companion to leave if the Christian did not forsake Christ, he has replied, "Let him depart; you are not a slave to him so that you must forsake Christ to hold him. Your children will be much better off—without their ungodly father at home—with a mother who truly loves them and the Lord."

(d) *deō.* The word deō does not appear in I Cor. 7:15, but nevertheless, it is important to the problem involved. This is the case because, in the only places in the New Testament where the word "bound" undoubtedly refers to marriage bond, the word is from deō—not from douloō! (Rom. 7:2; I Cor. 7:27; 7:39). If there is any occurrence of the word douloō in which it refers to the marriage bond, then I Cor. 7:15 must be that passage. However, there is no ground for holding that it does refer to the marriage in that passage.

As Roy Deaver points out, "In this very chapter (I Cor. 7, T.B.W.) in referring to the marriage bond, Paul twice uses deō, but in verse 15 he uses a different word. This fact must be significant. The word douloō (in some form) occurs 133 times in the New Testament and not a single time—unless I Cor. 7:15 is the exception—does it refer to the marriage bond. This word refers to slavery—the lowest term in the scale of servitude. The Christian—the deserted Christian—does not stand and—in fact—never did stand under that kind of bondage."[2] Roy H. Lanier, Sr. says, "He (Paul, T.B.W.) simply means that the believer is not so bound to the unbeliever that he must give up Christ to hold to the unbeliever."[3]

Harvey Floyd says, "Paul uses dedoulōtai in I Cor. 7:15 because he wishes to say that for a Christian to yield to pressure to give up his Christianity to preserve his marriage would mean slavery of the most abject kind. The Christian must never consider himself in such bondage."[4]

Conclusion

The doctrine that I Cor. 7:15 gives to the Christian some ground other than fornication for divorce and remarriage, is simply false. This is the case for at least the following reasons:

1. *Matthew 19:9 is a universal instruction; all men (whether in or out of the church) are amenable to it.*

(1) The "exceptive" element in John 3:5 teaches that there is one—and only one—"door" into the kingdom. It is simply not possible—given this exceptive statement—that any other passage could set out another "door" without contradicting John 3:5.

(2) In the same way, the "exceptive" element in Matt. 19:9 makes clear that there is one—and only one—ground for divorce and remarriage; viz., fornication. (This has been discussed in detail in preceding material.)

(3) In the same way, no passage—not even I Cor. 7:15—could set out another ground for divorce and remarriage (i.e., in addition to "fornication" which is shown, by Matt. 19:9, to be the one and only ground for divorce and remarriage) without contradicting

Matthew 19:9.

(4) To assert that I Cor. 7:15 gives a ground for divorce and remarriage which Matt. 19:9 does not give is to charge Jesus with contradicting (through the Holy Spirit and Paul) what he (Jesus) taught during his earthly ministry (as recorded in Matt. 19:9).

(5) To charge Jesus with such contradiction is to:

a. Charge Jesus (and the Holy Spirit—thus, God) with lying—but God does not lie, Tit. 1:2; Heb. 6:18; I Sam. 15:29.

b. Charge the Bible with being self-contradictory and, thus, not the word of the infinite God.

c. Charge the Bible with implying any and every conceivable proposition—e.g. that God does not exist, etc., etc.

(6) Thus—the position must be false! (Any doctrine which implies a false doctrine is itself false.)

2. *The doctrine that I Corinthians 7:15 gives another ground for divorce and remarriage is false because:*

(1) It implies that the Lord deals unjustly in similar circumstances:

a. In Matthew 19:9, the Lord does not give the innocent party (unjustly put away) the right to remarriage.

b. Yet—some claim that in I Cor. 7:15, the Lord gives the deserted believer the right to marry again.

c. This would make God a "respecter of persons" (which Peter said he, God, was not, Acts 10:34,35).

(2) I Corinthians 7:15 gives no basis for assuming that Paul is setting out or allowing a second ground for divorce and remarriage.

Some Special Questions

Some questions on I Cor. 7:15 and Matt. 19:9. How would liberal thinkers on divorce and remarriage answer? (Put ✓ mark in proper spaces.) H = husband; W = wife; ~C = non-Christian.

Situation No. 1

H	W	
(~C)	(~C)	(1) W departs
		(2) No fornication by H or W.

___ Both H and W = free to marry again.
___ H—but not W = free to marry again.
___ W—but not H = free to marry again.
___ Neither H nor W = free to marry again.

Situation No. 2

H	W	
		(1) W departs
(C)	(~C)	(2) No fornication by H or W.

___ Both H and W = free to marry again.
___ H—but not W = free to marry again.
___ W—but not H = free to marry again.
___ Neither H nor W = free to marry again.

Situation No. 3

H	W	
		(1) W departs
(C)	(C)	(2) No fornication by H or W.

___ Both H and W = free to marry again.
___ H—but not W = free to marry again.
___ W—but not H = free to marry again.
___ Neither H nor W = free to marry again.

Situation No. 4

H	W	
		(1) H and W married before either baptized.
(C)	(~C)	(2) Then H baptized.
		(3) W departs.
		(4) No fornication by H or W.

___ Both H and W = free to marry again.
___ H—but not W = free to marry again.
___ W—but not H = free to marry again.
___ Neither H nor W = free to marry again.

Situation No. 5

H	W	
		(1) H and W married before either is baptized.
(C)	(C)	(2) Then H and W are baptized.
		(3) W departs.
		(4) No fornication by H or W.

___ Both H and W = free to marry again.
___ H—but not W = free to marry again.
___ W—but not H = free to marry again.
___ Both H and W = free to marry again.

Situation No. 6

H	W
(C)	(~C)

(1) H and W married before either is baptized.
(2) Then H is baptized.
(3) Then W commits fornication.
(4) H puts W away for fornication.

___ Both H and W = free to marry again.
___ H—but not W = free to marry again.
___ W—but not H = free to marry again.
___ Neither H nor W = free to marry again.

Situation No. 7

H	W
(C)	(C)

(1) H and W are baptized.
(2) Then they are married.
(3) He puts away W on some ground other than fornication.

___ Both H and W = free to marry again.
___ H—but not W = free to marry again.
___ W—but not H = free to marry again.
___ Neither H nor W = free to marry again.

The exponents of the view that I Cor. 7:15 gives an acceptable (to God) ground other than that given by Jesus in Matt. 19:9 (fornication) cannot consistently answer the foregoing questions. This is significant because teachers of false doctrine cannot consistently answer crucial questions—they will contradict themselves and the Bible.

Conclusion

The view that I Cor. 7:15 does not give another ground for divorce and remarriage is in harmony with the view that all men (whether Christians or non-Christians) are amenable to Christ's law, including Matthew 19:9 (Mk. 16:15-16; Acts 17:30-31) and with the view that Matt. 19:9 gives one—and only one—ground for divorce and remarriage: fornication. The view that I Cor. 7:15 gives another ground—i.e., in addition to fornication—for divorce and remarriage is not in harmony with the plain teaching of Matt. 19:9.

Footnotes

[1]See Appendix C for details.

[2] Roy Deaver, *Marriage, Divorce, and Remarriage* (Cookeville, TN., Roy Deaver Publishers, being the Harding Forum of 1977 notes), p. 17.

[3] Quoted by Deaver, Ibid.

[4] Harvey Floyd, see *Spiritual Sword*, Vol. 6, No. 2 and *Your Marriage Can Be Great*, edited by Thomas B. Warren, (Jonesboro, AK., National Christian Press, 1978), pp. 498-503.

APPENDIX E

I CORINTHIANS 6:9-11; I CORINTHIANS 9:20-22

According to I Cor. 6:9-11, some of those who had become Christians had been guilty of adultery before they were baptized into Christ—i.e., before they became Christians.

Since no one can be guilty of sin if there is no law (Rom. 4:15; I John 3:4), it is clear that the Corinthians had violated some law before they became Christians.

Obviously, in sinning before they became Christians, they violated either (a) the law of Christ or (b) some other law.

Bales recognizes this truth—and the problem which it poses for him in upholding the doctrine which he has espoused—so he tries desperately to do something about it. What he does is wrong. He tries to prove that he (Bales) can do the same thing (in exactly the same detail) in proving to men living today that they are guilty of sin that Paul did in proving the need for the Old Covenant (the law of Moses) to be abolished and the New Covenant (the gospel) to come into force (Heb. 10:9; cf.: Rom. 1:18-3:20).[1]

Since Bales had already admitted the truth of the point which is now to be made[2] and since the problem has already been discussed in previous chapters, it will suffice here to deal only with the law of Moses.

One crucial element of Bales' contention is that non-Christian Jews were amenable to the law of Moses until after the destruction of Jerusalem in A.D. 70.[3] (In another place, he implies that non-Christian Jews living today are amenable to the law of Moses—not to the law of Christ.[4])

Bales' doctrine can be shown, in many ways, to be false, but one simple way is sufficient. It must be noted that Bales, in contending that some of the Corinthians (Jewish ones) had violated the law of Moses (in committing the sins enumerated in I Cor. 6:9-11) and that non-Christian Jews were still under the law of Moses at the time Paul wrote I Cor. 9:20-22. Bales claims that I Cor. 9:20-22 proves that at the time Paul wrote that passage, there were three classes of people: (a) those under the law of Moses, (b) those without the law—i.e., Gentiles; who were not under the law of Moses, and (c) those (including himself) who were under the law of Christ.

While many things might be said about all of this (and much has been in other parts of this book), as noted above, Bales' argument is easily refuted. Here is that refutation.

1. If Ⓐ Bales' doctrine is true, then both Ⓑ the law of Moses was in effect after Pentecost until (at the earliest) the destruction of Jerusalem and Ⓒ the law of Christ was in effect from after Pentecost on to the present time.

2. But it is false that both Ⓑ and Ⓒ could be true. This is the case because two covenants could not be in force at the same time and on the same people (Heb. 10:9,10). And, it is crucially significant that Bales (in former times, and when he was not writing on divorce and remarriage) admits, by implication, that it is false that both proposition B and proposition C are true.

Note the following statements from Bales.

> The Old and New Testaments or Covenants could not co-exist and both be binding at the same time and on the same people. The first, or old, Covenant had to be taken away that the second, or new, Covenant might be established. "Then said he, Lo, I come to do thy will, O God. He taketh away the first, that he may establish the second. By the which will we are sanctified through the body of Jesus Christ once for all" (Heb. 10:9, 10). The "first" is the first covenant or Old Covenant (Heb. 9:1-4; 8:7-13), and the "second" is the New Covenant (Heb. 8:7,8-13). The second could not be established before the first was taken away.
>
> If the two covenants were bound on the same people at the same time they would be in spiritual adultery, since one cannot be joined to Christ and to the law at the same time.[5]

Thus, since the law (gospel) of Christ came into force on the day of Pentecost and since the law of Christ could not be established (come into effect) before the first covenant (the law of Moses) was taken away, it is clear that the law of Moses was abolished before the law of Christ came into force. Thus, it is false that both the law of Moses and the law of Christ were in force between Pentecost and the destruction of Jerusalem (at A.D. 70).

Thus, Bales' doctrine on I Cor. 6:9-11 is false. He must know—but he cannot know—that the Corinthian Christians who had committed the sins listed in I Cor. 6:9-11 had committed those sins by violating the law of Moses.

Again, Bales' failure is obvious.

The foregoing argument can be seen in symbolic terms in the note below.[6]

A summarizing argument which proves that Bales is wrong in I Corinthians 6:9-11.

The following logically precise argument proves

that Bales' contention that at least some of the Corinthian Christians were Jews and, being still under the law of Moses, were guilty (in committing the sins listed in I Cor. 6:9-11) of violating the law of Moses —not the law of Christ. That none of the Corinthian Jews were still under the law of Moses at the time Paul wrote I Cor. 6:9-11 is made clear by the following argument.

(1) If Ⓐ the New Covenant came into force (was proclaimed as an existing reality) on the first Pentecost after Christ's resurrection, and if Ⓑ the New Covenant could not come into force until after the Old Covenant (the law of Moses) was done away, and if Ⓒ none of the Old Covenant was done away until the entire Old Covenant was done away, then Ⓓ the entire Old Covenant (the law of Moses) had already been abolished at the time Paul wrote I Cor. 6:9-11. (Obviously true)

(2) Ⓐ the New Covenant came into force (was proclaimed as an existing reality) on the first Pentecost after Christ's resurrection. Acts 2:1-47. Bales admits this truth.[7]

(3) Ⓑ. The New Covenant could not come into force until after the Old Covenant was done away. Heb. 10:9; 8:4. Bales admits this truth.[8]

(4) Ⓒ None of the Old Covenant was done away until the entire Old Covenant was done away. Matthew 5:17-18. Bales admits this truth.[9]

(5) The conjunction of Proposition A and Proposition B and Proposition C is true. This is the case because any conjunction of true propositions is also true.

(6) Therefore, Ⓓ the entire Old Covenant had already been abolished at the time Paul wrote I Cor. 6:9-11. (Follows from premises (1) and (5) by Modus Ponens argument[10]).

The proof of the conclusion of the argument just above makes way for the final argument:

(1) If Ⓓ the entire Old Covenant had already been abolished at the time Paul wrote I Cor. 6:9-11, then Ⓔ Bales' doctrine that the Jews were still under the Law of Moses after the day of Pentecost is false.

(2) Ⓓ the entire Old Covenant had already been abolished at the time Paul wrote I Cor. 6:9-11. (Proved in argument above)

(3) Therefore, Ⓔ Bales' doctrine that the Jews were still under the law of Moses after the day of Pentecost is false.

And, if his doctrine on that matter is false, then he has no way of refuting the truth that non-Christians are amenable to the law of Christ. Of course, other—and positive—proof of this point is given in other chapters.

Footnotes

[1]Along with Patriarchy. See Bales' admission on both points in his book, *The Kingdom Prophesied and Established*, p. 181.

[2]Ibid.

[3]See *NUB*, pp. 148-154.

[4]Unpublished notes in reply to questions by T.B.W. This has been discussed earlier.

[5]Bales, *The Kingdom Prophesied and Established* p. 149; cf.: 181.

[6]

1.	$B^D > (M_L^{EAP} \cdot C_L^{EAP})$	Obvious
2.	$\sim(M_L^{EAP} \cdot C_L^{EAP})$	Heb. 10:9-10, and Bales admits.
3.	$\therefore \sim B^D$	1,2, M.T. (Modus Tollens)

Where B^D = Bales' doctrine is true.

$>$ = "If. . .then. . ."

$\cdot$ = . . .and. . .

$\sim$ = it is false that

M_L^{EAP} = The Law of Moses was in effect after Pentecost (at the same time as the law of Christ).

C_L^{EAP} = The Law of Christ was in effect after Pentecost (at the same time as the law of Moses).

$\sim B^D$ = Bales' doctrine is false (the conclusion of the argument).

[7]Bales, *Instrumental Music and New Testament Worship*, p. 16; *WCAC?*, p. 41.

[8]Bales, *Nature of the Word*, p. 43.

[9]Bales, *WCAC?*, p. 12.

[10]The form of the Modus Ponens argument is: $p>q$; p; $\therefore q$.—i.e., if the antecedent of an if. . . then. . .type argument is affirmed and proved to be true, then the consequent must be true. These things are true of this argument.

APPENDIX F

REPENTANCE

So far as this author knows no gospel preacher (at least no "gospel preacher" who is not a modernist) has any trouble with the problem of repentance at all—that is, not until he comes to the problem of divorce and remarriage. However, it seems that divorce and remarriage is such an emotional problem that even some men who ordinarily are strong, faithful Bible-preaching men (i.e., men who are willing to follow where God, through the Bible, leads) will desert that role and try to write Scripture rather than to merely follow it.

All men who know anything at all about the Bible doctrine of repentance know that, in the New Testament, the word repentance is translated from the Greek word *metanoia*.[1] This word means "a change of mind." And, it is a change of mind which always leads to a reformation of life, with restitution being made insofar as it is possible for restitution to be made.[2]

Brother J. W. McGarvey well said that he had never met a truly penitent believer that raised any question about being baptized.[3]

Jesus, Peter and Paul all made clear that without repentance there can be no salvation (Lk. 13:3-5; Acts 2:13; 3:19; II Pet. 3:9-10; Acts 17:30-31).

It must be kept clear that repentance is a change of mind. It is not mere sorrow—after all, there is such a thing as "worldly sorrow" (II Cor. 7:10). But, even though there is "godly sorrow," repentance is not godly sorrow. Rather, "godly sorrow worketh repentance unto salvation" (II Cor. 7:10). Thus, repentance comes as a result of godly sorrow. Neither is repentance reformation of life. Genuine repentance leads to (always results in) reformation of life. It is true that some change of life can occur without genuine repentance being the cause of it. But genuine repentance (as enjoined in the gospel of Christ), when coupled with knowledge of the will of God, always results in the correct reformation of life.

Thus, if a man has stolen a horse, if he genuinely repents, he will not keep the horse. If a man steals a watch, if he genuinely repents, he will not keep the watch.

It seems that people easily understand repentance and its results (reformation of life—ceasing all sinful practices, getting out of all sinful relationships) except in the one topic of divorce and remarriage. But on that topic people say that a man may steal another man's wife and be free (with God's approval) to keep her as his own wife merely saying, "I'm sorry that I did it; I won't do it anymore."

To give an example of what can happen to a man on

this emotional subject,[4] I call attention to the words of brother Jimmy Allen, a man whom I love sincerely and deeply respect, who—in a city-wide meeting in Dallas in 1964—correctly defined "repentance" as a "change of will."[5] He set out this definition after a lengthy discourse in which he explained what repentance was not. This good treatment certainly well set the stage for his explaining what repentance is. He made clear that one's failure to repent of sinful practices, states, or relationships will result in his spending eternity in Hell. He also made clear that if one does not reform his life after alleged repentance, then that failure constitutes proof that he has not truly repented. So, brother Allen made clear in the Dallas meeting that *both repentance and reformation of life are necessary to salvation!*

In order to make his point clear, brother Allen said, "If one really repents, he will bring forth the fruits of repentance. If he steals $10.00 from another and repents, he will give the money back. *Everybody understands that* (emphasis mine, T.B.W.).

"What if he steals another man's wife? A lot of times we simply wink at that sin. I know a Christian man who lost his first wife because of death. Naturally he was lonely, so he began to seek companionship. However, he became interested in a married woman. He took that woman from her husband. He destroyed another man's family. The only thing he did about it was trot down the aisle in a church building and say he had sinned. *If that is right with God, I am reading the wrong book* (emphasis T.B.W.)." Allen goes on to say that the congregation "should have withdrawn fellowship from him. We understand this point in dealing with money. We can understand it if one steals another man's horse, but it seems to be perfectly all right to steal another man's wife. *I refuse to subscribe to such a view* (emphasis, T.B.W.)." (Note: in a letter, Feb. 6, 1980, to this author, brother Allen said that the view he now holds in regard to this matter is different from the one he preached in the Dallas city-wide meeting of 1964. This implies that whereas he once refused "to subscribe to such a view" {as that described in the quotation from him, just above} he now does subscribe to it! This, in turn, implies that he now subscribes to the view one man may (with God's approval) "steal another man's wife"! All faithful Christians should pray for brother Allen to repent and go back to the truth which he preached in Dallas in 1964!) There is more, and this author urges everyone to read, with appreciation, brother Allen's sermon on "Repentance" in the Dallas meeting of 1964.

So, brother Allen, in accepting the doctrine of brother Bales, has now repudiated the statement quoted just above in regard to divorce and remarriage. Since brother Allen himself told this author that he no longer believed what he preached on repentance—at least as regards divorce and remarriage—in that "Campaign for Christ," which was held in Dallas in 1964,[6] in which hundreds of people responded to the gospel invitation, some more questions are in order: (1) Has brother Allen repudiated the definition of repentance ("a change of the will") which he set forth in that Dallas meeting? (2) If so, has he repudiated that definition in regard to *every sin or only in regard to the sin of marrying a woman in violation of Bible teaching* (i.e., as he put it, the sin of stealing another man's wife)?

Surely, he has not repudiated the definition of "repentance," which he gave in that meeting, for such a repudiation would mean that a drunkard could be saved without ever changing his will (mind) about getting drunk, a liar would not have to change his mind about lying, a prostitute would not have to change her mind about selling her body for sexual intercourse, a murderer would not have to change his mind about murdering; a polygamist would not have to change his mind about polygamy, etc.

If brother Allen has repudiated that true definition of "repentance"—and will not repent of that repudiation—then a faithful brotherhood will be forced to repudiate him as a preacher of the gospel, for no man can truly preach the true gospel of Christ who does not recognize and preach that genuine repentance means a change of mind (will) which leads to or results in a reformation of life. Brother Allen preached this truth in 1964. It is simply incredible to even imagine that brother Allen, under whose preaching so many have responded to the gospel invitation, would even consider repudiating the true definition of "repentance" which he gave in the Dallas campaign. In fact, this author rejects the very idea that brother Allen has repudiated that true definition of "repentance."

But, to say this is to say that, if he does still hold the true definition of repentance (that is, that it is a change of will which leads to a reformation of life in conformity to the word of God), he now simply refuses to apply that definition to the problem of divorce and remarriage! No doubt, he will sincerely and honestly deny that he is doing any such thing. No doubt he will say that Bales' doctrine (with which he agrees) entails that Matthew 19:9 applies only to Christians married to Christians and, so, many marriages which he (Allen) formerly thought were of such nature as to require one "to give up his sinful pursuit" (as he put in the Dallas campaign) he now sees as acceptable to God. To be consistent with his present position, brother Allen would have to say that, given the circumstances of the divorce and remarriage which he described, in the Dallas campaign, his statement that the brethren "should have withdrawn fellowship from him" was simply false—that is, that he (Allen) simply taught false doctrine in the Dallas campaign!

Having changed his mind on such a crucial matter, does brother Allen not owe it to the brethren (especially those in Dallas) to let them know that he no longer believes and preaches most of what is on p. 167 of his book *What Is Hell Like?*

And what of brother Bales? He is in the same "hole" of theological chaos that brother Allen is in. If not, let him explain how he differs from Allen on this matter of repentance. And what of brother Jerry Jones? He is in basic agreement with brother Bales. Is he in basic agreement with brother Allen?

Repentance is truly a crucial matter in the totality of the gospel message. It does mean (as brother Allen taught in Dallas, 1964) "a change of will." It does demand (as brother Allen taught in Dallas, 1964) a reformation of life in conformity with the will of God.

Both brother Allen and brother Bales once understood the meaning of repentance as "a change of mind or will" and the force of that meaning to entail reformation of life as a result.

The late brother R. L. Whiteside, whom Bales claims was in basic agreement with him (Bales), also understood the meaning and consequences of genuine gospel repentance. While he was serving as "Queries and Answer Department" editor of the *Gospel Advocate*, brother Whiteside received this question:

> Does an alien sinner, after repenting of his sins, making the confession, and being baptized, according to the Scriptures, if he has stolen from his fellow man, have to replace the things he has stolen before he can be saved?[7]

Brother Whiteside replied as follows:

"A thief is a person who appropriates to his own use property to which he has no right. A man who makes no effort to restore stolen property is still a thief, no matter what his professions may be. I might pick up another man's hat by mistake; that is not stealing. If I persist in keeping the hat because it is better than the one I left, I am a thief. The querist states an impossible condition. *That alien sinner did not repent of his sins if he makes no effort to repair the damage he has done to others* (emphasis T.B.W.). Does the querist think that a man could drive a stolen automobile to the place of his baptism and get forgiveness for his theft if he meant to keep the stolen car?"[8]

Obviously, Whiteside did not believe that a man can drive a stolen automobile to the place of his baptism and get forgiveness if he meant to keep the stolen car after he was baptized! Brother Jimmy Allen—at least during the 1964 Dallas campaign—also believed this. He said in that Dallas campaign, "If one really repents, he will bring forth the fruits of repentance. If he steals $10 from another and repents, he will give the money back. Everybody understands that."[9] Does James D. Bales understand that? Does Jerry Jones understand it? Does Jimmy Allen still undertand it? He said in a letter to this author (referring to repentance in regard to divorce and remarriage) that the view he now holds is different from the one he preached as Bible doctrine during the 1964 Dallas Campaign. This author again asks: Has he repudiated what he taught in 1964 in regard to what repentance will lead a man to do in regard to $10 which he has stolen? Does J. D. Bales agree with Allen in the repudiation which Allen has made in this matter? Does Jerry Jones agree with him?

During the Dallas campaign, Allen—with consistency—forcefully taught that repentance demands, in principle, the same thing in regard to divorce and remarriage that it demands in the case of stolen property; that is, one must give up that to which he does not have a scriptural right.

This question is now posed to brother Bales (and to brethren Allen and Jones): "If a man 'steals' (seduces away) another man's wife—i.e., he 'marries' her—may he take her with him to the place of baptism, knowing full well that his having her is not in harmony with the teaching of Matt. 19:9, with the full intention of keeping her after the baptism and have God's approval in doing so?" The doctrine of Bales, Allen, and Jones implies that the question should be answered "Yes"! Consider the tragedy that men of such ability and influence should now be preaching such a doctrine!

During his 1966 Campaign in Dallas, brother Jimmy Allen preached a sermon entitled, "What is Sin?" In studying Allen's answer to the question "What is Sin?," this author found no reference whatever to the view (presently held by Allen and Bales) that non-Christians sin by violating some "law on the heart" which is different from and other than the gospel (law) of Christ. So far as this author could find, Allen—as did E. C. Fuqua—used the Bible in every instance in showing that sin today is a violation of Christ's law. He made clear that men (any and all men) sin when they "go beyond that which the Lord authorized."[10] He used the Bible to establish that point. Since Allen's (and Bales') position on repentance in regard to divorce and remarriage is inextricably bound up with their view that non-Christians are amenable to a "law on the heart" which is different from and other than the gospel (law) of Christ and not to the gospel this point is pertinent here.

In that same sermon, Allen taught that the use of instrumental music is sinful because it is not authorized by the New Testament. He clearly implied that all men (whether Christian or non-Christian) must have Bible authority for what they do in worship. If he and Bales would apply that same truth to the problem of divorce and remarriage, this problem would be over and done with—at least so far as they and this author are concerned.

In that same 1966 campaign in Dallas, brother Allen preached a sermon entitled, "The American Crisis." In that sermon he said, "We have finally reached the point where so-called ministers of the gospel actually justify fornication and adultery. When men change their concept of God they must also change their views concerning morality."[11]

Since brother Allen—no doubt honestly and sincerely, trying only to do right—now is trying to justify what the Bible brands as adultery, is he himself—to use his own words—a "so-called minister of the gospel?" Since he (in his letter to this author of Feb. 6, 1980) made clear that he had drastically changed his position on a moral question (that of divorce and remarriage), in the light of the statement quoted just above from brother Allen, the question arises: has brother Allen changed his concept of God?

If brethren Allen, Jones, and Bales will go back and again espouse what brother Allen taught in Dallas in 1964 (on repentance) and in Dallas in 1966 (on sin, adultery and the concept of God), they will repudiate what they now hold on divorce and remarriage.

Also in the Dallas campaign of 1966, brother Allen, in a sermon entitled "Eternal Punishment," said, "Nero was married to a woman named Octavia. He wanted another woman named Poppaea, however, *he had no real grounds for divorce* (emphasis, T.B.W.). Eventually, he did divorce and dismiss Octavia. Twelve days later he married Poppaea. The Romans were not happy with his action so Nero had one of the men who participated in his mother's murder to testify that he and Octavia had engaged in adultery."[12]

Thus, it is clear that in the 1966 campaign, brother Allen implied that non-Christians were amenable to Christ's law in general and to divorce and remarriage in particular. (Otherwise, what did Allen mean by his statement that Nero "had no real grounds for divorce"? Given Allen's present position, Nero would not have needed any "real grounds" for divorce and remarriage. Would he, brother Allen?)

The presentation of such material from the pens of Allen and Bales could be multiplied many times over. It is clear that they have now rejected truth which they once clearly and forcefully preached.

Conclusion

It is the sincere prayer of this author that these three brethren will repudiate their repudiation of what genuine repentance will lead one to do in the case of anyone whose "marriage" is not in harmony with the teaching of Matthew 19:9 and go back to preaching as they once did. If they would do so, this one thing alone would go far toward bringing into being the unity which once prevailed in the church on the divorce-remarriage question.

Footnotes

[1]There is also the word *metamelomai*, which basically means "regret," which can mean either: (a) "godly sorrow" (son who repented and went, Matt. 21:28-32) or (b) "worldly sorrow" (Cf. Judas, Matt. 27:3).

[2]For example, no one can restore the life of a person he has murdered.

[3]This assumes that the penitent believer understood New Testament teaching on baptism (Acts 2:38, et al.). McGarvey, "Repentance" *Sermons*, p. 97.

[4]Emotional because the closest of human relationships are involved: wife, husband, children, brethren in Christ, friends.

[5]Jimmy Allen, *What Is Hell Like?* (Dallas: Christian Publishing Co., 1965), p. 167.

[6]In the letter referred to above the quotation is from Allen's sermon in that series on "Repentance," in the book *What Is Hell Like?*

[7]R. L. Whiteside, "Queries and Answers Department," *Gospel Advocate*, January 20, 1938.

[8]Ibid.

[9]Allen, *What Is Hell Like?*, pp. 166-167.

[10]Allen, *The American Crisis*, p. 33.

[11]Ibid., p. 21.

[12]Ibid., pp. 165-166.

APPENDIX G

OBLIGATION AND QUALIFICATION

A crucial element in Bales' doctrine is that if a person is not qualified to do a certain act, then he cannot be under obligation to do that act.

So far as this author knows, this is a doctrine which Bales has espoused only recently. (See his position on "the will of God" as constituting "the only safe rule of faith and life."[1]) In the same book, Bales asserts that "the Bible is all we have."[2] He also says, "The Scriptures constitute our rule of faith and practice because besides them there in no other rule. Since there is no other rule of faith, this one must be complete for it is the only one. It alone is the revelation of the truth for we do not have direct revelation today."[3] He further says, "There is no immediate revelation today, therefore the written revelation must have the final word in all controversies."[4] "The Scriptures are not the judge of controversies, but they are the 'sentence of the Judge concerning controversies.' Man, to whom God has revealed his judgments, does not constitute the judge."[5]

Bales goes on to affirm that while man must use his powers of ratiocination (reasoning powers) in order to determine what the standard (by which God will judge him) is and what that standard teaches, it is still the case that the reasoning power one uses is not the rule (standard) but is only that which "enables us to see and apply the rule."[6] He argues further that the Bible must be recognized as final authority.[7]

It is important to note that Bales does not restrict these matters to Christians. Rather, he emphasizes that all mankind must recognize the Bible as final authority.[8] Bales affirms that the Bible is the only revealed word of God which man has.

He says, "The Scriptures alone constitute the God-given rule of faith and practice for *mankind*"[9] (emphasis mine, T.B.W.). Note carefully that Bales says that "the Scriptures" alone constitute the God-given rule of faith and practice for mankind" (i.e., for all mankind)! He did not say—as he now says on the divorce-remarriage question—that the Scriptures are the rule of faith and practice for Christians only! He has now rejected the truth he formerly taught and has accepted error in his effort to try to be consistent with his view that Matthew 19:9 applies only to Christians who are married to Christians.

All brother Bales would have to do to settle this matter is to go back and accept the truth which he formerly taught that "The Scriptures alone constitute the God-given rule of faith and practice for mankind." In contradiction to that truth brother Bales now holds that no non-Christian is under (amenable to) the law (gospel) of Christ. Rather, Bales now says (at times), that non-Christians are under "the law on the heart" (as he, Bales, describes it) and not under the Scriptures at all. It would be difficult to imagine a more flagrant contradiction of self[10] and of the Scriptures.[11]

Thus, it should be clear to every reader that while brother Bales is now making a grievous mistake (error) in denying that all "mankind" is under (amenable to) the law of Christ, he has not always made this error.

Why is this point important to the proper answering of the crucial question for Appendix G—viz. that of the relationship of obligation and qualification?

The basic question to be answered here is: "Can men be obligated to do that for which they are not qualified to do?" Bales answers, "No"; this author answers, "Yes"—that is, the Bible teaches that one can be under obligation to do what he is not yet qualified to do.

To make clear that Bales is wrong about this matter, it is necessary to look at only a few of his affirmations (past and present) in the light of a few relevant passages of Scripture.

For example, Bales asserts: (a) that "baptism is a part of the New Covenant, but it was not a part of the Old Covenant,"[12] (b) "The birth of water and Spirit was not required in the patriarchal or the Mosaic dispensations. It *is required* for those *under the* New Covenant (emphasis mine, T.B.W.)."[13] (c) "*We are commanded* to *be baptized* but *they* were not (emphasis mine, T.B.W.)."[14] and (d) "On the first Pentecost after Christ's resurrection, He was proclaimed as reigning at God's right hand (Acts 2:34-36). Beginning then *people* were *required* to undergo the new birth, for the kingdom was now established (emphasis mine, T.B.W.)."[15]

As has been the case in so many instances, Bales here faces a dilemma from which he cannot escape. He must hold either (a) that people can be obligated to do what they are not qualified to do or else (b) that saved people (Christians) are to be baptized rather than lost people (non-Christians).

Now, it is surely the case that not even Bales is ready to openly and avowedly espouse the Baptist doctrine that Christians—not non-Christians—are to be baptized. If he does, who besides the liberals[16] will go along with such a view? In fact, it is appalling that James D. Bales, long known—and justifiably so—as one of the most conservative, sound, faithful, and able men among us, has now become the object of the praise of such men as the editors of *Restoration Review* and *Integrity*.[17] As was stated in the Preface, it seems that the liberals among us were looking for a man of unquestioned conservative reputation to carry at least a big load of their banner, and—it seems—they have found him in James D. Bales.[18]

At any rate, if brother Bales is not ready to affirm that Christians are to be baptized (as some of his statements imply—this has been noted in an earlier chapter as well as just above), then he must admit that a proposition which destroys his whole case is true: viz., that all men (unbelievers and believers) are commanded to be baptized:[19] (a) "We are commanded to be baptized. . .," (b) Beginning at Pentecost, "people were required to undergo the new birth. . ." The words "we" and "people" refer either to Christians or to non-Christians. (a) If Bales says that they (the words) refer to Christians, then he has espoused the Baptist position that Christians are to be baptized. (b) If Bales says that they (the words) refer to non-Christians, then he gives up his whole case by admitting that non-Christians are under (amenable to) the law of Christ.[20]

It is obvious, surely, that what brother Bales means to say in one of the statements quoted is that all people who are not yet Christians are required—note that "required," it places one under obligation—to undergo the new birth. This means that the following are under obligation to "undergo the new birth" (i.e., ". . .be baptized unto the remission of sins. . .," Acts 2:38): (a) non-Christians who do not even believe in God (they are under obligation—as Bales puts it, they are "required"—but are not qualified to undergo the new birth, (b) non-Christians who believe in God but who do not believe in Christ as His Son are obligated—but not qualified—to be baptized, (c) non-Christians who believe in God and in Christ as His Son but who are not penitent of their sins are obligated—but not qualified—to be baptized, and (d) non-Christians who believe in God and in Christ as His Son, who are penitent of their sins and who have confessed His blessed name are both obligated and qualified to be baptized in the name (by the authority) of Jesus Christ.

Bales' admission, in the light of plain Bible teaching, ought to settle the matter for all careful and honest readers. His admission here is an admission of defeat!

Thus, Bales' argument that the law of Christ (the gospel) simply could not be addressed to all men (because there are some required things which some people are not qualified to do—such as an unbeliever to be baptized) simply does not meet the test of sound argumentation (valid arguments with true premises). But because this particular point lends itself to sophistical treatment in a rather unusual way, the author wishes to say even more about it.

Bales asks such questions as: (1) Is the Christian commanded to be baptized?[21] (2) Is the non-Christian instructed to eat the Lord's supper? (3) Is a woman allowed to be an elder? etc., etc. All such questions are based on the same erroneous proposition (affirmed by Bales—and on which his case depends): no person who is not qualified to do a thing can be obligated to do it even if the Bible (as it does) teaches that obligation is to be laid upon "every creature" in all the world (Mark 16:15-16).

It is certainly true (a) that a non-Christian who is not a penitent believer in Jesus Christ as the Son of God is not qualified to be baptized (both belief and repentance must precede baptism), (b) that Christians are not to be baptized to be saved, and (c) that non-Christians are not to merely repent, confess, and pray —as Christians are—for the forgiveness of sins (they must be baptized to be saved, Acts 2:38).

But do these—or any other premises—necessitate the conclusion that one cannot be under obligation to do what he is not qualified to do? Absolutely not! Brother Bales has certainly not given the sound argument of which that proposition is the conclusion. First, he has not even made a respectable effort to set out such a precise, logical argument. Second, he could not do so even if he tried.

But this author can give a sound argument (a valid argument with all true premises) which proves that it is true that one can be under obligation to do what he is not qualified (at a certain point in time) to do.

1. If the Bible teaches that Ⓐ now (during the New Covenant dispensation) God commands (obligates) all men everywhere to repent and that Ⓑ God makes it clear that all those who do not repent will be lost forever, and that Ⓒ He makes it clear that even though all men are obligated (by the law of Christ—the New Covenant) to repent, He also makes it clear that one is not qualified to truly repent without first believing on God as the Father and Christ as the Son, then the Bible teaches Ⓓ that men can be obligated (by the law of Christ) to do something which he is not qualified to do.

2. Ⓐ Now (during the New Covenant dispensation) God commands (obligates) all men everywhere to repent (Acts 17:30-31).

3. Ⓑ God makes it clear that all those who do not repent will be lost forever (Acts 17:30-31; II Pet. 3:9).

4. Ⓒ He makes it clear that even though all men are obligated (by the law of Christ—the New Covenant) to repent, He also makes it clear that one is not qualified to truly repent without first believing on God as the Father and Christ as the Son. (Acts 17:30-31; 2:36-41; John 8:24; 20:30-31).

5. Therefore, the conjunction of propositions A, B, and C is true. (2,3,4,conj.)

6. Therefore, Ⓓ man can be obligated (by the

law of Christ) to do something which he is not qualified to do. (1,5,Modus Ponens. Cf.: Acts 17:30-31; John 8: 24).

But it must be seen that the matter is a universal one. Such requires another sound argument.

1. If the Bible teaches that Ⓐ men can be obligated to do what they are not qualified to do, and that Ⓑ all men everywhere (including unbelievers, who are not qualified to repent until after they believe) are commanded to repent, and the Ⓒ "repent" in Acts 17:30-31 is used figuratively (i.e., as a synecdoche) to stand for all of the gospel (New Covenant) message, then the Bible teaches that Ⓓ all men everywhere are under obligation to the whole law of Christ even when they are not qualified to do certain acts. (Obvious)

2. Ⓐ Men can be obligated to do what they are not qualified to do (proved in the argument just above).

3. Ⓑ All men everywhere (including unbelievers who are not qualified to repent until after they believe) are commanded to repent (Acts 17:30-31).

4. Ⓒ "Repent" in Acts 17:30-31 is used figuratively (i.e., as a synecdoche, in which a part is put for the whole) to stand for the all of the gospel (New Covenant) message (Cf.: Acts 11:18; I John 4:7; Romans 5:1, et al.).

5. Therefore, the conjunction of propositions A, B, and C is true. (2,3,conj.)

6. Therefore, Ⓓ all men everywhere are under obligation to be in submission to the whole law of Christ even when they are not qualified to do certain acts (1,5,Modus Ponens).

The conclusions of the two arguments above (especially the second one) are relevant to the material in Chapter X. It will be recalled that the basic thesis of that chapter was: there is one—and only one—body of doctrine to which all men are amenable today. It was proved in that chapter that the law (gospel) of Christ—the New Covenant— is that one body of doctrine. Therefore, this leaves no room for the additional law ("the law on the heart") which Bales alleges that the non-Christian is under. The expression ". . .in that they show the work of the law written in their hearts . . ." refers not to some law which was either innately in hearts (i.e., that, as babies, they were born with the knowledge of God, etc.) or to some philosophical system which they had reasoned out. Rather it refers to the law of Moses. Even when the law of Moses was in force (before Pentecost), the Gentiles were not under it, but—Paul says—when the Gentiles "do by nature the things of the law (the law of Moses, T.B.W.), these not having the law, are the law unto themselves: in that they show the work of the law (the law of Moses, T.B.W.) written in their hearts. Note: it was the work of the law which was written in their hearts.

In Jeremiah 31:31-34, the prophet says, among other important things, ". . .I will put my law in their inward parts, and on their heart will I write it. . ." In Hebrews 8:8-12, the writer quotes this prophecy from Jeremiah and clearly refers it to the law (gospel) of Christ—i.e., to the New Covenant. Obviously the law of Christ can be written on the heart of a man. How can this be done? By (a) his studying it or (b) by being taught it.[22]

It was also obvious (from Romans 2:14-15) that the work of the law of Moses could be written on the heart of a human being. How? Innately, at birth? Obviously not. How then? By being taught to the children by the parents. God gave explicit instructions for such (Deuteronomy 6:4-9).

If Bales holds that "the law on the heart" is a set of moral rules (e.g., like the Ten Commandments) which God puts into every child's heart at birth, it seems obvious he did not put the same set of rules into every human because moral codes differ not only between (or among) individuals but also between (or among) nations. Thus, if "the law on the heart," as Bales envisions it, is innate (but not objective and uniform) then Bales has espoused subjectivity (just as atheists do). (One atheist well said, "If there is no God then anything is permitted."). It was proved in two recent debates with atheists[23] that the mere fact of subjectivity proves atheism to be false.[24]

If Bales accepts this innate view, then he throws himself into subjectivity. This move sets him up for one of the same arguments which was destructive to Flew and Matson. Here is the argument:

1. If Ⓐ Bales claims that all non-Christians[25] are under "the law on the heart" is some sort of rule(s) which each baby has innately, and if Ⓑ there is contradiction in the moral codes of individuals and societies, and if Ⓒ if the situation in which contradictory moral codes are acceptable to God (and are the means by which God judges all non-Christian people) and if Ⓓ proposition C implies subjectivity, and if Ⓔ subjectivity implies logical contradiction, and if Ⓕ all logical contradictions are false, then it follows that Ⓖ subjectivity is false and Ⓗ therefore, Bales' doctrine is false.[26]

The truth of the matter—as was set forth in Chapter X—is that the law (gospel of Christ) is the one—and only—body of doctrine which God has for men today. It is true that men may—without studying the Bible—come to know (a) that God is, (b) something of what God would have men to do, but it is also true that man can learn of God from the Bible; i.e., man can reason from the various attributes of the Bible to the existence of God. Or, one can reason from some contingent empirical fact (such as a man himself) to the existence of God. He then can reason from what he knows of God to determine that the Bible is God's word. He then must use the Bible to test every phase and facet of his life.[27]

Every principle by which God ever acted is a part of the law (gospel) of Christ. Every moral principle which has ever been in any covenant (or dispensation) which God had with man in previous dispensations is now a part of the gospel of Christ. Every morally and spiritually right thing that man can learn by the combined functions of his conscience (a God-given faculty which always—unless "seared" by disobedience, I Tim. 4:1-5—urges him to choose what he himself is convinced is right—in harmony with God's will) and his powers of observation and reason is now a part of the Gospel (law) of Christ.

Thus, there is neither need nor authorization for "the law on the heart" upon which Bales bases his doctrine of divorce and remarriage.

Given Bales' view, "the law on the heart" cannot be either the gospel or a part of the gospel—it must be something different from and other than the gospel of Christ.

All men are under obligation to worship God.[28] And those that worship Him must worship in spirit and in truth. Every man on this earth is under obligation (a) to become a Christian, (b) to worship God in spirit and in truth, and (c) to live as the law (gospel) of Christ demands (Phil. 1:20-21; Acts 21:13; Revelation 2:10). This includes abiding by what the law of Christ teaches on the relationship of the sexes, including marriage, divorce, and remarriage. (The argument given above on Acts 17:30-31[29] on "repent" being a synecdoche—and standing for all of the law of Christ—made clear that all men are under obligation to do these things.)

If such were not the case—and it would not be if Bales' doctrine is true—then non-Christians would not have the slightest obligation to worship God in spirit and truth. They could do all of their worshipping—if any—in a "church" of mere human origin rather than as members of the church which Jesus purchased with His own blood (Acts 20:28); they could use instrumental music in worship without sin; they could use bacon in the Lord's Supper.

An important argument in regard to the foregoing follows.[30]

1. Either it is true that non-Christians living today are under obligation to worship God or it is false that non-Christians living today are under obligation to worship God.

2. If it is true that non-Christians are under obligation to worship God then either it is true that

non-Christians are under obligation to worship God "by faith" (according to His authority) or it is false that non-Christians are under obligation to worship God by faith (by His authority).

3. If it is false that non-Christians are under obligation to worship God by faith (according to His authority), then subjectivity for the non-Christian is acceptable in worship to God (i.e., every non-Christian is free to do what is right in his own eyes—e.g., Baptists, Roman Catholics, Moslems, Pentecostals, et al.).

4. If subjectivity in worship for the non-Christian (i.e., if every non-Christian is free to do in worship what is right in his own eyes), then it is true that when a non-Christian uses instrumental music in the worship of God such pleases God and it is also false that when a non-Christian uses instrumental music in the worship of God such pleases God.

5. It is false both that it is true that when a non-Christian uses instrumental music in the worship of God such pleases God and that it is also false that when a non-Christian uses instrumental music in the worship of God such pleases God.

6. Therefore (by modus tollens, from premises 4 and 5 above), it is false that subjectivity in worship for the non-Christian (i.e., that every non-Christian is free to do in worship what is right in his own eyes) pleases God.

7. If Bales' doctrine is true, then it is true that subjectivity in worship pleases God.

8. Therefore, (by modus tollens, from premises 7 and 6 above), it follows that Bales' doctrine is false.

In Appendix G, at least the following things have been accomplished. It has been shown: (1) that a man can be obligated to do what he is not (at some given moment) qualified to do, (2) that there is no such "law on the heart" which is different from and other than the law (gospel) of Christ (Hebrews 8:8-13) as Bales affirms, (3) that in inventing this "law on the heart" (in addition to the law of Christ) (as something different from and other than the law of Christ during this dispensation, Hebrews 8:8-12) Bales, by implication, dethrones Christ as the "King of kings and Lord of lords" and, thus, denies that He (Christ) has all authority in heaven and on earth, (4) that Christ does not (as the Bible plainly teaches, John 17:2) have power (authority) over all flesh, (5) that in denying the universality of Christ's authority (and, thus, of His law, the gospel) over all men, Bales (by implication) affirms either that no non-Christian has the obligation to worship God or that, if the non-Christian does have the obligation to worship, a purely subjective way of worship on his part is acceptable to

God, and, also (in the same connection) (6) that Bales must affirm either that the non-Christian has an obligation to worship God but is not qualified to do it or that the non-Christian is obligated to worship God and is qualified (in spite of the fact that he is not in the kingdom of God) and, thus can eat the Lord's Supper with God's approval.

Bales' doctrine is obviously false.

Footnotes

[1]Bales, *The Sufficiency of the Scriptures* (Searcy, Bales Bookstore, n.d.), p. 9.

[2]Ibid., p. 9.

[3]Ibid.

[4]Ibid., p. 11.

[5]Ibid.

[6]Ibid.

[7]Ibid., p. 6.

[8]Ibid.

[9]Bales, *The Nature of The Word*, p. 3. (*NOW*)

[10]*NOW*, p. 3.

[11]Mk. 16:15-16; Matt. 28:18-20; Lk. 24:44-49; Acts 1:6-8; 17:30-31.

[12]*WCAC?*, p. 57.

[13]Ibid.

[14]Ibid.

[15]Ibid.

[16]Such as some (at least) of the writers of such journals as *Mission, Restoration Review, Integrity*, et al.

[17]Perhaps, given the position brother Bales is now taking, it is not so surprising after all.

[18]Let all faithful brethren lovingly pray that such shall not long be the case.

[19] *WCAC?*, p. 57.

[20] Actually Bales' argumentation on this entire matter is really quite a "muddle" which has been explained in an earlier chapter.

[21] Given the implications of some of his own statements, Bales is obviously not the right person to even raise this question!

[22] John 6:44-45; II Tim. 2:15; Acts 2:22-41; 5:42; Mk. 16:15-16; Matt. 28:18-20, et al.

[23] *The Warren-Flew Debate* and *The Warren-Matson Debate*.

[24] The argument set out in symbolic terms is: (1) $A>S$, (2) $S>(X\cdot\sim X)$, (3) $\sim(X\cdot\sim X)$, (4) $\therefore\sim S$, (5) $\therefore\sim A$. See the two debates for explanation of these terms.

[25] Bales crosses himself here by implying that non-Christian Jews living today can violate the law of Moses. (Answer to T.B.W. question).

[26] The import of this argument is so obvious, it needs no further explanation.

[27] II Tim. 3:16-17; II Cor. 13:5; II Cor. 5:7; Rom. 4:20-21; II John 9-11, et al.

[28] Even before Pentecost, there were prophets among Gentile nations. Also, Cain and Abel worshipped God (Heb. 11:4). Men of old acted by faith (Heb. 11:1ff).

[29] Cf. "Repentance" in Acts 11:18.

[30] Set out in symbolic terms, the argument looks like this:

(1)	$O^{WG}_{\sim C} \vee \sim O^{WG}_{\sim C}$	obvious
(2)	$O^{WG}_{\sim C} > (W^{BF}_{\sim C} \vee \sim W^{BF}_{\sim C})$	obvious
(3)	$\sim W^{BF}_{\sim C} > S^{W}_{\sim C}$	obvious
(4)	$S^{W}_{\sim C} > (W^{IM}_{\sim C} \cdot \sim W^{IM}_{\sim C})$	obvious
(5)	$\sim(W^{IM}_{\sim C} \cdot \sim W^{IM}_{\sim C})$	law of contradiction
(6)	$\sim S^{W}_{\sim C}$	4,5,M.T.

(7)	$B^D > S^W_{\sim c}$	shown above
(8)	$\therefore \sim B^D$	7,6,M.T.

APPENDIX H

"HOMOSEXUAL MARRIAGES"

This matter needs to be treated here in a special appendix for at least the following reasons: (1) to expose how Bales has misrepresented this author on the matter, (2) to show how he himself is inconsistent in regard to the matter, and (3) to set forth the truth on the matter. (These matters will not be discussed in the order listed.)

1. *What this author (T.B.W.) has always taught in regard to marriage.* It would be good for the reader to re-read Chapter V in this book, which thoroughly discussed the questions "What is marriage?" and "When does marriage occur?" No fair-minded person could read that chapter and believe for one moment what Bales has implied.[1]

Those who have heard this author (T.B.W.) preach and teach orally and who have been honest readers of what he (T.B.W.) has taught on marriage, divorce and remarriage over a period of some thirty-five years (1979) could not have the slightest trouble in understanding what he has taught on the matter. In special series of sermons, in lectureships (both with colleges and churches) all over this nation, he has made this clear. It is clear from what he has written and told this author that J. D. Bales knows what this author's position has been and is in the matter. The significance of this fact will be seen later in this appendix.

For all of this author's preaching life—since he has studied the matter very closely early in his preaching career—he has taught:[2]

(1) That the only people who can marry with God's approval (i.e., without committing sin)—provided they marry people who are eligible to be married are:

(a) Those who have never been married at all.

(b) Those who have been married but whose companion is dead.

(c) Those who have been married but who (as an innocent party) put away their spouses because of the fornication of the spouses put away.

Each case, of course, entails recognition of the fact that in the beginning God made one male and one female—each for the other, not two of the same sex for each other.[3]

(2) Those who cannot marry with God's approval[4] —i.e., those who cannot marry without committing sin:

(a) Those who have been put away for fornication (i.e., the put-away guilty party).

(b) Those who have been put away for grounds other than fornication (the put-away innocent party).

(c) Those who have put away their spouses for grounds other than fornication.

(d) Those who marry a person who is not eligible (as per Bible teaching) to marry.

It will be helpful to the reader to understand the truth (which this author teaches) in regard to: (1) God's will—as regards man and sin and (2) God's will—as regards marriage. The two will now be discussed.

(1) *God's will—as regards man and sin.*

(a) *God's ideal will:* that no human being would ever be guilty of committing even one sin (Gen. 2:15-17; I John 2:1, et al.)

(b) *God's circumstantial will:* that, having sinned, man would be saved (through faith and obedience, by God's grace) from his (man's) sin through the blood of Christ (Eph. 2:8-9; Mk. 16:15-16; Matt. 28:18-20; Lk. 24:44-49; Tit. 2:11; Jas. 2:24-26; Heb. 5:8-9; Eph. 1:7; Rom. 8:1-5).

(c) *God's ultimate will:* {1} to eternally bless the obedient (Mk. 10:28-30; Matt. 25:46), and {2} to eternally punish the wicked (Matt. 25:46; Rev. 21:8).

(2) *God's will on Marriage:*

(a) *God's ideal (general) law for people living today (as to marriage):* every marriage is to be between two people (a man and a woman)[5] who are eligible (according to God's will as set forth in the New Covenant) to be married and is to last until the death of one of the parties to the marriage contract (Mk. 10:2-12; Matt. 19:6; Lk. 16:18; Rom. 7:1-3; I Cor. 7:39).

(b) *God's circumstantial will (as to marriage):*[6] if one of the parties is guilty of fornication (marital infidelity), then the innocent party may put away the guilty party and marry another person (who is eligible to marry according to New Covenant teaching) but the guilty party is not free to marry again. (To be saved, such a person must become "a eunuch for the kingdom of heaven's sake" (Matt. 19:12).

(c) *God's ultimate will (as to marriage):* {1} to eternally bless every righteous person—which will not include those who live in adultery (Col. 3:5-7; Rev. 21:8; Gal. 5:19-21)—(Rev. 2:10; Matt. 25:46) and {2} to punish eternally every wicked person (including all whose lives have ended while they were living in adultery, Col. 3:5-7; Rev. 21:8; Gal. 5:19-21).

2. *Bales' charge against this author (T.B.W.).* Bales charges, in a blatant implication that this author believes what he does not believe, that "Thomas B. Warren is the only gospel preacher whom I know who says that a homosexual relationship is a marriage." He bases this allegation on the fact that, in an article in which I was pleading with brethren to recognize the terrible consequences of holding the position (based on the misinterpretation of I Cor. 7:20) that every person can stay in any relationship in which he might find himself at the time he was baptized into Christ.

I pointed out that, given this erroneous

position, it would allow one to stay in any relationship in which he might find himself at the time he was baptized. If this terrible doctrine were true, then, of course it would allow "homosexual marriages,"[7] "group marriages," "open marriages," "trial marriages," "polygamous marriages," etc.

Because in one article (at least) I did not put "marriage" in quotation marks when I referred to "homosexual marriages," Bales accused me of believing that such relationships are marriages.

There are a number of things which need to be said about Bales' charge: (1) this author will try to be as charitable as possible with his efforts (my Christian responsibility would demand that I do such), (2) that he is simply wrong in regard to his understanding of the use or non-use of quotation marks, (3) that he himself uses expressions which are not what they say they are (as per Bible teaching) (4) that he does not make similar charges against a man who agrees with him on divorce and remarriage, and (5) some conclusions about the matter.

(1) This author will try to be as charitable as possible with brother Bales on this matter and say that he simply misunderstood him (this author) and did not mean to leave a wrong impression with his readers. (Nevertheless, he did leave, by implication, a wrong impression, which will be explained more fully below.)

(2) Bales is wrong in his understanding of the use or non-use of quotation marks. Wooley and Scott's *Handbook on English Composition* makes clear that words do not have to be labeled with quotation marks when the intent of the use of the word would be (or should be, T.B.W.) obvious to the reader. Such is the case with the expression "homosexual marriage." I can, if I like, use quotation marks to make clear that I do not regard such a relationship as really a marriage—except in the sense that many people call them marriages. I have books in my library which refer frequently to "open marriage," "liberated marriage," "trial marriage," "group marriage," and "homosexual marriage." None of the authors—as far as I am aware—put the expressions in quotation marks. I have consulted scholars in the field of English grammar and punctuation about this matter, and they agree that when an expression has come into such common usage that the ordinary reader would understand the writer's meaning even if quotation marks are not used, then such marks <u>may</u> be used, but—note carefully—*do not have to be used!* So, that takes care of point (2).

(3) Bales himself uses words in senses which cannot be found in the Bible (Bales insisted that I find a <u>Bible</u> use of homosexual marriage[8]). For example, Bales has, in a multitude of cases—likely thousands of cases—used such terms as "the Roman Catholic Church"

without putting "church" in quotation marks even though the word "church" is not any more used in the Bible in connection with "Roman Catholic" than the word "marriage" is used in the Bible in connection with the word "homosexual." As has been well said, "The legs of the lame are unequal"—i.e. Bales is grossly inconsistent. As Paul said, ". . .for wherein thou judgest another, thou condemnest thyself." (Rom. 2:1).

(4) Bales does not make similar charges (i.e., similar to that which he made against this author) against those who agree with him.[9]

Jimmy Allen, a fellow faculty member with Bales in the Bible department of Harding University (who agrees with Bales on the divorce-remarriage question), made the following statement in one of his books of sermons, "Nero was a sexual degenerate who actually lived with a man as his wife for a short period of time."[10] It must be noted that Allen did not label "wife" with quotation marks. If Bales was right in his charge against me, then he should make the same charge against brother Allen.

But, of course, if he did, he would be just as wrong in charging Allen as he was in charging this author. Brother Allen could say that he was under no obligation to put the word "wife" in quotations or else face the charge of believing that a man can actually be the wife of another man! All readers (of brother Allen's book) who had ordinary intelligence would need no help from Bales or anyone else in understanding the true situation. It is Bales who is wrong on this point—not Allen!

But this author does urge brother Bales to be as fair to him (this author) as he is to those who agree with him and is certain that brother Allen would urge the same thing upon him.

Bales further manifests his inconsistency when he himself sent me a copy of *Christian News* which had an article entitled, "Marriage of Homosexuals: Minn. Church Ceremony."[11] Neither "marriage" nor "Homosexuals" was in quotation marks in the article. Yet, Bales made no comment about it. The truth of the matter is such words and/or expressions and/or terms as "homosexual marriage," "group marriage," "open marriage," "gays," et al. have come into such common usage as not to demand—though such <u>may</u> be used—quotation marks on such terms.

As noted earlier, Bales gives proof that he himself has long recognized that truth of what this author (T.B.W.) has argued in refutation of his charge. He uses many words such as "church" in connection with such other words as "Roman Catholic" when the word "church" is not one time used in the Bible in such a way.

I am sorry to have to have spent so much space instructing brother Bales on something which he surely already knew—and allowed for himself and at least one who agrees with him. But, lest some do not have access to the facts, I have felt that this particular appendix—though somewhat useless—had to be written. Some men—when they do not know how to answer the sound arguments against their own unsound ones, do what some have called "drag a 'red herring' across the trail"—that is, they try to divert attention away from the real issue to something else.

Surely, as concerns brother Bales, it was simply a case of a good man who unknowingly "got off the track." (Please note the quotation marks!)

Surely brother Bales knows, as well as any man on earth, that this author not only condemns any "marriage" (note quotation marks!) between two men or two women, but I also brand as adulterous many marriages which Bales upholds as pleasing to God but which violate plain Bible teaching.

And we surely cannot close this chapter without noting that brother G. C. Brewer, who fought—as an ungodly relationship—"companionate marriage" in his debate with Judge Ben Lindsey, in at least one instance used the expression "companionate marriage" without putting it in quotation marks![12] Why has Bales not attacked Brewer on this matter?

Then, in a popular Sunday newspaper supplement[13] reference is made to the fact that a famous actress is undergoing a trial marriage with a certain actor. This is given only to show—again—that such expressions are in such common usage in our society and their meaning is so well and widely known that it is not necessary to use quotation marks.

The reader is urged, again, to re-read Chapter V of this book to see more on this matter and to see more of this author's true view of marriage.

Brother Bales could better spend his time in trying to figure some way out of *his implication that Christians can live in "polygamous marriages"* (note quotation marks!).

One last note: As to the matter of Bales' charge that this author is inconsistent in asking that "homosexual marriages" (note quotation marks) be broken up even if no fornication occurs (I suppose he means: one homosexual partner being "unfaithful" to another), the answer is simple: *all homosexual relationships* (just like most of what Bales regards God-approved marriages when they are adulterous marriages—remember the Bible says that Herod married his brother's wife (Mk. 6:17)!) *are sinful* and must be dissolved if the people involved are to be saved. It is not necessary that a relationship be a marriage in order for it to be sinful.

The difference is: this author says all sexual relations other than those within marriages contracted in harmony with the law (gospel) of Christ are sinful, while Bales actually has no ground for saying that anything which can rightly be called a marriage is not sinful (provided the parties in an unscriptural marriage say that they are "sorry" for any wrong they have committed).

The truth of the matter is: even the Bible itself, at times, refers to sinful relationships as marriages and every marriage is either authorized by the law of Christ or it is not. If any marriage is not authorized by the law of Christ, then it is sinful! If any marriage is authorized by the law of Christ, then it is not sinful. The whole matter is really just that simple. Note the following:

1. The Bible says that Herod had married his brother Philip's wife (Mk. 6:17). The Bible does not use quotation marks in so doing. Does Bales say that Herod was—in the sense that God had joined them together as husband and wife—really married to Herodias (the wife of Philip)?

Bales will have to choose either (1) to hold that the word "marriage" is sometimes used to refer to relationships which are *not really marriages in the sense that God has joined together as husband and wife* or (2) to hold that every occurrence of the word "marriage" refers only to cases in which God has joined together a man and a woman as husband and wife (i.e., the marriage is authorized by God's word). If he chooses (1), then he, in effect, admits he was wrong in his attack on this author. If he chooses (2), then he contradicts plain Bible teaching.

Recognizing that God joins together only those who are eligible to be married to each other, it is clear that any relationship which is not authorized by the gospel (law) of Christ is not really a marriage (i.e., in the sense that God has not joined them together).

Recognizing (1) that the only "real" marriages are those in which God has joined together a man and a woman as husband and wife and (2) that God joins together only those who are eligible to be married to each other, it is clear that any so-called "marriage" which violates the instructions of the Bible is not really a marriage but is an adulterous relationship.

This truth recognizes (1) that God has a standard for marriage and (2) that some men—willing to reject God's standard—have a standard which they themselves have invented.

2. While there is no doubt that a greater degree of degradation is involved in a homosexual "marraige" than in a legal heterosexual "marriage" which violates Bible teaching (cf.: Matt. 5:31-32; 19:3-12), it is nevertheless true that an adulterous heterosexual relationship (even if it is recognized as a legal

marriage by some civil government) will as surely send one to Hell as will a homosexual relationship (even if such should be recognized as a legal marriage—as brother Jimmy Allen did in the case of Nero). Rev. 21: 8; Gal. 5:19-21; I Cor. 6:9-11, et al. make this clear. The Bible clearly teaches that any and all sexual relationships which are not authorized by the law of Christ are sinful—and are not marriages in the sense that God has joined them together (Matt. 19:3-6). This would apply both to any unauthorized heterosexual "marriage" and any and all homosexual "marriages." Let Bales apply the standard he sought to "saddle" on this author to his own use of such words as "church," "baptism," et al.

The Bible uses the word "married" to refer to the relationship of Herod and Herodias (his brother Philip's wife) (Mk. 6:17), yet the Bible also makes clear that that relationship was "not lawful" (Mk. 6: 18). John said to Herod that it was "not lawful" for Herod to "have" (i.e., be married to) his "brother's wife" (Mk. 6:18). Thus, the Bible itself uses the word "married" to refer to relationships which are not lawful!

All homosexual "marriages" violate the law of Christ and, thus, will cause one to be lost eternally if not repented of. Some heterosexual "marriages" are unlawful and, thus, will cause one to be lost eternally if not repented of.

Thus, the Bible condemns *all homosexual relationships* ("marriages") and *some heterosexual relationships* ("marriages"). But James D. Bales defends (as acceptable to God) some (heterosexual) relationships which the Bible condemns!

In gross inconsistence with his practice of publicly denouncing this author and other men (such as Roy Deaver especially) simply because they teach that all men are amenable to the gospel (including Matt. 19:9), brother Bales has not—so far as this author knows—written or uttered one public word of condemnation of the false doctrine on divorce and remarriage taught by brother James S. Woodroof (the preacher for a number of years for the congregation of which brother Bales is a member) even though Woodroof, in trying to uphold a false doctrine on divorce and remarriage, has (1) implied that the Bible contradicts itself and (2) said that (a) ". . .to assume that the reference in Heb. 13:4 to 'honorable marriage' envisages only what may be termed 'scriptural marriage' is a false assumption."[14] and that (b) ". . .marriage is an institution which is honorable in the eyes of God and should be in the eyes of men."[15]

Statements (a) and (b) from (2) above, in connection with what Woodroof said in other parts of his book (especially in connection with I Cor. 7:20), make clear that Woodroof implies: (1) that any and every relationship that is, in any sense, a "marriage" can be continued in after baptism, (2) that this includes any and every "marriage" which violates Bible teaching, and (3) that a relationship may be unscriptural and yet be an "honorable marriage."

Thus, Woodroof holds (and, apparently Bales does not oppose, for he says nothing publicly against this position of the local preacher where he, Bales, is a member) that a marriage which is unscriptural may still be an "honorable marriage." This, by implication, is a rejection of the Bible as the authoritative word of God! Let Bales give his reaction to such.

A burning question: Why has Bales been silent in regard to the writings of (1) James Woodroof and (2) Jimmy Allen (in regard to Nero having a man for a wife —without putting "wife" in quotation marks?).

Conclusion

The above shows that brother Bales' efforts in connection with the use of the term "homosexual marriage" by this author to show an implication of some writing on divorce and remarriage amount to nothing. His efforts along this line constitute a diverting of the issue. He could better spend his efforts in facing up to the fact that his doctrine implies false doctrine and logical contradictions. His public expose of the doctrines taught by brethren Woodroof and Allen (who has now repudiated what he taught in Dallas in 1964 on repentance in regard to divorce and remarriage) would be much more appropriate and, thus, more valuable.

Footnotes

[1]Bales' implication will be quoted and explained just below.

[2]See: Thomas B. Warren, *Your Marriage Can Be Great,* pp. 353-355.

[3]Gen. 1, 2; Matt. 19:4-6.

[4]They may have Bales' approval, but they will not have God's.

[5]The reader should bear in mind that Bales had this information in his hands when he wrote *Not Under Bondage*. It appears in my book of *Charts* on divorce and remarriage, Chart no. 4.

[6]A more detailed discussion of this matter is set out in Appendix C.

[7]Note, please, that this author almost always puts such in quotation marks. Bales basically ignores this fact and misuses a few instances in which the term was used without quotation marks. Bales—inconsistently with his own rule—uses such terms as "the Baptist Church," "the Roman Catholic Church," without putting "church" in quotation marks even though the word "church" is never used in the New Testament in such a sense.

[8]Bales' unpublished notes sent to T.B.W.

[9]Bales also does this with Brother Jim Woodroof, minister of the College Church of Christ in Searcy, AK, who, even though he teaches very serious error on divorce and remarriage, differs in very crucial matters with Bales on divorce and remarriage.

[10]Jimmy Allen,"Eternal Punishment," *The American Crisis And Other Sermons* (Searcy, AK., Jimmy Allen, 1971), p. 165.

[11]*Christian News*, Sept. 18, 1978, p. 14.

[12]See pp. 17, 18 on that debate.

[13]*Parade,* October 14, 1979.

[14]James S. Woodroof, *The Divorce Dilemma*, p. 51.

[15]Ibid. See also: Thomas B. Warren, *Charts,* 229, 230.

APPENDIX I

LOGIC

It is beyond the scope of this book for any effort to be made to teach a course in logic. For a full treatment of the subject, one should consult any standard textbook in logic. For a brief treatment, the reader might consider the various relevant charts in *Charts You Can Use in Preaching, Teaching and Studying on Divorce and Remarriage* and discussion material in *When Is An Example Binding?*, both by Thomas B. Warren.

No one can really understand the Bible without (1) gathering the evidence which is relevant to a given problem or question and (2) reasoning in a valid way about the evidence (i.e., handling the evidence correctly), drawing only such conclusions as are warranted by the evidence. Many of the charts in that book are relevant to the logical problems involved in this present volume.

The Bible, when presenting God's will (rather than the devil's or some mere human's—e.g., the Sadducees or the Pharisees or Greek philosophers) is always precisely logical. Every argument is valid; all of the premises of the various arguments are true.

Below is a specific example of an argument (used in Chapter XII) set out in symbolic terms. The logical precision of this argument is characteristic of argumentation in the Bible itself.

1.	$B^{P} > (B^{WG} \vee G^{L})$	obvious
2.	$\sim\sim B^{WG}$	II Tim. 3:16-17; II Pet. 1: 20-21.
3.	$\sim G^{L}$	Hebrews 6:18; Titus 1:2.
4.	$\sim\sim B^{W} \cdot \sim G^{L}$	2,3,conj.
5.	$\sim(\sim B^{W} \vee \sim G^{L})$	4, DeM.
6.	$\therefore \sim B^{P}$	1,5, Modus Tollens.

*Explanation of symbols:

B^{P} = Bales' proposition is true.

$\sim B^{P}$ = Bales' proposition is false.

B^{WG} = The Bible is the Word of God.

$\sim B^{WG}$ = It is false that the Bible is the Word of God.

$\sim\sim B^{WG}$ = It is false that the Bible is not the Word of God.

$\sim G^L$ = It is false that God is a liar.

Some other specific examples of symbolism in logic (from Chapter XIII) is set out below:

(1) $\{(X)[\sim F_x > E_x]\} \cdot \{(X)[F_x > \sim E_x]\}$

This symbolism should be read as follows, "Given any student, if that student is not a freshman, then he is eligible to attend the party—and—if any student is a freshman, then he is not eligible to attend the party."

(2) $(X)[E_x \equiv \sim F_x]$

This symbolism should be read as follows: "Any student is eligible to attend the game if and only if he is not a freshman."

(3) $\{(X)[F_x > E_x]\} \cdot \{(X)[\sim F_x > \sim E_x]\}$

This symbolism should be read as follows: "Given any divorced man (X), if X is a man who has put away his wife because of fornication, then X is a man who is eligible to be married to someone else and given any divorced man (X), if X is a man who has put away his wife on some ground other than fornication, then X is a man who is not eligible to be married to someone else." This proposition can be the first premise in an argument which proves that fornication is the one—and only—ground for divorce and remarriage.

Conclusion

Brother Bales has—during past years—emphasized to this author in numerous conversations that he recognizes the crucial role which logic plays in any adequate approach to Biblical hermenuetics (interpretation). Yet, in his own material he has not set out precisely stated, sound arguments to prove his basic proposition. The reader will surely be struck by the difference of approach between that of brother Bales and that of this author at this point.

Some men hold that one can gain knowledge by logic apart from experience and others claim that one can gain knowledge by experience apart from logic. Actually, as noted in the second paragraph of this present appendix, one gains knowledge by gathering evidence (including learning what the Bible says) and by properly handling that evidence after it is gathered (i.e., by reasoning about it correctly—and that is using logic).

When one rejects logic, he rejects a necessary element of what is required to gain knowledge. Thus, men are told to "prove all things" (I Thess. 5:21).

APPENDIX J

WHAT ABOUT JEWS AND GENTILES WHO WERE MARRIED BEFORE THE DAY OF PENTECOST?

1. *Bales argument re this question.*

Bales thinks that he has a point of some force in regard to Jews who were already married when they were baptized on the day of Pentecost. He holds that there is nothing in the New Testament which demands that the Jews who were already married did not have to dissolve those marriages even if they were not in harmony with Matthew 19:9 but were in harmony with what was taught in the law of Moses.

On this point, Bales and this author are in agreement. But Bales draws an unwarranted conclusion from this truth. He argues,[1] in effect, in this fashion:

(1) If Ⓐ the Jews who were already married when they were baptized on Pentecost were not forced to dissolve those marriages even if they were not in harmony with Matt. 19:9 but were in harmony with the law of Moses, then Ⓑ people living today who are already married when they are baptized are not required (by the law of Christ) to dissolve those marriages even if they are not in harmony with Matt. 19:9.

(2) Proposition Ⓐ is true (both Bales and this author(T.B.W.) agree that the Bible teaches this.) (3) Therefore, Proposition Ⓑ is true. (Bales affirms that Proposition B is true, but this author (T.B.W.) denies that Proposition B is true). This is the case because Premise (1) of the above argument is false. Thus, his argument is unsound and, therefore, does not prove his conclusion. Proposition B simply does not follow from Proposition A.

2. *Explanation of T.B.W.'s answer.*

(1) *A crucial point.* One cannot understand the truth on this matter without understanding that, during the early days of the church, the Apostles and prophets preached to people who, just a few days previously, had lived under the Old Covenant (the law of Moses). But, then, suddenly, beginning on the day of Pentecost, they were living under a New Covenant—the law (gospel) of Christ (Col. 2:14-17; Gal. 3:23-25; 4:21-31; Heb. 9:11-17; 10:9).

It is very important to note the import of the Great Commission (see Mk. 16:15-16; Matt. 28:18-20; Lk. 24:44-49; Acts 1:6-8; and cf.: Acts 2:1ff). Repentance and remission of sins in the name of Christ (by His authority) were preached for the *very first time in all of history* (as actually in effect) on the first day of Pentecost following the resurrection of Christ from the dead (see Lk. 24:45-49). See also: Acts 1:1-8; 2:22-47; 3:11-26.

(2) *There were some important matters to consider:*

(a) No doubt, some of the people (both Jews and Gentiles {who were baptized later, Acts 10,11}) had been married in harmony with the law they were under at the time they married.

(b) Although the accounts of such are not given in the Scriptures, it is very likely the case that at least some of these people had been married in violation of the law they were under at the time they were married.

(c) But, during their lifetimes, the laws under which they (the Jews and the Gentiles) lived, respectively, were repealed, and a new law—a universal law (one which was addressed to all men)—the law (gospel) of Christ came into force.[2] There is not one adult now living on earth who is not under (amenable to) the law (gospel) of Christ. This was discussed thoroughly in Chapter X and is made clear in the following passages of Scripture: Isa. 2:1-4; Jer. 31:31-34; Heb. 8:8-13; 10:9; Gal. 3:23-25; 4:21-31; Mk. 16:15-16; Matt. 28:18-20; Lk. 24:44-49; Acts 1:6-8; 2:14-47; 14:14-17; 17:30-31; 15:6-9. (The hearts of both the Jews and the Gentiles were cleansed by the faith, the law of Christ.)

{1} Those who had married in harmony with the law they were under at the time they were baptized could continue in those marriages. Otherwise God would have been imposing an *ex post facto* law on them.

{2} Those who had married in violation of the law they were under had to repent of that sin and get out of those sinful relationships (cf.: the principle involved in repentance: Matt. 3:8; Mk. 1:4-5; Lk. 24:44-49; Acts 2:38; 3:19; 17:30-31). This is the case, then, because repentance is necessary to salvation, and repentance is a change of will (or of mind) which leads to a reformation of life! As brother Jimmy Allen put it during the Dallas Campaign in 1964, "If a man repents of his drinking, he will quit drinking, if he repents of his stealing, he will quit stealing. If young people repent of petting, they'll quit it. . .If one really repents, he will bring forth the fruits of repentance. If he steals $10 from another and repents he will give the money back. Everybody understands that. (Note that Allen says that everybody understands that![3]—T.B.W.)

Allen then went on to apply that same demand of repentance (that is, a reformation of life) to a man who steals another man's wife! This he did in accordance with the truth which he preached in the 1964 Dallas Campaign and in the book which is the record of the sermons which he preached at that time. But, now, he has told this author that he has repudiated what he said in that sermon on "Repentance" in regard to its demanding a reformation of life as concerns what he said, on p. 167, on divorce and remarriage. (It is the prayer of this author that he will repent of his repudiation of the truth on repentance and once again preach the truth which he preached in the Dallas Campaign—a campaign in which 222 were baptized and 505 restored, with it likely being the case that many of that number responded after the sermon on "Repentance" had been preached!)

(d) *Liberals on divorce and remarriage have no point here.* Let it be clearly noted that the truth stated in (c), {1} above affords Bales no comfort whatever for his doctrine. This is the case because—in contrast to those who had been living in either the patriarchal or the Mosaic dispensations—no one living today is in the situation which they were in; i.e., of having been married while one law was in effect, and—then—later having a new law to come into effect (with the old dispensation being abolished). Bales formerly admitted that both the Patriarchal and Mosaic systems ended at Pentecost.[4]

A very obvious truth should be noted by everyone: viz., that every person living today is living under the gospel dispensation—not one person living in the world today is now living under either the Patriarchal dispensation or the Mosaic dispensation or ever has lived under either of those dispensations! Every person living today who is married was amenable to the law (gospel) of Christ before he (she) married, at the time he (she) married, and after the time he (she) married. As was demonstrated (proved) in Chapter X, there is now in force one—and only one—body of doctrine to which all men are amenable.

As was pointed out above, Bales himself admits that the patriarchal system ended with the establishment of the New Covenant (the law of Christ). The Patriarchal system did not end with the establishment of the Old Covenant (the law of Moses) and it did not continue past the establishment of the New Covenant.[5] The reason for this, Bales admits, was that the law of Moses "was not for all mankind, but the gospel dispensation was for all mankind."[6]

This is a most crucial and devastating (to Bales) admission! In it, Bales admits (a) that the Patriarchal system did not continue past Pentecost, (b) that the law of Moses did not continue past Pentecost, (c) that the gospel dispensation is for all mankind (whether Christian or non-Christian), and, thus, (d) that his present doctrine on divorce and remarriage (which depends upon his present view that no one is amenable to the gospel except Christians and that the law of Moses continued in effect after Pentecost) is false. As surely as the gospel (the law of Christ) is for all mankind (as Bales once clearly taught), his present doctrine on divorce and remarriage is false.

Bales sent out material which contained a poem

which implied that this writer (T.B.W.) taught that if a Jew whose marriage was acceptable (under the law of Moses) went to sleep on the night before the day of Pentecost, he might awaken on the day of Pentecost with his marriage changed from an acceptable one into an adulterous one. Of course, this is simply not true; I have never taught such a doctrine. What I have always taught on this matter is taught right here in this Appendix J.

See Chart no. 244 for a graphic discussion of this matter. See this chart on p. 274.

Conclusion

The "Jew-Gentile before and after Pentecost" question affords no comfort whatever to Bales' false theory. This is the case because: (1) it uses people who lived the first part of their lives under one covenant and the last part of their lives under a different covenant to conclude what is the case with people today, but (2) no person living today has lived under any covenant other than the gospel. The gospel is addressed to all!

Footnotes

[1]Although, this author feels that it is fair to say that brother Bales almost never sets out an argument in precise logical form.

[2]This truth, of the universality of the gospel, was discussed thoroughly (and proved) in Chapter X.

[3]Allen, *What Is Hell Like?*, pp. 166-167. But, since brother Allen has now espoused the Bales doctrine on divorce and remarriage, the question has become: Does brother Allen himself understand it?

[4]Bales, *The Kingdom Prophesied and Established*, p. 181.

[5]Ibid.

[6]Ibid.

244

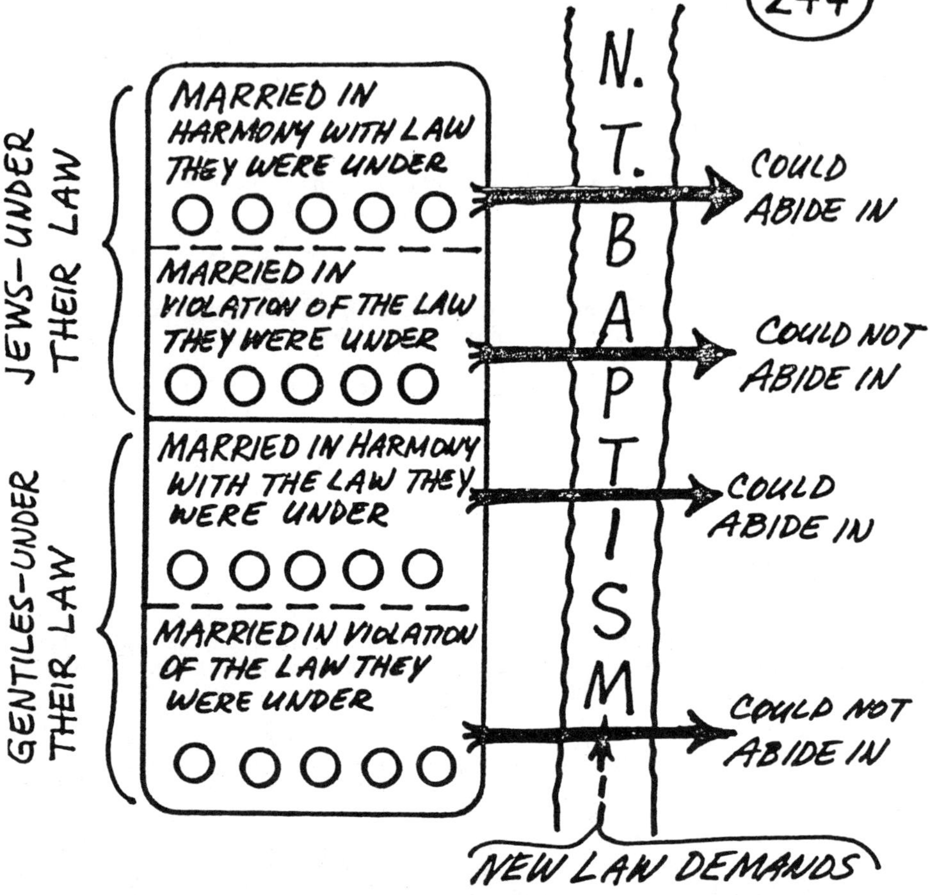

★ NOTE: NO ONE LIVING TODAY IS IN THE SITUATION THEY WERE IN—I.E., OF HAVING BEEN MARRIED WHILE ONE LAW WAS IN EFFECT AND—THEN—LATER HAVING A NEW LAW TO COME INTO EFFECT. SO—THE "JEW-GENTILE" QUESTION DOES NOT UPHOLD THEIR FALSE THEORY!!

APPENDIX K

ETERNAL PRINCIPLES

THE LAW (GOSPEL OF CHRIST)
(THE *NEW* COVENANT—HEB. 10:9)

Addressed To

ALL MEN

(Whether Christian or Non-Christian)
Mk. 16:15-16; Matt. 28:18-20; Lk. 24: 45-49; Acts 2:39; 15:7-11; 11:18; 17:30-31

Involving

HOW TO LIVE (ABOVE SIN)	HOW TO BE SAVED (FROM SIN)	HOW TO LIVE AS A CHRISTIAN (SAVED FROM SIN)
When one violates the Law of Christ, he sins. When he urges other men to violate it, he sins.	When one obeys the Gospel, he is saved by the blood of Christ (Mk. 16:15-16; Acts 2: 38; 20:28; Eph. 1:7.) When one rejects it or fights it, he sins.	When one "walks in the light" (of the Law of Christ—the Gospel), he will be saved eternally (Rev. 2:10). When one rejects or fights it, he sins.

**Note: ALL ETERNAL PRINCIPLES* (God does not change His nature) which have been in effect in any and every preceding dispensation are now in force (i.e., during the GOSPEL DISPENSATION). This is the case because they are constituent elements of the *GOSPEL—not* because they were in force in preceding dispensations. (The Bible—and Bales admits, *Christ: The Fulfillment of The Law And The Prophets*, pp. 64-74—contains all the principles man can learn by reasoning from evidence.)

*NOTE FURTHER ILLUSTRATION:

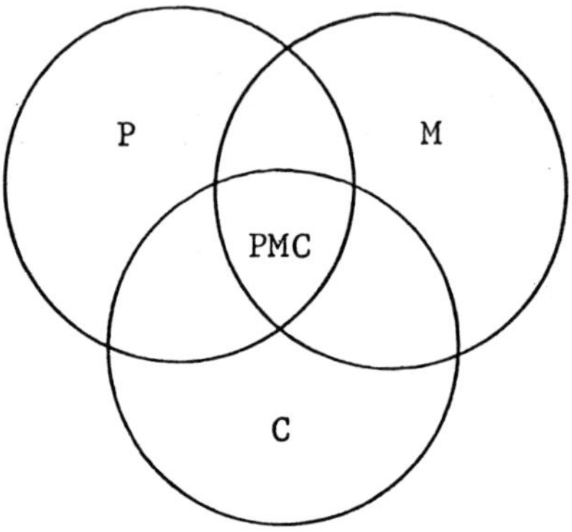

P = Patriarchal Dispensation.

M = Mosaic Dispensation.

C = Christian Dispensation

PMC = the *eternal principles* which have been in force in every dispensation—Men are to obey them *now* (today) *because* they are a *part* of the *gospel (law) of Christ, not* because they have been in other dispensations.

APPENDIX L

BALES AND DENOMINATIONALISM: "NEO-FUQUAISM"

In preceding material, it has already been pointed out that brother Fuqua, when writing on divorce and remarriage—not at any other time—claimed that all non-Christians are under (amenable to) civil law only. Yet, in his debate with L. S. Ballard (renowned Baptist debater) he claimed to have proved that men sin when they enter the Baptist church by showing that such action violates the law of Christ! Thus, he was in hopeless contradiction to the truth (and to what he himself had formerly taught) in his debate with this author (T.B.W.) on divorce and remarriage.

Although Bales rejects Fuqua's position that all non-Christians are under civil law only, he does join Fuqua in affirming that no non-Christian is amenable to the law (gospel) of Christ.[1] Bales, thus, by implication, teaches that denominationalism (with all of its human inventions of religious matters) is not sinful for a non-Christian. This point has been discussed earlier, but it is so crucial, so devastating—in that it undermines the message of Jesus Christ—that it must be given special attention.

It will be important, therefore, for the reader to see for himself just what position Bales has taken—now that he has espoused this anti-Biblical position on divorce and remarriage—in regard to denominationalism!

This author affirms that whenever a preacher takes a position such as that of either Bales or Fuqua logically it will follow that he must say that—for the non-Christian—denominationalism is not sinful!

So, in what follows this writer will do two things: (1) set out some crucial statements from Bales himself and (2) show how statements make clear that Bales has espoused a false doctrine.

1. *Some crucial statements from Bales on this matter.*

(1) Bales said that it is false that "there is a 'middle ground' between the world and the church into which men go when they do what they call 'accepting Christ.'"[2]

This answer admits that every person is either a Christian or a non-Christian. Thus, Bales cannot use his quibble that Baptists, et al. are not "unbelievers." He thus admits that denominationalism is a crucial element of this (the divorce and remarriage) question.

(2) Bales said, "People *outside the covenant* are guilty because they have sinned against *the law on the heart* (emphasis, T.B.W.)"[3] This answer implies that no non-Christian can violate the gospel of Christ because, by the expression "people outside the

covenant" Bales means non-Christians.

(3) Bales admits it is false that "Baptism is not the dividing line between the 'world' and the church."[4] Thus, Bales admits that baptism is the dividing line between the world (non-Christians) and the church (Christians). He thus admits that all people—including many religious ones—are non-Christians until they are baptized. He thus clearly takes the position no person who has not been baptized is amenable to the gospel. He thus espouses "Neo-Fuquaism."

(4) When this author (T.B.W.) asked Bales to answer whether the statement "Children of the devil are not amenable to the law of Christ" is true or false, Bales did not answer either "true" or "false," but his answer makes clear that he holds that the statement is true.[5] Thus, since he has admitted (a) that all people are either Christians or non-Christians, (b) that all people remain non-Christians until they are baptized, (c) that all non-Christians are not under (amenable to) the law of Christ, and (d) that demoni-nationalists (Baptist, et al.) have not been baptized into Christ (and, thus, are all non-Christians), he has taken the position that no non-Christian who is in a denomination[6] is amenable to any tenet of the law of Christ.[7] Since it was proved (in Chapter X) the law of Christ and the gospel of Christ and the doctrine of Christ are one and the same body of truth, Bales has here clearly implied that non-Christians are not amenable to any law from Christ on any subject. It follows that, according to Bales, non-Christians are not amenable even to the gospel plan of salvation.[8]

(5) Bales affirms that "the world today" (non-Christians living today) "is under the same law that non-covenant people were under while the law of Moses was in force."[9] By this statement, Bales affirms again that no non-Christian is under the law of Christ in any sense. It follows, therefore, that Bales implies that when a non-Christian living today (such as a Baptist preacher) urges people to reject the gospel plan of salvation[10] and to accept the Baptist doctrine that men are saved at the point of faith in Christ before and without being baptized unto the remission of sins, he (the Baptist preacher) would not sin in so doing.[11] Further, Bales' position implies that if a non-Christian (such as Billy Graham, Oral Roberts, "the Pope" of the Roman Catholic Church, et al.) were to urge people to reject the church which Jesus bought with His own blood (Acts 20:28) and to join "churches" of human origin, he would not sin in so doing.

This puts Bales in contradiction with the apostle Paul, who strongly condemned Elymas.[12] Why did Paul condemn Elymas? Because after Paul had preached "the word of God" ("the faith") to Sergius Paulus, the proconsul, Elymas tried "to turn aside the proconsul from the faith."[13]

It must be carefully noted that Elymas (being a non-Christian) was a man who, according to Bales' doctrine was not under the law of Christ on any point but was under what Bales calls "the law on the heart."[14] Therefore, since even Bales admits that his "law on the heart" says nothing about persuading or not persuading people to accept or reject the faith (the gospel, the law of Christ), then, given Bales' doctrine, Elymas did not sin in urging a non-Christian to reject the gospel!

This fact puts Bales in direct contradiction with the Holy Spirit and Paul and is enough, within and of itself, to prove that Bales' doctrine is false! This is the case because (a) if Bales' doctrine on divorce and remarriage is true, then no non-Christian sins when he urges men to reject Christ's plan of salvation and His church and to accept denominationalism. (b) But Acts 13:8-12 proves that a non-Christian commits sin when he tries to persuade men to reject the faith (and all that is implied by such). (c) Therefore,[15] it is false that Bales' doctrine on divorce and remarriage is true.

(6) Bales further admits that the following statement is false: "It is possible for Jones to genuinely repent of all of his sins without sincerely intending to reform his life (cease all of his sinful practices and sever all of his sinful relationships) and without doing his very best to bring about the required cessations and severances." Here Bales admits that *genuine repentance requires reformation of life*. Since in (5) above, this author (T.B.W.) proved (by the use of Acts 13:8-12) that non-Christians are amenable to the law of Christ, this present admission by Bales implies that any and all relationships (which violate the law of Christ) which are entered before or after being baptized will be severed by all who genuinely repent with understanding of the matter involved. This constitutes, for Bales, an incontrovertible admission of defeat.

(7) Bales declined to answer either "true" or "false" to T.B.W. question no. 58, p. 43 which reads, "One is not required to sever (come out of) any of the relationships which (1) violate the law of Christ and (2) are entered before one is baptized into Christ."

Even though this is a precisely stated proposition (no ambiguity is involved), it is surely evident that brother Bales could not answer either "true" or "false" without putting himself into big trouble on the divorce-remarriage question.

If he had answered "true," then he would have been saying that those who were polygamists before baptism could remain (with God's approval) polygamists after baptism.[17] He is also on record as saying when one is baptized, the law of Christ is not retroactive to cause any change in any marital relationship one may have entered before baptism.[18]

On the other hand, if Bales had answered "false," then he would have put his stamp of approval on the doctrine that repentance (a change of mind or will) does not demand reformation (a change of life—of practice, of relationship)! If he accepted this, he would accept "shacking up" (as he puts it), "trial marriage," and so on and so on to any evil relationship which might be entered before one became a Christian.

What Bales did do (rather than answering "true" or "false" was to avoid the issue at point by simply restating his position that Matthew 19:9 is addressed only to Christians who are married to Christians—a statement which is not only false but which does not answer the question which was asked.

He further said that "when one comes into Christ one is to cease divorcing and remarrying." But, given Bales' explanation of Biblical passages on divorce and remarriage (it must be remembered that he clearly implies that the guilty party—in fornication—is as free to remarry as the innocent party[19]) and that if two Christians who are married to each other divorce on grounds other than fornication, when (if) either of them ever married (even if ten years later) then, since fornication has then occurred, both are free to marry some one else. Given his doctrine, Bales has no way of demanding that any "married" couple sever their relationship. (See Chapter V for more details on what constitutes marriage. Also, see Appendix H).

(8) In response to T.B.W. question no. 63, Bales admits that a non-Christian who is a polygamist (a man with a multiplicity of wives) cannot keep a multiplicity of wives after he becomes a Christian.[20] For this position, Bales offers—in contradiction of his own doctrine—the rationale that after one is baptized into Christ, he must abide by the commands of Christ and make that rule such that it is "retroactive" to demand the severance of "marriages" he contracted before he was baptized.

Although Bales did not offer a precise logical argument, this author (T.B.W.) proposes to do such for him—i.e., set out the argument which is implied by Bales' answer to question no. 63 by T.B.W. Here is that argument.

(a) If Ⓐ once one is in Christ one from there on abides by the commands of Matt. 28:18-20, and if Ⓑ proposition A (just preceding) means that one must sever all marriage relationships which are in violation of the law of Christ, even if they were entered before baptism, and if Ⓒ polygamy is in violation of the law of Christ, then Ⓓ no polygamist can keep a multiplicity of wives after he is baptized.[21]

(b) Premise (a) is true. (Bales affirms)

(c) Proposition A (Premise {b}) is true. (Bales affirms)

(d) Proposition B (Premise {c}) is true (Bales affirms)

(e) Proposition C (Premise {d}) is true (Bales affirms)

(f) Therefore, the conjunction of Proposition A and Proposition B and Proposition C is true. (Bales affirms)

(g) Therefore, conclusion D is true. (would follow by Modus Ponens argument form.)

Thus, although Bales himself has not done such, his statements can be used to set up a valid argument. But it must be noted that by admitting that Proposition (B) is true, Bales gives up his whole case. Why? Because he admits that marital relationships which are entered before baptism and which violate the law of Christ must be severed because of the teaching of the law of Christ. If Bales denies this, then he must accept polygamy among Christians. Applying this truth to Matt. 19:9 will bring Bales out of his false position on divorce and remarriage. Applying this truth to Acts 13:8-12 will bring Bales out of his position that denominationalism is not sinful for non-Christians.

2. *Brief conclusion from the foregoing.* It must be repeated: as did Fuqua, Bales—in his desperate effort to liberalize New Testament teaching on divorce and remarriage—has been willing to renounce the truth, which he taught for so many years, that denominationalism is sinful for non-Christians (as well as Christians). Knowing that his "law on the heart" does not condemn denominationalism, its false doctrines, and its unauthorized practices (e.g. the use of instrumental music in worship), rather than admit that he is wrong on divorce and remarriage (which he must be if denominationalism and instrumental music in worship are sinful), Bales has chosen to affirm that non-Christians do not sin when they enter a denomination and practice and preach its false doctrine in urging people to reject the true gospel and the true church and to accept false doctrine and human "churches." (Note: Bales uses the term "Latter Day Saints" without using quotation marks.)

What a pity that such a spiritual giant as James D. Bales has now espoused doctrine which he has so valiantly fought for so many years.

Summary

It should be noted that there is much other material, both in the Bible itself and in Bales' writings, which would be highly useful in showing Bales' error on divorce and remarriage by the studying of the relation of denominationalists (non-Christians) to the law of Christ, but the above is more than adequate to show his error.

As a valuable summary, let the following be noted:

(a) Saul of Tarsus (who became Paul the Apostle) was guilty of sinning by violating the law of Christ—not "the law on the heart," as claimed by Bales. He lived in all good conscience even while persecuting Christ by persecuting the church.[22] He even referred to himself as the "chief" of sinners.[23] Bales argues that the law of Moses was still in effect at the time Paul wrote I Corinthians. Yet, as has already been documented, Bales also admits that *two covenants cannot be in effect at the same time* and that the entire law of Moses had to be done away before the New Covenant (the law—the gospel—of Christ) could come into effect. Yet, the law of Christ was in effect before Saul became a Christian. Therefore, he violated—not the law of Moses (Heb. 10:9)—but the law of Christ, when he sinned by trying to persuade Jews to reject the gospel (and the church purchased by the blood of Christ) and to accept his (Saul's) view that they should stay in Judaism.

Everyday on the television and radio stations of this nation thousands of denominational preachers do—in principle—what Paul did before he became a Christian, viz., they try to persuade people that they are saved "by faith only" or "by faith before and without being baptized in the name of Christ." Thus, they oppose true gospel preaching which is done by faithful preachers in the Lord's true church! This is what Paul was doing before he became a Christian and for which action—as he later referred to it—he branded himself not only as a sinner but the chief of sinners!

If it was a sin for Paul—to try to persuade men to reject the Lord's gospel and the Lord's church—then it is a sin for Billy Graham, Oral Roberts, Rex Humbard, "Pope" John Paul !!,[24] and multiplied thousands of other non-Christians to try to persuade people to reject the gospel of Christ and the church of Christ and to accept the false plans of salvation and the unauthorized "churches" which have been invented by mere human beings.

But, if it is the case that these denominational people can violate the law of Christ, then—since they are non-Christians—it follows that non-Christians can violate the law of Christ. And, if non-Christians can violate the law of Christ, it follows that they are amenable to the law of Christ (Rom. 3:19). And, if non-Christians are ambenable to the law of Christ, it follows that Bales' doctrine is false.

(b) Elymas was a non-Christian who violated the law of Christ when he was a non-Christian.[25] This case has already been discussed in detail.

(c) Paul clearly taught that it is sinful for any man (whether Christian or non-Christian) to preach any gospel other than the true gospel (i.e., that of Christ.)[26] Since such is not a violation of Bales' "law on the heart," and since Bales admits that both the patriarchal system and the Mosaic law ended with the establishment of the New Covenant (on Pentecost),[27] and since Gal. 1:9 is a part of the law of Christ, then it is clear that Gal. 1:9 proves that Bales' doctrine is false.

Conclusion and Appeal

This author lovingly and sincerely prays that brother Bales and those who have accepted his doctrine may see the "pit" into which they have fallen—and soon!

May the Lord's church be spared the spread of this doctrine.

This author debated brother E. C. Fuqua on divorce and remarriage more than twenty-five years ago. Since that time, so far as this author knows, he has not met even one man who will unequivocally admit that he holds to the doctrine brother Fuqua taught on divorce and remarriage.[28] This author prays that such may soon be the case with the doctrine of brother James D. Bales. May he and all those who have accepted what he teaches soon renounce such statements as, "However, neither the Jew nor the denominationalist is under new covenant law." (Then, is baptism not a part of the new covenant law? Or, are "the gospel" and "the New Covenant Law" two different laws—as per Ketcherside-ism?[29]) Bales has clearly taught false doctrine here. Denominationalism constitutes a "waterloo" for the doctrine taught by Bales—just as it did for Fuqua and his doctrine.

The word *diastrephō* (translated "pervert" in Acts 13:10), used by Paul in branding Elymas as having sinned, means "to oppose, plot against, the saving purposes and plans of God." (Thayer's Lexicon, p. 142, on Acts 13:10.)

Thus, if Bales is right in holding that no person is amenable to Christ's law until he is a Christian ("in the covenant," as Bales puts it), then non-Christians do not sin when they plot against and actively oppose the preaching of the true gospel. Given such a doctrine, Christians should praise, rather than condemn, the doctines taught by Billy Graham, "the Pope," et al.

May brother Bales and all who agree with his doctrine recognize the significance of this fact.

With men such as Bales teaching such a doctrine, it is not surprising to see even elders in the Lord's church striking out strongly against faithful preachers who expose the sin of denominationalism!

Brother Bales formerly exposed such sin. May the day soon come when such is again the case.

Proof that Bales formerly taught that Non-Christians sin when they enter and/or preach the false doctrines of denominationalism.

An honest reading of the material which brother Bales has written in years past on the subject of denominationalism would drive one to the conclusion that he (Bales) at least formerly taught that denominationalism was sinful for all men (whether Christian or non-Christian).[30]

For example, Bales has plainly taught that the New Testament (the gospel, the law of Christ) is "the only rule for there is no other word of God given to man" today.[31]

Bales has clearly taught (in years past) that non-Christian men today sin when they accept something other than the New Testament as authoritative in religious matters. He thus condemns (as being guilty of committing sin) Roman Catholics, Christian Scientists, Latter Day Saints (Mormons) Seventh Day Adventists, et al. (Note carefully: Bales did not put the names of any of these groups in quotation marks!) He condemns these groups for rejecting the law of Christ as authoritative and accepting some mere human doctrine as authoritative.[32]

Bales flatly condemned denominationalism by saying, "Paul condemned the division that existed in Corinth, a division of affection with reference to leaders and a forming of parties around them. This division had not ripened into the open denominationalism which we see today and neither did it support *the multitude of false doctrines which are being propagated by religious groups today* (emphasis, T.B.W.). How much more so is the denominationalism that exists today to be *condemned* (emphasis, T.B.W.)."[33] But it can be condemned only because it violates Christ's law. A fatal fact for Bales. Bales plainly taught that the denominationalism that exists today is to be condemned (that is, branded as sinful). Thus, since one cannot violate a law to which he is not amenable (Rom. 3:19), it is clear that Bales formerly taught the truth that, since non-Christian men sin when they enter a denomination and uphold denominational doctrine, non-Christian men are amenable to the law (gospel) of Christ.

Sadly, this truth which he formerly taught (that non-Christian men are amenable to the law of Christ) he now rejects (by implication) with the theory on divorce and remarriage which he now teaches. It is indeed a matter of sorrow to this author to see this great and good man (who has fought so valiantly against the errors of denominationalism) be so blinded by his zeal to propagate his theory on divorce and remarriage as to be led to his renunciation of the truth he formerly taught.

Other than the liberals among us (such as Garrett, Ketcherside, et al.), I know of no gospel preacher other than brother Bales who holds (either explicitly or implicitly) that denominationalism is not sinful for non-Christian men. (It may be the case that brethren Jimmy Allen and Jerry Jones, since they apparently accept Bales' book *Not Under Bondage* as teaching the truth, agree with Bales on this point. Because of their crucial positions with a Christian college, this author calls on them to clarify this point for the brotherhood. This is too important a matter to be "swept under the rug;" let them speak out in no uncertain terms.)

Brethren Bales, Jones, and Allen all know that, as Bales puts it, "he who puts the word 'only' after" the Biblical statement that men are justified by faith "does so without authority from God and in the face of God's word to the contrary."[34] Thus, in accepting Bales' view, brethren Jones and Allen put themselves in the position of logically accepting the fact that brother Bales, in espousing his doctrine on divorce and remarriage, has rejected the truth which he formerly taught that denominationalism is sinful for non-Christian men. If they reject the logical implications of Bales' view and admit (as the Bible plainly teaches) that denominationalism is sinful not only for Christian men but also non-Christian men, then they thereby admit that Bales is wrong on divorce and remarriage. But, if they accept the logical implications of Bales' doctrine on divorce and remarriage, then, to be consistent, they must also accept Bales' doctrine that denominationalism (with its preaching of false doctrine) is not sinful for non-Christians. Since these brethren are in such influential positions, it is certain that the brotherhood will be anxious to know just what their reaction to this state of affairs will be.

Bales Condemned "Pentecostalism" for Non-Christian Men

In years past, brother Bales unequivocally said (in regard to "Pentecostals" promising men that God would miraculously heal them of physical disease today) "Third, it is wrong to promise what God has not promised."[35] By "wrong" he meant sinful. Thus, he admitted that non-Christians are amenable to Christ's law.

In the same book, Bales also said, "But someone may object; How can these people be wrong since they do these things in the name of Christ? This overlooks the fact that a thing is not done in Christ's name unless it is done by His authority."[36] Note that Bales taught that "Pentecostals" do wrong (are guilty of sin) in promising miraculous healing.

This was written during days when Bales wrote the truth about non-Christian men being under (amenable to) the law (gospel) of Christ. He knew at that time that no one can violate Christ's law unless he is under (amenable to) it (Rom. 3:19). He (Bales) said nothing at that time about non-Christian men (such as "Pentecostals") being under "the law on the heart" and not under the law of Christ. But now—today—in order to have some semblance of a case for his doctrine that non-Christians are not amenable to Matt. 19:9, he has "hatched up" the doctrine that non-Christians are not under the law (gospel) of Christ but are under "the law on the heart." To be consistent with this doctrine, he must now renounce all of his wonderful work of the past in which he *proved the sinfulness of denominationalism for both non-Christians and Christians!*

Let the reader note carefully the following statement from brother Bales' pen: "For men to claim powers which were manifested in the revelation and confirmation of the gospel; and the establishment of the church; is to claim that they are called upon to do the work that the apostles, and other inspired individuals, were called upon to do in the first century."[37] In this statement Bales clearly means to say that any man (Christian or non-Christian) living today who claims that they are called on to do the work that the Apostles were called on to do in the first century are guilty of sin in so doing. What will Bales say today? Will he now deny that it is a sin for a non-Christian to claim to do the work of inspired men? To be consistent, he must deny such.

Since even Bales acknowledges that strictures against such are not in his "law on the heart." It is clear that he meant to teach that non-Christians living today who claim to be called upon to do the work which the apostles were called on to do in the first century are guilty of sin by violating the law of Christ. Thus, his teaching in *Miracles or Mirages?* clearly implies that all men (whether Christian or non-Christian) are under (amenable to) the law of Christ. But he cannot hold both that position and his present position on divorce and remarriage. He, like Fuqua, has met his "waterloo" on denominationalism.

What will Bales do in the face of this truth? (1) Will he do as Fuqua did and, by implication, renounce a lifetime of faithful teaching against the sinfulness of denominationalism for both non-Christians and Christians? Or, (2) Will he renounce the false doctrine on divorce and remarriage which he has now espoused and again openly attack the sinfulness of denominationalism even for non-Christians—and unequivocally proclaim that all men are amenable to the law of Christ (including Matt. 19:9)?

Bales cannot consistently hold to both doctrines, for the affirmation of the two of them involves a logical contradiction.

An anxious brotherhood awaits his—and some of his colleagues'—decision on this crucial matter. This author prays that his decision will be in harmony with the truth which he taught during so many past years.

In 1956 Bales said of so-called "faith healers" that their "false teaching misleads multitudes."[38]

Let brother Bales, brother Jerry Jones, and brother Jimmy Allen answer this question, "Is it a sin for a man such as Oral Roberts to mislead multitudes by their false claims in regard to miracles?" If their answer is, "Yes," then they give up on divorce and remarriage. If their answer is, "No," then they give up the Biblical truth which brother Bales (and, no doubt, both brethren Jones and Allen as well) formerly taught so forcefully against the sin of such false teachers as Oral Roberts.

As surely as it is sinful for non-Christians to mislead multitudes by teaching false doctrines (as denominational preachers do), then it is sinful for non-Christians to violate Matt. 19:9. Neither one could be the case if non-Christians are not amenable to the law of Christ.

And, as surely as it is not sinful for non-Christians to violate Matt. 19:9, then it is not sinful for non-Christians to mislead multitudes by teaching false doctrines (as denominational preachers do).

In his book *Soils and Seeds of Sectarianism,* Bales clearly taught that Baptists, Pentecostals, Mormons, Roman Catholics et al. sin (violate the law of Christ) by urging men to reject the gospel (law) of Christ and to accept human doctrines and human churches.[39]

In this book (*Soils and Seeds. . .*), Bales made clear that all men are amenable to the gospel (law) of Christ.[40] He made clear that the law of Christ could not come into force until after the law of Moses was taken away,[41] that all men are under (amenable to) the law of Christ,[42] and that non-Christians sin when they reject the gospel plan of salvation and urge men to accept a human plan of salvation.[43]

But now, sadly, brother Bales has rejected the truth which he taught in years past on the sinfulness of denominationalism. But, if denominationalism is sinful, Bales is wrong on divorce and remarriage. Since denominationalism is sinful, Bales is wrong on divorce and remarriage.

Footnotes

[1]Bales contradicts himself by implying in some statements that non-Christians are amenable to the gospel. But he never affirms that non-Christians are amenable to the doctrine of Christ. Thus, he espouses a tenet of Ketchersidism—i.e., what this author calls "Neo-Ketchersidism". Answer to T.B.W. question no. 26 p. 24 of Bales' manuscript.

[2]Bales' answer to T.B.W. question no. 41, p. 28 of Bales' typed manuscript.

[3]Bales' answer to T.B.W. question no. 42, p. 28 (Ms.)

[4]Bales' answer to T.B.W. question no. 49, p. 37 (Ms.)

[5]T.B.W. question no. 50, p. 38 (Ms.)

[6]Bales holds that Christians who, in apostatizing, have joined a denomination, have sinned in so doing. But, it still remains that he holds that non-Christians do not sin in entering a denomination.

[7]Remember: Fuqua held that no non-Christian is under any law from God (Christ) on any subject! In fact, Bales and Fuqua are so close that Bales' doctrine can be accurately labeled "Neo-Fuquaism."

[8]Although, in other places Bales contradicts himself by saying that Christ "invites" non-Christians to be saved and, thus, to obey the gospel. But, given Bales' position that no non-Christian is amenable to the law (gospel) of Christ, this simply will not do. (More on this in Appendix N)

[9]Bales' answer to T.B.W. question no. 55, p. 42.

[10]See Appendix R for an interesting "sidelight" to this problem.

[11]See earlier discussion. See also Acts 13:8-12.

[12]Acts 13:8-12.

[13]Acts 13:8.

[14]Bales' answer to T.B.W. question no. 55, p. 42.

[15]By logical argument form Modus Tollens ($p \supset q$; $\sim q$; $\therefore \sim p$).

[16]Bales' answer to T.B.W. question no. 57, p. 42 of Bales Ms.

[17]But Bales rejects explicitly polygamy for Christians (*NUB*, p. 187), although his doctrine implies that it would be acceptable for Christians. (See also T.B.W. question no. 63, p. 44 of Bales' Ms.)

[18]Bales' answer to T.B.W. question no. 58, p. 43, Bales' Ms.

[19]A.C.C. Lectures, 1961.

[20]Bales' answer to T.B.W. question no. 63, p. 44, Bales' Ms.

[21]Put into symbolic terms, it would be as follows:

(a)	(A·B·C)>D	
(b)	A	
(c)	B	
(d)	C	
(e)	A·B·C)	b,c,d,conjunction
(f)	∴D	a,e,M.P.

[22]Acts 23:1.

[23]I Tim. 1:15.

[24]Bales writes "Pope" without quotation marks! Truly, consistency is a "jewel" most rare!

[25]Acts 13:8-12.

[26]Gal. 1:6-9.

[27]Bales, *The Kingdom Prophesied and Established*, p. 181.

[28]Although Bales' doctrine is very close to that of Fuqua, he rejects Fuqua's view that non-Christians are under civil law only. Bales holds that non-Christians are under "the law on the heart."

[29]See Appendix N for more on this matter.

[30]See Bales' *Soils and Seeds of Sectarianism* (Shreveport, Lambert Book House, 1947), passim.

[31]Ibid., p. 23. Cf.: pp. 19, 22, et al.

[32]Ibid., p. 36.

[33]Ibid., p. 40.

[34]Ibid., p. 57.

[35]J. D. Bales, *Miracles or Mirages?* (Austin, Firm Foundation Publishing House, 1956), Introduction. Also, passim.

[36]Ibid.

[37]Ibid., p. 227.

[38]Ibid., p. 231.

[39]*Soils and Seeds of Sectarianism*, pp. 56-170.

[40]Ibid., p. 62.

[41]Ibid.

[42]Ibid.

[43]Ibid., pp. 66-170.

APPENDIX M

"THE LAW ON THE HEART"—PER BALES

It has already been pointed out and discussed that brother Bales leans heavily (in his effort to establish his liberal doctrine on divorce and remarriage) on his affirmation (a) that all non-Christians are under "the law in (or on) the heart" and (b) that no non-Christian is under (amenable to) the law (gospel) of Christ. (He has, in at least one statement, implied that non-Christian Jews living today are under the Law of Moses {Bales Ms.}).

In Appendix M the following will be set out (1) a listing of what Bales must know in order to demonstrate that his position re "the law on the heart" is true, (2) proof that he cannot know what he must know, and (3) reference to matters set out in other chapters and/or appendices which refute Bales' position on this matter.

1. *A listing of what Bales must know in order to demonstrate that his position is true.* In order to know that his position on "the law on the heart" is true, Bales must know at least the following: (a) that there is such a thing as "the law on the heart" (as he uses the expression), (b) that "the law on the heart" is objective (or absolute)—that is, that "the law on the heart" is not merely subjective, (c) the contents of "the law on the heart" are known—or at least can be known—by every non-Christian without any (miraculous) revelation from God, (d) that the contents of "the law on the heart" are addressed to him (the non-Christian)—and only to him, (e) that the law (gospel) of Christ is not addressed to the non-Christian—i.e., he must know that the law (gospel)[1] of Christ is not addressed to non-Christians, (f) that the contents of the law (gospel) of Christ, are not addressed to the non-Christian, (g) that even if non-Christians (e.g., Baptists, Catholics, Methodists, et al.) are thoroughly convinced that they are amenable to the law of Christ, they are not amenable to it, (h) that the contents (tenets) of "the law on the heart" are different from the contents (tenets) of the law of Moses and from the tenets of the law (gospel) of Christ, (i) that no matter how much a non-Christian (such as a Baptist) may know about what the gospel (law) of Christ teaches about divorce and remarriage and no matter how thoroughly convinced a non-Christian (Baptist) is that he is amenable to the teaching of Matt. 19:9, he is nevertheless not amenable, and (j) that no matter how little two Christians may know about what the gospel (law) of Christ teaches on divorce and remarriage—even if they are totally ignorant of Matt. 19:9—they are nevertheless amenable to Matt. 19:9.

Can Bales know all of these things? No, he cannot. Proof that he cannot follows.

2. *Proof that Bales cannot know what he must know in order to know that his position on "the law on the heart" is true.*

(a) *Bales cannot know that there even is such a thing as "the law on the heart" as he envisions it.* It is true that all responsible persons have a conscience. The conscience is God-given, not developed by training or environment. The conscience is that capacity within each person which urges him to follow that course of action (do those things) which he is convinced (has sincere conviction concerning) is right. The conscience involves the sense of oughtness—the realization that one ought to do what is right. But the conscience does not tell man what is right—i.e., it does not give the contents—the definite tenets of what is right.

From his sense of oughtness (conscience), man can use his reasoning power to deduce the existence of God. This is the case because, realizing that the sense of oughtness cannot be taught or learned, one realizes that it must have been given to each individual by the Supreme Good—infinite Good; i.e., God. Realizing the existence of God, one can "make sense" of his conviction that he ought to act in a certain way—i.e., to do what is right. This simply means that, realizing the existence of the infinite God, the individual can form a rationale for the existence of his own sense of oughtness. Then, using his powers of ratiocination (reasoning), he can determine some definite things which he ought to do and some definite things which he ought not to do. Realizing that every man owes his ultimate existence to the miraculous creative activity of God and, from that great truth, he further realizes the value of neighbor and something—not everything—of how he should treat his neighbor.

There are other things which could be said about this basic truth,[2] but it must suffice here to point out that all of the truth which man can learn (by means of the way just described—i.e., without direct revelation from God) has been made a part of every covenant God has had with man—e.g., the law of Moses and the law of Christ.

This is the case because God is infinite in all of His attributes—He does not change in His nature; He does not change—(in what is surely an inadequate way of saying it)—as to the principles by which He acts. To say that God is omnibenevolent is to say that He always acts in harmony with His own infinite nature (e.g., He does not lie, Tit. 1:2; it is impossible for Him to lie, Heb. 6:18; He is not a man that he should repent or lie, I Sam. 15:29).

Thus, every principle by which God has ever acted has been a part of every covenant He has had with man. Every principle by which God acted during the Patriarchy was also a part of the law of Moses. But Jews, during the time the law of Moses was in force, were under obligation to act in harmony with those principles because they were constituent elements of the law of Moses (the law which the Jews were under)—just as the Gentiles during that time—and before—were under obligation to act in harmony with those principles because they were constituent elements of the Patriarchal dispensation.

In the same way, those same principles are constituent elements of the law of Christ, and men now living are under obligation to act in harmony with those principles—not because they were constituent elements of the Patriarchal and/or Mosaic dispensations—but because they are component parts of the law under which all men are now living: the law of Christ (Mk.16:15-16; Matt. 28:18-20; Lk. 24:45-49; Acts 14:17; 15:6-9; 17:30-31; John 6:44-45; Heb. 8:8-10; 10:16).

But, for Bales to have any point at all in his use of "the law on the heart," that expression must refer to some law the contents of which are not a part—i.e., not constituent elements—of the law of Christ. This means that, for Bales to have any point with his "law on the heart," that "law on the heart" must be a law which is different from and other than the gospel (law) of Christ. But any one who teaches some law other than the gospel rests under the anathema of God (Gal. 1:9). Bales himself taught in years past that "the Bible alone constitutes the rule of faith for it is the only word of God we have" (*Soils and Seeds of Sectarianism,* p. 19. See also: *The Sufficiency of the Scripture* and *The Nature Of The Word* by Bales). Thus, Bales' whole effort on this point is doomed to failure. It has been shown to be false.

(b) *Bales cannot know that "the law on the heart" (as he envisions it) is objective (absolute) and not merely subjective.* If Bales contends that the contents of "the law on the heart" are not constituent elements of the Patriarchal dispensation, the law of Moses, and the law of Christ (which he must do to sustain his case), then he thereby implies that "the law on the heart," as he (Bales) sees it is not objective but subjective. This means that there is no objective standard to which non-Christians may refer in order to evaluate their thoughts and actions. This means that, for non-Christians, it is the case that Jones (a non-Christian) in all good conscience holds that polygamy is right (in harmony with God's will) and Smith (also a non-Christian) in all good conscience holds that polygamy is wrong (not in harmony with God's will). This is a situation in which Bales must affirm a logical contradiction because Bales has no standard by which to say that either Jones or Smith is right or wrong.

Thus, since any doctrine which affirms a logical contradiction is false itself, then since Bales' doctrine affirms a logical contradiction, it follows that Bales' doctrine is false.

(c) *Bales cannot know that the contents of "the law on the heart" (as he envisions it) are known—or at least can be known—by every non-Christian.*

Since Bales has no objective standard for non-Christians living today—even though he formerly taught that the Bible is the final authority for all men now living[3]—there is no way by which Bales can know the definite contents of "the law on the heart" (as he uses the expression). Thus, he fails in a fundamental way.

(d) *Bales cannot know that the contents of "the law on the heart" (as he envisions it) are addressed only to non-Christians.* Given Bales' doctrine, the non-Christian must know {a} that there is such a thing as "the law on the heart" (as Bales uses the expression), {b} the contents of that law, {c} that the contents of that law are different from and other than those of the law of Christ, and {d} that the contents of "the law on the heart" (as per Bales) are addressed only to non-Christians.

From the material set out in preceding sections, it is obvious that Bales has no way of knowing these four things. But, not knowing this, his case must fail.

(e) *Bales cannot know that the law (gospel) of Christ is not addressed to non-Christians.* The New Covenant plainly teaches that the law (gospel) of Christ is addressed to every adult in every nation in all the world during all of the gospel dispensation (Mk. 16:15-16; Matt. 28:18-20). This has already been proved (demonstrated) beyond doubt in this book.[4]

(f) *Bales cannot know that the details of the law (gospel) of Christ are not addressed to the non-Christian.*[5]

Bales' case depends upon his being able to prove—not just "think so"—that Matt. 19:9 is addressed only to Christians who are married to Christians. But, since Jesus taught Matt. 19:9 during His earthly ministry before He gave the Great Commission, and since, in giving the Great Commission He made clear that, as a part of their "making disciples" the Apostles were to teach men to "observe all things whatsoever I commanded you," and since Matt. 19:9 is a part of what He had commanded them, the Apostles had the obligation of teaching Matt. 19:9 to "every creature" in all the world ("of all the nations"). Thus, the very detail (of the law of Christ) which Bales is most concerned to proclaim as not being a detail (of the law of Christ) which is not to be addressed to non-Christians turns out to be incontrovertibly addressed to them.[6]

(g) *Bales cannot know that even if the non-Christian (e.g., Roman Catholics, Baptists, Lutherans, et al.) who may know a great deal about the Bible are thoroughly convinced that they are amenable to the law (gospel) of Christ, they are still not amenable to it.*[7]

This point has been briefly discussed earlier in this appendix and thoroughly discussed in other parts of this book[8] and, thus, really needs no further discussion here. Suffice it to say that Bales is hung on the cross of denominationalism. He has already given some indication that he intends to exclude Baptists, Methodists, et al. from the non-Christian realm and invent—as did Fuqua—another "in-between" realm for them. (He chided this author for asking questions about denominationalists rather than "unbelievers.")

(h) *Bales cannot know that the non-Christian can know that the contents of "the law on the heart" (as Bales sees it) are different from the contents of the law of Moses and the contents of the law of Christ.* Since this point—and its impossibility for Bales—has been discussed above, there is no need for further discussion here.

3. *References to matters set out in other chapters and/or appendices which refute Bales' position on this matter.* What Bales needs here is a passage which plainly teaches (either explicitly or implicitly) that there is such a thing as "the law written on the heart of non-Christians." He tries to supply this by citing Rom. 2:14-15, but in doing so, he fails to accomplish what he must in order to prove his case. This is the case because Rom. 2:14-15 says, "(for when the Gentiles that have not the law do by nature the things of the law, these, not having the law, are the law unto themselves; in that they show the work of the law written in their hearts, their conscience bearing witness therewith, and their thoughts one with another accusing or else excusing them)." Bales sees what is not there! This passage does not say that non-Christians have a law written in their hearts which is different from and other than the law (gospel) of Christ.

Let it be supposed—i.e., *ex hypothesi*—(a) that before God gave the law of Moses to the Jews, all people lived by "the law written in the heart" and (b) that after God gave the law of Moses to the Jews, all non-Jews kept on living by "the law written on the heart." If such were the case, then "the law written on the heart" allowed polygamy from earliest times of history of man (as soon as there was more than one woman on earth) until Pentecost! But, Bales insists on going even further; he insists that all non-Christians[9] living today are not amenable to the law (gospel) of Christ but to this same "law on the heart"!

If such be the case, then it would follow—although Bales contradicts himself here[10]—that Bales holds very strongly that the law of Christ is "not retroactive" (that is, to have binding force to cause severance of) to marriages which were contracted before the parties involved were baptized. And, further, if such be the case, then Bales would accept into Christian fellowship any man with, say, ten wives or more since the law he was under (according to Bales) before baptism (i.e., "the law on the heart") allows polygamy.

Since Bales' doctrine forces him—if he is consistent with the tenets of his own doctrine—to accept such views as (a) being involved in denominationalism is not sinful for non-Christians, (b) the use of instrumental music in worship is not sinful for non-Christians, and (c) polygamy is not sinful for either non-Christians or Christians.

If these things do not follow, why do they not? Will Bales say "the law on the heart" is now different from what it was in Abraham's day or in David's day? If so, who wrote the new "law written on the heart"? Since Jesus now has all authority in heaven and on earth, He must have written it. But, as was shown in Chapter X, the law (gospel) of Christ is the one—and only—body of doctrine which Christ addressed to men living today.

Again, brother Bales is wrong.

Before Appendix M is closed it would be good to: (1) raise one more crucial question and (2) make one more crucial affirmation.

1. *Another crucial question:* "Does 'the law on the heart' (as Bales envisions it) include the knowledge that God exists?" If Bales' answer to the question is, "Yes," then other questions arise:

(1) "Is the knowledge that God exists innate in every person (since Bales alleges that every non-Christian is under 'the law on the heart' and has knowledge of it)?" If Bales' answer to question (1) is "Yes," then Bales' doctrine does away with Paul's argument in Rom. 1:18-32 and, in fact, with all natural theology. If Bales' answer to question (1) is "No," (even though "the law on the heart"—as per Bales—includes the knowledge of God), then is it the case that all non-Christians have knowledge that God exists by unwritten, miraculous revelation—was knowledge that God exists gained by written miraculous revelation? Was it gained without observing evidence and reasoning correctly about that evidence?

(2) If Bales' answer to question (1) is "No," then, since Bales' alleged "law on the heart" depends on all men having knowledge of God (how could there be real (objective) moral right and wrong if there

were no God?), there could be no "law on the heart" for the non-Christian until—somehow or other—he gained knowledge of the existence of God. And, since a negative answer implies that knowledge of God is not innate then it would follow that Bales would have to hold that such knowledge came either by miraculous direct revelation or by deduction from some objective fact(s). Bales would deny that knowledge that God exists comes by miraculous direct revelation. He would also surely deny that knowledge that God exists is innate in every person. That leaves only the way of reasoning from evidence. But Bales cannot prove that men can reason to any moral or spiritual law which is binding (by God) on men today which is not a constituent element of the gospel (law) of Christ. (If Bales thinks he can present such a law, let him put his hand to the task—and let him do so in the light of Mk. 16:15-16; Matt. 28:18-20; Gal. 1:6-9; Eph. 4:4-6.)

The truth of the matter is: Bales' doctrine of "the law on the heart" is false; there is no such thing as a "law on the heart" which is different from and other than the gospel of Christ (Eph. 4:4-6; Gal. 1:6-9; Mk. 16:15-16). Thinking counterfactually, if there were such a law (i.e., "the law on the heart" which is different from and other than the gospel), then it would have to be either (1) innate or (2) a miraculous direct revelation or (3) reasoning from evidence. Since none of these can be the source of a moral or spiritual law which is approved by God and which is different from and other than the gospel (law) of Christ, then Bales is simply wrong about this matter.

The "law written in (or on) the heart" today is the gospel of Christ (Heb. 8:8-10; cf.: Jer. 31:31-33).

Whatever a man can learn of moral or spiritual laws by reasoning (from evidence) which are approved by God, as binding on men living today, will be what is already a part of the gospel. *In short, there simply is no "law on the heart" as affirmed by Bales*. Since this is the case, Bales' effort to "take the lock out of wedlock" fails; Bales' doctrine is false. Set out in precise logical form, the argument involved in the above material is as follows:

1. If Bales' doctrine on divorce and remarriage is true, then it is true both that there is a "law on the heart" which is different from and other than the law (gospel) of Christ and that men come to knowledge of that law either (1) by being born (i.e., knowledge of the law is innate), or (2) by some miraculous direct revelation, or (3) by reasoning validly from evidence.

2. It is false that men can come to knowledge of such a "law on the heart" by birth (no such law is innate or else Paul could not have lived "in all good

conscience," Acts 23:1, and have been guilty of sin while doing so).

3. It is false that men come to knowledge of such a "law on the heart" by a miraculous direct revelation. (As Bales will readily admit, the days of miracles are over, I Cor. 13:8-10.)

4. It is false that men come to knowledge of such a law by reasoning from evidence. (While it is true that men can reason from available evidence to knowledge that God exists and that some things are right and some things are wrong, it remains the case that everything which can be so learned is already a part of the gospel of Christ. Appendix K, with its discussion of eternal principles (by which God acts) as being a part of every dispensation, is relevant here and should be restudied if necessary.)

5. Thus, it is false that men can come to knowledge of a "law on the heart" (as Bales alleges, which is different from and other than the gospel of Christ) by either (1) birth, or (2) miraculous direct revelation, or (3) reasoning from evidence. (If any disjunctive proposition has all false disjunctive elements, then that entire proposition is false.)

6. Thus, it is false both that there is a "law on the heart" which is different from and other than the law of Christ and that men come to knowledge of that law either (1) by being born (i.e., knowledge of the law is innate) or (2) by some miraculous direct revelation or (3) by reasoning validly from some evidence. (If even one conjunct of a conjunctive proposition is false, then the conjunctive proposition as a whole is false.)[11]

7. Therefore, Bales' doctrine on divorce and remarriage is false.

This argument is set out in symbolic terms in a footnote below.[12]

Since Bales' entire case depends upon his alleged "law on the heart" which is different from and other than the law of Christ, this one argument destroys his entire argument on divorce and remarriage.

Footnotes

[1]See Chapter X for proof that the law of Christ and the gospel of Christ are one and the same message.

[2]See *The Warren-Flew Debate* and *The Warren-Matson Debate* (both on the existence of God) (Jonesboro, Ak., National Christian Press, 1977, 1979). passim.

[3]Bales, *The Sufficiency of the Scriptures* pp. 5-12.

[4]See Chapter X (as well as various other chapters) for detailed proof that all men (whether Christian or non-Christian) are under (amenable to) the law (gospel) of Christ.

[5]See Chapters XVI-A, XVI-B, and XVII in regard to such passages as Matt. 28:18-20 (. . .all things. . ."). Also see Appendix T below.

[6]Ibid.

[7]Bales, like Fuqua, has "hung" himself by espousing a doctrine which implies that, for non-Christians, being in a denomination and preaching and practicing denominational doctrine is not sinful.

[8]For example, see Appendix L.

[9]Although in a manuscript statement he implies that Jews living today are amenable to the law of Moses. This has been documented earlier.

[10]As has already been discussed and documented. See also Appendix P.

[11]Set out in symbolic terms, this premise looks like this: $\{[(p \cdot q) \cdot \sim q] > \sim(p \cdot q\}$; that is, by showing that one conjunct is false, one shows that the conjunctive proposition, as a whole, is false.

[12]The argument, set out in symbolic terms, is as follows*:

1. $B^D > [L_H^{D \cdot O} \cdot (IvMvR)]$
2. $\sim I$
3. $\sim M$
4. $\sim R$
5. $\sim(IvMvR)$ (If every disjunct of a disjunctive proposition is false, then that disjunctive proposition is false.)
6. $\therefore \sim [L_H^{D \cdot O} \cdot (IvMvR)]$ from 5. (If even one conjunct of a conjunctive proposition is false, then that proposition is false.
7. $\therefore \sim B^D$

*Meaning of the symbols used above:

B^D = Bales' doctrine on divorce and remarriage is true.

$L_H^{D \cdot O}$ = There is "law on the heart" which is different from and other than the law (gospel) of Christ.

I = men come to knowledge of the "law on the heart" by being born. (i.e., it is innate).

M = men come to knowledge of "law on the heart" by some miraculous direct revelation from God.

R = men come to knowledge of "the law on the heart" by reasoning from some evidence.

$\sim$ = It is false that. . .

APPENDIX N

NEO-KETCHERSIDISM"—
BALES ON "GOSPEL" AND "DOCTRINE"

For many years Carl Ketcherside (along with his fellow-worker, Leroy Garrett) has taught a false doctrine which involves the implication that "the gospel of Christ" is to be distinguished from "the doctrine of Christ."[1]

The view entails the claim that "the gospel" refers only to the death, burial, and resurrection of Christ and/or all that is involved in leading the non-Christian to be baptized.[2]

On the other hand, the view entails the claim that "doctrine" refers only to instructions as to what one is to do after he becomes a Christian (i.e., post-baptism activities).

The view further entails the basic claim that, as to "the gospel", there must be unity[3] and that, as to "the doctrine", there does not have to be unity—rather, even though Christians may hold contradictory views in matters of "doctrine," there can still be unity simply on the basis that all baptized believers are united in Christ. The basic affirmation is, in effect, that they will fellowship all baptized believers as their brothers in Christ—even if the baptism is not according to Acts 2:38 and even if they do hold contradictory positions on "doctrine."

Let it be made clear that—at least as far as this author knows—brother Bales has never agreed "down the line" (i.e., completely) with this viewpoint just explained. Yet, it is the conviction of this author that Bales' doctrine is close enough (in its fundamental basis) to "Ketchersidism" to brand Bales' view as "Neo-Ketchersidism."

This point is made because Bales—as do Ketcherside and Garrett—holds that the gospel and the doctrine of Christ are not one and the same body of doctrine.[4]

1. *Statements from Bales which show that he distinguishes between "gospel" and "doctrine."*

(1) *Bales refers to Matthew 28:18-20 and says that "this passage shows that the gospel is to be preached to people to save them, and after they are saved they are taught to observe all things whatsoever Jesus has commanded converts (Matt. 28:20)."*[5]

It should be noted that while Bales does not use the word "doctrine" to refer to what he says is to be taught to Christians, it is very clear that he agrees with Garrett and Ketcherside that "gospel" and "doctrine" are to be distinguished from each other. The reader should, if his memory needs refreshing, study carefully Chapter X in this book to see that the distinction which Bales makes is a false one.

(2) *Not surprisingly—in the light of his many self-contradictions—Bales contradicts himself by saying that "through the gospel Christ comes both to Jew and Gentile now that the new covenant is in operation. (Eph. 2:17)"*[6] Here he regards the gospel as a part of the New Covenant.

In the midst of the answer just referred to, brother Bales says ". . .if *we* (emphasis, T.B.W.) through faith obey the gospel."[7] Since Bales is a Christian, just whom does the "we" include? Is he not saying here that Christians obey the gospel by being born of water and the spirit (i.e., by being baptized)? Or, does he use "we" in the sense of "all men"? Or in the sense of "non-Christians only"? In a preceding chapter, Bales' "mix-up" on this matter has been explained in detail.[8]

Also, his perversion of Matt. 28:18-20 has also been explained in a previous chapter.[9] Matt. 28:18-20 does not teach—as Bales alleges—"Go baptize those you have taught and then teach those you have baptized." Rather, recognizing the function of the modal participles involved, it can be seen that Jesus is telling the Apostles to go make children of God out of children of the devil by baptizing and teaching them all things that Jesus had commanded them.[10] Thus, all men are amenable to Matt. 28:18-20.

(3) *In a special section on denominationalism, Bales made some significant statements.*

(a) He said, "However, neither the Jew nor the denominationalist is under New Covenant law."[11] Yet Bales holds that the non-Christian, to be saved, must respond to the invitation which Christ extends to them (i.e., he says, they must obey the gospel). It should be noted that Bales alleges that neither the Jew nor the denominationalist is under New Covenant law. Yet, he also holds, to be saved, the non-Christian must obey the gospel.[12] Since one cannot obey a law which he is not under (Rom. 3:19), and since Bales alleges (a) that *no denominationalist is under new covenant law* and (b) that to be saved, the denominationalist must obey the gospel, it follows that, according to Bales, the gospel is no part of the New Covenant of Jesus Christ. What a pity that such a brilliant mind as that of brother Bales should come to such an anti-Biblical position!

It should be noted Bales again has made a distinction between the gospel and the law (doctrine) of Christ—or the New Covenant of Christ. The detailed study set out in Chapter X shows that such a doctrine had its origin in the mind of an uninspired man and not with the Holy Spirit and His word (the Scriptures)!

Bales makes—if possible—an even more explicit statement on the matter when he says[13] that "denominationalists who have not obeyed the gospel are not in the New Covenant, therefore they are not amenable to the laws bound on converts (Matt. 28:18-20)."[14] (It can be seen that Bales leans heavily on his perversion of Matt. 28:18-20.)

It is a crucial element in Bales' entire case that he alleges that only one who is "in the covenant" can obey the covenant. Now, since it is clear that in the quotation (from Bales) just above, he strongly affirms that denominationalists who have not obeyed the gospel are not in the covenant (i.e., not saved, not Christians), then would it not be pertinent to ask Bales, "If one cannot obey the New Covenant until he is in the New Covenant, is it not also the case—given your view—that no one can obey the gospel until he is in the gospel?" (Whatever that might mean!) What does Bales mean when he says that one cannot obey the New Covenant until he is in the New Covenant? What would it mean to say that one cannot obey the gospel until he is in the gospel? Is it not the case that both of these are actually very foolish—even absurd—positions? Isn't it the case that to say that one cannot obey the New Covenant until he is in the New Covenant is just another way of saying that you cannot obey the New Covenant unless you have already obeyed it? If not, what does it mean? Further, since Bales admits that one can—even must—obey the gospel before he can be saved, is Bales not thus admitting that one can obey the gospel without being in the gospel? And, if—even given Bales' view—one can obey the gospel without being in the gospel, why is it not also the case that—even granting, for sake of argument, the counter-factual hypothesis (which Bales affirms)—one can obey the new covenant without being in the New Covenant? And, let it be remembered that all persons who obey the gospel are saved. And that one cannot obey the gospel unless he is amenable to it (Rom. 3:19). In the same way, one cannot obey the New Covenant unless he is amenable to it. So, Bales has based his entire case on an arbitrary assumption (i.e., that one cannot obey the new covenant unless he is already in the new covenant) which he, in self-contradiction, refuses to apply to obeying the gospel (cf. Mk. 16:15-16; II Thess. 1:7-9).

So, Bales, having conjured up an arbitrary distinction between "the gospel of Christ" and "the doctrine of Christ," has now conjured up another arbitrary distinction between "the gospel of Christ" and "the covenant of Christ." The proof that these assumptions are arbitrary and these distinctions are false has already been set out in detail in Chapter X. In that chapter, it was shown that there is one—and only one—body of doctrine from Christ to which all men (whether Christian or non-Christian) are amenable. That one body of doctrine is referred to in various passages of

Scripture as, the gospel of Christ, the truth, the faith, the word, the word of God, the new covenant, the doctrine of Christ, etc. These are not different messages but are simply different ways of referring to one and the same body of teaching! To affirm—as do Bales, Garrett, and Ketcherside—that the gospel is something different from and/or other than the doctrine of Christ is simply to affirm that which is false. In the same way, to affirm—even by implication, as does Bales—that the gospel of Christ is something different from and/or other than the covenant of Christ is to affirm that which is false.

But Bales' entire case depends upon this false distinction (that the gospel is something different from and other than the doctrine and/or the new covenant). The gospel of Christ and the doctrine of Christ are one and the same thing. The gospel of Christ and the covenant of Christ are one and the same thing. All men are amenable to the gospel; all men are amenable to the doctrine, all men are amenable to the new covenant. All men can obey the gospel (Mk. 16:15-16); all men can obey the doctrine (Matt. 28:18-20; Acts 5:42), and all men can obey the new covenant (Heb. 8:8-13).

It has been shown that it is sheer assumption—and a false one at that—to say that one cannot obey the covenant until after one is in the covenant (i.e., is already a Christian).

It is sheer human invention to brand Matt. 19:9 as a "covenant passage,"[15] as Bales has done (and builds his case upon). Anyone who can see the error made by Bales in calling Matt. 19:9 a "covenant passage" should have no trouble in seeing the falsity of his position on divorce and remarriage, for that position depends upon his use of the expression "covenant passage" and then also inventing the idea that a so-called "covenant passage" is addressed only to those who are already in the covenant (i.e., already Christians).

In the light of the foregoing, it should come as no surprise to anyone that Bales has not even tried to set forth a precise, logically valid argument with true premises, the conclusion of which is: "Therefore, Matt. 19:9 is a 'covenant passage' and therefore it applies only to Christians who are married to Christians." The view that there even is such a thing as a "covenant passage" implies that part of Christ's message to man in this dispensation is the new covenant but that the rest of it is not the new covenant. There is no Bible evidence for such a conclusion.

2. *Significance of the foregoing.* The foregoing shows that—at least as far as any alleged distinction between gospel and doctrine[16]—Bales has espoused what might be called "Neo-Ketchersidism" rather than the truth. It is sad to see such a valiant and able soldier

of the cross, who in the past has fought so boldly against the doctrine advanced by such men as Leroy Garrett and Carl Ketcherside, now, in effect, join them in the espousal of the proposition which is so fundamental to their case—viz., that the gospel of Christ and the doctrine of Christ are not one and the same body of doctrine.

It is sad to see—but now easily understood—that the time has now come that James D. Bales is the object of the praise of such false teachers as Leroy Garrett and Hoy Ledbetter.

It is the prayer of this author (T.B.W.) that brother Bales will soon see the error of what he has taught in this matter.

Footnotes

[1]Ketcherside, in *Mission Messenger,* passim., and Garrett, *Bible Talk,* passim; and *Restoration Review,* passim.

[2]But the view has been modified recently (at least by Garrett) to include recognition of people such as Baptists to be Christians.

[3]But there is evidence that even this view has been modified so that, for example, there does not have to be unity as to the purpose of baptism.

[4]In Chapter X of this book, it was proved that there is one—and only one—body of doctrine, the gospel.

[5]Bales' answer to T.B.W. question no. 26, p. 24, Ms.

[6]Bales' answer to T.B.W. question no. 25, p. 24, Ms. See entire answer.

[7]Ibid.

[8]But Bales cannot sustain his doctrine on divorce and remarriage if he cannot sustain the point that non-Christians are not amenable to the gospel.

[9]Chapter XVI-B.

[10]See previous detailed study of Matt. 28:18-20, Chapter XVI-B.

[11]Special section in Bales Ms. on "Denominationalism," p. 1.

[12] Ibid.

[13] Ibid.

[14] Ibid.

[15] *NUB*, passim.

[16] See also Chapter X.

[17] And of Hoy Ledbetter, editor of *Integrity*, a doctrinally liberal journal.

APPENDIX O

NON-CHRISTIANS AND WORSHIP

Brother Bales tries to counter the truth (set forth in such passages as Mk. 16:15-16; Acts 17:30-32; Matt. 28:18-20; et al.) that all men (whether Christian or non-Christian) are amenable to the one body of doctrine—the gospel, the truth, the faith, the word, et al.—by arguing that such cannot be true because, he says—if it were true,—then non-Christians would be under obligation to eat the Lord's Supper and do other acts of worship authorized and/or demanded by the law (gospel) of Christ.

That Bales' point here advanced is false has already been shown in Appendix G. There it was shown that he overlooks (denies) the truth that one can be obligated to do what he is not yet qualified to do. To avoid needless repetition, the reader is urged to study carefully Appendix G for the details of the truth on this matter.

However, just a bit might be said here in a positive way.

All men (whether Christian or non-Christian) now living on earth are under obligation to worship God. But to worship God acceptably (i.e., without sinning in so doing) one must worship God "by faith"—i.e., doing only what is authorized by the law of Christ.[1] To worship God acceptably, one must act by faith in worshipping Him "in spirit and in truth."

The principle—that men, to be pleasing to God, must do what He has authorized—is made clear even in the Old Testament (Lev. 10:1,2; I Chron. 15:1-15; Cf.: Heb. 11:4).

All men (whether Christian or non-Christian) who use instrumental music in the worship of God, sin in so doing. And, Bales fails to refute this truth when he calls attention to the fact that such non-Christians as Baptists are already lost so they are no worse off (Bales says) even if they do use instrumental music in worship. Bales urges others to recognize that non-Christians are lost any way. But Bales dodges the main point.

The point in asking, "Do Baptists sin when they use instrumental music in worship?" is not to ask, "Are non-Christians lost?" Of course, all adult non-Christians are lost, but the question is: "Do they sin when they use instrumental music in worship?" Of course, they do, because such is not authorized by the law (gospel) of Christ, and even non-Christians are amenable to the gospel (law) of Christ (Mk. 16:15-16; Matt. 28:18-20; Lk. 24:45-49; Acts 17:30-31; 15:6-9; 14:15-17, et al.).

May the brotherhood know that brother Bales'

implied position is that Baptists, Methodists, et al. do not sin when they use instrumental music in worship—just as he says they do not sin when they divorce and remarry again and again on some ground other than fornication (even if they know that Christ taught Matt. 19:9).

Thus, if Bales' present position on divorce and remarriage is true, then he and every other gospel preacher who has ever preached, taught or written that denominationalists sin in using instrumental music in the worship of God, should repent of all of that action and sincerely apologize to denominationalists for having said that they sin in using instrumental music in worship.

While the worship of God by faith (i.e., according to what the New Covenant authorizes) is obligatory upon all men now living, it is nevertheless true that one is not qualified—for example—to eat the Lord's Supper until after he has become a child of God. The eating of the Lord's Supper is both an obligation and a privilege: (a) it is an obligation of all men now living and (b) it is a privilege only of those who have qualified themselves to eat that Supper by becoming members of God's family.

Every man now living who fails to worship God by faith (according to what the New Covenant authorizes) sins in so failing. Even those in ignorance of the truth of this matter sin in so failing.

The reader should note that the Jews who led the Romans into crucifying Jesus, sinned in so doing even though Peter said to them of that crucifixion, "And now, brethren, I know that in ignorance ye did it, as did also your rulers" (Acts 3:17).

So, it is clear that Bales' assertions in regard to worship do not help his case on divorce and remarriage at all. It remains true that law (gospel) of Christ is addressed to all men (Mk. 16:15-16). And, so Bales himself admitted in days gone by, all men—this would include unbelievers—are required (under obligation) to be baptized, but those who have not yet both believed and repented are not qualified to be baptized (Mk. 16:15-16; Acts 2:38; 3:19; Cf. Matt. 3:8 to see the same principle in effect in connection with the preaching and baptizing of John the Baptist).

It is clear that Bales acknowledges—when writing on subjects other than divorce and remarriage—that all men are amenable to the law of Christ.[2] He said, "The Scriptures constitute our rule of faith and practice because besides them there is no other rule."[3] It is clear from the book that Bales was not confining the "our" to Christians only. If he did, he would make the colossal blunder—which, by implication, he actually does in a number of places, as has already been shown in this book—of affirming that the Scriptures have nothing to say to the non-Christian. And, if such be the case, then no non-Christian could be saved. And, since all of us were at one time non-Christians, it would follow that no one could ever be saved!

Bales thus faces this dilemma: either (a) admit that he is wrong on divorce and remarriage or (b) brand the gospel of Jesus Christ as being completely worthless to mankind.

It would be difficult—if not impossible—to imagine a more untenable position for any disputant.

Footnotes

[1]Study carefully *Ascertaining Bible Authority* by Roy Deaver.

[2]Bales, *The Sufficiency of the Scriptures*, pp. 5-11.

[3]Ibid., p. 9.

APPENDIX P

POLYGAMY

This topic is so devastating to brother Bales that, in his efforts to fit it in with his theory of divorce and remarriage, he involves himself in theological chaos, including admissions of defeat. Since this has already been explained in great detail, it has been decided to simply refer the reader to the material which has been presented on the matter in preceding chapters. Suffice it to say here that in cases of a polygamist being baptized, Bales makes the law of Christ on divorce and remarriage "retroactive" (as Bales refers to it) in such fashion as to demand that the polygamist give up his multiplicity of wives, but he (Bales) denies such "retroactivity" in regard to other pre-baptism marriages which violate the law of Christ. But it is important for the reader to study carefully the earlier detailed material on this topic. In that material it was shown that Bales must hold either (1) that polygamy for non-Christians and even for Christians (provided the "marriages" took place before the people involved became Christians) is acceptable to God or (2) that he, Bales, is wrong in what he affirms on divorce and remarriage (i.e., in regard to Matt. 19:9; I Cor. 7; et al.).

Bales hits a "theological brick wall" on the questions of polygamy and denominationalism, and there is no way he can avoid that "brick wall" except by giving up his doctrine on divorce and remarriage.

APPENDIX Q

"THE 'GUILTY PARTY' CAN REMARRY" THEORY

In his 1961 A.C.C. lecture,[1] brother Bales implies that, in a case of fornication on the part of one member of a married couple, the guilty party (the one guilty of the fornication) is just as free (in God's sight) as is the innocent party.

The basic effort which Bales makes to sustain this view is to raise a series of questions which, rhetorically, imply the following propositions:

1. If a marriage is broken so that one of the two parties is free to remarry, then, since the original marriage no longer exists, the other party also would be free to marry again.
2. Thus, even in a situation in which a man has been unfaithful to his wife, then, if she puts him away for fornication, he is just as free to marry again as she is.

Some, apparently following brother Bales' lead, have used an analogy involving police handcuffs. The analogy goes like this, if when Jones is handcuffed to Smith and Jones is freed (unhandcuffed) from Smith, then Smith of necessity must be freed from Jones. They make the application to divorce and remarriage by arguing that if Mr. Jones is married to Miss Smith and Smith (now Mrs. Jones) is freed from Jones (because of Mr. Jones' fornication) so that Smith (Mrs. Jones) is free to marry someone, then it must be the case that Smith (Mrs. Jones) is free to marry someone else because the marriage with Jones has been destroyed (the marriage no longer exists). But, these advocates continue, if Jones' marriage to Smith (Mrs. Jones) no longer exists, then Jones is just as free to marry again as is Smith (Mrs. Jones)—even though Jones has been guilty of marital unfaithfulness.

In response to this doctrine, this author (T.B.W.) wishes to point out a number of things.

First, it should be noted that human illustrations or analogies should be used to explain or illustrate—not to prove. The "handcuff" analogy proves nothing as to divorce and remarriage.

Second, it is possible that Smith and Jones could be handcuffed together and Smith be freed but Jones not. For example, the handcuffs could be unlocked and Smith allowed to go free, but Jones would remain handcuffed to a steel bar to which the two of them (Jones and Smith) had been handcuffed (as well as to each other). When God joins a man and woman in marriage they are not "handcuffed" (bound) only to each other but also to God's law (to which they were bound even before they married). God's law allows Smith (Mrs. Jones) (the innocent party) to remarry but forbids Jones (the guilty party) to remarry. So, in the "handcuff" analogy on divorce and remarriage, the following should be noted: (1) the husband is "handcuffed" to the wife, and the wife is "handcuffed" to the husband, (2) the husband is "handcuffed" to the law of God, and he remains so even if the "handcuffs" to his wife are broken, (3) the wife is "handcuffed" to the law of God, and she remains so even if the "handcuffs" to her husband are broken, and (4) according to the law of God, if the marriage bond is broken by the innocent party putting away the guilty party for fornication, then the innocent party is free to marry another, but (5) the guilty party is not free to marry another (Matt. 5:31-32; 19:9).

Third, the guilty party is not free to remarry because: (1) he is not one who has put away his (her) spouse "for fornication" (Matt. 19:9); (2) Jesus made clear that one is free to divorce and remarry if and only if one has put away his (her) spouse "for fornication" (Matt. 19:9; cf. Matt. 5:31-32). It is rebellion against Christ to hold that the guilty party is free to marry again. (Cf. I Sam. 15:22-23.)

Fourth, if the "guilty party" is free to marry, then "except" (in Jesus' statement in Matt. 19:9) does not really mean "except." (1) Jesus taught: all persons who put away their companions are free to marry if and only if they have put away those companions for fornication. (2)—Or—the same thing can be said in another way: all persons who put away their companions on any ground other than fornication and marry others are persons who keep on committing adultery. (3) But note: men deny (contradict) Jesus' teaching by teaching: it is false that all persons who put away their companions on any ground other than fornication and marry others are persons who (keep on committing adultery.)

Fifth, if both the guilty and the innocent parties are free to marry again, why did the Lord give any instruction about the matter? (1) If the "the-guilty-party-is-free" theory is true, then the phrases "except for fornication" and "committeth adultery" would have no meaning. (2) Note: According to Jesus, someone is guilty of adultery in Matt. 19:9! Who is it? The innocent party, when he (she) marries again? The guilty party, when he (she) marries again? (3) The truth is, it could be only the guilty party!!

Sixth, the "The-guilty-party-is-free" theory implies that the Lord was guilty of an incredible injustice! Who can believe it? (1) Note: Even the "The-guilty-party-is-free" theory advocates (at least most of them, anyway) hold that the unjustly put away innocent party is not free to marry again. (They hold that fornication must occur.) (2) Note further: This view has God forbidding the innocent party unjustly put away to marry again—but—giving to the man who deliberately plans and commits fornication for the express purpose of freeing himself to marry again (the right to marry again). (3) This is an incredibly low moral view. It is indescribably unjust. It is false! God never taught it!

Conclusion

The very idea of ascribing to the Son of God the doctrine that Mr. Jones (a 50 year old man) who has been married to his wife for thirty years could deliberately and with "malice aforethought" (that is, for the express purpose of freeing himself to marry a young woman or any other woman) commit fornication so that his wife would put him away and thus free him to marry the young woman, is repulsive to contemplate. It degrades marriage, it degrades God's word, and, in the eyes of those who accept it as true, it must surely degrade the Lord Himself! It is thus not surprising to see in our society today such practices as "wife-swapping."

Given brother Bales' theory, two men in a congregation could commit fornication with the wife of the other, then after the two marriages had ended in divorce, each one of the two could then marry the other's wife—if he will only say, "I'm sorry—and then live in that new relationship with God's approval, for the rest of their lives. Brother Bales' doctrine clearly implies this degraded consequence.

May it be remembered that every doctrine which implies a false doctrine is false itself!

Footnote

[1]As well as a number of other places.

APPENDIX R

DOES MORE KNOWLEDGE ENTAIL MORE AMENABILITY?

Brother Bales faces an "ungetoverable" problem in facing the above question. As a matter of fact, he flatly contradicts himself in trying to deal with the matter. In one statement, he answers the question "Yes," and, in another statement, he answers "No."

1. *Bales answers "Yes" to this question in the midst of answering a question posed by this author (T.B.W.)*[1] The question asked by T.B.W. was to be answered (by Bales) as either "true" or "false." Bales failed to answer directly that the statement was either "true" or "false," but, in a written answer which he gave to the question, he made it clear that he held the position that as a non-Christian gains additional knowledge of Christ's law, he becomes amenable to that part of the law of Christ which he has learned and does wrong (i.e., guilty of sin) if he does not accept and obey it. In reference to non-Christians who have come into contact with evidence which proves that Jesus Christ is the Son of God, but who refuse to believe that He is the Son of God, among other things, Bales said,[2] "Second, they seal their doom if they reject the only way of pardon. Third, the obligation to accept additional light or truth, when the gospel is preached to them means that they do wrong (sin, T.B.W.) in rejecting the additional light."[3]

But—note carefully—they would not "do wrong" (sin) in rejecting this "additional light" unless it was (is) the case that in learning more of the law (gospel) of Christ, they did become amenable to (under) at least that portion of the law of Christ which they had learned. This is the case because sin is the transgression of law (I John 3:4). Bales admits (a) that where there is no law, there can be no sin and (b) that no one can violate a law to which he is not amenable.

Thus, in answering T.B.W. question no. 56, Bales takes the position that as a non-Christian gains more knowledge of the law (gospel) of Christ, he does become amenable to those parts of it which he learns. Since Matt. 19:9 is a part of the law of Christ and since many non-Christians (for example, (a) some professors and students of Biblical ethics in denominational colleges, universities, and seminaries, (b) some denominational preachers, (c) some people who are not even religious, but who yet study the Bible a great deal, know what Matt. 19:9 says, it follows that, given this "Yes" answer in this statement, Bales admits (by implication) that millions of non-Christians are amenable to (under) the instructions of Matt. 19:9. In making this admission, he admits that his doctrine is false, and, thus, he admits defeat in regard to the whole question of divorce and remarriage.

2. *But, Bales also answers "No" to the same question.* In his book, *Not Under Bondage*, Bales raises the question (the same question considered in point 1 above): "When a person outside of Christ {any adult non-Christian, T.B.W.} learns that Christ taught Matt. 19:9, does that law then and there become binding on him?"[4]

Bales answers the question (which has been raised for him by others) by saying, "*First*, no, because they are not yet under the Covenant."[5] By this answer, he plainly teaches that, no matter how much of the law of Christ (the gospel, the New Covenant) a non-Christian may learn, none—not even one tenet—of the law of Christ is addressed to him. Even if a non-Christian knew the entire New Covenant by memory and understood it perfectly, given this answer by Bales, that non-Christian would still not be amenable to one word of it as long as he remains a non-Christian. Yet, Bales holds that if two Christians are married to each other, they are amenable to Matt. 19:9 even if they never have read it, heard it read or even heard it referred to!

Thus, Bales absolutely contradicts the answer which he gave to T.B.W. question no. 56 with the statement which he made on page 195 of *NUB*. Such is the inevitable fate of any man who espouses a false doctrine (such as brother Bales has on divorce and remarriage). Truth is consistent with itself; error is not.

3. *Significance of the foregoing.*

In giving the answers cited above, brother Bales has contradicted himself and, in so doing, showed that his doctrine on divorce and remarriage is false. This is the case because any doctrine which involves a self-contradiction is false.

Bales cannot answer T.B.W. question no. 56 by either "Yes" or "No" without getting himself into trouble.

If he answers "Yes," he makes at least millions of non-Christians amenable to Matt. 19:9. This defeats his basic position that no non-Christian is amenable to the law of Christ.

If he answers "No," he gives up his position that non-believing non-Christians are not under obligation to repent and be baptized even if they learn what the Bible teaches about Christ and the gospel plan of salvation but do not believe on Christ as the Son of God. Yet the Bible teaches that God commands all men everywhere, Acts 17:30-31 (this would, of course, include atheists and other unbelievers). Thus, a "no" answer by Bales would contradict Acts 17:30-31. (For more on this point, see Appendix G and Appendix X).

Footnotes

[1]Bales' answer to T.B.W. question no. 51 to Bales—answered by Bales on p. 39 of Bales' Manuscript.

[2]Ibid.

[3]Ibid.

[4]*NUB*, p. 195.

[5]Ibid.

APPENDIX S

DID MATTHEW 19:9 BECOME EFFECTIVE ON PENTECOST?

Actually, the answer to this question has already been given—at least by implication—in preceding material. The Bible answer is, "Yes."

During His earthly ministry Jesus taught Matt. 19:9. Then, in giving the Great Commission, (Matt. 28:18-20[1]), Jesus commanded His apostles to teach Matt. 19:9 by commanding them to teach all things that He had commanded to those who were yet to be baptized. Since this has already been discussed in such detail, no further discussion will be given here.

It must be remembered—as has already been thoroughly discussed—that since a change of covenants occurred on Pentecost but no such change has occurred since, then all men who live today live all of their lives under one covenant: the New Covenant—the law of Christ. Therefore, today the marriages of all men (whether Christian or non-Christian) are governed by the law of Christ (including Matt. 19:9).[2]

However, on Pentecost, some Jews heard and obeyed the gospel. They were in a different situation from men are who live today—so far as marriage, divorce and remarriage are concerned—since many of them had married while they were amenable to a different law. No one living today is in that kind of situation; i.e., no man living today has lived a part of his life under (amenable to) one covenant but then (with that first covenant having been abolished) is now living the rest of his life under a different covenant.

The reader should be certain that he has studied carefully the relation of the above truth to the time of the conversion of Saul and the truth stated in I Corinthians 7:12.

Of course, the really crucial point is this: *that Matthew 19:9 is addressed to all men living today.*

Footnotes

[1]See earlier discussion of Matt. 28:18-20 which proves that "all things" which Jesus had commanded was to be taught to those who were yet to be baptized.

[2]See fuller discussion in earlier chapters and appendices.

APPENDIX T

MATTHEW 28:18-20 AND MATTHEW 19:9

Even though Matthew 28:20 has been thoroughly discussed in earlier material[1] and Matthew 19:9 has been discussed in earlier chapters[2] and in a preceding Appendix,[3] it seems wise to add at least a brief note here in regard to the relationship between Matt. 28:18-20; 19:9 and I Cor. 7:10-15.

Bales, in failing to understand the force of an exceptive statement, holds that no one can know from Matt. 19:9 that fornication is the one and only ground which Christ authorizes for divorce and remarriage. Bales claims that some men "prove it too soon"[4] by failing to wait until they read all of the New Testament (especially I Cor. 7:10-15) before drawing their conclusion as to what ground(s) are authorized by the New Covenant. As noted just above, this position of Bales has already been answered in detail, but there is an additional point which should be made.

It should be recalled that during his earthly ministry Jesus taught to His disciples the doctrine set forth in Matt. 19:9 (also 19:4-12). Then, shortly before His ascension, He gave to His Apostles the Great Commission. In Matthew's record of that Commission Jesus told the Apostles, as an essential element in making disciples (leading men to become sons of God) to teach them to observe all things that He (Jesus) had commanded them. Thus, since Matt. 19:9 was among the "all things" which Jesus had taught the Apostles, the Great Commission laid upon them the obligation to teach the doctrine set forth in Matt. 19:9 to their auditors. The New Testament does not contain the record of every word spoken by every Apostle during their work on earth. It does not even record every word spoken by every apostle on the day of Pentecost. The New Testament does say of Peter's preaching on Pentecost, "And with many other words he testified, and exhorted them saying, Save yourselves from this crooked generation" (Acts 2:40).

Thus, men now living have no way of knowing that Matt. 19:9 was not preached from Pentecost on—long before I Cor. 7:10-15 was written.

If the Apostles did not preach Matt. 19:9, then they disobeyed the Lord's instructions set out in Matt. 28:18-20. And, if they did preach it—but without "knowing" the "modification" of Matt. 19:9 which Bales alleges occurs in I Cor. 7:10-15—then they were, given Bales' doctrine re Matt. 19:9 and I Cor. 7:10-15, preaching false doctrine.

But it is false that the Apostles taught false doctrine in preaching Matt. 19:9 (which they had to do according to Matt. 28:18-20) and, so, it is Bales' doctrine which is false.

And, it will do Bales no good to claim that I Cor. 7:10-15 was preached from Pentecost on because, given Bales' doctrine, at least some of I Cor. 7:10-15 was not taught until after Paul became a Christian (which may have been as long as three or four years after the day of Pentecost).

Since the Apostles surely did what Jesus told them to do (in regard to preaching Matt. 19:9), Bales' doctrine must be false.

In I Cor. 7:12, Paul said, "But to the rest say I, not the Lord. . ." This makes clear that there was at least something in regard to the entire matter of divorce and remarriage which had not been stated (or written) before Paul became a Christian. But Paul did not become a Christian until approximately three years after Pentecost.

Therefore, if what he revealed (i.e., which had not been stated before) modified Matt. 19:9 in such fashion as to make clear that Matt. 19:9 is not a "universal passage" (i.e., one addressed to all men), then, since the Apostles had to be preaching Matt. 19:9 during those three years before Paul's conversion, they would of necessity have been preaching false doctrine—given Bales' position. But, given the true position—which has already been set forth in Appendix C (viz. that I Cor. 7:10-11 is a re-statement of the general law set forth in Matt. 19:6 and that I Cor. 7:12-15 sets out applications of that general law to specific cases, not previously covered in detail, no such problem arises.

Bales' position re Matt. 19:9 and I Cor. 7:10-15 is thus seen to be untenable. The position set forth in Appendix C and throughout this book is thus seen to be true.

Since brother Bales admits (by implication) that he could not know (without I Cor. 7:10-15) that Matt. 19:9 is not a universal passage, then, since Paul is the means by which this revelation was known (and Bales depends upon I Cor. 7:12-13 for his conclusion that I Cor. 7:10-11 refers only to Christians married to Christians), then not even the Apostles could have known and/or preached that Matt. 19:9 is not a universal passage until after Paul's conversion and revelation of the material in I Cor. 7:10-15.

But, since the Apostles, because of the obligation laid upon them by the Great Commission, had to have been preaching Matt. 19:9 during the time between Pentecost and Paul's conversion, they would have, given Bales' doctrine, been preaching false doctrine.

So, since either (1) Bales is now preaching false doctrine or (2) the Apostles were preaching false doctrine, and since the Apostles did not teach false doctrine, it is clear that Bales is the one who is preaching false doctrine.

Footnotes

[1]Chapter XVI-B.

[2]Chapters XII, XIII, XIV, XVI-A, XVI-B, XVII, XVIII, XIX.

[3]Appendix A, Appendix G.

[4]This has been refuted in preceding material.

APPENDIX U

DOES BAPTISM "SANCTIFY" A SINFUL RELATIONSHIP?

Apparently, Bales does not see fit to criticize one of his close associates, James S. Woodroof, who preaches for the congregation of which brother Bales is a member for teaching that baptism "sanctifies" a marriage (contracted before baptism) which violates the teaching of the law of Christ (Matt. 19:9 in particular).[1] Brother Woodroof holds that there is ground for accepting the view that "Matt. 19:9 was not held as requiring the dissolution of that marriage (though contrary to Matt. 19:9) that was formed prior to conversion."[2] Woodroof then admits—in contradiction to Bales' view—that Matt. 19:9 is "applicable to and binding upon all" men.[3] (It is strange that brother Bales does not critique the doctrine taught by brother Woodroof! Given brother Bales' integrity and love of truth, it certainly could not be because Woodroof preaches where Bales is a member.)

Rather, Bales holds that non-Christians are simply not under (amenable to) the law (gospel) of Christ, and, so, given Bales' view that neither Christ nor Paul legislated on the marriages of non-Christians, marriages involving only non-Christians are acceptable to God even if they violate Matt. 19:9 because non-Christians are under "the law in the heart" (which is, according to Bales, different from and other than the law of Christ) not the law of Christ.

Since some people seem to "stump their toes" on this theory, it seems wise to consider it briefly in this appendix.

Note: It is alleged by some that since baptism washes away all sins, it sanctifies marriages which existed at the time of baptism—so—those involved in adulterous marriages (those which violate Matt. 19:9) do not have to separate after baptism. But some crucial facts should be noted.

1. *Baptism does many things* (Mk. 16:16; Acts 2:38; Gal. 3:26-27; et al.)—but—*baptism will not*: (1) change a sinful practice into a righteous one. (2) Change a sinful relationship into a righteous one.

2. *"Baptism" is not even baptism* ("in the name of Christ," Acts 2:38) without *preceding repentance*. (1) Repentance is necessary—Acts 2:38. (2) Repentance is a change of mind. (3) Repentance leads to a reformation of life which involves cessation of sinful practices and severance of sinful relationships. (Matt. 3:8; Rom. 6:2; I John 3:6-10; I Cor. 6:9-11; Acts 8:5-13; 19:18-19).

3. *Marriage* is not a "church ordinance". (1) Marriage did not begin on the day of Pentecost—it began with Adam and Eve. (2) If marriage cannot occur

until those involved are baptized, then all unbaptized people are living in adultery (but this is false). (3) To hold such is to imply a false doctrine—and, thus—to hold a false doctrine. (4) Baptism does not destroy a sinful marriage and create a righteous one. (5) Question: What if only one spouse is baptized—would the baptized spouse be married and the unbaptized one not be married? The Bible answer is "No." (6) Question: Would the children of unbaptized "married" people be illegitimate? The Bible answer is "No."

Conclusion

May no one be misled into accepting the theory that baptism "sanctifies" an unscriptural marriage!

Footnotes

[1]James S. Woodroof, *The Divorce Dilemma*, p. 48.

[2]Ibid., p. 48.

[3]Ibid.

APPENDIX V

MURDER AND ADULTERY

Some attempt to justify their unscriptural position on divorce and remarriage by referring to murder and adultery. They think that by referring to murder they can show that one does not have to give up an adulterous marriage. Following are some points which are involved in that attempt.

1. Some allege that since a murderer can repent of that murder, be baptized (and, thus, be saved), but cannot raise his victim from the dead, then it follows that those who are involved in a marriage which violates Matt. 19:9, may continue—even after being baptized—with God's approval in that marriage which violates Matt. 19:9. Such teachers hold (1) that it is obvious that there are some wrongs which cannot be righted, (2) that murder is one such wrong, and (3) that unscriptural marriages are another such wrong.

2. *Some things to be noted in response to the above allegation.*

(1) It is true, of course, that no murderer can raise his victim from the dead, but the question which this truth answers is not the question which should be asked in regard to this matter as it relates to the problem of divorce and remarriage. The important question is: "Can one, after repenting and being baptized in the name of Christ (Acts 2:38), continue to committ additional acts of murder and have God's approval while doing so?" The answer is, of course, "No" (Rom. 13:9). Repentance (a change of mind or will) demands a reformation of life. No man could spend eternity with God if he continued until death to commit murder.

(2) The same basic principle applies to the question of committing adultery by living in an unscriptural marriage. Those who live and die in the state of being an adulterer will be lost (Rev. 21:8). Repentance demands a reformation of life. In the case of an unscriptural marriage (one which violates Matt. 19:9), repentance demands that one get out of that marriage.

3. A sound argument which refutes the liberal's position in regard to murder and adultery:

(1) If Ⓐ one can, with God's approval, keep on committing adultery after being baptized, then Ⓑ one can, with God's approval, keep on committing murder after being baptized. (Premise one is obviously true.)

(2) It is false that Ⓑ one can, with God's approval, keep on committing murder after being baptized (Rom. 13:9). (This denies that proposition B—the consequent of Premise One—is true.

(3) Therefore, it is false that Ⓐ one can,

with God's approval, keep on committing adultery after being baptized (Rev. 21:8; cf.: Rom. 13:8). (This conclusion follows, by Modus Tollens, from Premise One and Premise Two.)

4. Some crucial facts about the argument:

(1) The argument is valid.

(2) All of the premises are true.

(3) Therefore, the conclusion must be true.

(4) Therefore, the effort of the liberals to use the question of murder to justify adulterous marriages fails.

APPENDIX W

EMOTIONALISM, HARDSHIP, STRONG SEXUAL DRIVE, ETC. AND DIVORCE AND REMARRIAGE

Some men try to justify unscriptural divorce and remarriage by appealing to such things as (1) emotionalism, (2) hardship, and (3) strong sexual drive. But such matters cannot justify rebelling against Christ (Heb. 5:8-9; II Thess. 1:7-9; Matt. 7:21-27; et al.; cf.: the principle in the Old Testament period: Lev. 10:1-2; I Sam. 15:22).

I. *Emotionalism and Divorce.*

1. *An argument:*

(1) If Ⓐ one may continue to be involved in a practice or relationship which violates Christ's law solely on the basis that the cessation of such practices and the severance of such relationships could cause deep emotional response, then Ⓑ practices or relationships would could cause deep emotional response actually set aside (nullify) the law of Christ (at least in those cases).

(2) Proposition B (the consequent in Premise One) is false. (I John 3:4; Rom. 6:23; II Cor. 6:14) (Cf.: I Cor. 5).

(3) Therefore, Proposition A (the antecedent in Premise One) is false. By Modus Tollens, from Premise One and Premise Two.

Note: The argument is valid. (2) The premises are true. (3) Thus, the conclusion must be true. Our hearts are touched by many human difficulties—but this does not give us the right to violate God's word.

2. *A situation described:*

(1) *Situation number one: Family X:*

(a) A and B have married each other in violation of Bible teaching (Matt. 5:31-32; 19:9; Rom. 7:1-4; Mk. 10:2-12; Lk. 16:18; I Cor. 7:39).

(b) Question: Does the fact that children are involved allow A and B to continue to live in a relation which violates Christ's law? Bible answer: "No" (Lk. 14:26-33; Rev. 2:10.)

(2) *Situation number two: Family Y:*

(a) C and D are married according to scriptures.

(b) C robs a bank of $50,000—and has it.

(c) Question: should C be allowed to live in violation of God's will (no repentance, no reformation, keep the money) because he has a wife and children to support? Bible answer, "No." (Lk. 14:26-33; Rev. 2: 10).

II. *Hardship and Divorce.*

1. *An argument:*

(1) If Ⓐ it is right in at least some instances to set aside (live in violation of) Christ's law on divorce and remarriage—then— Ⓑ there are at least

some things more important in human life than obeying Christ's will.

(2) Proposition B (in Premise One) is false. (Lk. 14:26-33; Rev. 2:10; Lk. 9:23; Acts 21:13; I Cor. 5; Matt. 22:37-39; Mk. 10:28-30).

(3) Therefore, Proposition A (in Premise One) is false. (From Premises One and Two by Modus Tollens).

2. Note: (1) The argument is valid (M.T.) (2) The premises are true. (3) Thus, the conclusion must be true.

3. The fact of human heartbreak must not blind us to God's truth!

III. *"Strong Sexual Drive"*

1. *An argument:*

(1) If Ⓐ God has created men and women with such a strong desire for sexual intercourse that it is simply impossible for them to live without sexual intercourse—then— Ⓑ God has given to every person (no matter what he or she has done in the past by way of marrying and divorcing) the right to marry (i.e., with His approval).

(2) Proposition B (of Premise One) is false. (Matt. 5:31-32; 19:9; Lk. 16:18; Mk. 10:2-12; Rev. 21:8; I Cor. 5:1-13).

(3) Therefore, Proposition A (of Premise One) is false. (From Premises One and Two by Modus Tollens. Note also: I Cor. 10:13.)

2. Note: (1) The argument is valid (M.T.) (2) The premises are true. (3) Therefore the conclusion must be true.

3. Note: One can live without sexual intercourse. (I Cor. 10:13! Cf.: Rev. 2:10.)

IV. *"Another Divorce—Your solution is worse than the problem."*

1. If Ⓐ the Bible teaches that, to be saved by the grace of God, one must repent of his sins—and—if Ⓑ repentance, being a change of mind, demands the cessation of sinful practices and the severance of sinful relationships—and—if Ⓒ men living today live under the New Testament, not the Old Testament—and—if Ⓓ Jesus made clear that the concession made by Moses is no longer in effect—and—if Ⓔ Jesus made clear that there is now one and only one ground (fornication) for divorce and remarriage (and, thus, the second divorce question is a matter of legally dissolving that which God never approved)—then— Ⓕ —the charge that "the solution is worse than the problem" is false.

2. Proposition A (in Premise One) is true. (Tit. 2:11; Acts 2:38; Acts 17:30-31.)

3. Proposition B (in Premise One) is true. (Acts 3:19; Acts 8:12ff.)

4. Proposition C (in Premise One) is true. (Heb. 9:15-17; 10:9; Gal. 4:21-31.)

5. Proposition D (in Premise One) is true. (Matt. 19:3-11.)

6. Proposition E (in Premise One) is true. (Matt. 19:3-12.)

7. The Conjunction of Propositions A, B, C, D, and E is true. (From Premises 2,3,4,5,6 by Conjunction.)

8. Therefore, Proposition F (in Premise One) is true. (From Premises One and Seven by Modus Ponens.)

V. *"Celibacy is unnatural"*

An argument:

1. If Ⓐ marriage is regulated by God's will, not merely by man's desires—and if—Ⓑ the Bible teaches that there are some who abstain from sexual relations for the kingdom's sake—and if—Ⓒ believers are separated they must remain unmarried or else be reconciled to their mates—and if—Ⓓ Jesus taught that some lose their right to marry—and if—Ⓔ one can so act as to forfeit certain rights—then—Ⓕ the theory that "celibacy is unnatural, so God gives the right to marry to everyone" is false.

2. Proposition A (in Premise One) is true. (Mk. 16:15; Mt. 5:31-32; 19:9).

3. Proposition B (in Premise One) is true. (Mt. 19:10-12; 6:33; Lk. 14:26-33.)

4. Proposition C (in Premise One) is true. (I Cor. 7:10-11; Cf. Matt. 19:9).

5. Proposition D (in Premise One) is true. (Matt. 5:31-32; 19:9.)

6. Proposition E (in Premise One) is true. (Heb. 12:14-17; Num. 12-14.)

7. The conjunction of Propositions A,B,C,D, E is true. (From Premises One, two, three, four, five, six and seven by Conjunction.)

8. Therefore, Proposition F (from Premise One) is true. (From Premises one and seven by Modus Ponens.)

Conclusion: Some Crucial Points

1. *Prison, death—and sex.*

(1) God requires us to put Him before every thing and every one (Lk. 14:26-33; Matt. 6:33; Matt. 22:34-40).

(2) He requires us to be willing to go to prison rather than to be unfaithful (Acts 21:13).

(3) He requires us to be willing to die rather than to be unfaithful (Acts 21:13; Rev. 2:10).

(4) Surely, then, it should not surprise us to learn that He requires some—because of a past marriage—to have to live without sexual relations (Matt. 19:3-12).

2. *God's grace and divorce.*

An argument:

(1) If Ⓐ God's grace "sanctifies: (renders acceptable to God) an adulterous marriage,—then—Ⓑ

God's grace annuls His laws relating to sinful relationships which were entered either before or after one is baptized.

(2) Proposition B (from Premise One) is false. (I Cor. 6:9-11; Gal. 5:19-21; Rev. 21:8; I Cor. 5:1-13).

(3) Therefore, Proposition A (from Premise One) is false (From Premises One and Two, by Modus Tollens.)

Note: (1) The argument is valid. (2) The premises are true. (3) Therefore, the conclusion must be true.

As God is gracious and forgiving, so ought men to be—but—this does not mean that they are given license to violate God's law!!

There are other matters of this sort which are dealt with in other publications of this author.[1]

Footnote

[1]Thomas B. Warren, *Charts On Divorce and Re-Marriage,* and Thomas B. Warren, editor, *Your Marriage Can Be Great.*

APPENDIX X

ROMANS 2:14-15

Brother Bales thinks (1) that he has found, in Romans 2:14, a passage which explicitly refers to his "law on the heart" and (2) that because this author (T.B.W.) has argued as he has, he (T.B.W.) has no right to use Rom. 2:14 as a part of the gospel. As usual (on divorce and remarriage), Bales is wrong on both counts.

As did brother Fuqua, brother Bales alleges that non-Christians have no written laws from God on any subject. (It must be remembered that he argues, throughout the great mass of material he has produced on divorce and remarriage, that no one can be amenable to the New Covenant until after he is "in" the Covenant—and by that Bales means until after he is baptized into Christ {a self-contradictory position}.) Thus, non-Christians—according to the implications of Bales' doctrine—are not amenable even to the plan of salvation.

If it is the case—as Bales alleges—that non-Christians have no written law from God, then, since the Gospel is written, then the Gospel is not addressed to non-Christians. If, in his effort to get out of this "logical hole" into which he has plunged himself, Bales wants to recant what he has implied by the above and say that non-Christians living today do have a written law from God, then since he holds that such a written law could not be the law of Christ, Bales must produce the written law from God which present day non-Christians are under! Of course, he cannot do such. His position is chaotic, untenable, self-contradictory, anti-Biblical and should be rejected by all. This author prays that brother Bales himself will reject it.

Bales simply does not understand Rom. 2:14-15. The passage says nothing about a law which is different from and other than the gospel (law) of Christ being written on the heart of the non-Christian. The context of Rom. 2:14-15 shows that the expression "have not the law" refers to the fact that Gentiles did not have the law of Moses. The Jews had a written law (the law of Moses); the Gentiles (at that time—i.e., before the day of Pentecost) did not have a written law from God. Since Pentecost, all men (whether Jew or Gentile, whether Christian or non-Christian) have one—and only one—written law from God: the Gospel (law) of Christ. But Bales fails—as did Fuqua—to see that Rom. 2:14-15 refers to the time anterior to the Gospel dispensation. Now, neither Jew nor Gentile has (is under) the law of Moses. In Rom. 2:14-15, Paul was not contrasting Christians with non-Christians (as Bales alleges). Rather, he was contrasting the ante-Pentecost Jew with the ante-Pentecost non-Jew (Gentile).

Of course, the Gentiles did not, before Pentecost, have a written law from God, but it must be noted that: (1) the Jews, who did then have a written law from God (the law of Moses), do not now have (i.e., are not under) that same written law (and they have not been under that law since the first day of Pentecost after the resurrection of Christ {Heb. 10:9; Mk. 16:15-16; Acts 2:1-47}).

However, the Jews do now have another written law from God addressed to them—and to the Gentiles—the gospel (law) of Christ. There is now no distinction between Jew and Gentile—both have the same law addressed to them—the gospel of Christ (Rom. 10:12; Acts 15:7-9; 17:30-31; Mk. 16:15-16; Matt. 28:18-20; Lk. 24:45-49; Acts 2:1-47).

Again, these crucial points are noted: (1) Bales alleges that no non-Christian presently has a written law from God addressed to him; (2) but the instruction to be baptized "unto the remission of sins" is a part of the gospel of Christ (Acts 2:38); so, it follows by implication, that, (3) according to Bales, (a) non-Christians cannot be baptized and (b) Christians are instructed to be baptized. Of course, both of these implications of Bales' doctrine are false. It is amazing to this author that brother Bales, who possesses a brilliant mind and who for such a long time has taught the truth on baptism, should now have espoused a doctrine which implies these two false doctrines.

Hebrews 8:10 makes clear that the gospel (law) of Christ is now written on the hearts of some men. In order for men to "go" to Christ, they must learn the law of Christ, the gospel (John 6:44-45).

In Romans 2:14-15, Paul said of the Gentiles (in that context—see above) that they "show the *work* of the law written in their hearts" (emphasis, T.B.W.). This refers to the law of Moses at a time anterior to the gospel dispensation—not to some presently-in-force law which is different from and other than the gospel (law) of Christ.

Brother Bales and those who agree with him face the fact that their "law on the heart" theory involves a logical contradiction. (This point has been discussed somewhat in preceding material.) Note how the contradiction develops.

Bales must admit that Ⓐ it is sinful to act out of harmony with what one's conscience urges him to choose (Rom. 2:14-15; 14:23; James 4:17), and Bales also holds that Ⓑ it is not sinful for a non-Christian (e.g., a Baptist who believes (a) that he is amenable to the teaching of Matt. 19:9 and (b) that Matt. 19:9 teaches that fornication is the one and only ground for divorce and remarriage) to act out of harmony with what his conscience urges him to do (i.e., to divorce his wife on some ground other than fornication and marry someone else).

It must be noted that Proposition B is the logical contradiction of Proposition A. Yet, Bales affirms both of them. Thus, if Bales' doctrine is true in regard to Rom. 2:14-15, then a logical contradiction is true. But no logical contradiction is true (the law of contradiction). Thus, since any doctrine which implies a logical contradiction is itself false, and since Bales' doctrine implies a logical contradiction, it follows that Bales' doctrine is false. Again, this one point should be all that is necessary to cause all men to reject Bales' doctrine.

It should also be recalled that in Appendix R, it was shown that (in regard to material relevant to the problem considered in this present Appendix) Bales affirms both (A) that the gaining of additional insight into God's will brings more responsibility and (B) that the gaining of additional insight into God's word does not bring more responsibility. Since Proposition B is contradictory of Proposition A, and since every doctrine which implies a logical contradiction is false, and since Bales' doctrine affirms a logical contradiction, then Bales' doctrine is false.

The reader is urged to re-read Appendix R to review the material there.

Thus, again, Bales is wrong. He is wrong on Rom. 2:14-15; he is wrong on "law on the heart." (See Appendix M for more material on this.)

The situation is clear: the doctrine taught by James D. Bales on divorce and remarriage is false. All men are amenable to the law of Christ, that law includes Matt. 19:9, and Matt. 19:9 clearly teaches that there is one and only one ground for divorce and remarriage: i.e., fornication.

Footnote

[1]See Appendix M for more on "the law on the heart" as Bales sees it.

APPENDIX Y

A FINAL WORD

For more than forty years, brother James D. Bales has been in the forefront among God's people as a man of great intellect, outstanding ability, love of truth and dedication to the propagation and defense of the gospel of Christ. He is known among God's people around the world as a strong conservative Biblical scholar.

Because of his reputation as a conservative scholar, likely many will listen to and, sadly, accept what he now teaches on divorce and remarriage even though they likely would not accept it if such were taught by such liberal teachers as Leroy Garrett, W. Carl Ketcherside, et al.

Because of his past credentials as a conservative scholar, brother Bales has thus become—for those who wish error to advance and spread—a "tool" for the rapid spread of false doctrine which liberal preachers could never become (unless the whole—or almost the whole—church should come to accept such liberalism as advanced by such journals as *Mission, Integrity, Mission Messenger,* and *Restoration Review*).

It is the sincere conviction of this author that brother Bales would not knowingly teach anything out of harmony with the will of God. Yet, he has now espoused a doctrine which contradicts (either explicitly or implicitly) almost every fundamental truth he formerly taught (and, no doubt, still does teach when he is on any subject other than divorce and remarriage). Thus, as stated elsewhere in this book, it is a sad day for the Lord's church that such a conservative scholar as James D. Bales has become the object of praise of such liberals as Leroy Garrett, Hoy Ledbetter, et al.

The final plea from this author to brother Bales is: *Come back* home to where you once were. *Come back* to the truth on divorce and remarriage which allowed you to consistently condemn denominationalism, claims of miraculous healings, claims of adventists, human plans of salvation without contradicting yourself. *Come back*, my dear brother, to the truth of the gospel.

What Has Been Done In This Book?

In this book at least the following has been done: (1) "Proposition TBW" (which involves the affirmation that for all men now living {whether Christian or non-Christian} *fornication* is the one and only ground for divorce and remarriage) has been proved to be true and (2) "Proposition JDB" (which includes the affirmation that only those who are Christians are amenable to the law of Christ and—more specifically—that non-Christians are not amenable to Matthew 19:9) has been proved to be false.

May God bless the truth to His glory and to the salvation of men.

As the author comes to the final words of this book, he does so with a broken heart—a broken heart because he has had to expose the error of a dear and respected friend and brother in Christ; a broken heart because the liberal position on divorce and remarriage was forced on the church at a most unfortunate time: a time when liberalism is already "running rampant." This author is deeply sorry that such a conservative scholar as brother James D. Bales is presently contributing to the advance of the liberal cause.

Now is the time for "all good men to come to the aid of" the cause of Christ.

Evaluation

Warren evidently has misunderstood Bales' position for he does not deal with his arguments set forth in 'Not Under Bondage'